EVOLUTION OF COST ACCOUNTING

TO 1925

ACCOUNTING HISTORY CLASSICS SERIES

EVOLUTION OF COST ACCOUNTING TO 1925

S. PAUL GARNER, Ph.D., CPA
Dean and Professor Emeritus of Accounting
The University of Alabama

𝔗𝔥𝔢 𝔄𝔠𝔞𝔡𝔢𝔪𝔶 𝔬𝔣
𝔄𝔠𝔠𝔬𝔲𝔫𝔱𝔦𝔫𝔤 𝔥𝔦𝔰𝔱𝔬𝔯𝔦𝔞𝔫𝔰

THE UNIVERSITY OF ALABAMA PRESS
University, Alabama

The Academy acknowledges the financial assistance
of The Arthur Andersen Foundation in making this
Series available. Dr. Garner has graciously
waived his royalties on this printing to assist
in making this publication available at a modest price.

Library of Congress Cataloging in Publication Data

Garner, Samuel Paul, 1910-
    Evolution of cost accounting to 1925.

    (Accounting history classics series)
    Bibliography: p.
    Includes index.
    1. Cost accounting-History.   I. Title.
II. Series.
HF686.C8G3   1976   657'.42'09   76-41238
ISBN 0-8173-8900-8

TO

R. B. G.

AND

G. H. N.

EDITOR'S FOREWORD TO
THE REPRINT EDITION

Few works published in accounting history in the last quarter century deserve to be called classics. *Evolution of Cost Accounting to 1925* first published over two decades ago continues to merit attention as a primary work for instruction and reference in the area of management accounting. The book and its author have become internationally known.

Before and since the formation of The Academy of Accounting Historians, there has been a growing number of inquiries as to how and when this important work would again be made available to students, teachers, and scholars.

Through the cooperation of the author, The University of Alabama Press, and the Arthur Andersen & Co. Foundation, The Academy is pleased to initiate a series of accounting history classics publications to meet the demand for this and other works which continue to maintain a fundamental relationship to the study of the history of accounting and accounting thought. It is with both pleasure and appreciation that The Academy inaugurates this series with the republication of this genuine classic, S. Paul Garner's *Evolution of Cost Accounting to 1925*.

July 15, 1976

Gary John Previts
Series Editor

PREFACE

UNTIL A FEW YEARS AGO, THE EVOLUTIONARY ASPECTS OF COST ACCOUNT-
ing had been neglected almost entirely by students of the history of accounting. With few exceptions, and these exceptions are quite limited
in scope, the topics treated in this book have failed to receive adequate
attention from the several writers who have from time to time devoted
their energies to the more general phases of accounting evolution. The
principal purpose of this volume, therefore, is an attempt to remedy
that neglect. In carrying out this aim, particular emphasis is placed
upon the origin and development of cost practices and theories which
are generally agreed to be rather basic, although some of the more advanced doctrines and procedures are discussed wherever necessary for
the sake of completeness. The cost accounting practices considered
in this study are for the most part those concerned with the ascertain-
ment of the so-called actual (accounting) cost of production. More
specifically, the line of demarcation is drawn so as to include a rather
comprehensive discussion of the following topics: the accounting for
raw material, direct labor, and manufacturing burden (from several
aspects), the question of the integration or nonintegration of the factory and financial accounts, the accounting for interdepartmental
transfers of product, the costing of by-products and co-products, the
handling of waste materials and scrap, the development of job order
and process cost systems and the problem of valuing factory inventories. Certain features of estimated and standard costing arrangements are also treated, especially in those instances where it is felt that
their neglect would cause a definite break in the continuity. However,

this book does not purport to be a history of standard costing; this aspect of accounting evolution deserves a separate volume.

No particular effort is made to bring strictly up to date the developmental aspects of the topics treated. Several reasons were involved in making the decision to ignore a considerable number of the authorities who wrote after the early years of the decade of the 1920's. These reasons should be enumerated at this point. In the first place, so far as the writer can ascertain, very few contributions of an original nature were made after 1925 in regard to the subjects discussed in this volume. This last statement, obviously, is subject to some exceptions, and wherever necessary, significant theories or techniques which were developed after the period referred to are briefly considered. All of this should not be taken to mean in any way that cost authorities since 1925 have neglected the subject matter of this study; on the contrary, some of the most thorough and comprehensive expositions have appeared since that date. These latter have been more noteworthy, however, for synthesizing the available material on the subject than for the inauguration of new theories or procedures. In view of this fact, they require comparatively little attention in this study, which is more concerned with the evolution of cost accounting than with its synthesis.

The second reason for partially ignoring the cost authorities who wrote after the early 1920's is that there seems to have been a shift in emphasis after the First World War. Comparatively less attention was devoted to actual costing and more to the advanced theories, such as standard and distribution costs and their attendant problems. The period referred to, then, provides a rather convenient concluding point, especially in view of the fact that the development of accounting procedures for deriving so-called actual factory costs had attained at least a temporary climactic stage by that time.

A third reason for limiting the time element of the study is centered around the fact that it is very difficult, if not impossible, to evaluate carefully, and to place in the proper historical perspective, contributions to which all discussions of the present type are subject. Serious errors of judgment could easily be committed by attempting to carry the evolutionary aspects of cost accounting down to a more recent date. Such a task, therefore, is not essayed here. Certain exceptions to the preceding limitation are made where it is believed that truly significant contributions are involved, but these were found to be relatively rare.

The locale of this study is confined to the United States and England, with only incidental reference to other countries as the opportunity affords. This concentration has considerable justification. As is treated in detail in later chapters, the English cost authorities were among the first to deal comprehensively with industrial accounting problems; and although they lost their relative standing in the period after 1900, they continued to contribute new techniques and theories from time to time. The cost experts in this country, on the other hand, made few contributions in the earlier period, but soon thereafter forged ahead of their contemporaries in Great Britain. Cost practices and procedures in other industrial nations were patterned, for the most part, after those in England and the United States. In view of this general trend, therefore, no serious deficiency results in limiting the principal discussion to English and American cost authorities. The two groups are treated simultaneously in the more important chapters in chronological order. Considerable effort has been made, however, to indicate the nationality of the authority under review at the moment, in order that the least possible confusion may exist.

The general plan of the study might also be indicated in this introductory section. The first chapter is concerned with some examples of the rather early adoption of the principles of double entry to workshop record keeping. This development took place during the mediaeval period and illustrates particularly the adaptability of the then new science of accounting. Several instances of the use of industrial accounts in that era are cited; some details of their operation are also described. The main point of emphasis, however, is to indicate that the cost of production concept was recognized and even fairly well understood several centuries before the Industrial Revolution. Some authorities, incidentally, would have it otherwise.

The second chapter continues the exposition of the slow evolution of cost accounting by pointing out the principal contributions to the subject in the period 1700-1885, with particular emphasis upon the English authorities. The available material on the subject is presented in chronological order, with little regard to its topical development, since the references are so scattered and nonconclusive in nature.

Beginning with the third chapter a more orderly arrangement is permitted in that some nine cost accounting theories or techniques are discussed from the standpoint of their origin, evolution, and development. The nine rather broad topics are divided into as many chapters. Each one of these attempts to summarize the most significant contributions to the subject (in order of time) which were made up to the period of the early 1920's. At intervals throughout these sections an effort is made to review the cumulative results of the work of the authorities up to that point in regard to the topic under discussion. This is done to give the proper perspective and to prevent possible duplication. No particular significance should be attached to the order in which the topics are discussed. Obviously, however, a logical arrangement would call first for a consideration of the so-called three elements of factory cost (material, labor, and burden), and that plan has been adopted here. No emphasis is intended in connection with the numerical order given to the last seven chapters.

The last chapter (Chapter XII) presents some inductions which seem to be justified from this study and the rather extensive investigation which has accompanied it. The remarks in Chapter XII, however, should not be considered conclusions, the reason being that cost evolution by its very nature is dynamic rather than static, and no statements made in regard thereto can be final or definitive.

Before concluding this Preface the author desires to express his appreciation to the several individuals who made this study possible. First, to Professor George Hillis Newlove, of the University of Texas, he owes a debt of gratitude for continued assistance and encouragement as well as numerous suggestions throughout its entire development. The outstanding and lasting contributions to accounting evolution made by Professors A. C. Littleton, R. S. Edwards, David Solomons, Raymond De Roover, and his wife Florence Edler De Roover gave the initial impetus for this study. Some of these scholars read parts of the manuscript and others helped with their comments. Professor Larry Benninger of the University of Missouri and Professor C. Aubrey Smith of the University of Texas read much of the volume and made useful suggestions. The Research Committee of the University of Alabama made its resources available by furnishing financial assistance. And, finally, the author's wife, Ruth Bailey Garner, made the work lighter with her infinite patience and encouragement. It is a pleasure to express my gratitude for all this aid and assistance.

Tuscaloosa, Alabama   S. Paul Garner
January, 1954

CONTENTS

CONTENTS (Continued)

CHAPTER I

INDUSTRIAL ACCOUNTING IN THE MEDIAEVAL ERA

UP UNTIL THE LAST FEW DECADES THERE WAS A GENERAL BELIEF THAT industrial accounting had its origin in the rise of the factory system in the Industrial Revolution. One authority, for example, has stated:

> Cost accounting is not old by several centuries as is mercantile bookkeeping by double entry. It is, in fact, of quite recent origin, essentially a product of the nineteenth century, which has been greatly extended and developed in the twentieth. . . . Cost accounting, therefore, is one of the many consequences of the industrial revolution.[1]

A second authority has written:

> Accounting has been developed to furnish management with better means of control than have been available in the past. This, accounting has done through a development of internal accounts. Before the Industrial Revolution, accounting was mainly a record of the external relations of one business unit with other business units, a record of relations determined in the market. With the advent of large scale productive operations . . . necessity arose for more emphasis upon the accounting for interests within the competitive unit and the use of accounting records as a means of administrative control over the enterprise. . . . The appearance of cost accounts in manufacturing is an example.[2]

Still a third authority has stated:

> Cost accounting is largely a product of the twentieth century though some of the causes of its growth operated much earlier.[3]

While each of the preceding authoritative quotations rightly emphasizes the fact that *cost* accounting came into existence after 1800, many *industrial* bookkeeping practices and techniques are much older than the Industrial Revolution. In fact, as will be shown later in this chapter, they date back to about the fourteenth century when, as a result of the rapid growth of Italian, English, Flemish, and German commerce, industrial enterprises began to be established by various individuals and partnerships to engage in the manufacture of woolen and silk cloth, books, coins, and other items in common use at the time. Several economic historians have pointed out, incidentally, that wherever capitalism began to show its head, better and more accurate accounting practices followed within a short time. The following is typical of the views of one of the keen students of this aspect of the subject:

> Though instances to suggest the contrary may be found, most merchants of the period we are considering did not use their bookkeeping, whether by double entry or otherwise, to keep a regular and accurate check on their capital and profits. . . . Double entry bookkeeping, to the extent that it was adopted in practice, could bring order and system to such records and so contribute to the "methodising" of business life. . . . The writings of the accountants contain some evidence to show that they were aware of those special properties of double entry that some economic historians have regarded as important in the development of capitalism. On the other hand, the evidence of early bookkeeping techniques gives little support to the views summarized at the opening of this study. . . . Moreover, it is quite likely that double entry bookkeeping came to be accepted by teachers and accountants as the standard or desirable system of bookkeeping, and that their influence and employment helped to introduce its use. . . . If this were so, then indeed double entry bookkeeping may have been, in small measure, an external influence on business practice.[4]

Although the specific origins of industrial record keeping are lost in antiquity,[5] one authority has offered the interesting suggestion that the earliest development in England took place in the time of King Henry VII (1485-1509), when a number of woolen workers, being resentful of the many guild restrictions, moved to country villages from cities, and established industrial communities, hoping to be able to sell their finished products through other than the organized guilds.[6] Costing had not been so essential among that group so long as all their industrial and selling activities were regulated by the highly monopolistic guilds; but, as many firms have since learned, when the owners of small central workshops found themselves competing now not only against the guilds, but also among themselves, more accurate records of costs became imperative and almost a prerequisite for success. An incentive was provided, then, for a careful study of many phases of the problem which had theretofore been neglected.

The principal purpose of this chapter is to show, therefore, that the beginnings of industrial accounting can be traced back to the period when capitalistic processes of production began to be substituted for domestic enterprise, putting-out and handicraft methods, rather than from the period of the Industrial Revolution.[7] In carrying out this purpose, several examples of the early use of accounting techniques in the mediaeval era are cited and discussed in subsequent sections.

THE GENOESE SHIPS' ACCOUNTS

While not concerned altogether with industrial or cost accounting, the records kept by Genoese ships' scribes in the twelfth and thirteenth centuries are interesting as indicating the early development of costing problems. The work and accounts of the scribe (really a sort of supercargo, or in modern terms, a purser) have been briefly described by E. H. Byrne.[8] The joint venture type of organization was used extensively, and some of the contracts between ship proprietors and merchants which have been preserved indicate that accurate records and accounts of the voyages were an absolute necessity if the shares of expenses and incomes were to be successfully accounted for. Some of the voyages were sponsored by as many as 25 persons, and in view of the complicated nature of the trade, even in the earlier period the patrons employed a clerk to record the expenses and incomes of the trip. "By the thirteenth century the responsibilities and burdens of accounting were so great that most maritime towns of importance in trade by law required the owners of ships crossing the seas to employ a scribe from the beginning to the end of a voyage as a permanent member of the crew; in Venice and Barcelona the larger ships were required to have two, but in Genoa one was apparently regarded as sufficient."[9] This individual had an official status and his records had to be deposited with the government as a matter of legal evidence in case of some dispute. He kept a careful record of the costs incurred on a voyage, as well as the amount of freight due from merchants who shipped goods overseas. From the standpoint of this study it is important to note that these costs were used to determine the equitable proportion of gain or loss to be allocated to each partner, or patron as they were called in those times. Moreover, shipbuilders employed scribes to keep records of costs of building vessels. Byrne thinks that the scribe may have even attained professional accounting standing, but H. Pirenne does not indicate any such position.[10]

As a matter of interest to indicate the care with which the accounts were kept towards the end of the thirteenth century, Byrne cites a passage which shows that the "scribes were familiar with the principles of depreciation and took them into account." The passage follows:

> The ship-owner borrows £200; he promises the creditor *tibi dare et solvere tantum quantum et ad eam rationem sive secundum quod processerit seu evenerit introitus seu proventus sive lucrum navis mee et Bernardi de Rivegno in viagio Neapolim in quod itura est ad presens dante domino deductis et computatis omnibus expensis non computando in predictis aliqua diminutione dicte navis vel sarcia ipsius excepto si immineretur vel rumperetur vel ex sarcia ipsius preter quam ex sarcia canabi qua rumperetur.*[11]

This sentence may be freely translated thus: He promises the creditor to give and pay him as much as is in accord with the account [the debt], or according to what is earned on the investment, on the voyage of the ship owned by Bernardi de Rivegno and myself, to Naples, to which [city] it is to go. [From the total income] as shown by the accounts of the master [of the ship], all expenses are to be deducted [including] in the things before mentioned [in the contract] loss [due to wear and tear] of the equipment of the ship as well as of the ship [itself]. [In case, however,] that the ship is injured [wrecked] or any part of its [rigging] equipment is broken or lost such [items] [are] not [to be] considered [as] deductions.

Since the scribes knew of and took account of depreciation, one must conclude that their record keeping was partly modern. Furthermore, it was apparently entirely adequate for their purposes.

THE FUGGER ACCOUNTS

As an introduction to the records kept by the Fuggers it might be mentioned that in the sixteenth and seventeenth centuries this famous family, in addition to their many other activities,[12] owned a few and operated some others of the then prolific silver and copper mines of Tyrol and Carinthia in Austria. The beginnings of this enterprise can be traced back to the middle of the fifteenth century; the records under review, however, are dated later. The first decisive movement in the direction of securing control over the mines took place in 1487 when one of the sons of Jakob Fugger the Elder, the best known member of the family, lent the Archduke of Tyrol, Siegmund, several thousand florins, taking a mortgage on the best of the silver mines as security for the loan. This transaction led to new and larger loans, and by the end of the fifteenth century the Fuggers were well entrenched not only in Tyrol but in Carinthia and other parts of Austria as well.

This business was extremely profitable, and according to the contemporary records the Fuggers financed several of the wars of Emperor Maximilian the First, which added much more to their wealth. The present chapter, however, is concerned with the records which were kept concerning the production of, and the cost of, operating the mines. In a monograph by Ludwig Scheuermann, which is a volume of *Studien zur Fugger-Geschichte,* one can find some evidence that rough cost calculations were made from time to time in order to arrive at the amount which was due the Emperor over and above the sum withheld to repay the loans owed to the Fuggers.[13] Scheuermann does not show any consecutive chronological accounts from the books which were kept under the direction of the Fugger managers; he does, however, select some typical reports and accounts of the period 1548-1655. An an example of the structure of a set of accounts for one of the several individual organizations, the following may be cited (1577) for the Bleiberger mine, and the foundry which was operated in connection with it:[14]

I. ORE ACCOUNT

"Soll uns" (debits)	"Sollen wir" (credits)
Balance of ore at end of 1576.	Proceeds of ore sold.
Year's production of ore valued at 1 florin per hundredweight.[15]	Balance of ore at end of 1577.
Profit on sale of ore over and above the "valuation" (as above).	

II. LEAD ACCOUNT

Balance of lead at end of 1576.

Commission on sales of lead.

Lead production 1577 valued at 2 florins per hundredweight.

Profit on lead sales over and above the "valuation" as above.

Proceeds of ore sold.

Balance of lead at end of 1577.

III. MINE AND FOUNDRY ACCOUNT

Valuation of foundry and equipment.

Cost of production of the ore (according to production of mines), subtracted from the above valuation of year's production, compared to the real prime cost.

Rent for the use of smelting works, furnaces, crushers, and forges paid by Bleiberger Lehenhauer, (compared with below).

Rent received for leasing out our mines and pit-heaps to Lehenhauer.

IV. GENERAL EXPENSES

Offices supplies.

Verehrungen (bonuses).

Alms and gifts.

Employees' salaries.

V. SMELTING ACCOUNT

Expenditures for burning materials.

Foremen and workers' wages.

Other wages.

Other current expenditures.

VI. FREIGHT AND TRANSPORT ACCOUNT

Cost for lead and ore transportation up to the main storage place at St. Anna in Gressach.

VII. IRON AND IRON-SLACK TRADE ACCOUNT

Balance at end of 1576.

Expenditures for purchases 1577.

Income from sale of goods in 1577.

Balance at end of 1577.

As the mining operations of the Fuggers increased in scope year after year the accounts necessary to give the details became more comprehensive. For example, in 1585, 35 summary accounts were needed, not all, however, concerned with mining. The debit side of one of these accounts, "The Rattenberg Smelter Account," contained 23 items, and the credit side, nine. This account was used not only to record the cost of operating the smelter, but also for shipments to other parts. The two sides were added each year and the difference was termed the net gain for the year.[16] The family, in addition, carried on an extensive grain trade in the Tyrol, and records were kept for each workshop (depot or warehouse) so that the headquarters in Augsburg would know the condition and value of the stock in each locality.

While the Fugger records cannot be considered cost accounting in the strict meaning of the term, they are a further indication of the adaptation of record-keeping to the needs of a particular manufacturing industry, namely the mining and smelting. Also, as can be easily seen from the above illustration, the accounts themselves were quite mixed in nature, with inventories, collections, sales, shipments, expenses, material costs, and labor costs all under one account. The important thing about these records, however, is not that the accounts were mixed but that the concept of a "cost of production" was evidenced. This latter point, then, is the significant feature of the bookkeeping for Fugger mining interests.

THE MEDICI ACCOUNTS

The accounts of the Medici offer an extremely interesting example of the early adaptation of bookkeeping to industrial establishments. This well-known family, in addition to its extensive banking activities,[17] was engaged in the production of silk and wool for many decades throughout the fifteenth and sixteenth centuries.[18] The partnership form of business organization was used, and a large number of the ledgers, journals, and other documents of those mediaeval firms have been preserved. These are now in the Selfridge Collection at Harvard. They indicate that a much more comprehensive control over the industrial operations and the processes was exercised than in the case of the Fuggers.

While the Medici produced much of their cloth in Florence, it was sold not only in that area but in many distant places. There was a constant emphasis on top quality since most of the customers were wealthy people. As was customary in those years, the "putting-out" or "wholesale handicraft" system was widely employed. As a consequence, the central establishment, where the material was stored, sorted, cleansed, combed, and carded, was quite small. This central workship should not perhaps even be dignified by calling it a factory.[19] Even though the employees worked in their own homes, and owned their tools and instruments, considerable skill was required to manage the operations successfully. Since the Medici were noted generally for their business acumen, it is little wonder that their accounting records reflect an unusually high degree of accuracy and completeness.

The Medici invited men of technical experience to join with them in their partnerships. [20] Keeping track of the numerous details of the cloth manufacturing and avoiding waste were no mean tasks; they required ability of a high order.

As early as 1431, some 63 years before Paciolo published the first printed text on double entry bookkeeping, one finds "rather complex sets of books in use in Medici industrial partnerships."[21] In those early years, four books of original entry were kept: (1) a stock book, used to record purchases of wool, alum, and dyestuffs needed in the manufacture of woolen cloth; (2) a cash book; (3) a book of income and outgo; and (4) a wage book. Incidentally, postings were made directly from the cash book and the special wage journal to the ledger —a distinctly modern practice used some 500 years ago. Edler illustrates the relationship which existed between the different books as follows: [22]

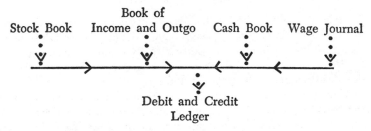

A statistical record was also kept of all the cloth manufactured by the partnership, as well as of the sales. Later on, about 1475, the wage journal was divided into two parts, each one being bound separately. One of these was used as a memorandum of material and work passed out to spinners, warpers, and weavers; the other one was used for dyers and all other workers.

Petty expenses for the shop were entered first in the cash book and then posted from there to a separate account in the general ledger. (The term "general ledger" is used because later on a "wage" ledger was also maintained.) Edler insists that the system used in 1431 was not double entry because it lacked the making of two entries for all transactions; but ten years later, 1441, another series of books show that double entry had begun to be used there in Florence. Inventories were also taken and a balance sheet drawn up.

An account called *panni lavorati e finiti* "cloth manufactured and sold" was drawn up. It seems to have been used to record all the cloth manufactured by each partnership. As an indication that the Medici accountants were familiar with the modern concept of "cost of production," Edler states that "on the last pages of these cloth accounts is found a statement drawn up to show the profit on all the cloth that has been sold. . . . On the debit side of each cloth account are the following items: (1) the sum total of all wool purchased and used in making of cloth during the period of the partnership, (2) the total amount spent for dyestuffs and the dying of wool and cloth, and (3) the total of all the other manufacturing costs—wages, materials used by the workman, such as oil, combs, cards, and teasels, and miscellaneous expenses. The total of the debits shows the cost of producing the finished cloth." [23] Such was the system in use in the fifteenth century.

In the sixteenth century (from 1520 on) some additional books were used as the operations became more complex. One of these was a special wage ledger, and another was entitled *Manifatture di Nostra ragione* "cost of manufacturing of our company." The book of income and outgo, containing the total income and expenditures of the enterprise, was also continued. It is not clear, however, just what connection this record book had with the cash book. Edler thinks the cash book may have contained summaries of the different sections of the book of income and outgo. [24] The book of income and outgo orginally had five sections, only four of which, however, are of interest from the standpoint of industrial accounting. One of the sections is called income of the general ledger, another outgo of the general ledger, another income of the wage ledger, and the last, outgo of the wage ledger. "All the money and services in terms of money received from workmen for purchases of cloth, etc., and from the shop expense account are found in the income from the wage ledger section and are posted to the wage ledger. In the outgo of the wage ledger section appear all entries for money paid out in wages, commissions, etc., the items being posted to the wage ledger."[25] A trial balance was taken annually of the total income and expenditures unless there was a change in cashiers, in which event they were balanced at that time.

The wage ledger contained accounts with "workmen, industrial factors, various apprentices" as well as a number of impersonal accounts, such as "cash, a general expense account, a brokerage account, a profit and loss account, a cost of manufacturing account and an account for the general ledger which is the controlling account for all the money paid out through the wage ledger."[26] The general expense account contained several sorts of debits, such as charcoal and firewood, wool-combs, and purchases of account books, as well as many other expenses. The source of entries was the book of income and outgo; and it was closed to the cost of manufacture account by crediting general expense and debiting the cost of manufacture account. In addition to this debit, the cost of manufacture account was charged with all wages, commissions, and salaries, being in turn closed out to the general ledger control account by a debit to the latter at periodic intervals. In effect, then, the wage ledger was a combined factory ledger and employees accounts receivable ledger.

This wage ledger is probably the most significant aspect of the Medici accounts, at least from the standpoint of the development of cost accounting controls. It was what we call today a subsidiary ledger. De Roover believes that "it is the earliest known example" of this now familiar accounting procedure and technique.[27] (Many people have the impression that controlling accounts and subsidiary ledgers were invented much later.) The wage ledger was tied in with the general ledger by a reciprocal account called *quaderno dei manifattori;* in the subsidiary ledger an account was maintained with the principal ledger. Following modern practice the two reciprocal accounts offset each other. It is interesting to note, however, that the wage ledger was kept in *lire piccioli,* the petty transaction monetary unit, while the main ledger used the gold florin (at that time worth seven times as much as the lire). Another interesting point is that the wage ledger, being "a key-book for purposes of control," was kept by the managing partner in his own handwriting, while the hired accountant kept the remaining records.[28] This arrangement was provided for in the partnership agreement.

In addition to the above books, three other journals of original entry were kept in the sixteenth century: namely, the book of spinners, the book of weavers, and the book of dyers. These were used to keep track of the work given out to individuals to be finished at home or some other place beyond the control of the Medici family or its agents, as well as some workers within the shop. Items were posted from these journals to both the general ledger and wage ledger depending upon the status of the worker. "The wool factors in charge of spinning, with dyers, fullers, shearmen, and stretchers, were posted to the general ledger,"[29] while all others were posted to the wage ledger. "Why this was done is not clear,"[30] that is, the basis used for division of the posting is not evident from the available data. The connection between the different books and the posting process may be more easily comprehended by the accompanying diagram:

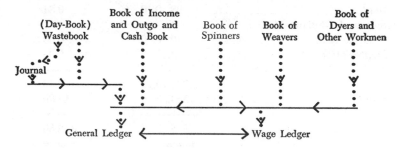

An interesting point arises here in connection with the wastebook noted in the diagram. It may be remembered that, as contrasted with what Paciolo had to say about the wastebook, that is, that the wastebook should be used for *all* transactions (Chapter VI of his *Summa*, 1494), "the purposes and usefulness of the wastebooks found in the Medici records are not clear, because the entries in these books are practically identical in form and substance with' these in the corresponding journals."[31] Certain entries were posted first to the journal and then to the general ledger (see diagram), while others were posted directly from the wastebook to the ledger. "It is not at all clear why certain types of entries are posted directly from the wastebook to the ledger. Some of the entries are for fixtures, a few are for expenses charged to real accounts, and most of them are for payments to creditors made by transferring accounts receivable to the creditors' accounts."[32] This is another of the many mysteries in the early development of bookkeeping by double entry.

The extent to which the details of the manufacturing cost were

made available to the partners can be observed from the accompanying
statement, based on the 1531 partnership general ledger:[33]

	Fl. s. d.	Percent of cost
Wool	3899.19. 0	34.60
Dyeing	1967.12. 5	17.50
Dyestuffs	219.12. 2	1.94
Soap	98.15.10	0.85
Napping and Shearing	6. 0. 5	0.04
Manufacturing Expense, detailed		
in wage-ledger	4920. 8. 5	43.60
	11112. 8. 3	98.53
Rent	98. 0. 0	0.84
Salary of Giuliano Medici,		
accountant	70. 0. 0	0.60
Depreciation	3.11. 5	0.03
	11283.19. 8	100.00
Profit	1554. 5. 6	13.80
Selling Price	12838. 5. 2	113.80

It is noteworthy that the manufacturing expense, a large item in
the cost statement, was separately shown and that the details thereof
were available in the so-called "wage-ledger." Even though depreciation was a negligible amount, it was present in the accounts of the
partnership.

Some time later, by 1556, the accounts had become even more detailed. If they had desired, the partners could have drawn up the
accompanying statement:

FRANCESCO DI GIULIANO DI RAFFAELLO DE' MEDICI &
CO., 1556-1558[34]

	Fl. s. d.	Ratio
Sales, 71 cloths	2970.15. 9	96.6%
Loss	105.19. 2	3.4%
	3076.14.11	100.0%

	Fl. s. d.	Fl. s. d.	Ratio	Ratio
Purchases of Raw Material (Wool)		921. 6.11		29.7%

Manufacturing Expense

		Fl. s. d.	Fl. s. d.	Ratio	Ratio
I.	Washing	19.14. 0		0.64%	
	Beating	56.19. 8		1.86%	
	Combing	106.15. 9		3.50%	
	Carding	90. 8. 7	273.18. 0	2.90%	8.9%
II.	Spinning		650.11. 1		21.2%
III.	Warping	22. 5. 0		0.75%	
	Weaving	365. 2. 3	387. 7. 3	11.85%	12.6%
IV.	Burling	18.17. 7		0.60%	
	Scouring	27.15. 5		0.90%	
	Fulling	13.19. 2		0.45%	
	Tentering	9. 8.10		0.33%	
	Shearing	23. 6. 0		0.77%	
	Mending	1. 8. 8		0.06%	
	Twisting of selvage	5.10. 9	100. 6. 5	0.19%	3.3%
V.	Dyeing		309. 5. 6		10.1%

Supplies

	Fl. s. d.	Fl. s. d.	Ratio	Ratio
Oil	53. 8. 5		1.74%	
Dyestuffs	36.12.10		1.16%	
Soap	33.14. 9	123.16. 0	1.10%	4.0%
		2766.11. 2		89.8%

Overhead

	Fl. s. d.	Ratio
Tools	12.10. 0	0.4%
Rent	52. 0. 0	1.7%
Administrative Expenses	98. 5.10	3.2%
Salaries (Staff members)	128.13. 4	4.3%
Brokerage	7.15. 0	0.3%
Lavatura di Guado (washing of woad)	10.19. 7	0.3%
	3076.14.11	100.0%

De Roover offers the following interesting comments regarding the statement:

It should be observed that the total direct charges, including raw materials, supplies, and labor amount to approximately 90 percent of the cost of goods sold. Raw materials represent 29.7 percent of the total cost; supplies, 4 percent; manufacturing expense, as high as 56.1 percent. This last item only includes outlay for wages. Spinning is the most costly process, with a ratio of 21.2 percent. Next comes weaving with 12.6 percent, dyeing with 10.1 percent, and preparing the wool with 8.9 percent. Finishing does not exceed 3.3 percent of the total cost.

Overhead charges, like rent, salaries and sundry administrative expenses, are relatively unimportant as they represent only 10 percent. The overwhelming importance of direct charges, as contrasted with overhead, was to be expected, because burden on fixed investments, like machinery, did not yet play any part in the computation of cost in the sixteenth century. Industrial enterprises were then highly flexible units and could adapt themselves readily to a slacker demand by simply curtailing their volume of production. Each curtailment engendered unemployment, but it did not necessarily turn profits into losses, as would be the case in a modern industrial concern with topheavy overhead. With regard to price reductions, mediaeval and early modern enterprises were perhaps less flexible because guild regulations and custom determined the scale of wages and thereby introduced an element of rigidity into the cost structure.[35]

The books of account used by some of the Medici dyers in the early part of the sixteenth century offer few new features over the ones used in the wool industry. In addition to the usual wastebook, journal, ledger, and book of income and outgo, two others were used; one had to do with alum purchases and the other was a record of cloth received for dyeing.

Such was the system of accounts used by the Medici industrial enterprises. Anyone at all familiar with modern cost accounting techniques will recognize immediately that some of the current practices are quite evident in the old Medici records. The methods used were crude, of course, but the astonishing thing is that the systems worked as well as they did. The development of a separate so-called "wage ledger" was quite original, and was a distinct forerunner of the modern factory ledger. Moreover, the bookkeepers who handled the complex records which were kept must have been experts because even today the system used by them would be considered complicated and technical in nature. As De Roover states it:

The bookkeeping system of the Medici was entirely adequate for their purpose and fitted perfectly their organization. It provided the means which the management needed to control the flow of material as well as the movement of funds. It was not yet a cost-finding system, but it came very close to being one. The account books give enough indication to permit one to assume that the Medici had a good knowledge of their approximate cost.

The use of special journals and of a subsidiary ledger reveals a far-advanced accounting technique. Neither Paciolo nor the sixteenth and seventeenth-century authors on bookkeeping contain any reference to industrial accounting or to the use of subsidiary books. The Medici account books prove beyond a doubt that the contemporary textbooks do not give an accurate picture, and that actual business practice was far ahead of theory. If accounting manuals were lagging behind, this was not equally true of contemporary technical treatises relating to the textile industry; for example, a fifteenth-century manuscript dealing with manufacturing of silk fabrics describes and gives examples of use of subsidiary books.[36]

THE DEL BENE ACCOUNTS

The accounts of the Del Bene firm of wool manufacturers offer another example of the early use of bookkeeping records in an enterprise which converted raw material into a useful and salable product. The headquarters of the firm were at Florence, Italy. While the system used was crude compared with later developments, the ingenuity displayed by the persons in charge of the records was remarkable. Only prime costs were derived, but considerable additional information was furnished to the owners and managers.[37]

The records of this firm go far back into the mediaeval era; one authority has even gone so far as to insist that they hold, "as far as is known, the origins of industrial cost accounting."[38] Since the accounts begin in the year 1318, there is little question that they represent some of the earliest examples of cost bookkeeping.

In the earlier decades of the fourteenth century the Del Bene accountants made little distinction between their merchandise and industrial transactions. The firm evidently grew out of humble circumstances and for a long while there was no need to separate the trading and work shop activities; the profits from the two phases were mingled. After a few decades, however, the need arose for more accurate and distinct cost data. So, beginning about 1350 the firm's accountants established, in a sense, two sets of books in order to show separately (1) the results of the trading or mercantile activity, and (2) the central workshop data.

The system originated by the persons responsible for the records consisted of opening up individual record books for each of the principal cost components, excluding overhead or burden. Thus, by 1368, there were (a) the *libri delle lane* "book of raw wool purchased," (b) the *libri dei lavoranti* "laborers wage book,," and (c) the *libri dei tintori* "dyers wage book." Peragallo explains the use of each book in the following manner: (1) In the raw wool purchases book the transactions are recorded in the form of bills. "Each entry bears the date of purchase, the name of the seller, the place of purchase, the mark (in the nature of a trade-mark) indicating the quality of the wool, and finally the price." (2) In the laborers wage book the "labor expenses necessary to manufacture a certain quantity and quality of woolen cloth" are recorded. For example, the combing and the wool carding operations were kept distinct and the processed quantity of each presented. (3) The dyers wage book was similar to the *lavoranti*, "except that costs here are not kept on the basis of quantity of cloth, but rather are kept in accounts opened for each individual *tintore* (dyer)."[39]   The following is a sample of the detail record kept in this book in 1368:

Ugolino di Marcho, skilled dyer

1 white 57	May 8	black	16, soldi 4
1 white	June 8	black	16, soldi 4
1 pale blue	July 8	light blue	16, soldi 10

Total fiorini 48, soldi 18

Obviously, the sum of the items entered in the three books just described would be the same as the now familiar prime cost. Records of consignments out and sales were kept in other account books. There is no evidence that double entry accounts were maintained for the separate industrial activities of the Del Bene firm, but it is certain that the three books were summarized at intervals and their totals carried to the ledger of the firm. This ledger had many of the attributes of modern double entry. As Peragallo explains it: "The manufacturing periods were divided in length according to the time necessary for the manufacture of a certain fixed quantity of cloth. All costs and sales were based on this quantity of cloth and anything over and above this was deferred to the next period. A *bilancio*, from which the profits or losses were ascertained, was drawn up at the end of each period. Each manufacturing period was named *ragione*, and was distinguished from the others by a letter of the alphabet."[40] There was much that was modern in those ancient records!

Space does not permit the reproduction here of the *bilancio*. It is sufficient to explain that the total of the liabilities, capital, and deferred sales was subtracted from the total assets in order to obtain the profit for the period. The profit was described on the statement as "net profit which God saw fit to allow us for the past 12 months ended today March 1, 1364, for the fiscal period 'h'."[41] This net profit was recorded in turn in a book especially adapted to the purpose. In a subsequent entry the income was divided between the owners in their agreed profit and loss ratio.

The Del Bene accounts are especially significant when they are contrasted with those of the Medici. It is surprising how many improvements had been originated by the time the Medici industrial partnerships began to operate. The Del Bene system of accounts, however, definitely foreshadowed the records maintained a hundred years later by the Medici. They also gave an impetus to the early growth of double entry bookkeeping by showing its adaptability to new and different situations. Many later authorities have pointed out the relationship between the growth of bookkeeping and capitalism.

THE ACCOUNTS OF DATINI AND NICCOLO OF PRATO

A large number (over 500) of the record books of these early business men have been preserved in the Datini Archives at Prato in Italy.[42] Some of them indicate that, just as in Florence, a flourishing woolen manufacturing industry was carried on in that city. Penndorf in "Die Anfange der Betriebsbuchhaltung," has given a short description of these early industrial records and accounts.[43] The first workshop in Prato was established by Francesco di Marco in 1382, and had a branch in Florence; a ledger is extant for the shop beginning with March, 1384. Single entry was used, and the wages paid to the workers for the twenty to thirty processes through which the wool was put were entered in the ledger. Other costs were also computed and entered in the so-called "day book," or *memorial*, and posted to the ledger.

In the spinners' books there was a special section for each lot of carded wool, containing the accounts of the different spinners. These accounts showed the name of the spinner, the weight of the carded wool received for spinning, the weight of the returned spun yarn, as well as the wages for spinning and remarks as to the manner of payment of the wages, with which the workmen were charged in the lower part of the account.[44]

The books of the weavers were somewhat similar. In the dye shops, on the other hand, were kept some journals, daybooks, and books for business relations with clothiers. As a matter of interest, one of the dye books began: "In this book I shall write the name of all clothiers who furnish me with wool, cloth, carded wool, dyer's woad, and anything else I need in my dye shop. Niccolo di Piero, dyer at Prato. Begun July 10, 1386 for profit."[45]

In one of the daybooks for 1395 there was a resume of the different costs incurred in manufacturing two pieces of white woolen cloth, each one 14 ellen (32.6 meters) long by 3½ ellen (8.1 meters) wide. The costs were:

	£.	s.	d.
Bought from Francesco di Marco and Stoldo di Lorenzo 95 pounds white carded wool marked eight-plus (refer page 2) for	12.	8.	1
Additional 9 pounds white yarn, marked plus-plus, needed for this cloth (refer page 86)	2.15.		6
Additional 3 pounds white spun wool, marked 7 plus-plus, needed for weaving (refer weaving book, page 5, and refer page 82 of the handbook of weavers and shearers)	1.10.		8
Cost of beating (refer workbook A page 15)	—.17.		2
Combing of the wool	3.—.		2
Carding of the two pieces	2.10.10		
Spinning of the worsted wool	2. 8.		3
Spinning of the ordinary wool	2.18.—		
Combing, carding, and oil	3. 8.—		
Clipping of the two pieces	—. 6.		5
Weaving	4. 5.		8
Cleaning and examining	—.18.—		
Edging	4.—.—		
Washing, carding, and soap	4. 6.—		
Stiffening and transportation	—.11.—		
Clipping of the front side	—. 6—		
Hire and expense of apprentices	2.10.—		
Other expenses	—.18.—		
Final clipping	—.12.		6
Arranging and folding	—. 7.		6
Dyes	8. 5.		8
Total costs of above named pieces	59. 3.		5

Deduct therefrom the remaining balance of filling and
   warp yarn ....—. 9.—

And there remains (a net cost of) ....58.14. 5[46]

This list shows that the now familiar "cost of production" was
well-known several centuries ago, and a hundred years before Paciolo
wrote his *Summa*, 1494. It is also interesting to note that the by-
products (filling and warp yarn) were deducted from the total costs
in order to arrive at the "net" cost of the two pieces of cloth. As far
back as 1395, then, cost accountants were being plagued by that perplexing problem!

THE BRACCI ACCOUNTS

Another example of the early use of accounts in workshops has
been described by Federigo Melis.[47] The full name of this firm was
Compagnia de Lazzaro di Giovanni de Feo Bracci, and it was located
in the city of Arezzo in northern Italy. Only one ledger manuscript
remains of the many which must have been used. This single manuscript was made from an unusual kind of strong paper; the pages were
large (fourteen by eighteen inches) and they show transactions dating
from 1415 to 1423. On the first page of the book someone has written:
"This book belongs to Lazzaro di Giovanni, and in it will be written
every evidence concerning the wool industry in my factory of
Arezzo."[48]

As contrasted with the Datini records, the Bracci bookkeepers did
not record in separate books the different activities of the firm. Yet
these different operations were clearly distinguished in the sections of
the manuscript. An index was prepared showing the page number
where the different matters could be found. Since only one book
was used, it seems obvious that the operations were quite limited as
compared with the competing Datini family in Prato. Some illustrative
entries are given below:

In the name of God, amen.   The 20th of July 1415.

1 dark grey cloth distinguished with number 1, to be carded and
combed

To be delivered to Mariotto di messer Giovanni at his disposition in
July, 64 pounds of carded wool of the above mentioned cloth at a

price of 12s. per hundred: total pounds s. seven d. eight

lb. — s. 7 d. 8

Received cash, on the 27th July, s. seven d. 8 according to the memorial
of the workers distinguished with an A at page

lb. — s. 7 d. 8

To be delivered to Antonio detto Gellosino, in July, 60 pounds of carded wool of the above mentioned cloth for d. two pounds, total s.
ten.

lb. — s. 10 d. —

Received on the 27th July, s. ten p. : in the book of worker A,
page 9

lb. — s. 10 d. —

[Next five entries dealing with combing, carding, and spinning are
omitted here to save space.]

Amount of the above expenditures for the above cloth

lb. 8 s. 19 d. 10

And for the spinning of the thread of the above cloth according
to page 17

lb. 9 s. 1 d. —

And for the assortment of wools of several kinds of cloth to
Pietro Paolo di Giugliano pounds 3 s. nine in special personal account, according to the book of workers distinguished by A, page 10

lb. 3 s. 9 d. —

Total amount of the above expenditures pounds 28 s. 15 d. 6.

Posted to bottom page 66, designated A.[49]

Even though this Bracci manuscript contains unusually complete
information for the time at which it was prepared, certain important
cost accounting data are missing. For instance, both the raw material
and the general manufacturing costs were entered in another book,
l'arte de la lana, now lost. It is important to note that the pages of
the ledger from which these illustrations were drawn have horizontal
lines enclosing each entry. Further, these entries were limited to the
accounts with each separate worker and each phase of the making of
the cloth (except for the combing process—this had two separate
accounts).

Another book, now lost, referred to as *libro di lavoranti,* was evidently kept. It would probably be referred to as a pay roll book today,

since it contained the accounts concerning the workers. In order to obtain the totals shown in the last illustrative entry given here, there must be included certain sums from other accounts on other pages of the ledger; these sums include the raw material and other general costs. Further, the total of lb. 28. 15. 6, excluding the weaving cost (lb. 13) was posted to another place designated by A.

The entries were recorded by Bracci at odd dates, except for weaving transactions; in the case of the Datini accounts the twelfth and twenty-fourth of each month were used.

The workers who conducted the spinning operations evidently belonged to some organized group, since no separate accounts of their indebtedness were kept. The accountants also used columns to record carefully the quantity of wool issued and received from the employees.

In summary, it may be stated that the early Bracci accounts contained many of the elements of a cost accounting system, especially in regard to the control of all cost factors leading to the production of the product. It is to be regretted that some of the important documents are no longer available, but enough remains to indicate clearly that these fifteenth century accountants were quite clever and original.[50]

THE PLANTIN ACCOUNTS

Florence Edler (de Roover) has made a study of the books of account of Christopher Plantin, a Flemish printer and publisher who lived in the sixteenth century.[51] These accounts further illustrate the fact that some cost accounting techniques developed concurrent with the rise of capitalism during and after the Renaissance, several centuries before the Industrial Revolution and the growth of the factory system on a large scale. The important account books of this printer were kept by double entry, and date from 1563 when Plantin, a Frenchman by birth, who had been in the printing business for several years prior to that time, formed a partnership with four influential men of the period, all living in Antwerp. This arrangement, unfortunately for later students of cost accounting, terminated in 1567, but in the four-year period the records of the enterprise were handled in such a manner as to be most interesting to later generations. It might be mentioned also that the Plantin accounts are available for a long period of time in addition to the years 1563-67, but the bookkeeping for all the remaining years was mediocre, a type of single entry being used. Edler thinks that the formation of the partnership gave rise to the

very accurate double entry records kept during the period under review.[52] Be that as it may, the ledger and journal (written in Italian)
kept under the supervision of one of the partners illustrated several
quite modern techniques. A description of the records follows:

For the sake of clearness it should be pointed out first that in
reality two sets of accounts were kept. The partner responsible for
the correct accounting evidently employed an Italian bookkeeper,
steeped in the best tradition of Paciolo, to make up the annual accounts
and reports. This the bookkeeper did from a journal and ledger (no
wastebook was used) which he kept in Italian and which was not made
or posted every day, "but at irregular intervals."[53] How did the latter
get his information for his entries? The answer is that Plantin himself
kept a second set of account books, mostly memoranda of various
sorts. The functions and nature of the books Plantin kept may be
summarized as follows: "(1) Some kind of a journal, called *journal des
affaires*, in which he made note of all his transactions: purchases of
equipment, paper, sales, receipts, and various expenditures; (2) some
kind of a ledger, called *grand livre des affaires*, wherein the same information was reproduced in a somewhat concentrated form; (3) a
wage book, containing detailed records of wages paid to compositors,
printers, proofreaders, artists, scholars, etc.; (4) a *livre des ustensiles*,
which today one would call a plant ledger";[54] and several others
which are not important in this connection. All of these were written
in French and Edler speculates as to the reason why the two different
languages were used; all that is known, however, is that the double
entry ledger was kept just as Paciolo explained in his *Summa*.

The Italian ledger also contained several other interesting accounts. For example, each type of what would be called now "fixed
assets" had its own special account; the different grades of paper
(raw material) also had individual accounts with special extension
columns so that the amount on hand at any time could be easily determined—a type of perpetual inventory. A manufacturing expense
account was established in which wages and other expenses were
recorded; even work-in-process accounts were used—on a job order
basis. Edler describes the operation of the latter as follows:

For each book, which Plantin undertook to print, a special
account was opened in the ledger, for example, 'Virgil in 16°,'
'Horace in 16°' etc. These accounts were debited for the paper
used and for the wages and other expenses of printing. The paper
account and the account, *spese di mercanzie* (expenses of manu-

facture), were credited. When the book came off the press, its special account was canceled and an account named "Books in Stock" (*libri in monte*) was debited. From this explanation it clearly appears that the accounts opened for each book which was printed were the equivalent of a goods-in-process account. The account "Books in Stock" is somewhat like the modern Finished-Goods account.[55]

Incidentally, like the paper accounts mentioned above, the books in stock account had special columns for recording the numbers on hand at any time—again, a type of perpetual inventory.

When a book had been completely printed, the total cost of publication could be determined by the addition of the debits in the account established for that purpose; nothing was said, however, about overhead or depreciation charges. As for the latter it is Edler's opinion that accuracy was not sacrificed even though no provision was made for wear and tear of the presses. Her reason for this conclusion is that "the equipment used was not very expensive, and there was no danger of its becoming obsolete, or even of wearing out within a foreseeable time."[56] It might be mentioned, however, that this is contradictory to the present-day explanation of the depreciation charge; that is, that the depreciation charge represents the recovery of the cost of an asset however insignificant, which, if neglected, causes the over statement of income (if there is any income).[57] Strict accuracy was sacrificed by the failure to record depreciation as a cost of carrying on the enterprise. But in view of Hatfield's often-quoted statement that all machinery is on the road to the scrap pile,[58] it is interesting to note that some of Plantin's presses were still in good working order in the 1930's, and that the City of Antwerp used them occasionally to print significant speeches of public officials.

Royalties were not paid to the authors of the works published by Plantin; the writer of a book, however, was given a flat sum for his manuscript, which sum was charged to the account established for each publication.

In concluding the discussion of the Plantin records it might be stated "that the problems of cost finding were not entirely ignored"[59] even in the Flemish territories. "This is rather surprising because neither Paciolo [1494] nor any of the subsequent Italian writers on bookkeeping refer to industrial bookkeeping in their works. The early treatises on bookkeeping deal only with ordinary mercantile accounting, but the Plantin account books confirm the statement that bookkeeping in actual practice was forging ahead of the textbooks."[60] The same statement could be made, however, in regard to the development of cost accountancy for the past hundred years; it is a well-known fact that current cost practices consistently keep a step ahead of text writers. This order of progress, though, is perfectly normal and logical.

THE ACCOUNTS OF THE MINT AT RAGUSA IN DALMATIA

Another example of the early (1422) use of accounting in an industrial enterprise is afforded by the records of the mint at Ragusa, the journals of which have been preserved in large part. These are dated in the fifteenth century and illustrate especially the flow of material (ore) from the crude metal to the finished coins.[61] The mint used special accounts which corresponded roughly with each step of the coining process. When a customer brought some metal to the mint, an account called "*argento de zecha*" was debited for its contrevaleur "exchange value," and a credit was made to the customer's current account for the same amount. When the metal passed to the smelter, the account *argento de zecha* was credited and a debit made to another account called "*fornelo*." The fornelo in turn was closed to the account *argento de lega* when the metal had been refined to its legal fineness and left the crucible. The metal was now ready to be struck into coins; and to preserve the flow of value as well as to show responsibility, the master of the mint's own personal account was debited when bars or ingots were taken from the *argento de lega* to be stamped into coins. The latter account, of course, was credited. After the coins had been struck, the master's account was closed, by a credit, for the value of the pieces, and the cash box or cash account was debited. As can be easily seen, one could follow the metal through the successive accounting manipulations without difficulty. The mint managers were able to maintain quite accurate control over the different processes, as well as to account for the responsibility over the valuable metals. In fact, the internal audit control feature was probably as important to the mint managers at the time as the determination of the cost of minting coins.

THE ACCOUNTING AT THE SILVER MINES AT KOSSEN AND KITZBUHL

The last example of mediaeval industrial records to be described in this chapter is concerned with the accounts of the Kossen and Kitzbuhl (Austria) silver mines. De Roover states that the accounts for the mines as such were not kept distinct from the accounts of the foundries operated in connection with the mines, and adjacent thereto. But when the ore was transferred from the mines to the foundry an entry was made debiting the foundry account and crediting the mines account for the transfer.[62] The interesting feature of these accounts, therefore, is their presentation of both the ordinary commercial transactions and the mutation of the silver from the rough ore to the finished product—fine silver.

SUMMARY

Even though the preceding examples of industrial accounting in the mediaeval era demonstrate that certain cost techniques and practices had their origin in the period 1350-1600, we should not hasten to the conclusion that cost accounting had gone through its growing pains period by the end of the sixteenth century. Far from it. As a matter of fact, there is no evidence that there was any widespread use of the techniques adopted by the firms described on the preceding pages of this chapter;[63] these firms were evidently forerunners in the developmental decades of cost accounting. It is also interesting and significant that while a hundred or more people wrote textbooks and treatises on bookkeeping topics during the era under discussion, not a single one, so far as the writer can ascertain, felt impelled to describe even the rudiments of industrial accounting.[64]

What, then, were the objectives of these early systems of industrial accounts?[65] One thing is certain: the records were *not* generally used to keep a regular and accurate account of the proprietorship and income of the individual enterprise. Furthermore, little use apparently was made of the cost determinations in the setting of product selling prices; this nonuse, however, can readily be appreciated when it is recalled how incomplete the cost records were.[66] Factory overhead was also indifferently handled, but this cost element was small in view of the fact that almost no machinery was used in the operations. In summary, it seems to have been the purpose of most of the systems to provide for (1) accounting control over the steps of production and for (2) the curbing of waste and spoilage in the use of materials, which are, however, two of the essential aims of present-day cost accounting. In the wool and silk cloth manufacturing enterprises, for instance, the numerous processes brought into existence the necessity for accurate control of raw material and labor, and this need was reflected in the Medici records, to give just one example. These, then, were the contributions of the mediaeval period to cost accounting theory and its techniques. They were sufficient, however, to permit one modern authority to state: "Indeed the more of bookkeeping history that is uncovered, the more the conviction grows that we moderns have added woefully little to the early foundations."[67]

COST DEVELOPMENTS TO 1885 WITH EMPHASIS UPON ENGLAND, FRANCE, AND THE UNITED STATES

EVEN THOUGH ONE MAY FIND EVIDENCE OF THE USE OF DOUBLE ENTRY bookkeeping in connection with manufacturing firms several centuries before the Industrial Revolution, the literature on cost accounting before that period is conspicious by its rarity. As a matter of fact, it may be safely stated that the examples of industrial accounting technique discussed in the previous chapter were the exception rather than the rule in so far as their widespread adoption was concerned. While they are important in indicating the adaptability of the then new science of double entry, the problems involved were rather simple as compared with the perplexing accounting questions raised by the Industrial Revolution. Before that time a person well trained in double entry could handle most of the records which needed to be maintained; there was relatively little necessity for highly complex record keeping. Mercantile transactions predominated. Expenses had to be summarized, of course, in the form of a profit and loss account, and records of certain types of assets and liabilities maintained, but no great problems arose from these tasks. Occasionally, also, the bookkeeper had to keep separate accounts of different consignments or perhaps of a series of ventures or voyages. In addition, some merchants wanted details showing the profit on the sale of several classes of merchandise

by types of goods. All of these needs of the day were met, as evidenced by the considerable variety of textbooks which have been preserved to the present time. These books were written not only by the
English but also by Dutch, German, Italian, and French writers.[1]

The same relative simplicity existed in regard to the accounting
for engineering, coal mining, and textile firms in the latter part of the
eighteenth century. With the rapid growth of these industries, however, a number of problems arose which accountants and bookkeepers
had not previously needed to consider, except in a minor sort of way.
These problems arose mainly in connection with the large amounts of
capital sunk in plant equipment and transportation facilities.[2] Many
economic historians have pointed out the contrast between the old
and the new methods of production. For example, Ashton states:

> The typical concern of the new era was integrated in its struc-
> ture; it mined the ore and coal, smelted, refined, rolled and slit
> the iron into its finished form of plates and rods. From this
> time onward, therefore, very large capitals began to be sunk
> in the iron industry; and in 1812, to give an example, in one
> locality, there were in the neighborhood of Birmingham no
> fewer than ten iron works, each of which had cost over £50,000 to
> establish. It was by no means uncommon to find 300 or 500 men
> employed in a single works, apart from the colliers and others
> connected with supply of raw materials.[3]

The same authority states that in 1833 about one fourth of the
cost of bar iron was said to consist of interest on the capital sunk in
the foundry and equipment.[4] The relatively large investment required
in those early mills brought on many of the same problems which pro-
ducers have to face today, and which require such complex cost
records. For the sake of emphasis a few may be enumerated (some of
these were also significant in connection with the firms described in
the preceding chapter):

(1) An adequate supply of raw material and the records pertaining thereto would be wanted by the managers of the foundry, as
is was recognized that too much inventory might be kept on hand.

(2) The large payments made to employees required a system
which would tend to diminish payroll frauds or errors.

(3) The problem of depreciation became much more important
in view of the more expensive equipment used and the obsolescence
factor.

(4) In view of the keen competition which began to prevail, it
was essential that the managers know to what extent prices could be

cut in dull seasons, and yet cover "prime costs"; in other words, a knowledge of variable and fixed costs was required. This latter brought up the whole problem of overhead.

(5) The transfer of product from process to process needed to be watched carefully and costs compared from period to period.

Many other problems of like nature arose, not only in the iron and steel industry but in other industries as well.[5] For example, the accounting for the engineering and machinery trades offered many interesting perplexities. Steam engines began to be used in England in the latter part of the eighteenth century, and the production of textile machinery grew by leaps and bounds after the Napoleonic Wars. Railway equipment was needed after 1830, in both England and the United States. In all of these trades it was the custom to estimate costs and tender bids to prospective buyers. What was more logical than to take the next step; that is, after accepting a contract for a certain project, to keep some sort of collective details "as to the costs of executing the contract in order to ascertain the profit or loss thereon, and to provide information for future estimates"?[6] Obviously, this is what is known today as job order costing, and some of the modern cost accountants' most difficult problems grew out of those humble beginnings. All of the controversy concerning the allocation of overhead to jobs or contracts, whether or not to include interest as a cost, profit on unfinished contracts, and the coördination of the cost and the general financial records, can be traced back to the same source. By-product and joint product costs became increasingly important as industrial chemistry gained a foothold in the early 1800's. The extension of railway systems combined practically all costing problems, such as depreciation, obsolescence, heavy overhead expenses, shop costs, joint costs, and control of a far-flung integrated organization.

It is common knowledge that some of the problems listed have not been solved even at present. The economist J. M. Clark has aptly stated the situation thus: "The Industrial Revolution was so strangely slow in making men aware of what it was doing to them!"[7]

It is also a striking fact that cost literature of this period is very scarce. The persons who worked on the problems seemed to have been very practical, busy men who had no time to write concerning their problems and how they met them in practice. As stated by one authority: "The Industrial Revolution gave a real impetus to the growth of cost accounting but progress in machine technology was much more rapid than progress in cost accounting."[8]

There is also no doubt that most of the earlier firms managed to get along with only a modicum of accounting records even though their costing problems must have vexed them continually in more ways than one. It should be stressed, however, that the whole development of accounting has been a very gradual process—*natura non facit saltum*—and cost accounting is no exception. One cost accountant or bookkeeper passed on his methods to another for experiment and trial rather than writing textbooks or learned articles. On the other hand, it should be noted that perhaps another reason why so little was written on cost accounting before 1885 was the traditional attitude of business men towards divulging any comparative advantages in manufacturing techniques to possible competitors. The handling of a firm's accounts in an especially advantageous way was considered personal, a secret not to be let out to rival firms. As two authorities put it: "Rightly, in the circumstances of the time, the British Manufacturer did not wish to disclose the basis on which his prices were made up."[9] Then, too, there were very few theoreticians, and if some firm did happen to develop special and effective methods for dealing with its own costing problems, it is not likely that it would allow the facts to be broadcast. Possible solutions, therefore, to some of the problems mentioned above went unheralded. This conclusion is borne out by a statement made by Sir John Mann in 1903. Writing as late as that date, on the origin of costing, he was able to say: "Until recent years . . . individual managers who had evolved cost methods suited to their own needs generally kept these secret. . . . A more liberal spirit is gaining ground generally, as it is seen that publicity as to principles (of costing) aids each manufacturer in ascertaining his actual costs, leads to sound accounting, and therefore tends in time to lessen price cutting—a piece of commercial cruelty which sometimes happens from sheer ignorance of actual cost."[10] It is strange, however, that there is no dearth of texts on commercial bookkeeping during this period, several score having come down to the present; yet it is rare that any of them mention cost or manufacturing record keeping.

In view of what has been stated above, it is entirely natural that probably the first writer to mention factory accounting specifically should be an Englishman. The Industrial Revolution began, as is well known, in England, and that country was the first to be faced with industrial problems. Later on, it would also be natural for America to take over part of the lead, along different lines perhaps, but nevertheless the lead.[11] This will be treated in detail on subsequent pages.

Authoritative references to cost accounting in the 1600's are few and far between. The accounting text writers of that century either ignored the need of the manufacturer, or they simply suggested that the merchant's books would also serve the industrial firm. This does not mean, however, that the workshop owners of the seventeenth century were entirely unaware of the useful features of analytical cost records. One of the most interesting examples of a seventeenth century cost calculation is dated 1620 and was issued by the London members of the Worshipful Company of Bakers. The principal purpose of the statement was an attempt to demonstrate to all concerned that the selling price of baked bread at the time was inadequate to cover the cost of baking—a common enough complaint both then and now. The cost schedule in its original language is given on page 32.

(Comments originally attached to the statement)
Besides all duties to the Kinges Matie, charges in the Cittie and in the Warde, charges in his Companie, charges or reparacons of the howse, charges for howshould stuff dailie bought into the howse and amended. Also losses by stale bread, ill debtors, bad servants, and other like hindrances.

Item there is a penny in everie shilling given away for vantage.
Item many Bakers do scarce bake ten quarters a weeke and yf anie man do bake more his charge is accordinglie greater.
And so it plainlie appeareth that a quarter of Wheat cannot be baked with 6s. allowance for charges.

        ✧   ✧   ✧   ✧   ✧

While some of the items of cost appearing on the statement are amusing in the light of present day standards, e.g., "ill debtors," "bad servants," "children's food," "fee to parson," "duty to the poor," "pay of maidservants," etc., there is an air of accuracy about the computation which gives it dignity and a seriousness of purpose. It is also significant that some of the items represent expenses which in modern practice would be absorbed by the owner as personal outlays not related to the cost of production. The concluding sentence of the comments is in the best tradition of the cost accountant: "And so it plainlie appeareth that a quarter of wheat cannot be baked with 6s. allowance for charges."[12]

Upon the restoration of Charles II of England, business and commerce made rapid strides ahead. Urwick and Brech suggest two reasons for this surge of interest, one of which is pertinent to the discussion here, namely, the sponsorship by the Royal Society of inventors

A COMPUTATION OF A BAKER'S PERTICULAR CHARGES ARISEING UPPON THE BAKEING OF TEN QUARTERS OF WHEAT BY WEEKE IN LONDON.
Year 1620

	£	s.	d.
Imprimis for howsrent after the rate of 30£ per ann. is by the weeke	0	11	6
For 4 Journeymens wages att 2s. 6d. a peece per weeke	0	10	0
For meate and drinck for them and for two apprentices at 4s. a peece per weeke	1	4	0
For Yeist	0	10	0
For Woodde	0	12	0
For Salt	0	1	0
For Boulters	0	1	0
For Garner Rent	0	2	0
For Wheat bought att the waterside the porters and fillers have 2d. ob. per quarter	0	2	0
For Sacks	0	1	0
For Wages for two maidservants	0	1	8
For their dyett	0	8	0
For a dyett for a man's self and his wife	0	10	0
A commonlie man hath not lesse than three or foure children, which cannot be lesse then fourpence a daie a peece for their dyett	0	7	0
And for their apparell and teaching at Schole at 12d. a pece	0	3	0
For seacoles for fireing by the weeke after 4 Chauldron per year	0	1	4
For Basketts after 13s. per ann. is	0	0	3
For Water weeklie	0	0	8
Item the Miller hath for his Toll out of everie quarter for grinding half a bushell, which id in tenn quarters 5 bushells, after 24s. the quarter	0	15	0
Item for apparell for a man's self, his wife, and two apprentices after 20£. per ann. is per weeke	0	7	8
Item for duties in his parishe to the Parson, the Skavengers, for the Poore for watching and wardeing at the least weekle	0	1	0
Summa totalis is per weeke	6	10	1

and other persons capable of contributing to technical progress.[13] This spirit of innovation spilled over into the authorship of books to instruct interested parties in the techniques of bookkeeping. As noted previously in this chapter, several dozen volumes were published in the period 1675-1725; even though they generally neglected the accounts of the industrialist, they nonetheless made a contribution to the economic well-being of the country. This in turn led later to the Industrial Revolution, with its emphasis on the factory system.

One of the earliest works in English to recognize that factory accounting was not exactly the same as commercial accounting, and that the requirements of each were different, was written by John Collins in 1697. It was called *The Perfect Method of Merchants Accompts,* and was published in London.[14] A set of dyers' accounts was used as an illustration, and Collins showed a raw materials (argol) account which dealt with both quantities and values. When material was purchased, the account was debited; and when argol was used or sold, the account was credited. In case the material was used in a further process, material was credited and a sort of work-in-process, that is, a dyehouse, account was debited, along with various miscellaneous expenses (costs). The difference between the two sides of the dyehouse account was the net profit for the year. Both of these accounts are given below. It should be noted that the entries are dated 1664 and 1665, several decades before the book was published, and that the accounts show the flow of values and goods from one

THE LEDGER OF THE DYE-HOUSE PARTABLE ACCOUNT
Debit

1664	Argol	C.	qrs.	l.		£.	s.	d.
Jan. 15	To stock of Adam Barker for 10 Casks Weighing,							
	viz.: C. Qrs. 1. _____	90	00	27 at 30s.		135	07	00
1665								
June 10	To Cash for 5 Casks ___	80	00	00 at 30s.		120	00	00
		170	00	27				
	To the Dye-house for neat gains_____					1	09	00
						256	16	00

Credit

1665	Argol	C.	qrs.	l.	£.	s.	d.
June 7	By Cash for 2 CsKS.						
	Weight at 32s. per C ___	18	00	00	28	16	00
	Sold to J. H. by the Dye-						
	House for _____	72	00	00			
	Spent as per Particulars						
	at 30s. _____				108	00	00
	By Goods remaining						
	for _____	80	00	00			
	Left at 30s. _____				120	00	00
	Lost in Weight _____	00	00	27	000	00	00
		170	00	27	256	16	00

account to another. The same idea was illustrated in the last chapter in connection with the Medici accounts, but in the present instance the illustration is concerned with a hypothetical firm and not an actual set of accounts.

THE LEDGER OF THE DYE-HOUSE PARTABLE ACCOUNT
Debit

	£.	s.	d.	£.	s.	d.
Dye-house or Loss						
To wares for sundry Commodities spent, viz. in a year ending the 29th December 1665						
To coals for 40 Chaulder _____	40	00	00			
To Argol for 72 C. (See above) _____	108	00	00			
To Allom for 2 tuns _____	50	00	00			
To Brazil Wood for 1 Tun _____	28	00	00			
To Coucheaneel for 40 l. at 30s. _____	60	00	00			
To the said for 15l. at 28s. _____	21	00	00			
To Fustick for 18C. at 6s. 8d. _____	6	00	00			
To Coppras for 3 h. h. _____	8	00	00			
To Mather for 68C. crop at 41 _____	272	00	00			
To Shumack for 10 Baggs _____	56	08	00			
To Island Wood for 3 Tuns _____	45	00	00			
To Spanish Indigo for 3 Cask _____	100	16	00	795	04	00

	£.	s.	d.
To Stock of Adam Barker for Year's Rent	100	00	00
To John Garthwait for an abatement		13	04
To Cash for the total of Sundry Disbursements in the Outward Column	664	12	03
To the Stocks of the Partners for the Dividend, being the neat gains of one Year's Trade	497	10	09
	2,058	00	04

Credit

Per Contra Dye-house or Profit	£.	s.	d.
By Argol for the neat gains	1	09	00
By Coucheaneel for the said	4	00	00
By Mather gained thereby	3	08	00
By Bayes for the like	100	00	00
By Goods remaining for divers loose Goods left that are charged to Account in the Disbursements for Contra	10	00	00
By John Garthwait for Earnings	1,406	13	04
By Jericho Cudworth for the said	532	10	00
	2,058	00	04

The next book dealing with industrial accounting (using the term in a wide sense) was written by one "A Person of Honour" in 1714. It was concerned with a very pertinent problem of the time, that is, the recording of the results of operations of farms by large estates. The work was given the title of *The Gentleman Accomptant*. David Murray has identified the author as Roger North, who is perhaps more famous as the writer of *Lives of the Norths*.[15] The accounts illustrated were divided so as to show the operating results of each farm separately, as well as the various undertakings within each farm.[16] North showed how each account was kept, both in quantities and in value if necessary. For example, the "grazing and dairy" account had an inner column for the number of lambs purchased or bred as well as a column for their value. On the credit side of the same account the sales were recorded, and the value and number used for personal consumption carefully entered. The balance was the number and value of lambs remaining "in stock." North also illustrated an interesting report form which is still used today in some instances, namely, a weekly summary of jobs performed by workers. The report follows:[17]

Workmens' Names	Monday Nov. 8, 1709	Tuesday 9	Wednesday 10	Thursday 11	Friday 12	Saturday 13
A. B.		Lopping of Trees	Same		Filling Gravel	Half of the Same
C. D.	Dyking by the Rod	Same	Same	Same	Same	Half the Same
E. F.	Dyking by the Rod	Same	Same	Same	Same	Half the same both done 12 Rod
G. H.	Helping in the Garden	Cutting & Pruning	Same	Same	Same	Same
J. K.	Filling the Gravel Cart	Digging Gravel	Same	Same	Same	Helping in the Garden

Obviously this sort of accounting would only be needed by the larger estates, and was probably used only by a few of those. The illustrations do show, however, that the needs of the time were being met in characteristic fashion. North observed, too, that this type of bookkeeping was "useful to gentlemen and to some necessary; commendable in all, and fruitless to none."[18]

In 1750, the needs of the shoemaker for accurate accounting were recognized, for in that year James Dodson, "Teacher of Mathematics," published *The Accountant or The Method of Bookkeeping*. It is not necessary to reproduce his shoemaker accounts here. The significant features were that he showed clearly "the processes through which the materials went, and the division into different types of shoes."[19] His handling of materials was also particularly noteworthy. Entries were made showing the conversion of raw leather into soles and heels of varying sizes, as well as the uppers. It seems to have been the custom in those days to transfer to journeymen the unattached parts of the shoe. When these were returned, therefore, as finished shoes, a credit was made to their accounts for the cost of materials and their own wages, while at the same time a debit was made to the finished shoe accounts, by types of shoe. The sales of finished shoes were kept by types also, one account showing columns for five styles of men's shoes sold for "ready money" (his term) in the shoemaker's own shop. Dodson concluded that: "An intelligent tradesman may easily use the preceding accounts as a model whereby to form his own books; in doing which, he may enter the delivery of materials, and the receipt of them manufactured, on opposite pages of a book kept for that purpose; the sale of goods in the shop, for ready money, may make another separate book, and the payments to workmen, a third."[20] Dodson also discussed estate accounts in much the same form as North, with the additional feature that wear of equipment was transferred from the implements account to the "home farm account" as an expense.[21]

In *Bookkeeping Methodized* (6th edition), 1760, by the schoolmaster John Mair, there was a bare mention of the accounts which should be kept by plantations in the West Indies. The author did not recommend that double entry be employed[22] and stated that the books of accounts to be used were to be "filled up" by the plantation clerk, under the general supervision of the overseer. Three different books, however, were recommended: (1) the boiling house book, which contained an account of all the sugar that was put into the pots; (2) the still house book, which contained an account of all the rum produced; and (3) the plantation book, which contained an account of all the sugar, rum, and other produce shipped and to whom sold. "The accounts of this book too are commonly stated in a simple manner, without double entry, as in the following specimen":

Butler Plantation, Jamaica, 1760[23]

John Wright	Debit	Contra	Credit
To 1 hogshead sugar,		By 12 firkins butter,	
Weight 15C. 3 qrs.		Weight neat	
14 lb. at 33s. 6d. ____xxxx		602 lb. at 13d. ____xxxx	
To 1 puncheon rum,		By 4 barrels herring	
Containing 118		at 45s. ____xxxx	
gallons, at 3s. ____xxxx			

This particular section ended with this amusing sentence: "It is needless to insist further plantation accounts, because any person skilled in bookkeeping will at first sight understand them, and be able to conduct them with all the exactness commonly required, or even perhaps to reduce them to a more accurate form."[24]

In a later work[25] John Mair wrote in more detail concerning estate and plantation accounting, but his description at that time did not improve upon the illustrations prepared by the "Person of Honour"; thus there is no necessity for taking up his other ideas at this point.

A person who styled himself as "many years an Accomptant in London," one Wardlaugh Thompson, wrote the next work concerned with industrial accounting. It was dated 1777 and was given the title of *The Accomptants Oracle*. The last chapter, dealing with the accounts of a thread-hosiery manufacturing establishment, is the only one of interest here. The illustrations were purposely made simple in that it was assumed "that all the flax bought was of the same quality and price and also that the hose made were all of one size."[26] Thompson recommended two subsidiary books or ledgers (as in the Medici Accounts). Each of these was designed to relieve the general books of the tremendous amount of detail concerned with the affairs of the different weavers and spinners, since the "putting-out" system was still in general vogue. A total (control) account was maintained in the main ledger. Thompson's method of carrying costs forward from one account to another was rather interesting; he illustrated the flow of material from process to process, the cost being increased each time further work was done. Space does not allow the entries to be reproduced here in full.[27] It is sufficient at this point to state that the first journal entry of the illustration brought the flax into the flax stock account, kept both on a quantity and value basis. The next two entries showed the yarn returned from the spinners, part scoured and part unscoured. The spinners account was then relieved of the cost of the flax debited to it and the yarn accounts were charged with the cost of the flax and the cost of spinning. In addition, the cost price per hank was worked out for both scoured and unscoured yarn. The sixth entry dealt with scoured yarn being sent out, some to be dyed, some to be woven. The total cost per pair of woven hose was calculated, and the weavers account credited therewith. It is not only important to note that Thompson recognized the necessity of proper additions to cost of material going through the different steps of manufacure, but he was familiar with the procedure needed to carry out his objective. This is another instance of the surprisingly early introduction of cost accounting techniques which are generally thought to be dated much later.

In spite of the fact that Thompson and Dodson appear to have described a method of showing the flow of costs from one account to another, they treated transactions with persons outside the firm. Purely internal processes had not yet been considered in any great detail. What is important, however, is that in their time the so-called domestic system of manufacture was still in wide use, and there was a need for showing the flow of cost and the increased value of materials as they were worked upon by outsiders. The large factory with its many departments had not yet come into existence. As will be shown later, the accounting transition to a presentation of the flow of materials within one organization was a hurdle which took several decades to overcome; it was not so difficult to deal with outsiders as with internal transactions. Perhaps the essential reasons for this difficulty was the impersonal nature of the latter type of entries as contrasted with the personalities in the former. It is a well known fact in the history of accounting that the development of procedures for handling inanimate, impersonal objects or concepts came later than the accounting for persons.

It must not be thought that Thompson's or Dodson's techniques were immediately adopted. The manufacturers of the time appear to have been more concerned with the technical problems of production than they were with factory costing; secrecy as to costs was also widely practiced. Edwards suggests that it is very unlikely that the bookkeeping methods of these two authors were in general use, even many years after they wrote.[28] "These early writers were doubtless pioneers in a field which remained unreceptive for more than a century."[29] Proof of this statement is indicated by some remarks of Robert Hamilton in his *Introduction to Merchandise* first published in 1788.[30] He described the practice of the day in these terms: "Artificers and manufacturers sometimes keep only a day book and ledger; the former for entering goods sold, or work done on credit; the latter for personal accompts; and perhaps a cash book and an invoice book."[31] Even though Hamilton stated that he was dissatisfied with the then current methods of keeping the accounts of manufacturers, he adduced no illustrations of his preferred technique, choosing rather to describe it in hazy, confused terminology. For example, he recommended that at least three subsidiary books be kept by the processing firm. The first of these was a book of raw material where the quantities purchased and consumed were to be entered. This would appear to be a crude raw material stock ledger. The second book was a "book of work, where the quantities of materials delivered to journeymen, the quantities of wrought goods received in return, the dates of the delivery, and return, the value of the materials and wages, and the value of the wrought goods are entered in separate columns." This certainly looks like a cost ledger. The third book was a 'book of wages' for "the names of the employees, the work they are engaged on, the number of days and rate per day, or the quantity of work done and the rate paid by the piece."[32] As for the ledger, Hamilton wished to have a

> general accompt of the trade or manufacture. To the Dr. of this accompt, the balances of the accompts of materials, and other expenses, are transferred at the end of the year; on the Cr. the value of goods manufactured each month is entered. The balance shows the gain or loss, allowance being made for the value of goods not yet completely manufactured, and therefore not entered on the Cr. One or more accompts for manufactured goods, where the quantity made is entered monthly on the Dr. and the monthly sales on the Cr., these accompts will balance by the value on hand, if the prices be constant; but if the prices vary, the balance compared with the value on hand, per inventory, will show the gain or loss by the alteration.[33]

The Professor of Mathematics continued:

> When a person is engaged in several branches of manufacture, whether on different materials, or on the same materials through successive stages, he should keep his books in such a manner as to exhibit the gain or loss on each. Take the example of a linen manufacturer who purchases or imports rough flax, dresses it by his own servants, and sells such kinds as do not suit his purpose; delivers the rest to be spun, and receives the yarn from the spinners; weaves part in his own warehouse by journeymen and delivers the rest to other weavers; gives out the linen to be bleached, and receives and sells it when white. If all these branches of business were necessarily connected and the manufacturer had no other choice than to purchase the rough flax, and carry on the successive operations, it would be sufficient to keep his books in a form that should exhibit the gain or loss on the whole; but if he has an opportunity of beginning or desisting at any stage of the manufacture, his books should exhibit the gain or loss on each operation separately.[34]

Hamilton gave no details as to the actual bookkeeping necessary to carry out his ideas. He thought no illustrations were necessary because each scheme would be different, depending upon the individual firm. Edwards states that in his opinion Hamilton would have had no trouble putting his (Hamilton's) principles into actual use if the occasion arose, the reason being that Hamilton was unusually clear in the illustrations which he used for other lines of business.[35] Littleton, however, insists that Hamilton "comes perilously near to making a

sad mess of the explanations," and that if Hamilton had tried to put
his accounting scheme into practice he would have found it extremely
unsatisfactory.[36]   What the author of *Introduction to Merchandise* was
attempting to do was noteworthy, that is, to establish a "goods in process" account and a "finished goods" account; but "if this was his object, it is an error to say that the balance of the former would show loss
or gain; since it is debited for costs and credited for goods manufactured (at cost prices), the account should balance except for any
partly finished inventory."[37]

The author of this work also described certain specialized cost
records to be used by large farmers who wanted to keep an accurate
check on the advantages to be derived by rotation of crops and different methods of planting.   This record was called a "field book," and
several pages were devoted to each field.   In essence, the idea was to
account for the farm expenses and incomes, as well as production,
when any certain system of cultivation was used.

So much for Hamilton's contribution to the literature of cost accounting.   The methods he described must not have proved very
popular with his readers because when the "new modelled" edition
(these words appeared on the title page of the 1820 edition) was
published nothing was said at all about the accounting for manufacturers and artificers.   The "advertisement" to the new edition stated:
"It has been the object . . . of this Edition, so to enlarge the work, as
to adapt it to the state of Commerce at the present period. . . . The
most material alteration has been made in the system of Bookkeeping.
The plan which has been followed is nearly that invented by Mr.
Cronhelm, and published by him in 1818."[38]   (Cronhelm's contribution is discussed in later pages of this chapter.)

Hamilton's omission of the manufacturing section of his work in
1820 typifies the general attitude toward industrial accounting during
the Napoleonic period.   Several authorities have commented on the
unusual scarcity of cost literature during the entire period 1790-1850.
For example, Edwards states: "It is difficult to account for the absence
of works on industrial accountancy during the period 1790-1880.
Books on commercial accounts were turned out by the dozen, but . . .
writers on accounting neglected the problems of the industrial com-
munity at a time when the latter was being revolutionized by power,
the factory system and the growth of communications."[39]   And Littleton regrets "that more material is not at hand to permit further study of
the attempts between 1818 and 1887 to use double entry bookkeeping

in the treatment of manufacturing records."[40]   Urwick and Brech conclude that for nearly 100 years after the publication of Hamilton's book, "there seems to have been very little literature dealing with cost accounting. This may, in fact, have been due to the concentration of manufacturers on technical problems or to secrecy. . . . Another possible reason was the growing tendency to separate the engineering

COST CALCULATION
COOPER AND ANDERSON'S ENGINE[41]

	£	s.	d.
Total number of days: 170			
Charge for men's time	20	15	11
Charge for use of tools	3	16	10
Charge for use of machinery	8	16	3
Total amount, exclusive of percentage	33	9	0

INFERENCES:

	£	s.	d.
Total time 170 days: Amount of charge for do	20	15	11

= 2s. 5d. per day

	£	s.	d.
Amount for use of tools for 170 days	3	16	10

= 5½d. per day, or 18½ per cent on amount of men's time

	£	s.	d.
Amount of use of machinery for 170 days	8	16	3

= 1s. per day, or 43 per cent on amount of man's time.

Application

	£	s.	d.
Wm. Harrison's charge for the total fitting, turning, boring and labour, exclusive of packing	20	0	0

£20 = 400s. 2s. 6d. =

	£	s.	d.
Charge for use of tools, say 6d. per day on 160	4	0	0
Charge for use of machinery, say 1s. per day	8	0	0
Charge for weighing and loading	1	10	0
	33	10	0
Plus 40 per cent	15	0	0
	48	10	0

or, say £45   0s.   0d.

(i.e., production) function from the control or accounting (i.e., commercial) function, a process which became more and more emphasized as the importance of capital in industry grew."[42]

Even though most of the writers on accounting ignored industrial or cost accounting in the early years of the nineteenth century, there are isolated examples extant of cost calculations such as shown on page 42 (dated 1801).

One of the few striking exceptions to the absence of cost literature during the early 1800's is a book published in Paris in 1817, by Anselme Payen, entitled *Essai sur la tenus Livres d'un Manufacturies*. Payen was a magistrate of the old regime in France, who after the Revolution, launched several industrial enterprises. By 1814 he was at the head of an important sugar-beet factory in Vangirard. He maintained that position until about 1825, when he relinquished it to his son.[43] Both Littleton and Edwards have described the illustrations and the techniques used by Payen in his book.[44] Their discussions form the basis for the summary given below.

Payen illustrated the accounting necessary for two different industries, the first being a carriage manufactory engaged in the production of three vehicles; and the second, a glue factory. Although Payen did not, of course, mention the fact, the two industries he selected are perfect illustrations of what are today called job costing and process costing systems. The sets of records necessary to handle the first, according to this author, were two in number. There was to be a journal and ledger in money, and a journal and ledger for quantities. The latter journal "in kind" was really a summary of the cost of each sort of labor used in manufacturing the three carriages. (See the illustration on page 44.)

The "money" journal was drawn up in somewhat different form. Here was summarized the cash received and paid out, as well as the data concerning the sales of the three carriages, as shown on the accompanying table.

The "money" journal is noteworthy in that the finished carriages and their respective costs are carried from one section of the entry to the next with a clarity "which might easily be the envy of modern writers."[45] In addition it should be noted that Payen showed a transfer *within* the same enterprise, that is, from the workshop to the warehouse. This is a technique which previous authors had found difficult to master. Payen, however, did not indulge in purely modern manipulative transactions within one ledger, since he used a "ledger in

Journal in Kind[46]
For the Production of Three Carriages
Abstract of Memoranda

Carriage 1	305	Carpenter's
2	102	Memo 407
Carriage 1	475	Smith's
2	400	Memo 875
Carriage 1	440	
2	310	Lumber
3	222	Merchant's
Carriage 1	340	Memo 972
2	100	
3	205	Wheelwright's
Carriage 1	70	Memo 645
2	65	
3	55	Saddler's
		Memo 190
Carriage 1	345	
2	200	Painter's
3	30	Memo 575
	3,664	3,664

Factory Warehouse		Enterprise is
Carriage 1		discharged of
Amounting to 1,975		accountability
Carriage 2		by the transfer
Amounting to 1,177		to warehouse 3,664
Carriage 3		
Amounting to 512		
7,328		7,328

money" for transactions with outside persons, and a "ledger in kind" for transactions within the firm. The two types were never combined in the same ledger, as is done today.

This writer's second illustration was concerned with a glue factory, and here one finds even greater detail; in fact, his technique was not to be improved upon for several decades. Again, Payen used a

Journal in Money[47]

Debit		Credit	Profit	Loss
The business is ac-countable for	3,664	Carpenter 407		
		Smith 875		
		Lumber merchant 972		
		Wheelwright 645		
		Saddler 190		
		Painter 575		
The warehouse re-ceives 3 carriages	3,664	3,664		
		The business is discharged of 3,664		
A buys carriage No. 1, ...	2,045	Warehouse is discharged by carriage No. 1....1,975	70	
B buys carriage No. 2, ...	1,095	Warehouse is discharged by carriage No. 2....1,177		82
C buys carriage No. 3, ...	637	Warehouse is discharged by carriage No. 3.... 512	125	
Cash	3,777	Buyers A, B, C 3,777		
Paid the above mechanics	3,664	Cash 3,664	195	82
	18,546	18,433	195	82

(Warehouse lines bracketed to 3,664)

journal in kind and a journal in money. The money journal contained
not only the transactions for the factory (called "business" by Payen),
but the proprietor's personal transactions as well. This journal was
posted to a separate ledger, in which a considerable number of accounts appeared. One of these was headed "The Business" and involved the financial transactions of the factory. It is reproduced
on page 46.

The interest mentioned in the account was not interest on investment which is familiar to present-day cost theory, but was interest
paid to creditors for agreeing to wait for payment until sales had been
made. Evidently, therefore, Payen considered this payment a "manufacturing" item. It should be noted also that the account contained
assets, expenses, costs, and sales all mixed together. Of course, if
the author had deducted from the balance of the account (1) the

THE BUSINESS (OF MANUFACTURING)[48]

To proprietor for con-		To be used in the dis-	
struction work	1,000	charge of the account	
Materials	14,200		
Utensils	5,000	Product sold by Leroy	18,948
Coal	3,000	Product sold by Guerin	751
Interest	300		
Workers	2,000	Proceeds from the 24[49]	
Minor utensils	300	barrels of glue	19,699
Rent	500	Value of 2 barrels unsold	312[50]
Repair boilers	400		
Repair utensils	100		
	26,800		20,011

asset element, (2) the balance of raw materials on hand, and (3) the remaining stock of glue at cost, he would have arrived at the now familiar gross profit figure for the period; but the final step was not taken.

The ledger showing the factory accounts "in kind" is given on page 47.[51] Again there was considerable originality in the handling of the transactions.

It should be noted that depreciation was charged as a cost of production through the technique of pricing the final inventories of

MANUFACTURING SUMMARY[52]

Materials consumed	12,000	To cost of goods	
Depreciation on furnace	100	manufactured	
Direct labor	2,000	and sold	17,000
Depreciation on boiler	400		
Repair cost on boiler	400		
Repair cost on utensils	100		
Depreciation on utensils	100		
Coal consumed	1,000		
Interest paid to creditors	300		
Sundry utensils used up	100		
Rent	500		
	17,000		17,000

boilers, utensils, etc., at a figure smaller than the one used at the beginning of the period.

The transactions given in the illustration below would not miss being the modern technique if a "manufacturing summary" account had been used to accumulate the various items labeled "consumed" and "carried to cost," as shown in the adapted example on page 46.

Even though Payen did not extend his technique to the preparation of a manufacturing summary account, he came so close to it that much later writers did no better. In place of a manufacturing summary account this early cost expert recommended that an abstract be drawn up in the following form:

LEDGER IN KIND

Debit		Credit	
Storeroom: Raw materials	14,200	Consumed	12,000
		Inventory	2,200
Shop: Raw materials	12,000	24 barrels of glue manu-	
Storeroom:		factured	12,000
Manufactured merchan-		Sent to Leroy 6 barrels	
dise 24 barrels		Sent to Leroy 13 barrels	
		Sent to Guerin 5 barrels	
		24 barrels	
Furnaces:		As valued for the	
Mason's work	300	inventory	900
Iron	200		
Locksmith	150		
Bricks	200		
Plaster	50	Carried forward to the	
Lead	75	cost of manufactured	
Roughstone	25	glue	100
	1,000		
Workers: Wages in manu-			
facturing of glue	2,000	As used in cost	2,000
Boilers:			
2 boilers	4,500	As valued for the	
Repair cost	400	inventory	4,100
		Carried to cost	800

Utensils:

2 skimmers	225	As valued for the inventory	400
4 funnels	275	Transferred to cost	200
Repairs	100		

Coal:

		Consumed	1,000
25 loads	3,000	Balance, valued at	2,000

Sundry Expenses:

Interest paid to creditors	300	Transferred to cost	300

Sundry Utensils	300	Those remaining valued at	200
		Transferred to cost	100

Rent	500	Transferred to cost	500

ABSTRACT OF THE LEDGER IN KIND

Asset inventory, or balance of which the business is charged on new account:

Costs of glue:

Materials	2,200	Materials	12,000
Furnaces	900	Use of boilers	800
Boilers	4,100	Use of Utensils	200
Utensils	400	Coal Used	1,000
Coal	2,000	Interest	300
Sundry Utensils	200	Sundry expenses	100
		Rent	500
		Use of furnaces	100
		Wages	2,000
		The business has expended	17,000
	9,800		

Total to be charged to business	17,000
	26,800

The business has at its credit the proceeds of sales   19,699

> There are to be added
> the articles not sold ___ 312
>
> ___
>
> Total product _____20,011
> The merchandise manu-
> factured has cost _____17,000
>
> ___
>
> Profit produced ___ 3,011

Payen showed that he was acquainted with unit costs; in one of his abstracts he presented the following exhibit:

> The said 17,000 francs referred to in the book of glue made, with the weight of 20,000 lbs., will amount to 17s per pound, as shown below:[53]

Details

Raw material _____12s
Hand workers _____ 2
Utensils _____ 1
Charcoal _____ 1
Interest ⎫	
Rent ⎪ _____ 1
Use of furnaces ⎬
Miscellaneous ⎭

> 17s

Another feature of Payen's cost accounting technique is indicated by his treatment of waste. He allowed the waste to increase the cost of the final inventory, rather than to increase production costs (see example on page 50).

While the waste in the example increased the price of the final inventory of material, Payen indicated in another chapter of his work that there were two other varieties of losses in material: (1) those "foreign to management of the factory—and (2) others arising from accidents and faults in manufacturing and are part of the cost of the products."[54]

In subsequent chapters of his *Essai* Payen presented a considerably more intricate illustration dealing with the allocation of costs between two principal products. All elements of cost were divided, including material, labor, and factory burden. He neglected to mention, however, the technique which should be used to subdivide the

PAYEN'S EXAMPLE OF WASTE ALLOWANCE

Debit		Credit
Storeroom	Waste _____ 400	
Raw Material	Consumed _____24,000	
28,400 clippings at 50c __14,200	at prime cost	12,000
	Inventory _____ 4,000	2,200
	28,400	
Furnace		
Daily pay of masons _____ 300	On inventory value sheet __	900
Iron _____ 200	We will report on glue	
Locksmith _____ 150	made at prime cost _____	100
Bricks _____ 200		
Plaster (mortar) _____ 50		
Lead _____ 75		
Ashlar (shiver) _____ 25		
1,000		
Coal		
50 cartloads _____ 3,000	Consumed, 16 cartloads ___	1,000
	Remainder, priced at ____	2,000

burden between the two products; he contented himself with the observation that it was not easy to assign a value to the buildings, furnaces, and utensils, since these items have a use value to the individual firm in that they enable the manufacturer to produce his product more efficiently.

In order to show the joint cost allocation plan which Payen suggested, a summary, dealing with the furnaces, is presented on page 51.

In retrospect, Payen came very close to the discovery of the technique for integrating the cost and the financial records. "The key to the union of the two sets of accounts lay in the entry necessary to bring together the inventories from the 'ledger in kind' and the business-of-manufacturing account from the 'ledger in money'. But this key was not used. The practice of the time was content if the abstract at this point came into agreement with the business-of-manufacuring account through the equivalence of the two separately derived totals."[55]

PAYEN'S EXAMPLE OF JOINT COST ALLOCATION

Furnace A, mason	1,100	Valued	1,700
Bricks	300	Cost consumed	620
Plaster (mortar)	120		
Locksmith	300		
Iron	450		
Ashlar (shiver)	50		
	2,320		2,320
Furnace B, mason	700	Valued	1,678
Bricks	500	Cost Consumed	800
Plaster (mortar)	100		
Locksmith	200		
Iron	908		
Ashlar (shiver)	70		
	2,478		2,478
Furnace C, mason	500	Valued	1,361
Bricks	250	Cost Consumed	580
Plaster (mortar)	80		
Iron	681		
Locksmith	180		
Ashlar (shiver)	250		
	1,941		1,941
	2,478		
	2,320	Total Cost	2,000
		Final Inventory	4,739
Prime cost of 3 furnaces	6,739		6,739
Sum of cost on 3 furnaces	2,000	First Product	1,400
		Second Product	600

As Payen explained it, "The task which the business has to accomplish by its accounts is to distinguish between those expenditures applicable to the cost of the product made and those which remain as inventoriable value. There then only remains to deduct the sum of the costs from the amount received from the sale of the merchandise to calculate the profit."[56] This concise statement of the goal of product cost accounting has a modern ring; it indicates that Payen knew whereof he spoke.

As the reader may easily perceive, Payen went a long way toward showing an illustration of a costing scheme which would work fairly satisfactorily even today. It was clumsy, of course, but his originality is surprising in view of the relatively little that had been done in the way of costing up to his time. He seemed to have cut through many of the entanglements which befuddled later writers on this subject, and his system also avoided much of the pure red tape which was often found in the systems advocated by writers up to the twentieth century.

In a later section of his work, Payen showed still more clearly that he knew what he was doing, since he illustrated two additional "tie-ins" between the financial records and the factory or "business" records. He also reconciled the computation of the profit of his hypothetical firm by two methods: (1) By the use of asset and liability accounts (there was no original capital investment); and (2) by the use of cost of product and sales figures. This check is sometimes used even today. However, it is very doubtful that Payen's methods (like Hamilton's) were used on any widespread scale during his lifetime.[57]

A few years after Payen's work had appeared another Frenchman, L. F. G. de Cazaux, published a volume on farm accounting which distinctly recommended that the flow of monetary values be shown in the accounts, something which Payen had found troublesome.[58] De Cazaux's methodology may be summarized by stating that his system involved the setting up of accounts for each type of asset in the business. The values put into these accounts constituted the debits, while the values taken out periodically were credits. The differences between these two sets of values were indicative of the profit or loss for the period. Furthermore, every time a value was taken out of an account it had to be transferred to another; this rule was not to be broken even though the transfer involved no one outside the firm.

In order to illustrate his plan of accounting de Cazaux broke down the processes of large scale farming into the following operations:

(a) Pure agriculture or husbandry for which an account is required for each piece of land, classified according as it consists of fields, meadows, vineyards, woods, etc.

(b) Commercial speculation, sometimes unavoidable, resulting from the fact that products are stored instead of being sold at the time of harvesting. This speculation involves the opening (following the accounts for the various pieces of land) of accounts for each type of product in order to be in a position to judge the profit or loss on holding stocks. This profitability is measured for each product by the difference between the value at the time of harvesting and that at the time of sale or consumption after taking into account expenses and wastage.

(c) Lastly, accounts are required for the various factors of production which are converted from type of commodity to another, for example, into days of labor, into wool, meat, manure. This is the purpose of showing the gain or loss on each transformation.[59]

De Cazaux went on to describe rather clearly and accurately the problems of valuation and depreciation. In connection with depreciation, he anticipated later practice when he suggested that each type of asset be divided into its component parts; a different rate of depreciation would then be applied to each part (on a straight line basis). This early cost expert even recommended that the depreciation expense charge be subdivided between the operations which received the benefits from the use of the equipment, although he did state that this was a cost accounting refinement which could be safely passed over while a business was new.

In addition to the above features, de Cazaux urged that imputed interest at the rate of five percent be added to any asset which required several years to bring into full production, e. g., a vineyard. In summary, de Cazaux showed a grasp of certain cost problems which was definitely superior to that of his predecessors. Again, however, it is likely that his procedures were followed by only a small number of business enterprises.

The next major French contribution came in 1827 when M. Godard wrote his *Traité General et Sommaire de la Comptabilité Commerciale*. The author of this work was evidently a practical business man. In addition to a section on manufacturing accounts, he included some discussion of finance, farming, and public administration. Even though Godard was a manufacturer of glassware, which involves multiple products and multiple processes, he selected as his book illustration a simpler process costing situation.

After some preliminary discussion concerned with the recommended accounts for raw material, products in process, fixed assets, and wages, Godard for some unknown reason launched into a rather careful analysis of the proper treatment of deferred costs associated with the installation and rearrangement of machinery. This particular technical problem may have been of personal interest to him in his own plant, but he was nearly unique in his analysis. He recommended, incidentally, that these costs (as well as those we now call "organization costs") should not all be loaded onto one year, but should be divided out over several periods. As he expressed it, "it would be unfair to charge them to the first year of operations." This conclusion strikes a modern note.

Like de Cazaux, Godard was quite careful in his analysis of depreciation and labor costs. He urged manufacturers to classify their production machinery and employees by departments and processes in order to make the cost analyses more accurate. In the light of later developments it is interesting to observe some samples of his statistical cost summaries. The table on page 55 deals with a forge.

Godard offered the following general observations concerning the summary:

We have taken a forge for our example, and have made an application of the statistical record to a cash expenditure which is known every month and to a consumption of material the price of which cannot be established until the end of the year. But absolutely nothing can be concluded from the accounts whose existence we have assumed, nor of the significance of the expenses of labor or of the assumptions that we have made to correspond to each of them. Never having taken part in the management of a forge, we do not intend to indicate the organization of a typical establishment, nor to make evaluations; we have assumed some figures in order to fill in our hypothetical table. It is also possible to have three kinds of mineral coming from three different mines, the costs of which one may wish to account for separately. This cost determination may be made. We have selected the data also in order to give an idea of the manner in which one can divide the raw material accounts, in line with the type of firm and its management, even when the raw materials are of the same nature.

The same motive made us assume that there were two blast furnaces and two foundries, the products and the expenses of which we desired to keep separate in the accounts. If space permitted we could also demonstrate a slitting mill, a wire mill (hemp spinning mill, ropewalk), etc.

MAIN WORKS[60]

No. 14   Observation

Indicate at head of each chapter the object to which it is dedicated.

MODEL FOR STATISTICAL REGISTER

(With application to a forge)

Indication of the accounts to which the amounts and quantities refer	January	February etc.	Total by accounts	
	francs	francs	francs	centimes
Mineral No. 1	1,800	1,700	22,240	25
Mineral No. 2	1,250	1,300	15,205	80
Mineral No. 3	800	950	10,561	10
Charcoal	900	920	7,222	35
Blast-furnace No. 1	200	200	2,516	40
Blast-furnace No. 2	250	250	2,991	90
Melting furnace	120	125	1,475	40
Forge No. 1	130	135	1,556	45
Forge No. 2	125	120	1,510	30
Flattening-Mill	140	140	1,704	10
Stables	300	320	3,635	50
Miscellaneous expenses	350	310	3,755	60
Totals by months	6,365	6,470	74,375	15

After presenting these observations Godard digressed for a bit to make sure that his readers had available his technique for recording the cutting of timber for fuel. He recommended that an account be set up for each separate cut. Following modern practice he mentioned that this account should be charged for the timber cost as well as the labor and other costs involved in the cutting. Credits were then made to the timber account when the trees were cut; the debit was made to the department cost accounts using the fuel.

Godard was quite modern in his discussion of the accounting for raw material. After first mentioning that separate accounts should be established for each type, he noted that there was no constancy about material costs; these fluctuations, he observed, would cause endless trouble if the accountant attempted to keep track of all of them insofar as the pricing out of the material was concerned. (Contemporary cost accountants can certainly attest to this fact.) Godard's preferred solution to this "inextricable embarassment," as he

called it, was simply to suggest that the cost accountant wait until
the end of the year to determine the average raw material price-out
cost.

He did concede that if it were necessary to determine costs
monthly, "we must choose some value more or less inaccurate, and
make the necessary adjustment at the end of the year."[61]

This early cost authority was impressed with the necessity for
careful handling of work in process at its various stages of production. After first indicating that the factory manager should have
data as to the cost of each operation, he suggested that separate
accounts be opened for departmental work in process to which would
be debited the costs transferred from prior departments as well as the
new costs incurred in the department, e. g., direct labor, fuel, and
depreciation on equipment. Modern process cost accountants would
refer to this as "pyramided costs." While Godard was indefinite
as to how the final inventory in each department was to be priced,
he did recognize (1) that his plan of costing would present a "faith-
ful picture of the march and progress of manufacture" and (2) that
the total cost of the product as shown in the last stage work in
progress account would be the factory cost of sales for the period.
This result, he concluded, was to be contrasted with the bookkeeping
routine of a merchandising firm wherein the cost of goods sold was
calculated from data concerned only with purchases and inventories.

With experience as a manufacturer, Godard naturally emphasized the key role played by raw material records in any well-designed
cost system. The disappearance and waste of material were no less
important in his time than they are today; so we find him urging
that materials be inspected, classified by quantity and quality, and
the receipts and issues entered on "registers and notebooks regularly
kept, and under the responsibility of tried and tested accounting
employees." These registers, of course, are the familiar perpetual
inventories of more modern times; Godard cited their advantages
and stated that they "enable us to see the loss or gain in weight and
quantity of each process, and also give us monthly inventory figures
without an actual count, thus enabling the management to take steps
to replace before they run out of stocks."[61] This statement could
hardly be improved upon even now.

Even though Godard neglected to present the cost forms to accompany many of his techniques, he was distinctly ahead of his
contemporaries in regard to the presentation of monthly cost com-

parisons. These statements used the same average cost for materials throughout the twelve months; the profit shown on any single statement, therefore, was only a tentative one, subject to correction at the end of the year when the so-called actual cost of the material used was calculated for the entire fiscal period. Godard, however, did not consider this estimating of profit feature significant, since he was more interested in the comparative cost figures than he was in monthly income data. The table on page 58 is an example of his cost report.

While there was much that was modern in Godard's cost technique, he did not mention specifically a work in process account. The introduction of this account was not long delayed, however, since another Frenchman, Jeannin, published a book in Paris in 1829 in which he definitely mentioned an account called "d'objets en fabrication."[62] Debits were made to this account for raw material cost, direct labor, and other items; credits were made for the value of the completed goods as well as for losses and waste product. Completed product ready to sell was then debited to a finished goods account, while the waste loss was transferred to profit and loss—a quite modern treatment of this costing difficulty.

Not long after Jeannin's work appeared, another practical French accountant, F. N. Simon, wrote a two-volume work on bookkeeping which contained some discussion of forge accounts.[63] This cost accounting authority recommended that a dual ledger plan be adopted. The first of these would be referred to today as a general ledger, while the other was definitely subsidiary. In order to avoid complicating detail, Simon suggested that the monthly entries for the flow of the product be made in terms of quantities only, values not being inserted until the end of the accounting period, when the total cost and output of each process was known. The principal process accounts were those for the furnace and the forge. The furnace account was debited with opening stock of tools, wages, machine maintenance, charcoal or coal, and iron ore used. At the end of the year it was debited with its proportion of general expenses, interest, and water cost. Each month the account was credited in quantities only for the iron produced. At the end of the year the account was credited with the value of tools still on hand, leaving in the account the cost price of the iron produced. This cost price was subsequently transferred to an iron finished stock account.[64]

Simon's illustration is significant because he was one of the first to recommend the division of rent, administrative salaries, and taxes

COMPARATIVE TABLE[65]
Of Manufactured Products and of Monthly Actual or Estimated Expenses

Expenses	Quantities	Average Price f.	Average Price c.	Total f.	Total by Divisions f.
Raw Material:					
Mineral No. 1	1,600	1	70	2,720	
Mineral No. 2	1,400	1	40	1,960	
Mineral No. 3	800	1	50	1,200	
Special material to aid in fusion	1,000		50	500	6,380
Processing Items:					
Principal workers and their assistants at furnaces, forges, etc.				3,500	
Repairs and maintenance of furnaces, utensils, etc.				800	
Charcoal	4,500	2		9,000	
Coal	1,200	3	50	4,200	
Transportation charges inside and outside of the works				1,200	18,700
General Expenses:					
Maintenance and repair of real estate				600	
Cost of administration, contributions, insurance, etc.				2,000	
Cost of the "house"				400	
Miscellaneous costs				300	
Interest on capital				4,000	7,300
Total of the charges for month					32,380
Products Made:					
Castings from 1st "fusion"	500	12		6,000	
Castings from 2nd "fusion"	150	18		2,700	
Bar iron	800	20		16,000	
Wrought iron	320	25		8,000	
Sheet iron	180	30		5,400	
				38,100	
Less: Allowances and discounts				nil	
Estimated sale of products (net)					38,100
Estimated profit					5,720

between the operating processes of the factory, instead of closing them directly to profit and loss. Even though he stated clearly that this allocation should be made in accordance with the importance of each "manufactory," he used an arbitrary assignment of fifty percent to each of the two processes which he included in his example.

Three decades after Simon had published his volume another Frenchman, Louis Mézières, recommended that the raw material book be prepared and posted at least once each month. This book is of interest in that it showed both quantities and prices. Mézières suggested that the material be issued at cost prices, but the illustration he gave does not permit us to determine whether he preferred first-in, first-out, average cost, or some other basis of pricing.[66] The columnar arrangement is unusually complete (see form on page 60).

The monthly total of materials and stores issued was recorded in a summary journal entry in the main books, the credit being to raw material account while the debit was to finished goods. Individual job costs for material were also kept in a "book of orders"; this same book received postings from the wage record where the time spent on each job was detailed. Prime costs only were entered in the book of orders (job cost ledger). An example[66] from this latter ledger is given on page 61.

The discussion and techniques of Mézières would approach modernity if he had handled satisfactorily the problems of work in process and the application of burden. As it was, he stopped short of a complete illustration, even though he did present a finished goods stock ledger which included columns to show the quantity of each item on hand at any time.

Mézières' treatment fell disappointingly short of completeness, but he was followed three years later by C. Adolphe Guilbault.[67] This distinguished French authority described the underlying techniques of the process cost method in a manner which would do credit to most contemporary texts. His examples dealt with oil refining and mining, iron foundries, and sugar refining. Many samples of forms are given in the second volume of his work; he even gave a full illustration of the average cost method of pricing raw material into production (the average cost was determined at the time of each new purchase). His discussion of process costing is particularly noteworthy in that he made a distinction between fixed and variable plant

JANUARY 1862

Designation of objects of stores	Materials and Objects of Stores					Use of materials and objects of stores			Final Inventory Quantity
	Beginning inventory quantity	Received during month quantity	Date	Value	Total Quantities	Quantities put into works	Price per Unit	Total Price	
	Kil.	Kil.		£ c.	Kil.	Kil.	£ c.	£ c.	Kil.
Steel (refined)	250	100	6	210 0	350	14 50	2 10	30 45	335 50
Borax	2		6		2		3 50		2 00
Iron	1250	600	24	360 0	1,850	500 00	60	300 00	1,350 00
Zinc		104	4	52 0	104	57 00	50	28 50	47 00
Etc.				Etc.				Etc.	
				4,265 0				1,910 35	

Nature of order and names of persons to whom they are to be sent.	Material						Direct Labor				
				Per Unit		Total				Cost	
											Total
	Types	Quantity		f.	c.	f.	c.	Names of Workers	Days	Per day f.	f.
No. 1—The first of January 1862:	Iron	410			60	246		L.	16	3	48
M. Moreau orders 2 fire pumps, having sizes fixed by estimates which he will furnish to us. For each pump he will pay us 850 francs, without accessories. Delivery is to be made about February 1.	Coal	8		5		40		B.	16	3	48
	Charcoal	16		2	30	36	80	P.	16	3	48
	Oak	81			70	56	70	L.	16	3	48
	Ash	1		7		7		R.	16	3	48
	Copper	112		2	40	268	80	P.	16	3	48
	Zinc	56			50	28		N.	16	3	48
	Castings	17			30	5	10	A.	16	3	48
	Brass	51		4		204		S.	16	3	48
	Leather	4		3	50	14		A.	16	3	48
	Sheet-Iron	3			75	2	25	C.	17	3	51
	Oil	2		1	40	2	80	A.	17	3	51
	Paint					15					
	Misc.					6	90				
						933	35				582

	f.	c.	
Total cost of materials	933	35	
Total cost of direct labor	582		} 1,700
Net profit	184	65	

Recap, drawn up January 21, 1862

overhead costs. As examples of the fixed items, he cited rent, salaries, and office expenditures; the variable costs included general labor and fuel. Even though he did not explore the matter thoroughly, he indicated that the variability of costs was important in the comparative analysis of costs in periods of "good" and "bad" business. This astute Frenchman also was one of the first authorities to suggest that commercial, selling, and administrative expenses should not enter into the determination of factory product cost calculations. He was thus a forerunner of the English group which carried on with such vehemence a discussion of this matter in later years (see Chapter V).

By 1872 developments in cost accounting in France had reached the point where some writers were describing specialized cost applications, such as in the building industry. M. Dugué, for example, illustrated a plan involving the following steps: (1) set up an account for all direct costs associated with the contracts; (2) transfer these direct costs periodically to detailed accounts for each contract; (3) set up an account for general depreciation, rent, and other items; (4) upon the completion of a contract debit its separate cost account with five percent of the total direct costs, crediting this amount to the general expense account mentioned in (3).[68] Disappointingly, Dugué did not mention specifically what should be done with the possible difference between the two sides of the general expenses account. While his method of applying burden was criticized later it had much popularity in the 1880's.

It was also in the middle 1880's that M. E. Claperon, in describing the application of burden items to products, suggested that the monthly total of actual burden costs should not be used; instead, the cost accountant should use one-twelfth of the total for the entire year.[69] The adoption of this plan, therefore, involved a delay in the product costing until the end of the year, unless he meant that the "one-twelfth" was to be based on an estimate. If a firm produced more than one product, and if it desired to have data on the full factory cost of each type, Claperon admitted that experience was the only guide. (In his words: "We have not anything to say about it.")

Outstanding French contributions to the theory and techniques of cost accounting came sharply to an end by 1890. As one prominent English authority, R. S. Edwards, has well stated: "It appears . . . that French accountants towards the end of the century were not moving so rapidly as their contemporaries in America and Great

Britain in dealing with the complicated problem of oncost [burden]. Moreover, there had been some reaction against excessive analysis, according to H. Lefèvre.[70] He quotes, for example, M. Dobost, a teacher of the agriculture school at Grignon, as saying that many of the artifices employed in cost accounting analysis were mere fictions. . . . " Edwards states further:

I do not think the influence of French studies on English methods was anything but slight. It seems likely that the English speaking races worked out their own technique. . . . In the last decade of the 19th century much that was heralded as new [in England] had almost been forgotten by the French text-writers. Only in the detailed allocation of overheads to jobs and in standard costing were the English speaking countries first in the field, and this is probably due to difference in the types of industrial growth. In flexibility in the use of double entry technique the Continent was first; it adapted bookkeeping to the needs of departmental, process and job costing.[71]

Returning now to English developments we find F. W. Cronhelm discussing woolen manufacturing accounts in his *Double Entry by Single*, published in 1818. His description did not nearly approach that of Payen, the early French authority, from the standpoint of either accuracy or clearness. The work is noteworthy, nevertheless, in that it was probably the first text to discuss a perpetual inventory (by quantities only) to be kept for raw material, work in process, and finished goods. Like Payen, Cronhelm could not bring himself to the point of consolidating the internal and the external transactions of his hypothetical business into an integrated set of accounts.

The perpetual inventory records (of course, he did not call them that) were to be kept in a sort of warehouse ledger which was in turn divided into three parts. The first part showed an account for the wool purchased from different individuals, the account being debited for acquisitions and credited for wool put into process by both grades and quantities (in pounds). The balance was the wool unprocessed. The second part of the warehouse ledger was a manufactory record or account, in which the wool carried to manufacturing was recorded on the debit side, while the credits showed the finished product, which was in turn transferred to what we call now a finished goods ledger. The finished goods ledger made up the third part of the warehouse ledger, and was debited for goods finished and credited for goods sold—still in quantities only, the quantities, however, being pieces of cloth and not pounds as in the materials account.[72]

In addition to the above, Cronhelm recommended a manufacturing book, or perhaps it should be called an account, on the debit side of which appeared the beginning inventory of raw wool, the purchases for the period, salaries (general), discounts, postage, taxes, drayage, dyeing, and the sum of the following three books (to be kept by "overlookers"):

	£.	s.	d.
Book A: Sorting, carding, spinning, etc.	178	15	9
Book B: Weaving, milling, etc.	193	15	10
Book C: Dressing, finishing, packing, etc.	181	4	8

The three books were really wage records, and their summarized amounts were carried to the manufacturing account as debits. The sales and closing inventory were placed on the credit side of the manufacturing account. It should be mentioned, however, that the manufacturing account used by Cronhelm was not at all comparable to the manufacturing summary account used at present in cost systems. Rather, it was a sort of trading account somewhat like that used by bookkeepers in the last century. Absolutely no grouping of costs was present here, and the different processes were not systematically classified.

Lastly, Cronhelm illustrated a form for computing the value of the final inventory of raw materials and goods in process. The former were valued at the same prices shown in the "warehouse ledger" account for materials, and checked with that ledger; the latter were valued "as averaged at the middle stage," that is, as half completed. But the prices on a unit basis were not given—only the computed "total value" was shown. The total of these two types of inventories checked with the figure placed on the credit side of the manufacturing account.

Cronhelm did a somewhat better job of handling inventories than Payen, but taking his system as a whole it was much more cumbersome than that of the French author. However, both of these writers were far superior to any who wrote for the next fifty years, even though they had considerable difficulty in handling nonfinancial transactions. The latter point is a forerunner of all the controversy which was to rage in the period 1885-1910 concerning whether or not factory cost books should be kept distinct from the financial books.[73] Payen avoided some of the pitfalls when he advocated two separate sets of books, while Cronhelm recommended memoranda accounts in order to sidestep the issue. Payen was on the right track but he never solved the problem of the integration of his two different sets of books; Cronhelm became more confused the deeper he went into the details of his memoranda system.

English writers on accounting for the next fifty years generally slighted the industrial aspects. This apparent oversight is rather strange when it is recalled that the factory system was, during that half century, developing rapidly. The following (dated 1836) is indicative of the rare and skimpy treatment given to the subject in bookkeeping texts published in those decades:

> And in manufacturing concerns, the quantity of raw materials consumed should be made to correspond with that of the articles manufactured. For which purpose, it will be necessary to open accounts for each; for the steam apparatus; and for the workmen's wages in every branch; which last should be done by a proper classification of the printed weekly papers. At the close of the year, the amount of all these, together with the charges, under their various heads, are concentrated by being brought to the debit of the general factory; while the produce, in its several kinds, is carried to the credit of this account.[74]

There were no illustrations in this work, and nothing further was said about the interesting "printed weekly papers."

Even though little was written in England during this period on industrial accounting, its importance was not entirely overlooked. As early as 1823-1832, a famous English mathematician and scientist named Charles Babbage became interested in the workshops and factories of his country, with special emphasis on the management aspects. After engaging in independent study and research in England and other countries, he returned to his home and published an essay *On the Economy of Machinery and Manufactures* (1832). This work was perhaps the first treatise on the scientific management of factories to be published in the English language. Many thousand of copies were sold within the following ten years and the book was translated into several other languages. Because of his training and experience, we find Babbage stressing the use and organization of machines in a well-regulated factory; he was not concerned with machine design or cost accounting methods *per se*. There were almost no illustrations or examples in his volume, but his table showing the processes, time, labor cost, and other details involved in making pins strikes a modern note. Since this is a classical illustration of early English operation cost analysis, it is reproduced on page 66.

ENGLISH MANUFACTURE[75]

(178) Pins, *"Elevens,"* 5,546 weigh one pound; *"one dozen"*—6,932 pins weigh twenty ounces, and require six ounces of paper.

Name of the Process	Work-men	Time of Making 1 lb. of pins	Cost of Making 1 lb. of pins	Work-man earns per day		Price of making each part of a single pin, in millionths of a penny
		Pence	*Hours*	*s.*	*d.*	
1. Drawing Wire	Man	.3636	1.2500	3	3	225
2. Straightening	Woman	.3000	.2840	1	0	51
the wire	Girl	.3000	.1420	0	6	26
3. Pointing	Man	.3000	1.7750	5	3	319
4. Twisting and						
Cutting the	Boy	.0400	.0147	0	4½	3
Heads	Man	.0400	.2103	5	4½	38
5. Heading	Woman	4.0000	5.0000	1	3	901
6. Tinning or	Man	.1071	.6666	6	0	121
Whitening	Woman	.1071	.3333	3	0	60
7. Papering	Woman	2.1314	3.1973	1	6	576
		7.6892	12.8732			2,320

Even though Babbage was not interested in technical description, he was fully cognizant of the industrial potentials arising from the applications of scientific processes of thought. In one place, for example, he stated that "the great competition introduced by machinery, and the application of the principle of the subdivision of labour, render it necessary for each producer to be continually on the watch, to discover improved methods by which the cost of the article he manufactures may be reduced, and, with this view, it is of great importance to know the precise expense of every process, as well as the wear and tear of the machinery which is due to it . . . . One of the first advantages which suggests itself as likely to arise from a correct analysis of the expense of the several processes of any manufacturer, is the indication which it would furnish of the course in which improvement should be directed."[76]

But Babbage did not discuss the cost accounting necessary for the attainment of his excellently stated objectives.

Babbage's work, in spite of its wide circulation, made very little impression on his contemporaries; actually, his thinking was far ahead of the times.[77] At least fifty years were to pass by before his scientific approach was attacked again with renewed vigor by industrial engineers like F. W. Taylor, Oberlin Smith, H. R. Towne, F. A.

Halsey and others. Factory managers in England seemed to have been too excited over the potential of power-driven machinery to devote much effort to seeking out the answers to industrial accounting questions.[78] Furthermore, competition for markets was not as acute as it later became. Accurate costs, therefore, were not a necessity.

Even though developments in English and American industrial accounting were at a low ebb in the period 1840-75, several references have come down to us which have sections or chapters devoted to costing of factory products.

For example, in a book by John Fleming, *Bookkeeping by Double Entry*, published in the United States in 1854, the, at that time, usual merchandise trading account was made to serve the purpose of industrial accounting by changing its name to "factory account." His illustration (a textile mill) follows:

FACTORY ACCOUNT[79]

Cost of building	$ xx	Cloth, etc., sold	$ xx
Cotton purchased	xx	Cloth, etc., shipped on	
Wages of hands	xx	consignment	xx
Purchased coal	xx	Inventory (at end)	xx
Clerk and expenses	xx		
Profit or loss	xx		

In connection with the inclusion of the cost of the building in this account, it might be mentioned that this particular practice was very common in the period 1800-1850. The value of the building at the end of the period, after depreciation, was included in the credit item entitled "inventory," thus allowing the account to show a profit or loss for the period. More than likely, Fleming included in his "building" the equipment and machinery therein, as well as the structure itself.[80]

Frederick C. Krepp, an Englishman, who wrote *Statistical Bookkeeping* in 1858, discussed and illustrated some books which he called a "special system" for manufacturers. Upon close inspection, however, one finds that they were really just raw materials and goods produced books which were to be kept by quantities and kinds in two different columns. The first column was to be used for the quantity of raw material purchased or the finished goods produced, and the second column was to include the material used or finished goods shipped to customers, depending upon the nature of the transaction. The value of the quantity on hand could be ascertained by multiplying the quantity by respective average prices; but he neglected to state how the latter were to be computed, that is, what sort of an average to use.[81]

In a work entitled *Bookkeeping for the Tanning Trade,* [82] there are certain statements which indicate the sorry state to which cost theory had fallen in this Dark Ages[83] period: This author wrote as follows:

> The recognized principle that stock should be valued at cost price (unless depreciated in value) and that no profit should be estimated unless realized, much less upon goods only partly manufactured, and subject further to the contingency of a falling market, may be questioned if applicable to the case in question. Upon this plan, it would be necessary to value all hides in process of tanning, and the produce thereof, at their cost price, to which would be added the cost of tanning material consumed, the proportion of wages disbursed for the attendant labor, and a sum for rent and expenses. But, apart from the *insuperable difficulties attending* this, there are reasons why a tanner is justified, to some extent, in estimating a profit upon goods in process of manufacture, and in connection with which his time, skill, capital, and labor have for a period of six months been brought into requisition.[84]

In the engineering industry, where mistakes in costing were fairly easy to recognize, there were probably some firms which developed adequate systems during this period. For example, in a letter to the editor of the *Engineer* of December 23, 1870, a correspondent, in outlining such a system, stated that: "The entire outlay for all purposes (in a factory) may be said to be direct or indirect, according as the disbursements can be charged at once to the various jobs in hand, or only to interim accounts, from which they are deducted from time to time in portions, as may be required for the fulfillment of the work."

What the correspondent was attempting to state, of course, was that there was a certain prime cost of each job to which must be added some overhead in order to arrive at total cost. This writer recognized, too, that it was the overhead group of items which caused so much trouble in job cost systems for he stated that "they vary from year to year, in unequal ratio with the rest of the expenditures, unless the business fluctuates to a very small extent."

This last is a clear-cut explanation of the difficulty involved in allocating overhead. But the correspondent went further. He saw that it was illogical and incorrect to charge work in process with an equal amount of these indirect expenses, since the indirect costs were different in the various departments of the firm. This injustice gave rise to his suggestion that the accounts for each department should be kept separate; yet the system should be designed in such a way that the costs of all departments would agree with the total costs of operating the firm. Perhaps what he was struggling to explain was that there should be no unallocated overhead at the end of any certain period. This writer seemed to have a grasp of certain aspects of job costing which were considerably in advance of his contemporaries; yet he did not give any illustrations, nor did he describe the books of account necessary for attaining his objective.[85]

A few years later, a Newcastle (England) accountant discussed what he called a "Net Cost" system in a paper which he read at a convention of engineers in 1873.[86] This net cost technique involved the "charging off to each particular engine, order or contract, the amount of raw material used in its manufacture, together with its exact proportion of wages and charges, and of crediting respectively your accounts representing such materials and wages regularly."[87] This accountant also advocated a separate account for each job, on the debit side of which were to be posted not only the wages and materials used or incurred but also a charge for the use of tools. The tool charge was to be determined as follows: The total cost of tools lost and the wear and tear of tools which remained was to be divided up between the different cost accounts according to the time expired in manufacturing the different jobs, due regard being taken as to the relative expensiveness of the tools used in each department. Other overhead items, such as rent, taxes, and superintendence were to be allocated as a percentage of total cost of each job. This writer did not explain his system further, nor did he give any illustrations. It would be interesting to know what he meant by "exact proportion" and "percentage of total cost," since what he was obviously trying to determine was total cost. Perhaps he had in mind prime cost. Although very little study has ever been made of the actual books of account used by manufacturers during the period under review, the ambiguity and confusion existing in the above paper would probably be reflected in the cost practices of the time.[88]

So far as England is concerned this conjecture is well borne out by a review of current cost practices published by Thomas Battersby, a Manchester public accountant, in 1878.[89] His rather extensive remarks on the subject will be only summarized here. After stating that there was no uniformity in the methods of costing in general use at that time, the author noted that the "prime cost" rates charged for tools and workers were fixed on no definite principle; they varied according to the inclination of different authorities. In some instances, however, he had seen cases where the rates were fixed according to the respective values of the tools used on a certain job or in a certain department. He seemed to think this was the correct procedure. But even in those cases the rates had been fixed without regard to the actual data of "working" (his term) expenses, and were, therefore, just as incorrect as where no definite principle was used.[90]

Battersby's terminology, incidentally, is confusing in the light of present day definitions. For example, when he mentioned prime cost rates, as in the above statement, it would ordinarily be understood from the context that he referred only to material and labor costs; but later on he defined prime cost as including materials, wages, working, upholding (maintenance and depreciation?), and general expenses. The working and upholding expenses were supposed to make up the net prime cost in this instance, while adding on the general expenses would give the gross prime cost. What he was trying to do perhaps was to divide up expenses according to whether they could be directly applied to departments, or were incurred for the business as a whole. If this supposition is true, his idea was distinctly in advance of the then current thinking on the subject.

Battersby discussed six different methods of costing which he had seen in use in his public accounting practice. A summary of these techniques follows:

(1) In the first method the total amount paid to employees on a certain job was computed and 100% added for the use of tools and for other expenses incurred. Twenty-five percent of the preceding total was added on for profit, as well as 25% profit on all materials used. To this total Battersby added the cost of materials in order to arrive at the selling price.

(2) In the second method the wages paid to direct workers were first added to a *uniform* amount for the use of lathes and other tools. This uniform amount might be the workmen's wages plus two or four shillings or so. Then 25 percent of the total was added on for indirect expenses and profit, as well as the usual 25 percent for profit on materials purchased. All these sums plus the cost of the materials used gave the selling price.

(3) In the third method the wages paid to workers were added to a percentage of wages for the use of tools and other expenses. To

this total was added the profit to arrive at the selling price. This was really a forerunner of the percentage of direct labor cost method of allocating overhead. In regard to the procedure of calculating the "percentage," Battersby stated that in practice all the overhead expenses were summarized, and the percentage that they bore to the total yearly sales of product was the percentage to be used in every job.

(4) In the fourth method all the tools were "rated according to the purchase price and the power required to work them, plus the workman's wages, and every workman is rated at the wages paid him, and a percentage for indirect expenses and profit is added on the total and on materials purchased, which gives the selling price. (These rates, however, are not worked out on correct principles, as the direct expenses are not taken into account, and therefore the rates are to a great extent assumed.)"[91] Evidently what Battersby had in mind here was that the life of the machinery and tools was to be estimated and divided into their cost to get a type of machine hour method. However, one cannot be too sure of this supposition because of what he had stated in the last sentence quoted above.

(5) The fifth method was purely arbitrary. A so-called "rate" was fixed by some responsible person in the organization based upon the purchase price of the tools and lathes used. These rates then were "used as selling prices, both for contract work and jobbing work." The expert who set the rate was to draw upon his own experience as a guide, using no other data than the purchase price. The manager "does not consider it necessary to have other than selling rates, for the simple reason that every contract is made up at these rates, and a deduction taken off the total, in estimating contract work. This deduction, no doubt, varies according to circumstances, the object being to secure the order (from the customer) with the least possible deduction; but it must be evident that this method is most uncertain and unsatisfactory, and cannot but lead to disappointment and loss."[92]

(6) The sixth method was used where piecework was employed. The total cost of materials was added to the piece-rate wages paid to employees. Then a percentage was added for the use of tools as well as minor charges. Onto this total another percentage was added for the profit. Battersby gave some other details concerning this method: The expenses were collected in "nominal ledger accounts," and the total sales of finished product in a sales book. From these two sets of data the percentage of expense to total sales could be calculated, and added on to the other costs. This method could be

tested, according to its advocators, by summarizing what they called prime costs and selling prices for a year's time, and contrasting the "gain" thus shown with the profit as shown by the balance sheet. It was admitted, though, by this authority that the percentage to be used would vary, not only because of differences in firms, but also because of the differences of opinion of the principals (experts) who set the rates.

Battersby's criticisms of all the above methods of costing which he had seen in use are interesting, mainly because he himself ventured to suggest a "perfect" system. His "prime cost and profit" technique will be described later. At present it is necessary to examine the defects in the six methods. In the first place, according to this authority, the accountants did not know the "correct system," and they continued to use these methods because no one wanted to change. Their advocates hoped that the percentages and rates employed would be sufficient to cover all the overhead items and a profit as well. Battersby stated: "The expenses have not been ascertained from the bookkeeping, and in the absence of these data, the only course is that of adopting certain rates and percentages, based merely upon opinion and assumption."[93] But this procedure, according to him, contained a fundamental fallacy. The total costs could not be divided between different jobs unless they were definitely ascertainable at the time a job was finished. Battersby thought that it was a pure assumption, then, to say that certain percentages or certain rates, for tools or workmen, were all that was needed to operate a business successfully. Moreover, the costs of each firm would be different, and would need to be calculated for each firm separately, instead of using some precalculated percentage or amount based upon the experience or judgment of the "principal" (expert). Incidentally, this authority thought it wrong in principle to use the so-called prime cost method of allocating overhead, even though he stated that it was the general method in use at the time. The specific reasons for this objection, however, were not given. Battersby summarized his criticisms of the cost techniques employed in 1878 as follows: " .... they ignore the difference between materials and labour in relation to the working expenses, they confuse prime cost and profit, and, consequently, are so deceptive in effect, that more or less profit is charged than would be charged if prime cost and profit were worked out on correct principles and distinct in their natural order; in short, there is no true theory brought to bear upon the application of the expenses and the profit, and the consequence is that whilst the nature of the work and the expenses are similar in all engineering establishments, there is great variety in the methods in general use, and many of these methods do not even approach to correctness."[94]

After such a pithy criticism of other authorities one might expect that Battersby's own "Prime Cost" system would be rather modern in nature. Yet when it is examined closely it is found to be only a partial improvement over the methods he criticized. As a matter of fact, Battersby was considerably better in finding faults with the work of other authorities than he was in devising a more nearly perfect cost system of his own. How did his own system operate? The first feature of note is that he recommended certain subsidiary books which, however, he did not attempt to coordinate with the financial records. In these subsidiary books the materials used and the wages incurred were analyzed over the different jobs. The total for each job was collected in what he called a prime cost book, in which each individual contract or job had a distinct heading. These data were in turn to be transferred to a private cost ledger where certain percentages for overhead charges and profits were to be added on, giving the selling price and gross profit on each job. Battersby's illustration was concerned with a description of costing, on a per ton basis, the castings made in an iron foundry. The melting cost was recorded on a job basis, and included depreciation, direct departmental expenses, furnacemen's wages, and steam power used. The total was divided by the tonnage of the castings finished to get the cost per ton. To this total was added the wages paid to molders and other laborers. The foundry had also what would be called today three service departments: viz., steam power department, power department—lathes and tools, and smith's department. The cost of operating the steam power department per horsepower per year was to be computed as follows:

STEAM POWER DEPARTMENT[95]

Total value of Engine, Boilers, and Gearing_____ £_____
No. of indicated horsepower _____ No._____
To____% for yearly depreciation_____ £_____
 " Direct expenses, viz., coal, wages, etc., as per
      the Perfect Double Entry Bookkeeper_____ £_____
 " Direct expenses and upholding account as per
      the Direct and Indirect Expenses Book_____ £_____

   Total yearly Cost_____ £_____

This yearly cost was to be divided by the number of indicated horsepower produced during the period, to give the prime cost per horsepower on an annual basis.

The statement for the power department—lathes and tools follows:

POWER DEPARTMENT LATHES AND TOOLS[95]

Total value of tools_____£_____
To_____% for yearly depreciation_____£_____
  "   Direct expenses, viz., tools and steel for uphold-
       ing and repairs, belting, grindstones, oil, waste,
       etc., as per direct expenses and upholding ac-
       count in the direct and Indirect Expenses Book___£_____

     Total cost of tools per year_____£_____

     Equals _____% per £ value of tools_____£_____
Then No. 1 Tool, valued at £_____ at _____% per
£, equals its yearly cost_____£_____
_____ horsepower_____£_____

     Total cost per year No. 1 Tool_____£_____

This last total was to be divided by the number of working days in a year, to give the prime cost per day for tool number 1. To this was to be added the laborer's wage, and the total represented the prime cost rate per day to be used for work performed on this machine. A register of the numbers of tools as well as their prime cost rates was to be kept in a separate book.

The smith's department was to be handled similarly:

SMITH'S DEPARTMENT[95]

Total value of tools_____£_____
To _____% for yearly depreciation_____£_____
  "   Direct expenses, viz., coal, etc., as per the perfect
       Double Entry Bookkeeper_____£_____
  "   Direct expenses, viz., tools and steel for uphold-
       ing and repairs, as per direct expenses and up-
       holding account in the Direct and Indirect
       Expenses Book_____£_____
_____ horsepower required, at per horse_____£_____

     Total cost per year_____£_____

Again, this last figure was divided by working days in a year to arrive at the cost per day, and the cost per day was in turn divided by the number of smiths employed to give the cost per day per smith. To this last figure was added the smith's pay per day, plus his striker's pay, to give the prime cost rate to be charged for each day each smith worked on a certain job.

As noted in the last two statements the capital (relative) value basis was used to divide the total cost of machine (tools) maintenance and smithing between different machines within a department. General overhead items, on the other hand, which could not be directly apportioned to the above departments, were to be applied to jobs on a direct labor cost basis. For example, if total wages were £10,000, and general items £1,500, the rate would be fifteen percent.

Battersby did not make it clear whether all his discussion of rates and percentages was to be used (1) in a retrospective manner, that is, to cost of jobs already finished at end of a fiscal period, or (2) for allocating costs to jobs on the basis of past experience as soon as a particular job was completed. However, in a list of advantages of his system he implied that the former was his aim. This list is worth quoting in full:

(1) It shows the actual cost of work as a whole or in detail.
(2) It furnishes important data from which to estimate work.
(3) It shows by comparison whether work is costing too much, and in which department it occurs.
(4) It systematically applies and controls the percentages of profit.
(5) It secures a manufacturer against loss arising from this branch of his business, and it prevents *excess* of profit—extremes equally disastrous in effect.
(6) It is a wise and timely balance-sheet. It is the manufacturer's guide and surety, and consequently a continual source of safety and satisfaction.[95]

While the advantages named were admirable, Battersby's prime cost and profit system fell far short of their attainment. It did, though, anticipate some of the methods of applying overhead which were later to be used so frequently by cost accountants, for example, the direct labor cost and the machine hour or day bases. It might also be mentioned that in the financial ledger used by this author an account was established called "machinery." All the departmental costs of manufacture and the cost of the finished castings transferred from an "iron foundry" account were posted to the debit side of this account. The machinery account was credited with the sales (at selling price) and with the stock of finished product on hand at end of period (valuation method not given). After certain general expenses had been carried to the account the balance was transferred to the profit and loss account as the gross profit for the period.[96]

So much for Battersby's contribution; his work was not to fall on deaf ears because just ten years later, two Englishmen, Emile Garcke and J. M. Fells, were to write what they claimed to be the first systematized statement of the principles underlying factory accounts. Several of their ideas can be traced back to this Manchester public accountant.[97]

The writers of accounting and bookkeeping texts in the United States almost entirely ignored industrial accounting topics until around 1885. A careful student of one of the major industries of the time, glassmaking, has drawn the following interesting conclusions:

> One reason why bankruptcies were so frequent was the failure to adopt some reliable system of accounting. If books were kept at all, entries were not faithfully made nor was any one procedure followed throughout. Some of the books were more like diaries than business records and usually no allowance was made for depreciation and other capital charges. The individual or family who ran the shop as a proprietorship or partnership either was too careless or probably saw no reason for carefully calculating profits and losses. Even most incorporated firms had to render an account of their affairs only to small groups of stockholders who were often employees as well. Such corporations as the New England Glass Company and the Boston and Sandwich Glass Company, with relatively numerous shareholders drawn from the business world and with their complete set of accounting papers, were exceptions rather than the rule. After the Civil War noticeable improvement was made in bookkeeping methods, and many more firms kept adequate records than formerly.[98]

Typical perhaps of the period is a description of manufacturing accounts in a book by J. H. Goodwin of New York City.[99] This author merely carried over to his factory accounting technique the principles which he had previously used in illustrating ordinary merchandise accounting, but there were a few differences. He recommended, for example, that separate accounts be set up on the ledger for "all articles as we are going to buy to use in the manufacture of our goods"[100] during the coming year. Then during any one year any "articles" purchased were to be charged to the different accounts already established. At the end of each year an inventory was taken of each type of article in order to see what portion had not been used. (Goodwin did not state how the remaining portion should be valued.) The amount used or "lost" in manufacturing was carried to the debit side of "manufacturing" account. Goodwin neglected to mention, however, what would happen to items (or losses as he termed them) which could not by their nature be inventoried, for example, power charges; but, if questioned, he probably would have stated that they should be closed directly to the manufacturing account. In order to make his illustration specific he mentioned some of the accounts needed for a woolen mill, such as "wool" account, "oil" account, and a "dye stuffs" account. A "machinery" account was to be kept for all machinery bought; it was also to be used to record all repairs made on machines during any fiscal period. At the end of the year this account was to be credited with the "approximate" value of the machinery, considering an allowance for "wear and tear." The wear and tear and any losses of value were to be carried to the manufacturing account, while the "approximate" (his term) value figure was brought down as a debit balance in the machinery account. For labor, a separate account was to be established, and in turn closed at the end of the period to the manufacturing account. The freight and cartage account was to be treated in the same way, since Goodwin considered this item a factory cost. Perhaps a better understanding of this author's system can be gained from the accompanying illustration on page 78.

After these entries had been recorded, the balance of the account was carried to the "loss and gain" account. If the manufacturing were profitable, the loss and gain account would be credited; if not profitable, the account would be charged.

It is really stretching one's imagination to call the above technique "cost accounting"; yet Goodwin's book ran through several dozen editions, and was one of the very few in this country which mentioned manufacturing accounts at all.[101]

There is considerable evidence that procedures similar to those described by Goodwin were in rather wide use in the United States in the thirty year period before and after the War Between the States. This evidence has been brought to light only in the past decade, mainly through the pioneering research of a group of scholars working under the auspices of the Business Historical Society and published as *Harvard Studies in Business History*. While most of

MANUFACTURING[102]

Debit	Credit
(1) Debit, at commencement of business, for value of manufactured goods on hand, as shown by the inventory [method of valuation not given].	(1) Credit for all manufactured goods we sell [supposedly at selling prices].
(2) Debit for all goods returned to us after we have sold them [valuation not given].	(2) The "present worth" of the manufactured goods that are on hand at end of year [no method of valuation mentioned].
(3) The amount of "inventoried" articles "used or lost" in manufacturing during year.	
(4) The amount brought from machinery account, this being the estimated wear and tear plus any other losses of value.	
(5) The amount brought from labor account.	
(6) The amount brought from freight and cartage account.	

these studies deal with banking, merchandising, advertising, and the like, several of the more recent volumes have been concerned with well-known New England industrial firms established as far back as the 1820's. The records and account books of these manufacturing establishments have been described by the authors of the studies along with all the other aspects of the administration of the firms in question. While space does not permit a full discussion of the many interesting cost accounting features which have been presented in these excellent studies, a brief resume is given below.

One of the industries which developed rapidly in the New England states in the early years of the nineteenth century was silverware production. George S. Gibb has surveyed the records kept at Reed and Barton's.[103] He first makes the point that in the years before 1860 the plant was organized on a twofold basis, partly product and partly process. After about 1860 the operations slowly changed until they were altogether based upon products. This firm made product lines as follows: nickel, silver, sterling, plated white metal, and other products. Each of these lines had its own corps of skilled employees, with a foreman in charge. These foremen, the superintendent, and the principal owners maintained very close relations with the operations of the factory. Since there was a rather accurate subdivision of activity in the plant it would be comparatively easy for the book-keepers to keep track of direct labor costs by products and by operations, and, after 1860, this is what they did. The employee earnings were recorded both in terms of piece rates and hours worked.

Another interesting cost accounting practice in the Reed and Barton plant was the method of handling material. The actual quantity of metal used in each department was noted on the records; but apparently a unique pricing method (for this time) was followed, namely, "a standard price which had little relation to current market values," and no reserve accounts were utilized to carry the difference between actual and standard costs. To the intense annoyance of his salesmen and some of the foremen, George Brabrook, who supervised the costing, habitually placed a value on the metal used far above either the current market price or the price the company had paid for it. The inflated cost resulting from such a practice, Brabrook felt, was an excellent cushion against the inevitable cuts in the price of the finished article forced on him by company salesmen and company action. All costs of manufacturing, other than the direct labor and metal costs, and all administrative and selling costs were considered as overhead. No further attempt was made to assign them to different products or departments, nor was depreciation of equipment recognized as a current cost of doing business. To arrive at a selling price which would cover direct costs, overhead, and profit, Brabrook was accustomed to take the direct cost of an article and double it. The figure thus arrived at was the price which the dealer paid the company and on a percent-age basis contained the following elements:[104]

Direct costs	50%
Overhead	30
Profit	20
	100%

While the factory accounting methods used at Reed and Barton were of the rough and ready variety, the company was able to operate profitably in most of the years following the War Between the States. Gibbs suggests, however, that there was some evidence of dissatisfaction with the costing methods then in vogue. As he describes it:

In 1860 all costs were charged to two accounts, Manufacturing and Expense, where they disappeared forever in a meaningless total. The Manufacturing account contained all factory costs; the Expense account carried office and selling expenses, salaries, and miscellaneous indirect costs outside the factory. The Expense account was closed out to Manufacturing at the end of the year, and the balance of the Manufacturing account constituted the company profit. As time went on, the Expense account was gradually broken down into more significant and useful subdivisions. By 1870 separate accounts had been set up as follows:

Interest	Insurance
New York Office	Advertising
Royalties	Patents
Discount	Revenue Tax

By 1900 the following had been added:

Attorneys	Philadelphia Office
Building	Chicago Office
Payroll	New York Office—Union Square
Charity	New York Office—Maiden Lane
Liability Insurance	Supplies
Fire Insurance	Selling Expense
Commissions	Packing and Shipping

Little progress was made, however, in analyzing manufacturing costs, and throughout the whole period cost-consciousness was noticeably lacking in the factory. This factor was closely allied with the high-quality standards in force. A detail which might double the cost of an item was not rejected when it made possible a better product. Thousands of dollars were spent in the production of superbly wrought dies, many of which are still in use today. Many innovations were so costly that the company could never hope to profit by them, and yet such methods returned much to the company in the form of an enhanced market reputation. It might almost be said that the most effective advertising expenditures made by Reed & Barton at that time were made within the confines of the factory walls.[105]

A second example of the early use of the cost records by actual concerns has been furnished by T. R. Navin in his discussion of the Whitin Machine Works.[106] This early firm produced cotton and silk mill equipment, and began business about 1831. Navin has made the point that John C. Whitin, the founder of the company, was a specialist in making things, and like a majority of his contemporaries, he had little patience with selling and bookkeeping difficulties. "Occasionally he may have tried to persuade mill owners to buy Whitin products, but for the most part he ran what was essentially an order-taking business. Moreover, like most self-made men, he knew nothing of accounting. All but the most rudimentary forms of bookkeeping escaped his attention. Throughout his lifetime he kept no satisfactory financial records. To familiarize himself with what was going on in his business, he relied not on accounting reports, but on a direct, personal, and constant association with day-by-day affairs. Under such circumstances elaborate accounts probably seemed to him a wasteful expenditure of time and energy."[107] This attitude reminds one of the question raised by the noted fictional character, Sir Roger de Coverley, created in 1711-1712 by the English writers Addison and Steele. In *The Spectator*, No. 174, Sir Roger quipped: "What can there great and noble be expected from him whose attention is for ever fixed upon balancing his books, and watching over his expenses?"

After presenting Whitin's cost philosophy, Navin next described the type of management technique followed by the Whitin group in the years after 1850. As this authority stated it:

> The Whitin Machine Works possessed few of the sophisticated management techniques known to companies that could trace their ancestry to the merchant-era past. In a very general way, American manufacturing firms of the nineteenth century followed two management patterns. There were those which, founded by wealthy investing capitalists, were fair-sized institutions from the start; and there were those which, started by petty tradesmen or shop owners, were small in their beginnings but large in potentiality. Companies of the first group, having been promoted by experienced capitalists, were the beneficiaries of the business experience handed down to them through the ages of mercantile capitalism. Typically, companies in that group had well-developed double entry bookkeeping systems with such refinements as unit cost data and special manufacturing accounts. Companies in the second group, having been promoted by petty capitalists whose knowledge of business was limited to what they had learned from practical experience, usually kept their financial records on the same informal basis as their owners kept their personal accounts. Indeed, in such companies corporate and personal accounts were often indistinguishable.[108]

The Whitin enterprise undoubtedly belonged to the second group. It should be further noted that Navin referred to such now commonplace practices as "unit cost date" and "special manufacturing accounts" as "refinements." The present writer would certainly agree with him that unit cost determinations were a rarity in the 1800's, but special manufacturing accounts were well-known by 1850.

A third example of the early use of cost records by actual concerns has been furnished by George S. Gibb in his discussion of the Saco-Lowell Shops.[109]   Like the Whitin Company, this well-known firm produced cotton and silk mill equipment, and one of its predecessors, the Boston Manufacturing Company, began business about 1813. It was not long after that date that the management became curious about the elasticity and flexibility of the sales price schedule used by the firm in quoting its products to customers. As Gibb has explained it:

> The Boston Manufacturing Company experimented with prices, and found that the market was willing to pay more than the figures first set. After the first sale of machinery, prices on looms, warpers, and dressing machines were extended by inclusion of a patent fee. Once these initial adjustments had been made, prices and costs became well stabilized. The relationship of one to the other can be measured, but not explained. Prices after 1817 were set to allow an extremely generous profit margin, but a margin which varied considerably from one machine to another. Profits on individual machines, expressed as a percentage of selling price and usually reflecting the inclusion of a patent fee, ranged from 20 per cent on yarn beams to 50 per cent and more on warpers, dressers, drawing frames, throstle spinning frames and double speeders. Looms were usually priced to yield 28 per cent profit.[110]

This emphasis on profit margin would normally presuppose adequate factory cost data, but Gibb thinks otherwise. His reasons and conclusions are quite interesting and informative.

> Existing records do not clearly reveal the components of the cost figures against which sales were measured to arrive at profit margins. Inability to criticize the company's accounting in the light of present day concepts, however, is not a serious handicap. However they were made up, these profit figures are valuable because they represent what the company believed to be their profit. In spite of the existence in the record books of standard machine cost quotations, the company recognized and recorded the most minute variations in the day-to-day costs of building machinery. The concept of inflexible, standardized costs adhered to by generations of petty capitalist artisans was transcended.
> These costs and selling prices have only a relative significance in history and they are of value only to the extent that they can be compared with later costs and prices in the same company or with the contemporary costs and prices of other companies. There is no cost information on which to base comparisons between the Waltham machine shop and other shops in America and England, and very little comparative price information of a specific nature.

In 1820, prices of cotton machinery in America were said to be double those in England, and one competent observer states that in the American market the Waltham patents were being held at a high price. The Gilmour loom is known to have undersold the Waltham loom by as much as $55, but this is probably the only direct comparison possible between the machines of contemporary manufacturers. A comparison of Waltham prices with those of earlier machine-makers in an attempt to establish the trend of machine prices is subject to the same difficulties arising from lack of specific information. Rare price lists of cotton machinery in Philadelphia and New Jersey in the years from 1808 to 1815 are available. These data indicate that the Waltham prices on certain machines from 1817 to 1823 substantially exceeded those of the earlier period.[111]

Even though the management of this firm was definitely cost conscious in the 1820's, the accounting methodology employed was exceptionally crude in comparison with techniques already illustrated by text writers, such as Payen and Cronhelm. A sales machinery account was set up on the ledger.

This account was credited with machinery sales and income from patent fees and manufacturing rights. Charged against the account were standard costs of machines sold and a small number of miscellaneous items such as legal expenses in patent suits, drayage, etc. . . . The accounting controls of mercantile trade were here adapted with outstanding success to the requirements of an industrial system. Mercantile accounting could scarcely be applied to a manufacturing business without substantial alterations. These alterations were made, but the concept of close control through the keeping of adequate records was carried over intact. The accounting system of the Boston Manufacturing Company was a classic influence in the New England textile industry.[112]

That this firm was a definite forerunner in the matter of cost allocations to products is clearly shown in the following description and conclusions drawn by Gibb:

The question inevitably arises as to what the Boston Manufacturing Company considered as costs of building machinery. Unit costs which reflected allocation, on one basis or another, of all overhead costs were not computed for either cloth or machinery. Certain costs were not charged to the machinery or cloth accounts at all, but were posted, along with the machinery and cloth-account balances, to a central clearing account, which alone served to show what the over-all costs of doing business and the total profits from the enterprise were. The cost-per-machine figures are therefore artificial to the extent that they fail to include some overhead costs. The margin of error is not large, however, for the company allocated portions of a large percentage of its total costs to the production accounts. There was a painstaking tabulation of all direct costs, together with a careful allocation of such costs to the department of business in which they were incurred. Labor costs, for example, were not only broken down between cloth machinery, and other accounts, but were even further prorated to the various types of machines under construction or repair. A definite attempt was made to charge many overhead costs to the production accounts. An outstanding example of this attempt to assign such costs to the department in which they were incurred is provided by the company's treatment of executive salaries. The salaries of Paul Moody and Patrick Tracy Jackson were spread over several different accounts, and the allocations were varied from period to period as the supervisory attention of these men shifted. Presumably the basis employed in making these charges was the number of hours (probably estimated rather than tabulated) devoted by the agent and the treasurer to the various phases of the business.

There are few contemporary examples against which to measure the accounting methods of the Boston Manufacturing Company. A tentative appraisal which could be confirmed or denied only by an extensive study of American accounting practice, indicates that in bringing to manufacturing industry the conscientious record keeping of the merchant countinghouse the company made a vastly important contribution to American business techniques. This contribution should be assigned a value equal to that of the Waltham precedents in production organization, mechanical effort, and labor policy.[113]

A fourth example of the early use of cost records by actual companies has been furnished by Evelyn H. Knowlton in her discussion of the Pepperell Manufacturing Company.[114] This well-known cotton textile firm began business in 1850.

The first clerk of the company was a man named Haines. "In setting up his system of accounts Haines had the experience of many other textile companies to guide him. . . . Thus, long before 1850, the textile companies had worked out a system which they kept, with few changes, for about three quarters of a century longer. Haines kept daybooks, cashbooks, bill books, lists of cotton invoices, payrolls, production records, mill expense figures, and a record of the disposal of cotton waste. These were primary books. . . . Haines also compiled summary books. The most important of these comprised the semi-annual statements which he submitted to the treasurer. . . . "[115]

While there are suggestions to the effect that Pepperell's accountants computed semiannual cost of manufacture statements,[116]

Knowlton does not furnish any details as to the technique used. Her analysis of the data follows:

> Let us glance briefly at the records of the totals of other expenses of manufacture of similar periods—mill expense and general expense. Mill expense, as we have noted earlier, included only the pay of the employees—supervisory and operative—in the carding, spinning, dressing, and weaving rooms of the mills. This series of figures for December, 1870, through June, 1911, showed much less violent fluctuations than the series for cotton. This is as one would expect, even though changes in wage rates and in the schedule of hours upset the normal growth. From 1870 to 1899 the percentage of increase in mill expense was about the same as in the number of employees, 33 per cent. Wage rates were apparently about the same in the two periods, although they had fluctuated in the interim. After the figures for the two divisions had been combined, the total mill expense, of course, increased considerably. During the first World War the workers shared in the inflation of wages and prices, as they had done during the Civil War.
>
> Similarly, the general expense—salaries of the agent and the superintendent, wages of the workers outside the four major divisions of the mills, miscellaneous supplies, and various other expenses, such as taxes—showed little cyclical fluctuation but a gradual trend upward during the period December, 1870, through June, 1911. One part of this expense about which the treasurer and agent were concerned was taxes. Although it composed a minor part of the general expense, typically about 20 per cent, the agent not unlike most taxpayers, always felt it should be lower.
>
> The total cost of manufacturing, composed of the three series —cotton, mill expense, and general expense—increased during this period of fifty-four years. On the whole the total manufacturing expense remained divided as earlier—66 per cent for cotton, 22 per cent for mill expense, and 12 per cent for general expense.[117]

The fifth example of the early actual use of cost records is concerned with a small company. It has been furnished by W. W. Cauley in his discussion of the Shelby Iron Works.[118] (This is not a part of the Harvard Series.) As early as 1847 the accountant for this company calculated the cost of a ton of iron to be made up of:

For ore	$ 2.00
For charcoal	10.00
For limestone	.75
For labor	3.00
For repairs	1.00
Cost per ton	$16.75

There is no evidence that this firm's accounting system contained any bona fide cost accounts until around 1870. Many of the detail records, however, are reminiscent of modern practice. For instance, depreciation was recorded as early as 1875, and a furnace record book was used after 1869 to keep track of the production at each of the blast furnaces. The information recorded was of the following type: charges, weights of ore, bushels of coal, weight of flux, pressure of blasts, pressure of steam used, revolutions of engine, temperature of blasts, weight of iron produced each day, quantity of each grade produced, quantity of each grade of iron shipped, lost time—hours and cause, percentage of iron to ore, bushels of charcoal used per ton of iron, total iron on hand and shipped each day, and miscellaneous sundries.

Another record kept, which amounted to a perpetual inventory of the various grades of iron on hand in the yard of the company, was called "pig iron analysis record." This was a bound book with each page ruled for columns with these titles: date made, casting number, grade, tons, silicon, phosphorous, sulphur, carbons, and date shipped. The chemical analysis of each lot of pig iron made, as well as a grade number, and the number of tons in each lot, was entered in this record. When the lot was shipped the date was recorded in the "date shipped" column and the entry referring to that lot was ruled through in red ink. If only a part of a lot was shipped, the portion remaining on hand was recorded by a new entry.

The basis for the preparation of payrolls and the distribution of labor costs was the employee time book. These small books were ruled with two facing pages with columns for each day of the month. They were kept by foremen and timekeepers. Workmen's names were listed down the left side of the left hand pages of each book and a mark was made in the appropriate column according to the date. The unit of time used in computing wages was the day and the pay period was monthly. Each month the time books from all the departments were gathered together at the office and the time worked by each employee was added up and his wages calculated. These data were then used to prepare the payroll. The payroll was a large sheet on which was recorded much the same information as that appearing on the time books plus the amount of wages earned by the workers. Columns were provided on the payroll for "stoppages," i.e., deductions from the pay of employees for such items as store checks (which could be exchanged for merchandise at the company commissary), rent of company houses, doctor's bills payable to the company physician, or other items of a similar nature.

The method of distributing indirect labor charges and indirect material charges to the various asset and operating expense ledger accounts after 1868 is of cost accounting interest in that the accountant for the company attempted to obtain a high degree of accuracy. A "distribution of labor" book was used, as well as one for indirect materials and supplies.

The source of entries in the distribution of labor book was evidenced by a time ticket form posted to the flyleaf of the volume. The form of this ticket was as follows:

MACHINIST'S DISTRIBUTION

Name_____18_____

    Job_____ Time_____(hours)

_____

_____

_____

Material

_____

_____

_____

A notation written above the time ticket says:

> Blanks for distribution of time by foreman.
> Used as original entries in this book. Blanks
> furnished by T. H. Payne and Co.

Various general journal entries indicate that the direct labor payrolls at Shelby were charged directly to operating accounts in the name of various departments of the organization. For example, the wages of laborers engaged in the preparation of charcoal were charged to pig iron; miners' wages were charged to ore or to lime rock. A labor account received charges for earnings of clerical and supervisory employees not associated with any one productive activity and a salaries account was charged with salaries of officials of the company. These were the general ledger labor accounts which received charges for labor.

Entries in the distribution of labor book indicate that indirect laborers were divided into four classifications: machinists, blacksmiths, carpenters, and masons. Evidently, time tickets of the type indicated above were kept for each classification. When a black-smith did some repair work at the furnace, the furnace foreman made out a blacksmith's distribution ticket, giving the date, name of the workman, a description of the work done, the time required for the job, and the materials used. A similar procedure was followed when machinists, carpenters, or masons performed duties in the various parts of the plant. These tickets were then assembled at the furnace office and posted to distribution of labor and distribution of materials records.

The distribution of labor book for the year 1887 was in reality a sort of subsidiary ledger. A separate account was maintained for each asset or operating expense to which indirect labor costs were charged. There were 109 accounts to which indirect labor costs were posted during the year 1887.

Each account was ruled into eight columns with the titles:

>Date
>Workman
>Job
>Hours
>Machinists
>Blacksmiths
>Lumber (Carpenters)
>Masons

The use of these columns in posting the information contained on the indirect labor time tickets was demonstrated by the entries posted to the charcoal account on page 33 of the distribution of labor book. This page has been reproduced in an accompanying illustration. It can be seen from these entries that Horton was a carpenter; Seale and Stinson were blacksmiths who did some work on the retort covers where charcoal was prepared; Keel was a machinist, etc. The distributions were made weekly and evidently the totals of the postings to the various accounts by labor classifications had to agree with the payroll for the same labor classification.

The information in the labor and materials distribution records served as the basis for summary entries in the general journal charging ore, charcoal, lime rock, improvements and repairs, etc., with indirect labor costs and crediting labor which had been previously charged with the indirect labor sections of the payroll.

In summary, it may be stated that the Shelby accountants determined the cost of making a ton of pig iron by the following

CHARCOAL

1887	Workman	Job		Hrs.	Mach.	Bsmith	Lbr.	Masons
May 27	Horton	Cabs		8			1.40	
	Horton	"		3			.52	
30	Horton	"		3			.52	
31	Seale	"		1		.28		
	Stinson	"		1		.12		
31	Ranscheubey	Retort Cover		3			.52	
	Horton	Cabs		6			1.05	
June 1	Horton	Cabs		2			.35	
	Ranscheubey	Retort Cover		10			1.75	
	Labor week ending June 1					.40	6.11	
Iune 2	Ranscheubey	Retort Cover		8			1.40	
3	Seale	"	"	1		.28		
	Stinson	"	"	1		.12		
3	Ranscheubey	"	"	4			.70	
6	McLean	"	Ovens	1		.25		
	Sammel	"	"	1		.10		
7	Stinson	"	"	5		.63		
	McLean	"	"	9		2.25		
	Sammel	"	"	4		.40		
8	McLean	"	"	8		2.00		
	Sammel	"	"	8		.80		
	Labor week ending June 8					6.83	2.10	
9	McLean	Retort Ovens		9		2.25		
	Sammel	"	"	9		.90		
10	McLean	"	"	5		1.25		
	Sammel	"	"	5		.50		
	Horton	Cabs		5			.87	
11	"	"		2			.35	
14	Horton	"		2			.35	
15	Keel	Retorts		3	.30			
	Horton	Cabs		5			.88	
	Labor week ending June 15				.30	4.90	2.45	

technique: (1) The total amount of costs charged to each of the various departments or activities was calculated for a given period of time. (2) The total number of tons of metal produced during that same period was divided into these amounts in order to arrive at the expenditures incident to each activity per ton of metal made. The flow of cost through the ledger was not recognized. The primary objective of the bookkeeping was to produce a written record of the bookkeeping transactions which took place and to provide a basis for a periodic statement of the assets and liabilities of the company. The system used, therefore, was a modified assortment of mixed trading accounts. Even though costs of production were calculated, the ledger procedures adopted were not cost accounting techniques. The per unit cost determinations seem to have been made on an outside-the-ledger basis; this procedure, incidentally, is still used by many firms today.

CHAPTER III

EVOLUTION OF THE ACCOUNTING FOR
RAW MATERIALS

PART I. HANDLING AND CONTROL OF RAW MATERIALS

ACCOUNTING FOR MATERIALS PURCHASED AND CONSUMED BY A FACTORY, being part of the so-called "prime cost" of the manufactured product, was mentioned or discussed by practically all of the early cost theorists. In fact, as explained in Chapter I, it was fairly well understood by even the mediaeval industrial accountants, especially those in Florence and Venice. The early part of the nineteenth century brought further refinements in the skill with which raw material was treated in the accounting records. In this connection the work of Payen and Cronhelm was particularly noteworthy; Cronhelm even recommended the use of what is now called a "perpetual inventory" system.[1] It was crude, of course, but he deserves credit for his originality.

The reason for the early interest in this topic is not difficult to determine. Obviously, if a firm kept any records at all, they would be at least concerned with the amount and value of the raw materials and direct labor used in the finished goods, and prime cost systems of costing were the forerunners of the more complete techniques which later evolved. With this incentive, therefore, it is not surprising to find such an authority as Henry Metcalfe, an American Army Ordnance officer, devoting several chapters of his 1885 *Cost of Manu-*

factures[2] to the subject. In addition to his superior treatment of the problem of costing the material element, Metcalfe also made several recommendations as to a looseleaf recording arrangement which was one of the first suggestions along those lines. It was his idea that a card should be made out for almost every possible type of transaction or transfer of material. Each card, moreover, had a space for pricing the article used, as well as the order number to which it was to be charged. In those days, a large number of factory managers thought it unwise to let the employees know how much the material cost, but Metcalfe concluded that the disadvantages of such a scheme far outweighed the advantages. He suggested, therefore, that a list of the prices paid for each article be drawn up and copies passed around to all persons who would have occasion to fill out material cards. In this way, the prices could be shown on every recording. In case certain component parts, manufactured within the plant, were used in further processes, tables of estimated costs of such component parts were to be passed to each department concerned. The latter type of card, then, served the same function as an original price list to some other department. Only one entry was to be made on each card; that is to say, each type of material used on each production order was separated. This was done in order that the cost and storeroom clerks could sort the cards later as to the amount used on each order and as to type of material. After serving their purposes, the cards were filed away by orders on which used, or according to operations involved; Metcalfe did not make any definite recommendation about this point. The cards, too, were to be copiously distributed throughout the factory so that workmen would have no hesitancy in using them. All of the cards, though, had to be authenticated by a foreman, who, incidentally, was to use a hand punch instead of his initials or name; requisitions and purchase orders were also to be entered on cards. In addition a "ledger slip" was to be made out for each sort of material or supply, and all the issues and returns entered thereon. The ledger slip was really a stores ledger, but no provision was made for carrying forward the balances after each transaction; the balance was to be struck only at the end of the quarter. The slips were by quantities only, even though the price was entered in the heading of each.[3]

As can be easily seen, there was considerable modernity in Captain Metcalfe's system, although it lacked some of the polish and finish of later techniques. It is interesting to note, however, that it was criticized severely by several prominent engineers of the time, F. W. Tay-

lor and Oberlin Smith being two. Smith was alarmed at the immense
number of cards which would be floating around in a large shop,
and suggested that there ought to be methods devised which would
reduce the number. Taylor thought, on the other hand, that Metcalfe's
procedure was a step in the right direction, but from his own personal
experience he had found it to be only partially adaptable. He did,
however, approve of the card system and had used it for some ten
years in his own firm, William Sellers and Company.[4]

Two years later, 1887, the English authorities, Emile Garcke and
J. M. Fells, also treated at length the handling of the material element
of cost. Both of these men were important industrial executives and
accountants. Garcke held the position of managing director of British
Electric Traction Company, and Fells was general manager of Salt
Union Limited. Their system contemplated the issuance of work
orders to foremen, who in turn requisitioned the storekeeper for the
material needed. The latter order was called the "stores warrant,"
and a duplicate copy was kept by the storekeeper. The storekeeper
entered all his warrants in a stores issued book which had columns for
date, number of warrant, supplied to, articles, working number or
purpose, dimensions, number, weight, rate, amount, ledger folio, and
remarks. The warrant was sent also to the "counting house" where it
was entered in the prime cost book, and also in the stores account in
the commercial ledger. The stores issued book was periodically recorded in the stores ledger to the credit of the respective articles. A
stores rejected book was provided for all the materials returned to vendors, the entries being based upon the credit memorandums received
from such vendors. Garcke and Fells emphasized the importance of
returning to the storeroom any material which had been drawn in excess of requirements for a certain job; for this purpose a stores debit
note was provided. It had columns for article, number of order, purposes, number, weight, rate, and amount. After the note had been
posted by the storekeeper to shop returns book, it was sent to the central office where it was entered on the prime cost book as a reduction
of the cost of a job. Any entries in the shop returns book were later
posted to the debit side of the stores ledger.[5]

Garcke and Fells also provided for the receipt of materials by
showing an illustration of a stores received book. The entries therein
were posted periodically to the stores ledger on the debit side. They
compared these two books to the debit side of the cash book and the debit side of the cash account in the ledger; that is, they bore the same re-

lationship to each other. The stores ledger was unusually complete;
it had on the debit side columns for date, folio, firm's name, description, number, rate, amount, total; and on the credit side columns with
the same titles. This subsidiary book, therefore, was the same as is
used today except for the lack of a balance on hand column. Obviously, however, a balance could be drawn off at any time the necessity
occurred, such as a statement date. Garcke and Fells also contemplated the exact reconciliation in total of the stores account in the
general ledger with the several accounts in the stores ledger. This
was a very definite improvement over those systems which called for
the maintenance of separate cost books. Although they were hazy
as to certain details, these two English authorities did emphasize the
general importance of securing accuracy in the factory accounting by
tying in the cost records with the general books. As they stated it,
"the result of the periodical survey of the stores would under this
system agree not only with the stores ledger in regard to the particular
classes of materials, but should also agree collectively with the stores
account in the commercial ledger."[6] Several years passed before other
authorities began to recommend such a technique. In summary, it may
be stated that Garcke and Fells showed a thorough understanding of
the accounting for materials, and that their system has been little improved on since that time. As will be developed in Chapter V, however, they were not very clear on the handling of overhead costs.

    Another late nineteenth century Englishman, G. P. Norton, fol-
lowed for the most part the treatment of Garcke and Fells. He showed
a raw material stock and cost book with several columns on the
received side, and several on the issued side. Again, no balance column was provided; both the quantities and cost price, however, were
recorded. The total quantity issued, moreover, was made to agree
with the quantity received by adding in the inventory at any date.
Articles which were returned after being issued to the departments
were to be entered in the issued column in red ink, which quantities
were to be deducted when the total was extended into the final total
issued column. This last technique should be contrasted with that of
Garcke and Fells' stores debit note arrangement. Norton considered
this an unnecessary refinement.[7]

    Several years later, J. S. Lewis, an English accountant and factory
manager, in his *Commercial Organisation of Factories*, added an additional point by recognizing that when a physical inventory of each
type of material was taken, more than likely it would not agree with

the stores ledger account. This was a point that previous authorities had neglected. Lewis suggested as a possible solution that in case of a discrepancy the "trading" account be debited, while excesses would be credited to the same account; the stores ledger itself should then be adjusted to conform to the physical stock on hand. A survey sheet was to be used as a means of accumulating the various shortages and over-ages. The survey sheet had columns for balances as per ledger, balances as per survey, and deficiency or excess by both quantity and value.[8] Except for this point Lewis added little to the theory or technique underlying the accounting for the material used in a product. Lewis' countryman, E. Andrade, on the other hand, recommended the use of a stores issued book which had the following columns: date, account chargeable, stores issue sheet folio, issues stores A, stores issue sheet folio, issue stores B, and so on for each type of stores. The storekeeper rendered a list of all his issues to the cost clerk each day; and the clerk valued the issues and charged them to the proper job. For material which was needed on a particular job, Andrade suggested a special column in the purchases ledger, or a separate book if desired.[9]

In the United States, the topic received little attention after Metcalfe, who wrote, it will be remembered, in 1885. Around the turn of the century, however, H. L. Arnold published his *Complete Cost-Keeper* (1899) in which he described the procedures used by several prominent industrial firms of the day. One of these used a stores ledger card system in which balance columns were provided not only for the quantity on hand, but also for the value. These were kept on a current basis, that is, the balance was known at the end of each day. A maximum and minimum quantity notation space was also mentioned. In addition to this modern feature, the stores ledger clerk arranged for the continuous accuracy of his accounts by sending to the storekeeper each day a request for an actual count of certain items unknown to the storekeeper in advance. If any discrepancies were found, and Arnold noted that there would be some, the permanent inventory record was changed correspondingly. All the articles in the storeroom were to be checked and counted at least every sixty days.[10] Requisitions were used, as at present, and all the incidental records which accompanied them. In general Arnold's technique and description would compare favorably with much more recent discussions of the topic.

During the next year, another American, H. Diemer, published a system providing for a so-called "bill of material" to be compiled by the drafting department which drew the plans for the job. The bill had columns for name of part, material, size or pattern number, drawing number, quantity required, date ordered, date received, material drawn from storeroom, total weight, and cost of material. Someone outside of the drafting department was to see that there was no overstocking of material, yet make sure that there was always a sufficient amount on hand for current needs. This sounds very much like the duty of a planning man, especially since Diemer mentioned that he must also arrange for the maintenance of an orderly flow of production throughout the plant. Diemer's principal contribution, however, was his bill of materials, which later became a feature of a great number of costing arrangements.[11] This authority, incidentally, was opposed to the use of cards for stores ledger transactions. In fact, he was not at all in sympathy with the proposals which had been put forward to keep perpetual inventories of materials, insisting that it was entirely too much trouble and that only the actual amount of material on hand was a safe record. He seems to have been confused as to the purpose of the stores ledger technique; obviously the actual count was more accurate, but it was to be used to check the book records and not vice versa. Diemer thus condemned one of the most important techniques employed by the later, more modern cost accountant. It was his idea that the bill of materials, plus a slip signed by section foremen for withdrawals of materials from the storeroom, could be used in place of the stores ledger. Actual counts, he mentioned, would be conducted from time to time to determine the exact amount on hand. All of this suggests that Diemer was more of a theorist than a practitioner.

By 1904 cost authorities were referring to the perpetual inventory plan by its present title. A Detroit accountant, H. L. C. Hall, for example, gave an illustration of a stores ledger card which was designed to permit the easy balancing of the amount and value of individual articles each month—not after each transaction, however. He referred to it as the "perpetual inventory system," and stated that with its use monthly statements of profit and financial conditions could be quickly compiled. Again, the book records were to be checked at intervals with an actual count of the goods on hand. Hall also considered at length the purchasing and storing of materials, showing a thorough grasp of those important subjects.[12]

A few of the English cost theorists were also continuing the work of Garcke and Fells and the other early authorities. By and large, however, the English writings of this period were barren so far as the handling of material was concerned. H. Spencer, for example, in 1907, devoted a chapter to the topic, stressing particularly the work of the storekeeper. He gave an illustration of a stores ledger which was designed to keep a running balance of the quantity (but not value) of the different articles on hand. The supply ordered could be entered on the same card if desired, thus affording an indication of the quantity in the storeroom as well as in transit. A continuous checking or audit scheme which would enable the records of quantities to be verified at least every few months was also provided.[13] In addition, Spencer devoted several pages to the work of the purchasing agent, maximum and minimum stocks, and the receiving and requisitioning of material; there was nothing original in the latter, however, the same ground having been covered by previous authorities.[14]

By 1909 cost writers in the United States were considering the requirements of larger firms as well as the ordinary transactions and forms needed by small manufacturing plants. J. L. Nicholson, for instance, in that year proposed a summary of requisitions which would eliminate a great deal of the work in posting to the stores ledgers, as well as to the cost records. The summary was to be added at periodic intervals, say every week or month; the cost of materials used for the entire period could thus be ascertained at one time instead of by individual requisitions.[15] Nicholson also made some suggestions at that time for what he called a "report of material delivered," which had for its purpose the accumulation of the total amount of material delivered by the storekeeper during a month to the different departments of the plant, and was designed for use by a processing firm which handled no job lot orders. This served essentially, then, the same purpose for a manufactory which handled no job lot orders, as the summary of requisitions did for the engineering or contracting establishment. This authority, moreover, gave numerous forms for the different summaries and reports which he discussed in his work, but in general he failed to devote much attention to the ledger transactions involved in the accounting for materials. He did, however, recommend the use of a true perpetual inventory system in line with previous suggestions by a few prior experts, and illustrated a raw material card which had spaces for the amounts and values received, delivered, and the balance. Entering both quantity and price on the cards had been neglected by most of those who wrote in the period immediately preceding him; a considerable number had been satisfied with just the quantity record.[16]   In summary, it might be stated that Nicholson recognized more completely than any of his predecessors the importance of a proper control of the material element of cost, yet his discussion suffered somewhat because of its generality; his work was more of a handbook than a textbook.   Perhaps, however, that was what he intended it to be.

By the end of the first decade of this century, therefore, most of the theories and techniques in regard to the handling and control of raw material had been worked out.   From that time on, few contributions of an original nature were made.   This does not mean that there was any less attention given to the matter.   On the contrary, nearly all the authorities felt it imperative to go over the ground previously covered by preceding writers.   Attention began to be given, also, to certain of the finer details of procedures.   F. E. Webner, for instance, introduced an account which he called "variation in weights and measures" designed to be a "barometer of inaccuracy or dishonesty."[17] To this account were charged all the inaccuracies in the stores ledgers as they were found throughout the year; these differences could arise from lost or stolen goods, or from errors.   The credits to the account were absorbed in the burden account and were spread over at least an entire fiscal period; the account was thus a budgetary or equalizing device.   Webner's system in general involved several such accounts, this being an especially noteworthy characteristic of his work.

In his 1913 work, J. L. Nicholson again expounded at length the details of the proper recording of materials, and he illustrated a rather complete store card which had columns for amount ordered, amount received (both quantity and price), amount delivered (both quantity and price), balance on hand (both quantity and value), quantity reserved, and, finally, quantity available.   This form, therefore, provided for about as much information as would ever be desired.   Nicholson also showed other headings which might be adopted if a firm could not use the more complete series.[18]

The writings of cost authorities during and after the First World War became more and more comprehensive as to the details of handling the raw material, or stores, of a factory.   The treatment accorded the topic by E. P. Moxey, of Philadelphia, might be considered typical of the period before World War I.   After making the observation that the widespread use of detail records helps to distinguish cost accounting from ordinary factory bookkeeping, Moxey next described the physical inventory method of determining the cost of materials used or "lost" (his term) during any given period of time.[19] This physical inventory method, of course, was simply the familiar formula of beginning inventory plus purchases less final inventory equals the cost of material consumed. This Philadelphia accountant (he was also a professor) stressed the fact that under this method the factory manager would have to "infer" as to the leakage of material from the storeroom. Under the second method of material accounting, however, called the "book inventory" technique, there was much less guesswork in that the balance of material actually on hand could be checked at intervals with the perpetual inventory cards. In further description of his preferred method, Moxey, following Garcke and Fells, employed the later quite popular diagrammatic approach. One of his diagrams, for example, depicted the relation of stores records to commercial records; twelve different forms were shown with arrows pointing out the flow of charges, entries, etc.

Moxey presented a clear, yet very brief, description of the details associated with the receiving and issuing of stores. The following features of his system are notable: (1) he preferred to make monthly entries to the general ledger; (2) the creditor's ledger should be posted daily; (3) the invoices for sub-standard material should be permitted to go through the regular routine and at a subsequent time a credit memo would be issued; (4) the stores department should keep a stores rejected book which would serve as the posting media from which entries would be made to the stores cards; (5) the pricing problem involved in requisitions was slighted entirely by Moxey; (6) the factory employees should fill out a stores debit note whenever excess material was issued to them; (7) he recommended the use of an unusually complete looseleaf stores ledger card having the following columns: I. Stores ordered but not yet delivered—date ordered, number of pieces or quantity, date received, purchase order number, date to be delivered; II. Stores on hand in store-room — date received, number of pieces or quantity, amount, date issued, requisition number; III. Stores apportioned, number of pieces or quantity, amount, date issued, order number; IV. Stores available—date, number of pieces or quantity, amount; (8) he made passing reference to tally cards and bills of material; (9) he concluded his discussion by explaining the problems and difficulties associated with the taking of the physical inventory, with particular emphasis upon the timing of the physical count to coincide with the moment at which the minimum limit of items was on hand. As he stated it: "Not only is the taking of the inventory lighter at this time, but an actual inventory serves to determine accurately whether or not a new order for more material" should be sent to the vendor.[20]

The treatment accorded the topic by J. P. Jordan and G. L. Harris[21] might be considered typical of the period after World War I, so far as this country is concerned; while, in England, E. T. Elbourne exhausted the subject in his comprehensive *Factory Administration and Cost Accounts.*[22] Elbourne followed for the most part the authorities who had preceded him, and consolidated the various advantageous techniques that had already been developed. Beginning with the early 1920's the interesting practices of standard costing came to the forefront, not only for materials, but also for other elements of cost. Various authorities had proposed such plans for several years, but the matter seemed to have become more prominent in the years mentioned. This particular development cannot be considered at length here; certain aspects of it, however, will be discussed in the second part of this chapter.

In addition to the general cost books, which dealt with the problem of materials only incidentally, various specialized works began also to appear. Some examples are given in the reference notes at the end of this volume; their titles sufficiently indicate their nature.[23] In summary, therefore, it may be stated that by 1925 the techniques and theories involved in handling and controlling the raw materials of a factory had become fairly well known. About the only development since that date has been the increasing use of tabulating machine equipment in large plants, but no new theory was needed for that modern practice.

PART II. MATERIAL REQUISITIONS AND THEIR PRICING

The few authorities who considered requisitions and their pricing before 1885 implied that the "cost" of the material was to be used when charging the product with the material element. As a matter of fact, however, little was written before that date as to the specific techniques to be employed. None of the many complications had been mentioned, nor was there much interest in the matter. But beginning with 1885 the subject began to assume some importance. In that year Henry Metcalfe made the recommendation that the "true cost" (his term) prices of materials be freely promulgated around the factory and placed on all the cards which he suggested should be used.[24] The prices were to be the same as those on the bills or invoices accompanying the stores, and were to be shown on the face of requisitions and other material cards. This authority seems to have thought that there would be no difficulty in determining the cost price, and he bothered little as to possible doubtful items, such as storage or handling charges. The following is typical of his treatment: "At the end of the fiscal year, when the inventory is taken, the value of the material actually on hand is credited to the order under which it has been held during the past year. The order so stands charged with all omissions, and the undistributed burden falls naturally where it should most properly, because most probably be borne."[25] His work was noteworthy, however, in that he did make definite recommendations along the lines indicated.

Not long afterwards, the English authorities, Emile Garcke and J. M. Fells, made provision on their stores ledger and their requisitions for the "rate, amount, and total" of the raw materials issued to foreman for use on jobs; but they did not indicate just how the aforesaid values were to be derived, leaving the matter entirely unsettled. Supposedly, however, the cost price was to be used.[26] Their countryman, G. P. Norton, on the other hand, was a little more specific; he referred to a raw material stock and cost book which had a column for the price per unit. Norton stated that the price should also include carriage and any charges in connection with buying, such as commissions or brokerage. On the issued side of this book, however, the prices were omitted; the cost, therefore, seemed only for the purpose of inventorying the items at a balance sheet date. In fact, Norton placed himself on record as follows:

"In accounting for material . . . regard must be had to *quantities* and not *values*. The introduction of values will only lead to hopeless confusion, and will serve no useful purpose."[27]

This writer, therefore, was not particularly concerned with the topic under discussion.

F. G. Burton, an English engineer, recommended somewhat later the adoption of a stores issue book in the plants of engineering and machinery builders. It was to be used to record the amounts and prices of articles issued by the general storekeeper. The cost price, which he defined as the invoice price per unit plus an apportioned part of the freight and cartage incurred, was to be adopted. He sagely recognized that such an allocation might be at times very difficult to carry out, and he went on to mention that a large number of firms did not follow the suggested technique but included such charges in the overhead costs. Burton, however, felt that the "actual cost price" should be used.[28]   As for the requisitions themselves, Burton was rather indefinite, preferring to let each firm decide the matter for itself.[29]

In America a controversy was in progress around the turn of the century as to whether or not a percentage should be added to the cost of materials to cover interest on their cost, storage, inspection, handling, and freight charges before they (the materials used) were added to the cost of a job.   Henry Roland,[30] for example, was insisting that the correct practice was to add such a charge but that the difficulty in ascertaining the proper amount was to be considered a disadvantage of of the technique.   This authority did not discuss any of the details in regard to the calculation of such a percentage, merely mentioning that the exact figure was a matter of dispute.   The Canadians, Eddis and Tindall, on the other hand, recognized that certain types of raw material would fluctuate in price.   When this happened, they recommended the use of a weighted average, computed after the end of the fiscal period and applied to products at that time.   In another place, however, they seemed to reverse themselves when they suggested that if goods were purchased at different prices at different periods, it was proper "to fix the price of raw materials from previous experience, at the time being guided by the state of the market."[31]   This statement implies that they wished the manufacturer to use market prices, but such was really not the case, since they observed that "profit made by an increase in values of raw materials should not be taken into consideration . . . ."[32]   Perhaps only the decreases in prices were to be recognized in the stores accounts as the articles were charged into the cost of the product.   As can be easily seen, their views were very confused and it is difficult to determine just what they recommended.

B. C. Bean, who wrote in Chicago, adopted the suggestion of Eddis and Tindall as to the use of a fixed price for entering requisitions of materials.   One sort of fixed price was the "buying price," while another was the average determined over a series of years.   The average was termed the "market value," and Bean discussed at length its possible uses.   He disagreed, however, with those prior writers who had insisted that a charge should be included for transportation of the material; such a practice, in his mind, unduly inflated the value of the articles, since it was not always true that goods were worth more after being placed in the factory ready for use.   Bean seems to have been referring to the inventory valuation problem at this point although he wrote as though he were still thinking of pricing the requisitions; otherwise his argument was without merit.[33]

By the turn of the century, therefore, the methods of pricing requisitions which had been advocated included (1) ordinary cost, (2) cost plus transportation and other charges, (3) average costs, and (4) market costs. At about that time the so-called first-in, first-out method of pricing began also to be considered. So far as quantities were concerned, J. MacNaughton, an English accountant and paper-mill manager, had dealt with the matter in 1899 in his *Factory Book-keeping for Paper Mills*. He showed there a ledger which kept a record of quantities only—one side for receipts, and the other, put into process. He used the first-in, first-out technique in this book, but did not indicate whether or not the same principle was followed in the commercial books, where the values were maintained.[34] Two or three other authorities had hinted at the matter but had given it up as a more or less hopeless proposition. This was not true, however, of S. S. Dawson, an Englishman who wrote in 1897 on the accounting for a flour mill. Dawson did not refer specifically to the matter under review, but in his illustration of a "grinding account," which was used to accumulate the cost of wheat consumed each week, he mentioned that if the price of a particular type of wheat varied between purchases of different lots, care had to be taken in pricing such types into process.[35] Although he did not so indicate, it is the opinion of the present writer, based upon an illustration which Dawson gave, that he wished the first-in, first-out method to be used. Dawson's procedure will be discussed at greater length in Chapter VIII.

In 1903 the English accountant Stanley Garry, in a paper read before the Society of Chemical Industry, proposed a pricing system for process industries which was extremely novel for the time at which it was written, but became considerably more important later. After discussing the general problem involved in the accounting for raw material which fluctuated in price, Garry continued by stating that such price changes needlessly complicated his other proposal, which was to adopt a normal standard by which the effectiveness and efficiency of the factory might be measured. First, the amount of material needed for the plant was estimated, based upon an efficient output basis; and, second, a "normal standard price" was assumed. The normal standard price was to be based upon both past results and future prospects. As he stated it, the advantage of such a plan would be that "there is obtained a standard against which may be measured the output, not only in quantity, but also in quality of material, as also in like manner the quality of the product. By thus taking a normal standard for both quantity and quality, it is possible to show in the first place the results of the management; and secondly, after this has been ascertained, the further effect on such cost of—

(1) The increase or decrease of market price.

(2) Any decrease on standard in production."[36]

Both of the above are aims of present-day standard costing arrangements. While Garry did not show the complete ledger treatment, he did illustrate certain statements which indicated that he had his plan well in mind. Variations between standard and actual were separated both for the material element of cost and also for the total cost. In addition, this authority devoted several paragraphs to a discussion of the setting of the standards and the difficulties involved therein. For the scoffers who thought the technique impossible as well as impractical, Garry indicated that he had tried the plan; and while at first many problems did have to be solved, they were not insoluble. In his words:

> It is not to be assumed that it is possible to enter into a standard without either time or trouble, but there exists already a rule-of-thumb measurement of proportion of value between products in their raw material stages which can be collated for reference to the standards thus obtained.[37]

In another place he compared the standards for raw material pricing (into product) with the tables of mortality used by life insurance companies; that is, the prices were to be computed on an average which had a sufficiently wide basis to eliminate any short term or erratic incidents or fluctuations. In summary, it may be stated that Garry showed considerable originality in his proposals, which, however, probably struck on barren ground at the time so far as their adoption was concerned. It was not until some twenty years later that serious steps were taken in the direction which he contemplated. His discussion, however, has valuable historical significance.

In 1905, the first-in, first-out technique was definitely recommended for use wherever raw material was purchased at varying prices. S. Pedder, an English Chartered Accountant, suggested in that year that since, in his opinion, it was generally impossible to adjust prices (the average) continually each time a new lot was bought, the requisitioning and the pricing of goods should be re-

corded in the order of their receipt. He did not, however, refer to
the method by its present title, leaving it unnamed.[38]

In this country, the average cost basis of pricing requisitions
seemed to be the trend—with some refinements, however. For example, in 1906, John Whitmore advocated the use of an average
price based upon the average cost of the existing stock of material
at the time of issuance. This figure was only changed in case a new
purchase was made at a different price. In the end, however, Whitmore did not wish to commit himself too definitely upon any one
method; each firm, according to him, would have to use its own
judgment and experience as a guide—the aim of all being centered
upon the proposition that the "stock of material shall be such active
necessary stocks as will promptly meet all shop needs,"[39] whatever
that meant. Within a few years some English authorities were also
beginning to advocate the use of market prices in certain instances,
either when the price had declined or increased. W. Strachan might
be cited as an example of this trend of thinking. He insisted that
market prices would give the manufacturer the same advantage in
competitive bidding as those firms which had just made purchases
of material. A price list, maintained on a current basis, was to be
drawn up, therefore, and referred to whenever requisitions were made
out. Strachan did not discuss what should be done with any differences between the market and the cost figures, nor did he devote any
attention to all the difficulties which would be involved in handling
the stores accounts. Incidentally, it was his idea that the market
quotations should be used whether the price was above or below
what the material had cost.[40]

The next six or seven years were almost entirely barren of developments in connection with this topic. While the overhead element
of cost was discussed extensively, no contributions of importance
were made to the problem of pricing the material which went into
the finished goods. The various authorities seemed to take it for
granted that specific lot cost or some type of an average would be
used. In fact, very few of them even mentioned the question. For
example, in 1913 one rather careful student of cost accounting, E. P.
Moxey of Philadelphia, simply made the statement that "as the stores
requisitions are presented to the storekeeper, he issues the materials
called for, ascertains the price of the goods, and extends the amount
on the requisition."[41] He did not give any indication as to the pricing
method he preferred. During the early part of the First World War,

however, the subject assumed a tremendous importance. Prices were rising and many firms began to see the effect of their material pricing techniques upon their competitive position. More and more thought began to be given to the matter in the years 1915-25.

Several authorities in the United States during the first part of the decade of the 1910s continued to recommend the use of an average cost arrangement,[42] the issue price being changed whenever a new supply was received at a price different from the previous average. There was a tendency, also, to add on to the cost of raw material the freight charges, if the freight charges could be allocated in some equitable manner.[43] Although the average cost theory had its many adherents, some experts preferred the first-in, first-out technique,[44] while others insisted that only the market price should be used.[45] None of these cost accountants gave a comprehensive discussion of just why they preferred the method recommended; and few of them considered the possibility of other techniques being adopted. This cavalier manner of treating the subject should be contrasted with that accorded the topic in the early 1920's.

Beginning with 1920, cost authorities began to deal with the problem of pricing the material into product with more care and thoroughness. A considerable number of them discussed the question in some detail, giving the various possible methods which might be used, and their advantages and disadvantages. The work of J. P. Jordan and G. L. Harris in America should be mentioned as illustrative of the more complete analysis of the topic. These writers devoted a whole chapter to the different methods.[46] After first making the point that the cost of material included all delivery and handling charges (this theory had become well established by 1920), these authorities proceeded to the consideration of the following techniques of pricing requisitions: (1) The method which used the original prices of the oldest stock on hand; (2) the method which used the market prices at time of consumption, adopted in the pine lumber industry and the iron and steel industry; (3) the method which used the average cost, both current averages and end-of-month averages; and (4) the method which used the original cost of the highest priced material, considered the most conservative method. This list of methods was practically complete except for the normal or base stock method, which a few companies had adopted during the period, and the last-in, first-out method which also was beginning to be adopted by a few lines of business.

One other factor of importance in connection with the topic under discussion should be mentioned at this point. It is concerned with the treatment accorded the problem by the United States Income Tax Regulations and Laws. Indeed, perhaps one of the reasons why no more thought was given to the question after 1913 was the rather narrow viewpoint of the Treasury Department. This Department has consistently viewed with disfavor any novel or inconsistent scheme of pricing the material element of cost; and has, in general recommended the use of the first-in, first-out plan wherever practicable. The use of the normal or base stock method, first advocated around 1913, was finally declared illegal for tax purposes in the late 1920's, while the average cost principle is sanctioned for only a very few industries. Only recently has Congress allowed industries to use the last-in, first-out method. This does not mean, however, that companies cannot adopt any method they desire for their own purposes; it does mean that for income tax statements a method which is sanctioned by the Treasury Department must be used.

The English cost accountants during this period were considering the topic under discussion with more care. In an address which he made in 1919, A. C. Ridgway, an English Chartered Accountant, recommended the use of the "last price for the costing," since that would be the price at which the material would have to be replaced.[47] It was evidently his idea, therefore, that present market prices should be adopted for pricing the requisitions although he did not give any details as to how his technique would be handled on the books of a company. In the fourth edition of his *Cost Accounts* (1920), L. W. Hawkins, another English cost authority, treated with some preciseness the relative merits of the strict cost method as compared with the market price method, finally concluding that the market price method was preferable in most instances. Hawkins also mentioned two sorts of average pricing schemes which might be used, that is, the average price of purchases which had been made and the average price of the quantities still in stock. The latter was to be preferred, according to him. In connection with the use of the market price, Hawkins suggested that small variations or fluctuations be disregarded, and only major changes be taken into account. Obviously the use of this technique would require the setting up of an account representing the profit or loss due to the fluctuation in prices. Hawkins mentioned this possibility but did not elaborate upon it.[48] A year later, E. T. Elbourne, who also treated this topic at length, decided that the recognition of market changes would prove too cumbersome for practical use, and if a factory manager desired to obtain whatever advantage there might be in such a scheme, he might use a rate which was changed only after a six-month or one-year period of time—a sort of predetermined market price. In the end, however, this authority recommended that for most manufacturing enterprises the first-in, first-out method of pricing would probably prove most advisable.[49] By 1925, therefore, the English cost authorities had begun to handle the present topic with the care which it deserved; their discussions, however, lagged behind that of American authorities throughout most of the period from 1900 to the present. Very few contributions were made by them after that date.

During the early 1920's, the sharp swings in the prices of some types of raw material caused the controversy over the use of market prices versus cost prices to come again to the forefront in the United States. Several authorities began to advance more cogent reasons as to why the replacement value method should be adopted, especially by those plants which consumed large quantities of material fluctuating in price from time to time.[50] So-called standard costs or normal costs for materials began also to be advocated with renewed fervor. In addition, agitation continued for a change in the income tax requirements so that a manufacturing firm could use the base stock method of pricing, if it desired, even for tax statements. Thus far, however, the attempts in this direction have proved unsuccessful.[51]

CHAPTER IV

EVOLUTION OF THE ACCOUNTING FOR DIRECT LABOR

SINCE THE DIRECT LABOR ELEMENT OF COST IS RELATIVELY SIMPLE TO handle and record it has excited comparatively little discussion among the many authorities who have written on industrial accounting topics during the past fifty years. In fact, except for innovations in the types of wage plans (which are only of incidental interest here), the treatments accorded the subject by the cost experts of three or four decades ago still are standard with only a few modifications. Several new features, however, have been devised from time to time, and one of the purposes of this chapter will be to indicate those developments which have taken place.

The accountants before 1885 often wrote of the necessity of recording the amount of labor incurred in the completion of a certain job or process, even though no very thorough explanation had appeared. The reason for this attention is obvious; if any records at all were kept of the cost of the product turned out, such records would have to show at least the amount of material consumed and the labor involved. Incidentally, so-called "prime cost systems" were in vogue many years before the factory overhead element began to be considered. The accounting for labor, therefore, merited some attention by even the early cost authorities. The treatment was usually quite skimpy and vague, as indicated by the following remarks made by one of the popular American authors of the 1880's, J. H. Goodwin:

When we pay our [employees] weekly, semi-monthly or month-ly, the total amounts due them, it is not necessary to keep an account with each, but debit the amount paid them directly to the Salaries, or Labor, account. If we do not pay them regularly the amounts due them, but allow them to draw from their salary at pleasure, we then open an account for each of our employees, debiting them whenever they draw any money, or take any merchandise for their private pleasure use; and crediting them at the end of each month for their salary for the month. . . . We next close all accounts we have kept in the Ledger to show the amounts consumed in the different articles of manufacture, and transfer amount lost on all such accounts to the debit side of the Manufacturing account, designating the accounts upon which such amounts were lost. Also, close the "Labor account," and transfer amount lost on labor to the debit side of the Manufacturing account.[1]

Considerable progress was made, nevertheless, in those closing years of the nineteenth century, and by 1885, when Henry Metcalfe wrote his *Cost of Manufactures,* he was able to summarize a fairly comprehensive system of reporting and recording the labor time and cost of employees. As was mentioned in the previous chapter, Met-calfe recommended the use of cards whenever possible. Following this suggestion, workmen in the shop were to be given a book of cards, each with a stub. As the workman moved from one job to another, he would fill out a card, the most minute time division, however, being a quarter-day. Also, a card was to be filled in at least every day. On the card were to be shown the worker's num-ber, the symbol for the job or jobs on which he worked during the day, his fingerprint, and name. All the cards each day were sorted by the cost clerk, first by names of workers, and second by the shop order numbers under each name. A time book was provided for entering the laborers' time opposite the shop orders on which they had worked. Until a job was finished, the cards were left in a file under the job numbers; after the job was completed, all cards per-taining to it were summarized and entered on the shop order. The time book had columns for shop order number, remarks, days of month, number of days, wage per day, and amount. As can be readily seen, Metcalfe's system was quite modern in nature, the use of cards being distinctively novel. It must be remembered, how-ever, that time clocks were just beginning to come into use, and the technique advocated by this authority was designated to perform somewhat the same function as mechanical recording devices. It is not known how extensively his system was used. When he discussed the matter at the meeting of the American Society of Mechanical Engineers in 1885, it met strong criticism from those individuals who had found factory workmen to be proverbially poor bookkeepers and time recorders.[2]

The English authorities, Emile Garcke and J. M. Fells, a few years later suggested that each employee enter on a "time board" a record of how each day's labor was spent, as well as the order number on which he had worked. These records were to be signed by the foreman and copied by the time clerk into a time allocation book, the latter being totaled each pay date and forwarded to the commercial office for pay roll purposes. In addition, the time clerk would have to draw up an abstract at periodic intervals, showing the various orders on which time had been spent. This abstract, then, would be used for the purpose of posting to the so-called prime cost ledger the cost of the labor that had been expended upon the various jobs or operations during the period; it would also check with the wages book, maintained by the financial office. Garcke and Fells also treated very carefully the flow of labor costs through the ledger accounts, and were among the earliest cost accountants to recommend a strict tie-in between the cost accounts and the general accounts. Their discussion of the accounting for labor, therefore, was noteworthy on that account if for no other.[3]

The work of G. P. Norton is also deserving of consideration at this point. This English authority, in the latter part of the 1880's was particularly interested in the accounting for a textile mill and in connection therewith he recommended the use of pay tickets to help control and record the labor cost. Each week a book of these tickets was furnished the foreman, who filled one out for each man or woman under him, showing the amount due. The original was given to the worker and a copy sent to the "counting house" (his term), the latter being responsible for the actual paying of the wages. Before the tickets were torn out, however, they were all inspected by an official of the company who also verified the amounts shown thereon. In case the pay tickets were not convenient, there could be substituted a wages book with columns for number, name, rate or quantities, and then ten more columns corresponding to as many weeks. Also, since Norton's books were departmentalized, he recommended the use of a summary of wages per department, which again had columns for the different departments (thirteen in all), cash book folio, and the lateral total corresponding with the entry in the cash book, showing

the payment of wages. In the event, however, that the managers
did not desire departments, Norton showed a mill wages account
on the ledger which could be used to save space in the cash payments book. The total of wages paid was posted to the debit of this
account; and, at the end of the fiscal period, various credits were
made, exactly equalling the debits. The credits were for the transfer
of wages paid to the power plant employees, and the wages paid to
the stables account for cartage and transfer, the wages charged to
the trading account because of mill hands' wages, mill manager's
salary, mechanics, joiners, and plumbers, and the watchmen and timekeepers. The mill wages account, therefore, was a clearing and collection account for all wages paid. Norton, then, provided a variety
of techniques for handling the labor element of cost, which, incidentally was rather significant in the textile industry at that time.[4]

The work of these four authorities gives evidence of the fact
that the direct labor problem was treated with some respect and care
long before the burden cost question became pertinent.[5] The same
carefulness was characteristic of later writers. For example, in 1894,
an anonymous English author gave an illustration of an 1890 pay
roll book ruled (for each week) as follows:

Week ending, 7 January, 1890.

Number of worker	Name	Dept.	Monday Hrs. Job Fo. No.	Each day of week ruled as for Monday	Total Hours	Rate	Amount

Certain modifications could be employed if desired. For instance,
if the number of workers was quite large, and if there were only
a few jobs in process, a single posting of the total number of hours
spent on each job by all employees each day could be made in so
far as their rate of pay was the same. This technique would save a
large number of postings in a plant of considerable size.[6] Another
Englishman, J. Slater Lewis, described a much more comprehensive
scheme for handling the labor element of cost a few years later. It
was Lewis' plan to record the time of each employee on a separate
sheet each week, showing the job order numbers on which he had
worked. The columns were divided so as to show both ordinary
time and overtime, if any, one column for each day of the week. The
particulars recorded thereon were to be transferred each week to a
wages book, which consolidated all the time sheets. Columns were
provided on the wages book for check number (employee); name,

ordinary time (including overtime)—hours, rate, and amount; piece-work—job order number, debit, credit; total due; and departmental totals—folio and amount. The wages book was used by the pay roll office as a source of information for making up the pay roll; the cost clerks also used it to post to the job order ledger which summarized the prime cost of the jobs performed. Postings were made to the job order ledger once each week, and quite a large mass of information was contained therein, both as to the material used and as to the labor involved on the different jobs. In connection with the labor, columns were provided for number of hours payable, rate, ordinary time amount, overtime payable, paid on account of piece-work, monthly totals, piecework earnings—number of pieces, rate, per, and amount. Taken as a whole the system advocated by this authority was rather complicated. Incidentally, it should be mentioned here that all of the above was external to the financial books of the factory; various other transactions had to be shown for the actual paying of the employees.[7]

Lewis' contemporary, F. G. Burton, who was also particularly interested in the cost accounts of engineering works, recommended the use of a comparatively simple wages book. Since Burton subdivided his costing between the different sections of a job, such as building a ship, he showed the following columns on his wage sheet: name of employee, process (really the section of job), time (for each day of week), total time for week, rate per hour, wages per process, and total wages per man. This sheet, therefore, took the place of a payroll sheet and a labor allocation sheet such as Lewis had suggested. Abstracts were to be prepared weekly or monthly by the timekeeper of the amount chargeable to each division or section of the job, which amount was then posted to the respective cost sheets previously set up.[8]

By the turn of the century various specialized arrangements for costing the labor element were beginning to come into use. The American, H. L. Arnold, for example, discussed certain "detailed time cards," which could be used if desired. These had columns for man number, operation, days of week, total, rate, and amount. Under the operation column there was a list of all the steps involved in making the product (Hyatt roller bearings), and opposite each was a space for the number of pieces as well as the time in hours. The order number and date were given at the top of the card. The advantage of this card, according to Arnold, was that the time of one workman for a particular operation could be compared with that of others, and discrepancies noted. Another company whose cost accounting he described used an "overtime and half-time report," with the days of the week down the left side, and work done, overtime, half-time, and total across the top. The totals of these items were in turn transferred to a type of pay roll sheet showing the "debits" the workmen were entitled to, the "credits" (or deductions), and the amount paid each employee on pay day. For piecework, two books were provided. One was called the "piecework timebook," but it was in reality a comparative record of the time under a regular hourly wage plan as contrasted with that under piecework. The second was a piecework rate-book giving the catalog number, description, size, pattern number, weight, and rate per piece of each piecework job. The two taken together constituted an effective control over the labor cost involved under the processes which were costed in that way. In his volume Arnold gave some illustrations of time cards which could be used under machine work conditions; each of these had spaces provided for the time involved as well as the type of work that was performed on the machines.[9] A little later, Arnold recommended the use of what he called a "scatter-good weekly payroll" sheet. This had columns for total amount paid, reference number, deductions, hours time work, amount by time, hours piecework, amount by piece, and then one column for each day of the week. It is evident that this form was designed, also, to enable a contrast to be made between piecework and day-work, or perhaps the multiple columns were provided to satisfy the requirements of both types of pay plans.[10] Taken as a whole, Arnold's discussion of the handling of direct labor was quite advanced for the period, but the accounting for labor evolved much more rapidly than the accounting for the other two elements of cost.

Around 1902 some cost authorities, such as the Canadians, Eddis and Tindall, began to refer to the departmentalization of the labor charges, as well as to labor cost summaries. For example, where a large number of employees worked on the different jobs and where there were several departments, Eddis and Tindall recommended the use of a sheet which had columns for date, workman number, rate, particulars, and then several "tool" columns, each with a space for hours and amount. These columns were to be added at periodic intervals and posted to the cost ledger in toto. This technique saved a mass of individual postings to the job order sheets, as well as giving a summary of all the labor charges. It was also their suggestion that, in case piecework was done in the plant, a piecework time sheet should be drawn up every two weeks for each worker. This sheet provided information as to the order number, description of work, the quantity produced, the rate, and the amount earned. In addition, if the factory manager also wished the time involved to be recorded, proper spaces were left for that data. An inspector certified to the quantity of good pieces produced as well as to the pieces spoiled.[11]

The American, H. L. C. Hall, also considered the possibility of departmentalizing the labor or payroll items, suggesting that the employees should be given numbers which would indicate the department in which they worked. Following Metcalfe, Hall mentioned that for those workers who were shifted around from place to place, a card was to be filled out each day detailing the operations to which their services were to be charged.[12]

The accounting for labor, as has been indicated on the previous pages of this chapter, had, by the middle of the first decade of this century, been developed to a rather fine point so far as day-work and piecework wage plans were concerned. Machine time recorders had also been perfected and many cost accountants recommended their use. Proposals had been put forward, in the 1890's, for premium wage systems of various types, and certain cost authorities, especially in England, devoted parts of their discussions to the peculiar features of the accounting involved therewith. Henry Spencer, for instance, recommended the use of a "premium job note," showing the description of the work, the quantity of output, the payments on account, and the premium allowed. A premium ledger was also designed to accompany the job note giving the details of the earnings of each employee. Actual wages paid were recorded in a wages book, which was in reality merely a pay roll sheet. Spencer's discussion, in general, was rather complete for that period,[13] although he did not bother to give any of the ledger accounts or entries which would be required to operate his system.[14]

Another Englishman, G. A. Mitchell, consolidated in 1907 all the wage payments in his hypothetical factory into one labor summary book. Columns were provided therein for week ending, sheet number, order numbers(as many as necessary), foremen, staff employees, shop expenses (indirect labor), loose tools (assets), maintenance of plant, patterns, repairing department, new plant, and total. The order number columns were for the purpose of recording the direct labor applicable to each order, while the total column was the amount credited to the wages account. The details for this summary book were obtained from workmen's time cards, and, in turn, weekly labor sheets; the labor sheets merely summarized the time cards. Incidentally, Mitchell recommended definitely the use of time clocks for maintaining control over the hours spent by workers within the factory.[15] Some authorities during that period were rather skeptical as to their advantages, but in general favored their use.

In the latter part of the first decade of this century, proposals began to be made for the inclusion of the labor element of cost in the machine charge which would be applied to products passing through departments or processes. This technique was recommended, however, only for those factories which were highly mechanized and which produced a fairly uniform product. A. Hamilton Church, a noted English electrical engineer who moved to the United States about 1900, in a series of articles which he wrote in 1901,[16] had hinted at such a plan but he had not at that time developed it to any great extent. J. Lee Nicholson, on the other hand, described it fully in his compresensive work published in New York in 1909. In fact, there were really two techniques which could be employed. One was called the "new machine rate" and involved the collection of all costs, except material, by departments; these costs were later divided between the units produced on the basis of the time incurred in various machine processes. This particular procedure, however, is so intimately related to the problem of overhead allocation and distribution that a fuller discussion will be given in the next chapter. The second technique was referred to as the "new pay rate," and had as its central base the addition of the rates of pay of employees within a department to the burden rates which had been ascertained also on a departmental grouping arrangement. The total of these two elements of cost was then to be applied to the product by multiplying the employee's time incurred on a certain operation by the new rate, instead of taking the labor cost and factory overhead costs as separate items. This technique, incidentally, was really a special type of cost system, and was discussed in that way by later authorities, some of whom will be treated below. It was also criticized by some cost experts because it did not provide the necessary detail for controlling costs—too many items were grouped.[17] Nicholson, in addition to his contribution along these lines, illustrated some 28 time ticket forms and fourteen pay roll sheets, out of which the factory accountant could select the ones which best suited his own peculiar conditions. This collection was the most extensive that had been assembled up to that time and formed a valuable reference for the cost system designer. Nicholson also discussed the nature of seven different pay plans, giving their advantages and disadvantages. His treatise was notably weak, however, when it came to the ledger treatment of the labor element of cost; he preferred to describe, for the most part, the uses of the forms illustrated and certain modifications which might be adopted if desired.

Various other authorities soon began to extend and elaborate upon Nicholson's treatment. For example, the next year found John R. Wildman, also of New York, illustrating a labor summary sheet which had columns for department, total, indirect labor, and then various columns for the direct labor incurred on each job in each department of the factory. The cost clerk was to post only the direct labor columns to his cost sheets, whereas the total was the amount of pay roll for which the paymaster was responsible.[18]

In 1911, F. E. Webner, a practicing American accountant, published his *Factory Costs* in which several chapters were devoted to the problem of the proper handling of the direct labor element of cost. After giving a careful, though general, discussion to the matter of time records and the forms to be used in connection therewith, this authority next considered the composition of pay rolls and the actual paying of the wages, the latter being, he said, outside of the province of the cost system proper. Like Nicholson, Webner also discussed the relative merits of different types of wage plans, especially those grouped under the "premium" classification. But Webner's main contribution was in connection with his discussion of the methods of applying labor costs to products. While various authorities had, from time to time, advocated different techniques, no one had taken the trouble to summarize them. Webner gave a short exposition of some six general plans which were in common use at that time. Even though some duplication will be involved, these will be briefly discussed at this point. The first was titled the "order number estimate" plan, and contemplated the estimation of the cost of a shop order either by good guesses or by tests. For orders of like nature, then, the labor costs would be applied on the basis of the predetermined estimates. Webner did not recommend the general adoption of such a plan, stating that it was not safe under many circumstances. The second was the "specific order number charge" method, and used the exact production time of each employee (multiplied by his wage rate) for the labor charge per order. The third was the piece-work plan which has already been discussed. The fourth method was called the "averaged-hour plan" or the "sold-hour plan," and was comparable with Nicholson's "new pay rate" scheme in that the over-head costs were added to the direct labor charge to ascertain the departmental charge per unit or per hour as the case might be. The "list-percentage" plan, which was the fifth, contemplated the deriv-ing of the labor cost of the goods produced by taking the records of such costs in the past, and expressing the same "as a percentage of the list price of such goods." This percentage "is charged to the entire mass of product in each department for a given period, or to individual order number when preferable. Any variations between the actual costs and these list-percentage costs are subsequently de-termined and recorded."[19] Webner's sixth plan was the by then familiar machine hour technique which tied together not only the labor charge with the overhead charge, but was also a rather ac-curate method of distributing and allocating burden items. In ad-dition to the preceding six methods, there was also a "point plan" which could be effectively adopted wherever workmen took a certain piece of material, such as lumber, and made from it several different items. A certain number of points would be assigned to the largest product and a smaller number to the others. The employee's pay would then be divided among the items of output in accordance with the number of "points" which each totaled. Taken as a whole, Web-ner's discussion of labor accounting was the most comprehensive that had appeared up to that time. While Nicholson had given more forms, Webner's treatment included a more adequate description of the ledger transactions, even though it left much to be desired, at least from a beginner's viewpoint.

One observer of the period before the First World War, E. P. Moxey, came rather close to describing the standard cost methodology when he stated that:

> It can be readily seen that after the pay-roll has been made up and the entries posted from the commercial side—that is to say, the cash book—and the factory side—the manufacturing journal —into the "Labor" account in the general ledger, both sides of this account should be in balance. If, however, any difference should exist as between the amount of labor paid for and the amount of labor charged to goods in process, such balance will show directly in the general ledger "Labor" account. Many

manufacturers do not like this account to show this balance continuously, so a transfer is made to a "Labor Adjustment account" which shows by its balance the loss in labor.[20]

Moxey had previously explained that the "Adjustment" account should be closed directly to profit and loss.

English cost accountants, in the period immediately preceding the First World War, neglected for the most part this particular topic. Although L. W. Hawkins treated the subject in considerable detail, he added very little that was new. He did illustrate the entries which should be made on the "cost accounts" and the "general accounts," this discussion being especially valuable because the two sets of accounts were separate and not tied together in any way. Hawkins also gave some forms which he had devised for both the charging of direct labor time and for the pay rolls. There was, however, very little that was novel about their use.[21]

After 1915, in this country, the several cost authorities who wrote on the problem customarily gave an adequate discussion of the handling of the direct labor costs of a factory. Some, however, were more specific than others. In addition, certain specialized topics began to appear in the discussions. S. H. Bunnell, for example, thought the matter of "outside work" worthy of special attention. That particular sort of work was the labor performed by erectors and machine installers who helped place into position the large pieces of equipment which a firm might sell. Obviously, this would rarely, if ever, be considered direct labor, but Bunnell treated it along with that subject.[22] The necessary reports and time sheets were given as well as a discussion of their uses.

So far as the more complete treatises around 1920 were concerned, the work of J. P. Jordan and G. L. Harris may be taken as an illustration. These prominent American authorities devoted several chapters of their *Cost Accounting* (1920) to the topic, leaving little to be desired from the standpoint of thoroughness. The chief forms to be adopted were explained first, followed by a consideration of the procedure involved in case workers were loaned from one department to another. After that the technique of checking the labor cards was summarized, as well as their extension. Pay roll systems were taken up next, and different forms illustrated. Again the procedure for handling loaned workers was considered, this time with special emphasis upon their pay. Later on in their work they briefly reviewed the journal entries which would be made at intervals in connection with the handling of direct labor. Taken as a whole, therefore, their description of the accounting necessary for this element of cost will serve as an example of the better works published in the early 1920's in this country.

The general neglect of this topic by the English accountants of the 1920's was remedied to some extent by the new edition of E. T. Elbourne's *Factory Administration and Cost Accounts* which appeared in 1921. Even though his costing arrangements were external to the financial ledgers and not definitely connected therewith, his discussion of the handling of labor was noteworthy. A great deal of attention was devoted to the administrative and personnel problems involved as well as to the time sheets, pay roll forms, etc., which were necessary for the cost accounting data. A form called the "works cost allocation abstract" was used to collect the wage charges for each month; these charges were divided into the labor incurred on office orders, departmental process accounts, standing orders for plant additions, standing orders for works repairs, and various others.[23] Mechanical tabulating cards for labor might be used also, if desired. As a matter of information, however, mechanical tabulating cards had been recommended by certain cost accountants in the United States several years before 1921.[24] Elbourne's discussion of the direct labor problem ended with a checklist of the eight different methods of "time-booking" (his term) the worker's hourly employment. Since he was one of the few who thought it necessary to give such a summary, the specific techniques should be summarized here: (1) the worker could book his time daily on a chalk board or on a daily time sheet or card; or (2) a clerk could take down on a time sheet the time according to the worker's own verbal statement each day; or (3) the foreman could book each worker on a time sheet; or (4) the worker himself could book his own time on a job ticket by writing down the times "on" and "off"; or (5) the worker could stamp the times "on" and "off" on a job ticket for each job by means of a mechanical time recorder; or (6) the foreman could issue a new job ticket to each worker on each change of job; or (7) the foreman could make out a job advice slip at each change of job, giving the necessary particulars to the wages office; or (8) a clerk could book the time on job tickets from actual observation.[25] Such was the comprehensiveness with which this English authority dealt with the topic. Later cost experts, generally speaking, were just as thorough.

Thus has the cost accounting for factory labor evolved. From a humble though early beginning, a transition slowly took place, always keeping pace with the greater needs of the manufacturing establishments for which the various systems and techniques were designed. From the shops of perhaps a thousand workers in the 1870's to the gigantic plants of today, employing a hundred thousand or more people, there was as great a change in the accounting requirements as that which transpired during the earlier years of the Industrial Revolution; and, as has been developed in the preceding pages of this chapter, the labor element of cost was handled accurately and efficiently throughout the period, in accordance with the ever present demands of the factory managers and administrators.

CHAPTER V

EVOLUTION OF THE ACCOUNTING FOR MANUFACTURING BURDEN

PART I. ITEMS TO BE INCLUDED[1]

AUTHORITIES ON INDUSTRIAL ACCOUNTING HAD VERY LITTLE TO SAY ABOUT the items to be included in the factory overhead charge in the years prior to 1885.[2] Writing in 1913, one authority stated: "In the early days of factory accounting, manufacturers did not concern themselves with anything but prime costs. . . . All other production expenses were provided for in the amount of profit which they received over and above this cost."[3]

There were a few exceptions to the conclusions presented above. The Frenchman, Payen, for example, had a group of sundry expenses which he included in the cost of making glue (see Chapter II). These sundry expenses comprised such items as interest paid to creditors, rent, depreciation, "petty articles," and coal. Cronhelm, the Englishman, entered in a "merchandise book" (his term) all purchases which contributed toward the operation of his hypothetical textile mill. Thus one finds in the merchandise book not only the purchases of varying grades of wool, but also stamps and stationery, bankers' charges, coal, freight, salaries of foremen, taxes, and carriage. Both of these early authors, then, bothered little as to what the expenditures were for; all items were indiscriminately lumped together to arrive at unit costs. Robert Hamilton, who first wrote in the generation preceding Cronhelm and Payen, had said that ledger accounts should be established for the different expenditures of a manufacturing business. He mentioned specifically maintenance of machinery, rents, excise taxes, and incidental charges. These were closed out at the end of a year to a "general" (his term) account. The Manchester public accountant, Thomas Battersby, also referred to in Chapter II, divided his expenses into two groups, viz., direct expenses, such as coal and wages which could be allocated specifically to articles passing through a given department; and indirect expenses, which included those that could not be attributed directly to departments. The latter were collected in a separate book. Battersby was much more concerned with the problem of burden allocation than he was with the present topic; thus he had very little to say about the actual composition of the burden element of cost. The contributions made by other early nineteenth century writers have already been described in Chapter II.

Beginning about 1885, the subject assumed much more importance. In that year Captain Henry Metcalfe, an American Army Ordnance officer, published his *Cost of Manufactures* in which he considered "indirect expenses" under two headings: first, "those like rent, insurance, salaries, etc., which are fixed charges; and, second, those which like attendance, wear, and waste have a closer relation, say a direct ratio, to the number of men employed."[4] This division was obviously the now familiar fixed and variable cost separation.[5] In another place he expanded on the items which constituted his "miscellaneous expenses" and listed superintendence; clerk hire; power; use and wear of tools, machinery, and buildings; oil; heating and lighting; laborers; and watchmen.[6] It is obvious that Metcalfe thought the problem to be one of only passing interest, yet he did not include in his discussion the handling of the sales expenses and the general expenses of a firm. One cannot be too sure of just what he would have done under ordinary factory circumstances, however, because he was writing about the accounting for governmental workshops where there were no expenses connected with sales.

Emile Garcke and J. M. Fells, the English authorities, had considerably more to say on the subject. As early as 1887, they made a sharp distinction between what they called "shop expenses" and "establishment expenses"—two terms, incidentally, which were to be used by English writers on cost accounts for the next three decades.[7] The shop expenses comprised wages of foremen, rent of factory, fuel, lighting, heating, and cleaning. These items were to be distributed over the products turned out by the factory. Establishment charges, on the other hand, were to be closed to the profit and loss account at the end of each fiscal period. Some of these charges were: salaries of clerks, office rent, and stationery. The two authors had, in their opinion, logical reasons for not considering establishment charges as a part of their manufacturing burden. In the first place no advantage would be obtained by distributing those expenses over the articles made, and secondly, they did not vary in a fixed ratio with the volume of production. To quote: "They do not vary proportionately with the volume of business. . . . The establishment charges are, in the aggregate, more or less constant, while the manufacturing costs fluctuate with the costs of labor and the price of materials. To distribute the charges over the articles manufactured would, therefore, have the effect of disproportionately reducing the cost of production with every increase, and the reverse with every dimunition of business. Such a result is greatly to be deprecated. . . . "[8]

The distinction which Garcke and Fells made between shop charges and establishment expenses was not followed consistently by later English writers, and still less so by American authorities. The American, G. L. Fowler, thought that all the expenses incurred by the factory should be considered part of the manufacturing cost.[9] He mentioned specifically salaries of clerks, office expenses, depreciation, and interest on borrowed money. It made no difference to him for what the expenditure might be; the total was assembled and added on to the product turned out by the foundry, the accounting for which he was discussing. As opposing the views of Fowler, however, can be cited G. P. Norton's *Textile Manufacturers' Bookkeeping,* a rather authoritative English book for the time it was written (1889). Norton made a rather careful distinction between the costs which should be included in the processed cloth and those expenses which were extraneous. In the extraneous group was to be found the "warehouse and office standing expenses," viz., stables, rent, warehouse and office salaries, travelers' [salesmen's] salaries and expenses, commissions, and depreciation of fixtures. There were also certain "general charges," such as bank charges, discounts on sales, and bad debts."[10] All these were to be deducted from the gross profit in order to derive the net profit. Norton's procedure was followed for several subsequent decades.

Even though both Norton and Garcke and Fells had made a

sharp distinction between the charges, their ideas were not followed generally. In an address before the American Society of Mechanical Engineers in 1893, F. A. Halsey, the industrial engineer, listed certain items which he thought should be added together to attain the total "loading" (his term) for a certain period, but he went on to state: "If office expenses are considered as part of the cost of production, they may be included in the calculation; or, if the sales account is considered separate from the manufacturing account, these expenses may be omitted, in which latter case the result will be to give the cost of goods at the shop door."[11]

F. G. Burton, also one of the earlier writers on cost accounting for engineering works, included in his establishment charges the depreciation of machinery and tools, salaries of partners if the firm were a partnership, salaries of directors, managers, general foremen, storekeepers, and timekeepers.[12] The total of all these items was to be added on to any estimate made by the firm. It is evident that Burton wished to include all the miscellaneous expenditures in his establishment charge percentage, making no distinction between those applicable to the shop and those applicable to the office. As a matter of fact, though, this author was not particularly concerned with the composition of the burden element of cost, preferring rather to consider more carefully the allocation of the total to contracts handled by the ship builder or machinery maker.

In his rather complete work, published in London in 1896, J. S. Lewis devoted an entire chapter to establishment charges, which he divided into three classes.[13] The first was the expenditure of the firm for wages, material, and any direct item chargeable specifically to a job. The total of these three was the prime cost of the order, and should, in his opinion, be kept entirely separate from the establishment charges proper. The second class included all the expenditures incurred in each shop or department which could not be directly allocated to specific orders. This group he called "shop establishment charges," and he listed various items properly included in it. The third group, "general establishment charges," comprised expenditures for stationery, salaries of clerks, managers and officials, rents, taxes, insurance, gas, water, steam power, wages of storekeeper, gatekeeper, timekeeper and engineman, advertising, traveling expenses, catalogs, and expenses of maintaining branch offices.[14] From the above system of grouping it would seem that Lewis was rather careless in making the distinction between manufacturing burden, on the one hand, and selling and office expenses on the other hand. Yet he realized that such a distinction was significant because he stated that the essential manufacturing indirect expenditures should be separated from those of the commercial branch of the business.[15] The reason was that the commercial "may be adversely affected by conditions, the result of commercial blunders, which have nothing to do with the direct cost of production. The relative *manufacturing* efficiency of two rival firms may be precisely similar, but the *commercial* efficiency of one hopelessly behind that of the other."[16] When it came to their treatment in the cost accounting books, however, Lewis considered it proper to divide the entire total over the orders finished during the period. Thus, in the last analysis, his distinction was rather superficial; that is to say, he really did not have an understanding of their fundamental nature.

In the United States the question as to what should be included in manufacturing burden was discussed at length in 1897 by various members of the American Society of Mechanical Engineers at their semiannual meeting. H. M. Norris led the discussion with an address in which he recommended that all expenses "of whatever nature which are not chargeable to some specific order number" should be spread over the product manufactured.[17] Oberlin Smith, a prominent engineer of the time, seconded the Norris suggestion, but thought that bad debts (which Norris had not specifically mentioned) should also be included. Since Smith represented one trend of thought of the time, his views should be quoted more extensively:

> My own experience has convinced me that it is better to work by the year, put in a plenty high enough expense rate, and be sure to get every expense in. Some such . . . are telephoning, telegraphing, expressage, discounts for cash, etc. . . . . . It seems to me that the best way to get an expense account is to take all expenses, starting with . . . bad debts . . . and such as are mentioned here— insurance, taxes, depreciation, travelling, advertising, office expenses, repairs, power, heat, light, and the rest of it, including such amount of salary and wages account as is not directly productive. In some cases a part of the officers' salaries, especially in the engineering departments, can be charged directly to certain jobs— expense that is non-productive.[18]

In another place (page 895) he stated, however, that commercial expenses should be included in cost of production only where they were not excessive or remarkable in any way.

The views of Norris and Smith were not allowed, however, to

go unchallenged. F. A. Halsey, the originator of the Halsey wage payment plan, reasoned "that the items which are included in the cost of production include only those incurred inside the shop door and not those outside. The expenses incurred outside the shop door are properly considered cost of distribution and not of production."[19] When asked to elaborate upon this point Halsey showed a rather keen understanding of cost theory which seemed, however, to fall on deaf ears. This authority considered the distinction important because of the effect that the inclusion of office and sales expenses had upon inventory valuation. If a firm produced goods without specific orders therefor, and solely with regard to what the sales officials thought could be sold, it was very likely that at the end of a fiscal period it would have on hand a fairly large amount of stock ready for sale. It was Halsey's contention in such a case that the inventory value would be inflated improperly if office and sales expenses were considered a cost of production, as had been suggested by the principal speaker. This was a condition, in his mind, which had no justification. If a factory produced only for some specific order, and no stock was carried except what was in the process of manufacture, the inclusion of office and selling expenses would violate no practical considerations, yet even in that case it would be better, according to Halsey, to exclude the aforementioned items. He went on to state that the practice of inclusion was very common, "but it is as wrong in principle as it is common."[20]

Another speaker, W. S. Rogers, stated that he was in complete agreement with Halsey. His reason, however, was that if this were done, that is, if sales and administrative departments were separated, the cost of production figures could be calculated in an almost straight line tending downward, whatever that meant! "And the business department can follow its own bent without hindrance and add 10 per cent, or 100 per cent, to their costs, as they deem best."[21]

Norris did not, in the end, allow the views of Halsey and Rogers to change his opinion. In his closing statement he again insisted that the "true" (his term) cost of an article should include office expenses, even when it came to preparing the inventory figures. He admitted readily that such inventory values would be inflated, but to him that over statement did not matter. As a matter of fact, it might be suggested here that Norris did not really understand the basic contention of his critics because he concluded by stating that he failed to see why office expenses were not just as much a part of the cost

of goods delivered into the warehouse as to the customer.[22]   This was
beside the point that Halsey had made.   Then, too, Norris thought
that it did not make any difference, so far as what should be in cost,
whether the products were made for order or were stored for a month
or a year.   Obviously it did make a difference, as his opponents had
pointed out.

Also in 1897, an American engineer, with an inquisitive turn, sent
out a questionnaire to some forty prominent industrial firms asking
them to indicate what they considered to be the proper cost of production elements.   The consensus was that "shop cost" was the sum
of four items: (1) producer's labor, that is, what would today be called
"direct labor"; (2) cost of material, including hauling and waste; (3)
a plant charge, which was an hourly charge for depreciation, maintenance, and power consumed by the different machines used in
manufacturing product; and (4) burden, which he stated, was "an
appropriate term met with only in the reply of Fraser and Chalmers."[23]
Burden was "the sum of all expense chargeable to the shop except
producer's labor and material."[24]   He also made the statement that
office expenses were often added in as a part of burden, a practice
which Halsey had said was common at that time.   This author referred
to that practice, however, as "a slight modification."   In his reply to
the questionnaire, Oberlin Smith again described the method used by
his own firm, but he added nothing to what he had already said.[25]

Two years later, 1899, H. L. Arnold, an American practicing accountant, wrote a volume in which he summarized the factory accounting practices of several types of manufacturing firms.   One of these
firms was the Hyatt Roller Bearing Company, now a division of General Motors Corporation.   To the prime cost of articles, it was that
company's practice to add a percentage for shop expenses and office
expenses.   The shop expenses included interest and taxes on real
estate, depreciation, insurance, and repairs; while office expenses comprised office salaries, supplies, advertising, and traveling and sales expenses.[26]   Practically all the other firms described followed the same
technique.   Since the businesses selected by Arnold were supposedly
representative of the best accounting of the day, it may be safely said
that even though a few authorities, such as Halsey, partially perceived
the later popular view point, the general practice was quite varied in
that in most cases sales and administrative expenses were included
in cost of production.

The English thinking of this period was quite similar.   For example, Joseph MacNaughton, who described himself as a papermaker and accountant, included in his "fixed charges" (his term), which were to be allocated over the paper made in a paper mill, every item of expense incurred by the mill. Some of them were: bad debts, sales allowances, office expenses, rentals, interest paid, and others.[27] A. G. Charleton, writing on cost keeping for mines, recommended the same practice.[28] All sorts of expenditures were added together to arrive at the monthly total of mine costs. It was not even suggested that there could be any other method of treating the office and selling expenses. This technique would, of course, yield an acceptable net profit figure, but the cost of mining would not be accurately stated.

In a series of articles which he wrote in 1901, A. Hamilton Church treated this topic (as he did several others) in a more comprehensive manner than any authority prior to that time.[29] (Church wrote and worked for the most part in the United States.) Although he was primarily concerned at that time with the allocation and distribution of "establishment charges," it was of course necessary for him to define what he meant by the term. "Cost of production," according to Church, was made up of prime cost (material and wages) plus "shop charges" (depreciation, power, floor burden—insurance and taxes—supervision, and various sundry expenses, such as oil and repairs) plus the "general establishment charges." It is this last group which is of particular interest here. Church, like Lewis before him, thought that all of the items mentioned should be allocated over product or jobs, but that it was far more important to keep shop charges and general charges separate in the accounting records. The reason for such a distinction was that the operations of making and selling were naturally different and required different talents and instincts. "An undertaking may be most efficiently organized and managed on one of these sides, and yet be unsuccessful, because what is gained in one set of efforts is lost in another. What is more useful, therefore, than to make this natural division of work to be reflected by a similar division in the system of accounting?"[30] But Church went on to state that since his so-called general establishment charges were not "yet" capable of any great amount of analysis, he was not going to consider them in large detail; nevertheless, in the final article of the series he did discuss various methods of distributing the general charges. Since this study is not particularly concerned with that aspect of the problem, it may be passed over rather lightly.

Church's views may be summarized at this point by stating that he was thoroughly in agreement with the idea that selling and general expenses had no place in the concept of "works [factory] cost," yet he felt they should be distributed over the jobs handled, or products turned out—not, however, on the same basis, nor according to the same rules, as "shop charges." And what was more, they were not to be included in the same accounts. After the total factory cost had been ascertained, the general charges were to be analyzed and charged to the jobs on whatever basis seemed best. Church admitted that no matter what method might be selected, it would be rather arbitrary; nevertheless he insisted that the general charges should be distributed. In concluding, he aimed a few barbs at such authorities as H. M. Norris and Oberlin Smith, when he stated that any system of cost accounts which grouped all charges indiscriminately and then averaged them into a percentage charge was next to worthless, even dangerous perhaps, since such a technique induced a false security.[31]

The work of W. C. Eddis and W. B. Tindall, published in 1902, will serve to illustrate the Canadian thinking on the subject during this period.[32] In one chapter they made a sharp distinction between "workshop expenses" and selling and distributing expenses. Here they went so far as to advocate that the workshop expenses should be the only ones considered part of the cost of production. This group was made up of all items incidental to the workshop and primarily caused by the manufacturing processes. The selling and general expenses were here closed directly to the profit and loss account.[33] In spite of their clear distinction at this point, they turned to a different practice in a later chapter when they began to describe a system of accounts for a hypothetical factory. Here they stated that estimates of cost should include not only the "factory expenses" but also selling and management expenses.[34] This inconsistency seems to give evidence that when discussing cost theory it was perfectly correct to exclude the selling and management expenditures, but from a practical viewpoint they should be included.

Returning again to the English practice, John Urie in 1902 proposed that "oncost,"[35] the English term for burden, be divided into two broad groups of items, the first to be called "departmental charges," and the second, "general organization expenses."[36] Each group was to be collected separately in subsidiary journals unconnected with the accounts. The general organization (or establishment) charges included all of the items which today are considered under the heading of selling and general administrative expenses. Several of them, however, might be listed: salaries of clerks, messengers, and managers, stationery, catalogs, advertising, discounts, branch office upkeep, telegrams, and others. Both the departmental and the general establishment charges were to be distributed over the jobs finished—not on the same basis, however. The different method of allocation was the reason for the distinction made in their collection. Both were considered properly part of the cost of orders, and should be remembered particularly when making estimates for bids on jobs.[37]

Sir John Mann, writing a year later, 1903, followed Urie's grouping exactly,[38] but he added several theoretical considerations which Urie had neglected. He was rather doubtful of the wisdom and logic of allocating both groups over orders or jobs,[39] and he gave different names to his groups. The first was called "direct expenses" and included all those charges which could immediately be charged to some contract, piece of work, or department of a business. It should be noted that this group was much broader in scope than the term "direct expenses" as used at the present time, since it meant foremen's and superintendents' salaries, fuel, lighting, heating, rent, taxes, insurance, depreciation, and maintenance. It is evident that Mann considered this group synonymous with "manufacturing burden," since he stated that "strictly speaking, direct expenses are elements of prime cost, and in a proper system should be so treated; that is, they are expenses of production rather than of distribution."[40] The second group he called "indirect expenses." These were all the items which were not direct expenses, and generally were expenses of administration and distribution. Some of them were office salaries and expenses, bad debts, and interest on loans. Both classes were to be considered oncost, however, and both were to be divided or allocated to product, although, as Urie had pointed out, the method to be used was different in each case.[41] Then, too, direct expenses were "more clearly foreseen and estimated; each manufactured article, and, if necessary, each manufacturing operation, may have attached to it very close approximation of its proper share of power, rent, superintendence, and other expenses of production. Much of the indirect, on the other hand, is fluctuating, and is unconnected with the conditions of the particular business; it may vary with the state of trade, conditions of the money market, etc., and may be entirely wanting in concrete results."[42]

It would be interesting to know the extent to which the above distinction was observed by manufacturing firms of the time. Sir John Mann himself noted that the common practice was not to make any distinction—just lump all expenses together. The best theoreticians, however, were insisting that a separate grouping be made, and Mann himself thought it of considerable significance. Nevertheless, in many cases, firms which took the utmost care to handle labor and material costs properly, neglected to make any distinction between manufacturing overhead and selling and administrative expenses.

For the United States the same conclusion could be drawn. For example, J. E. Sterrett, in a paper read before the Pennsylvania Institute of Certified Public Accountants in December of 1903[43] stated that many highly reputable factories included both manufacturing expenses and selling expenses in the so-called third element of cost; that is to say, they considered as a part of their cost of production such items as traveling expenses, salesmen's expenses, and advertising. Sterrett admitted that there might be some justification for their inclusion, yet he felt that they should be excluded. As he stated it: "The manufacturing department is properly chargeable with all expenses incident to the production of an article until it has reached its finished state and is ready to be sold."[44] The better practice would be, then, to omit from the cost accounts commercial and selling expenses. Again, the later popular viewpoint had been expounded, but it took root very slowly. As a matter of fact, though, the editor of the English publication, *The Accountant,* thought the Sterrett address so significant that he devoted two of his editorials to it. In one of these he pointed out the fatuity of including distribution expenses in cost of production, and stated that such a practice violated "a fundamental principle of statistical accounting," which the expert accountant should have thought of years prior, but which the manager of a factory might never consider; that is to say, most of the manufacturing items varied, if at all, with production, while the expenses of distribution varied with shipments from the warehouse.[45] This was not, of course, a new idea, as several prior authorities had already made that point clear. The editor also arrived at the same conclusion as F. A. Halsey, that is, that it did not make any difference in the *final* analysis whether selling expenses were included or excluded, *if* practically no finished goods were carried in stock, or *if* the amount was constant from period to period. The last condition was satisfied in only a relatively few firms, so that a large majority of manufacturers had no "reliable" (the editor's term) costs of production so long as they continued to intermingle all sorts of expenses indiscriminately. The editor of this important English accounting journal thus put himself on record as favoring the entire elimination (from factory costs) of distribution and commercial expenses. He reiterated his idea the next year (1905) in commenting upon a prize essay by Stanley Pedder, in which Pedder had made the statement that to arrive at the total cost of production one must add the indirect expenses for selling, distribution, and administration.[46] These were, according to Pedder, to be distributed over product manufactured. Pedder was undoubtedly reflecting the current practice of the period.

The editor, however, in his second editorial called Pedder's thinking an "error of principle."[47] He considered useless, too, the attempt to include all expenditures in factory cost, especially those which had no relation to output. Then he advanced a view which later was to become the focal point of the many disputants; that is to say, he arrived at the conclusion that since the factory manager had no control over the "counting house" expenses (his term) he (the factory manager) should not be held responsible for them, and the best way to relieve him of that responsibility was to omit selling and distribution expenses from cost. In this way the cost accounts would explain what happened within the works or factory. In addition, the editor pointed out that selling and administrative expenses could not be apportioned on any scientific basis; wherever such attempts were made they had the effect of making the cost figures fluctuate violently, even though production conditions remained constant and uniform. At last, a clear statement had been made of the basic reasoning involved; and cost authorities began to build upon this thesis.

The suggestion of the editor of *The Accountant* soon bore fruit, for in 1906 Stanley Garry wrote his *Multiple Cost Accounts*, one of the units of the then very popular Accountants' Library. In this volume nothing was said about including selling and administrative expenses in cost of production. Manufacturing burden was divided (1) into factory expenses, such as coal, power, lighting, indirect wages, and taxes; and (2) into establishment expenses, such as patterns, timekeepers, store room expenses, and drawing office expenses.[48] Both of these groups were closed to a manufacturing account at the end of the fiscal period, while the selling and general expenses were closed to a trading account. With that statement the distinction was complete.

Even in the case of the accounting for engineering construction jobs, which one would have thought would have been the last to capitulate, for all practical purposes the division was soon made. A. G. Nisbet, for instance, divided all expenditures and charges into two classes which

he called shop expenses and establishment charges.[49] For an engineering firm the first included foremen's wages, repairs, coal, coke, oil,
water, depreciation, lighting, yard expenses, and the like. These constituted a part of the cost of building a bridge, railway, or some other
construction project, while the establishment charges (which required
a definite separation) were closed to the profit and loss account,[50]
being considered a charge against manufacturing profits. It should
be noted that Garry and Nisbet did not use the term "establishment
charges or expenses" in the same sense. Matters of terminology had
to be watched by readers in those days even more than at present.
In addition, in view of the intermittent character of the engineering
contracts, Nisbet recommended that when making an estimate for
tendering a bid on a proposed job a percentage should be added to
cover both of his groups of expenses. But this was for estimating
purposes only. The two classes of items were not to be intermingled
in the accounts.

          After 1900, the American authorities followed the lead of A.
Hamilton Church[51] when it came to discussing the content of the burden element of cost. John Whitmore, for example, was certainly influenced by Church's thinking. In a series of articles which he wrote
in 1906, Whitmore considered in detail what he called "machine rates,"
and the costs which were thereby to be absorbed.[52] These included
repairs, depreciation, heat, light, taxes, insurance, superintendence,
supplies, and tools. All of these were to be considered legitimate parts
of the cost of articles or product. Then, as Church had done before
him, this author discussed methods of allocating administration, general
office, and selling expenses,[53] just as though these were also part of
cost. Two years later, however, Whitmore came very close to giving
a clear-cut exposition of standard costing. His remarks on this
were so significant, for the time at which they were written, that they
are quoted at length below:

          Concerning the definition of cost I would say that true or correct
     cost does not necessarily include every expense incurred in the
     course of producing an article. Accidents and blunders occur and
     the cost, as in some instances the cost of unused factory capacity, may
     be so great that it would be absurd to state it as a part of the cost
     of the product. If this is established, it establishes the principle that
     improper costs may be separated and stated under a heading which
     will distinguish between these and manufacturing expenses properly
     and necessarily incurred. This principle is rather far reaching; its
     application may be of the greatest practical value; and it is suscep-

tible of abuse. The danger is of assuming an impossible perfect standard of working and of failing to allow for a certain unescapable average of accident and failure . . . .

It is possible to carry the application of the principle distinguishing between proper and improper cost so far as to use calculations of proper and improper costs, and then to direct the cost accounting to showing the variations of actual from calculated costs. This involves the setting up of complete standards for quality in materials and efficiency in working, and is not to be confused with estimates of probable cost which are arrived at by any superficial method, or except with the idea of continuously testing actual and calculated costs with each other.

Calculations of proper costs with provisions in the accounting for showing the variations of actual from calculated costs constitute a plan which may be adopted for another reason than the one just dealt with. In some industries the manufacturing orders are so numerous that it is scarcely possible to have a separate cost account fully worked out for every order, while it is still quite practicable to have a calculation of cost for every article and to show where and how the calculated costs are varied from . . . .[54]

Other writers also began to touch upon standard costs. Harrington Emerson, for example, gave a remarkably clear analysis of standard cost variations in 1908, even though he did not include journal entries in his discussion.[55]

The English authorities were not unanimous in their adherence to the sharp distinction which Garry and Nisbet had made in 1906. Just a year later, Henry Spencer, an engineer, made the bold statement that the various expenses incurred by the sales department should be collected, compared with the value of sales, a percentage derived, and then added to the product to get total factory cost.[56] He went on also to state that "by this means every item of recorded expense incurred by both manufacturing and selling departments in a given period is liquidated by distribution over the prime costs of the various jobs in hand."[57] This was reminiscent of the doctrine which prevailed in Great Britain around the turn of the century.

But G. A. Mitchell's *Single Cost Accounts*, published in 1907, again made the distinction clear. His manufacturing account illustrated the fact that he did not consider selling and general expenses as part of the cost of production,[58] and in a chapter on "stocktaking" he made the specific statement that distribution expenses should not be included in the valuation of any finished stock which might be on hand at a balance sheet date.[59] So-called "shop expenses" were, however, to be added in.

Returning now to the development of the concept in this country, we find that Clarence Day, whose *Accounting Practice* was published in 1908, refused to accept the distinction which the better English authorities had emphasized. In several places he stated that general and selling expenses should be distributed over the product manufactured just like "departmental and factory" expenses, except on a different basis. He did insist, however, that the cost of manufacture should be determined before any addition was made for selling expenses.[60] It would seem, therefore, that Day recognized the fact that distribution items were not part of factory cost; nevertheless they should be placed on the cost sheets as part of the cost of a production order. Thus he had perceived the later basis of cost classification partially but not completely.

C. E. Knoeppel, a prominent American industrial management consultant, divided the "expenses" into three groups. The first was called "shop expenses," and included repairs, power, heat, light, stock room expenses, and general expense labor and material. The second group comprised supervision and recording expenses and was called "administrative expense," while the third group included selling expenses only.[61] Each of these groups was to be distinguished on reports and in ledger accounts, but, like Day he used the total of all three to get his percentage of "productive" (his term) labor cost to determine the amount to add to the cost of jobs turned out.

In *The Engineering Magazine* there is an early expression of opinion on the part of F. E. Webner as to what constituted manufacturing expense.[62] His discussion here was incomplete,[63] but he mentioned that it should include "fixed charges of various kinds, nonproductive labor and other direct charges, also reserves for depreciation, repairs and renewals of plant and machinery, and numerous items under what has been called invisible expense."[64] The careless inclusion of "renewals" should, in the light of present-day thinking, be disregarded. The reader was left to guess as to the composition of the so-called "invisible expenses."

The next year, 1909, Gershom Smith, while writing more specifically on the application of burden, dismissed entirely the concept of including marketing and administrative expenses in the amount to be allocated over product.[65] His "manufacturing cost" was made up of material, direct labor, and shop expenses, and he only mentioned the fact that other expenses existed.

When J. L. Nicholson published his *Factory Organization and*

Costs in New York in 1909, the basis for the distinction between the types of overhead had already, therefore, been fairly well established in this country. His discussion of the topic left little to be desired. He called it a "vital distinction," and stated that even though he had found in practice that selling expenses were frequently included as a part of cost of goods, it was wrong so to consider them. The reasons were (1) that they added nothing to the value of the goods produced by a factory, and (2) that they bore "little or practically no relation to the manufacturing cost."[66] In other words, factory cost ended with the completion of the product. The second reason given by Nicholson was quite similar to the conclusion arrived at much earlier by the editor of *The Accountant*.[67] At last, then, the English viewpoint was beginning to prevail in this country.

A year later, 1910, even A. Hamilton Church subscribed to the fundamental distinction. It will be remembered that earlier he had recommended that selling and purely administrative expenses be allocated over orders or products and had discussed methods of carrying that out. In his *Production Factors* (1910) he changed his opinion about this practice and declared that selling expenses were so far removed from manufacturing, and were so varied, that they should never be mingled with manufacturing at all.[68] He stated further that selling expenses should be closed to profit and loss by themselves, and that he desired to emphasize the important principle that production costs ended when the goods left the factory for the stockroom. It is interesting to note that even at this early date so-called "distribution costs" were recognized as deserving of separate treatment.[69]

Sterling H. Bunnell followed Church when he came to the treatment of distribution and general administrative expenses.[70] That is to say, he pointed out the fact that those two groups of expenses were in no way connected with the factory operations, and thus should not be included in the items which went to make up the burden rates. He also made the point as several before him had done, that any finished product on hand at a balance sheet date should be valued at factory cost only, omitting any distribution expenses. But Bunnell did not stop with the preceding discussion. He went on to describe how administration and selling expenses should best be taken care of, even though they were no part of manufacturing cost. It would seem, then, that he reverted to the theory of those who wrote a decade before him in so far as the final results were concerned. In fact, he still attempted to add a percentage to the factory cost of an order to cover the distribution and general expenses, several pages being devoted to a discussion of how such a percentage should be computed or estimated.[71]

One of the clearest statements before World War I of the factors governing the choice of methods was presented by a popular writer of the time, H. M. Rowe, who began to write accounting textbooks in this country in 1899. To quote at length from his 1910 work:

> Factory expenses consist of all incidental expenses for *indirect labor, supplies* and *material,* and other items of expense necessary in operating the factory which are chargeable directly to the cost of manufacture. These expenses are known as "burden," doubtless for the reason that they must be borne and provided for as a part of the factory cost of the articles produced.
>
> Overhead expenses are those which are incurred in the administrative department of the concern but which have, in fact, increased the cost of production in the factory, works or plant, either in their management or in technical or clerical service rendered, although instead of being charged directly to factory expense, which is always preferable, are charged in the general or administrative expense accounts of the concern. These are known as "overhead" expenses, doubtless because they represent a manufacturing cost *over and above* those included under the head of factory expense, or burden.
>
> It is sometimes difficult to distinguish between what should properly be classed as administrative expenses and those which should properly be considered as manufacturing expenses. An illustration is where part of the services of officers or office employees are given to the manufacturing department and part to the selling or financial departments. Another illustration relates to the proper account to be charged for drawing and patterns.
>
> Just what overhead expenses should be included in "factory cost," or "work cost," or "cost of production," as it is variously designated, is a question about which there are differences of opinion. Some hold that all expenses outside of those incurred in effecting sales and in the management of the financial affairs of the concern are necessarily incurred in connection with the manufacturing processes, and that they should, therefore, be included in the manufacturing costs in ascertaining the "factory," or "works" cost, or the "cost of production." This view is opposed by the argument that it might very easily be carried to the extreme of including a larger part of the administrative or other general expenses in factory expense, which would, in fact, capitalize them by including them in the cost of the goods manufactured, as shown in the finished goods account, and would thus show them as assets in the final statements of the business instead of expenses chargeable against income.
>
> Others hold that manufacturing costs should include only those that are incurred in the factory or works proper, and that those

incurred in connection with the administration or financial departments of the business, even when including the cost of technical or clerical service rendered to the factory, should in no way be considered as factory expenses, and therefore should not be included among the elements of cost of production chargeable to orders, jobs or contracts. The point at which the line is drawn between factory and other expenses by those who hold this view is illustrated in a concern having its plant in the country and its commercial office in the city, where only the expenses of the former would be included in factory cost, the expenses of the latter being classed as expenses of conducting the business that, in a bookkeeping sense, should be charged against *income*.

There is general agreement, however, that the best practice is to charge all expenses that are classed as factory expenses directly to that account at the time the entry is made, which will avoid any later question as to their proper disposition and will eliminate all questionable items from the administrative or general expense accounts, so that these accounts will then clearly represent balances which should be charged against income and should appear only in the trading and profit and loss statement.

A careful consideration of these views would seem to indicate that the line between factory costs and administrative and other costs should be drawn at that point which would include as manufacturing expenses only those items that are clearly a direct element of cost in the production of the manufactured article, no matter in what account they may be found. In any event, what should be considered manufacturing costs and what should constitute administrative and other expenses, and the place at which the former should end and the latter begin, must be divided separately for each establishment in which a cost system is installed, either by the owners or by the accountant.[72]

In his more complete treatise on *Factory Costs,* 1911, F. E. Webner elaborated upon his earlier 1908 views.[73] As the very name of his book implies, Webner disregarded all items which he did not consider to be a proper part of the manufacturing cost of a product or order. In doing this he directed his readers' attention to the fact that a sharp line must be drawn between what he called the two broad classes of expense. The first class included only manufacturing expense, while the second was made up of commercial and selling expense. His insistence on the wisdom and logic of omitting the latter group from productive costs was quite emphatic. It was, according to him, entirely unwise to bother with "items which pertain purely and simply to the sale of product . . . . This is also true of those other commercial expenses which have to do more or less directly with the delivery of the product and with collections, such as cash and quantity discounts, crating, hauling, freight on outgoing products, allowances after product has left the factory, etc., etc."[74] Furthermore, "such expenses are a proper charge, direct and indirect, to loss and gain, but not through production, and any attempt to fasten them on production will be a purely arbitrary process, entirely without advantage and entirely destructive of accurate costs."[75] No clearer statement of the then current thinking on this topic could be made, yet it is surprising how many authorities who followed Webner overlooked the distinction which he made.

An illustration of the careless disregard of the more popular basis for the distinction is to be found in a paper delivered by R. R. Keely before The American Society of Mechanical Engineers in 1913. This speaker refused, for the most part, to make any fundamental division between manufacturing burden and selling and administrative expenses. It was his opinion that every individual length of pipe (his business was making cast-iron water pipe) should bear a proportionate part of the expense of supervision, taxes, insurance, depreciation, repairs, heat, light, selling and advertising, and general office expense.[76] Selling and advertising and general office expense should, however, be apportioned in a different way, either on the basis of material and direct wages, or wages alone. However, it was not always necessary to use a different method, for, according to his way of thinking, it would not matter very much if the selling and administrative expenses were merged with all the others mentioned above.

The views expressed by Keely were not allowed to go unchallenged. William Kent, in some comments, expressed the opinion that it was generally inadvisable to include any part of the selling expenses in the burden rates. In addition, the selling department of a business should be considered entirely separate from the factory, and what was more, it should even have a separate system of accounts.[77]

In his little book called *Cost Accounts,* which he wrote in London in 1912, L. W. Hawkins also reverted to the principle of including office and selling items in the rate which he stated should be added on to the cost of orders finished by a factory[78] In this way he derived what he called "gross cost." He did mention, however, that where this practice was followed, a deduction must be made when the goods in process, as well as finished, were valued for balance sheet purposes.[79] He did not point out, though, how difficult this would be to do, even if it had to be done only once or twice a year.

In spite of the opinions of Keely and Hawkins the later widely recommended technique of handling selling and administrative expenses seemed to make rapid headway. The University of Pennsylvania Professor E. P. Moxey, for example, did not think these items worth mentioning;[80] they were so entirely distinct and different that they were not even to be treated in the same category. A couple of years later, however, F. H. Baugh, while making a distinction between what he termed "production cost" and "supplementary cost"—the latter being office, administration, and selling expenses—showed by his specimen journal entries that he preferred to allocate both classes of charges over the product.[81] He did not even make an issue of using a different method of allocation, nor did he think it necessary to reduce inventory valuations at end-of-period closings.[82] This neglect seems all the more strange in the light of the fact that his work appears unusually complete in other respects.[83]

Beginning with 1915 the authorities who wrote in this country on the subject were fairly uniform in their treatment; that is to say, they made a careful distinction between production costs on the one hand, and selling and administrative costs on the other. N. T. Ficker wrote in that year a series of articles concerned particularly with overhead cost items.[84] In these he excluded entirely any consideration of what he termed the sales and general administration departments, being content to deal strictly with the shop proper. Thus, in effect, he divorced industrial cost accounting from what later became distribution cost accounting. Another example is furnished by C. H. Scovell's comprehensive work on *Cost Accounting and Burden Application*, 1916. In this contribution the author specifically defined "burden" as "everything in a manufacturing plant that is not direct material, or selling expenses."[85] The eminent authors of *Cost Accounting*, Jordan and Harris, observed, too,[86] that the distinction should be made because of the necessity of divided responsibility, that is, the manufacturing and selling organizations were usually under different persons; thus for control purposes, the division must be maintained.[87] This same point had been made by previous authorities.

In England, also, the distinction began to be made by nearly all the authors and lecturers after 1915. A. C. Ridgway, however, in an address before the Birmingham Chartered Students' Society, split oncost into works and commercial charges.[88] Both of these classes, though, were to be allocated over orders or product turned out, even though the selling expenses were not to be included in the valuation of any goods in process at "stocktaking." When a student asked him the reason for including commercial charges in the allocated burden, Ridgway replied that "these are matters on which opinions differ. . . . There is no reason why you should not put the administrative expenses on to the total. . . ." [89] All of this is strangely reminiscent of the evolution of the same concept in this country.

A second example of English trend of thought after World War I is afforded by the discussion in the very complete *Factory Administration and Cost Accounts*, by E. T. Elbourne.[90] The author of this work made a complete separation of commercial expenses from production costs and claimed that the differentiation was absolutely esential from a control viewpoint—the same reason given by Jordan and Harris.[91] Manufacturing efficiency could not be determined so long as there was an indiscriminate mixing of the two classes of items; moreover, the legitimate burden could not intelligently be applied when the commercial charges were included in the rates.[92] Nevertheless, according to Elbourne, the practice of combining the two classes was in wide use even at that late date.[93]

Both in this country and in England the basic distinction between production or manufacturing cost on the one hand, and distribution and administrative expenses on the other, continued to be drawn during the decade of the 1920's. Numerous illustrations could be given, but there would be little difference between them. It is sufficient to point out here that not only were the fundamental differences observed by most of the various authorities, but also that technical studies began to appear concerned almost altogether with what came to be known as "distribution and commercial costing." The early ideas of A. Hamilton Church along this line bore fruit in such treatises as *Cost Accounting for Sales, Overhead Costs in Theory and Practice,* and *Control of Distribution Costs and Sales.*[94]

PART II. IMPUTED INTEREST AND RENT

The literature on imputed interest and rent in the past sixty years has run the gamut all the way from vituperative personal expressions of opinion to scholarly, though possibly biased, treatises extending over hundreds of pages. Thousands of words have been printed, and many more thousands spoken both for and against the inclusion of interest and rent as elements of production cost, and still the question is far from settled. The torrent of ideas and opinions has somewhat abated in the past decade or so, but it seems only to lie smoldering, awaiting perhaps a recrudescence. The purpose of this section is not to review *all* that has been written on the subject—that would be as fruitless as it would be tedious—but to develop the trend of thinking from the earliest references to the time when authorities no longer either bitterly opposed the inclusion of interest as a cost, or rejected all reasons advanced for its exclusion.

Thomas Battersby, who summarized more completely the items to be included in manufacturing cost than anyone preceding him,[95] had absolutely nothing to say on this subject which later became so important. Evidently it was not much of a problem in the period before 1880. One reason for this immediately suggests itself. It is to be found in the fact that political economists, who have contributed considerably to the theoretical aspects of the matter, before that time rarely if ever made any distinction between interest and so-called "profits" as forms of return to the capitalist. Nassau Senior, the noted English economist, for example, did not mention interest in the list of overhead charges which he gave in his *Report of Inspectors of Factories*, October 31, 1862. The list, incidentally, was rather complete for such an early date. It included rent, rates, taxes, fire insurance, wages of permanent employees, and depreciation of machinery.[96] But beginning with Francis Walker, who wrote in the United States in the late 1870's and 1880's, such a distinction began to be made. Generally speaking, later economists considered interest an entrepreneur cost, and segregated profits as a residuum. With this lead, later writers on cost accounting began to treat the subject in their works.

While Captain Metcalfe did not mention interest and rent in his *Cost of Manufactures*, 1885, his English contemporaries, Emile Garcke and J. M. Fells, propounded some confused and sketchy remarks which should be summarized here.[97] In one place (page 73) they made the definite statement that interest on capital should not under any circumstances form part of the cost of production, and went on to state that no advantages would be obtained by its inclusion. On a later page (page 124) they reiterated this view when they discussed the proper valuation of finished goods inventory at a "stocktaking" date. Yet on another page (page 133) "the interest on fixed capital" was a factor which had "a constant tendency to increase," as factories became more and more mechanized. While this statement is true, it conflicts somewhat with those previously given. These prominent authorities believed also that it was proper under special circumstances to consider interest an element of cost. For example, "should an arrangement be made by which the work-people, in consideration of not paying rent for the houses they occupy, receive less wages than they otherwise would, then the interest on the capital invested in the buildings forms an element in the cost of production."[98] As a matter of policy, however, these authors felt it was generally better to pay "full" wages, and collect a rent from each tenant, the rent to be considered a miscellaneous revenue.

G. P. Norton, on the other hand, had an entirely different opinion. He considered interest on the capital "employed" (his term) in a business an item of great importance when it came to calculating the cost of manufacture. His reason for such inclusion struck a later familiar ring; that is, the proprietor of the business could get a return from the application of his funds in other directions. As a consequence, the firm in question should be charged with interest as a cost.[99] Another reason given was that if the capital were borrowed the business would of course, by necessity, have to pay interest on such borrowings. Therefore, there was no reason why the interest should not be charged when the proprietor himself furnished the capital. Norton did not state specifically, however, whether he would have considered such interest payments an element of cost of production,[100] although to be consistent in his reasoning he would need so to show it. Incidentally, this English Chartered Accountant showed his charge as a debit in the trading account and a credit to capital account. This treatment had the effect of reducing the amount reported as net profit. From a rapid calculation one can find that he used a rate of five percent, based upon the capital account of the owner of the firm; however, Norton gave no clue as to why he used that particular percent.[101]

A year later, 1890, an anonymous English writer made the statement that interest should be included in the list of items composing the burden element of cost. He did not, however, elaborate upon this view and he did not make it clear whether he was referring to imputed interest or interest paid out on borrowed money.[102]

In this country the question received early attention at the meetings of the American Society of Mechanical Engineers. For example, E. P. Bates, in 1893, asked a speaker to comment on whether or not he considered interest on capital invested as entering into the cost of the products manufactured.[103] The speaker, L. S. Wright, evidently was not very sure of his ground when he made his reply; he would not commit himself definitely. As a matter of fact, he belabored the question so much that it is difficult to determine just what he meant. To quote:

> I may say that in looking at the running of your plant you have the land, the buildings, the tools, the furniture and fixtures, the labor, and the material. If the plant is a new one, it is probable that a part of the land bought may be considered as an investment. It is therefore set aside as such. The balance, together with its improvements and repairs to improvements, is devoted to manufacturing. On this land are buildings. Each building on this land is looked upon as having to earn for itself its proportion of the land cost; i.e., it rents its proportion of the land, and therefore it is necessary to figure in the cost of operating expenses the cost of its proportionate value of the land.[104]

Such was the answer given to the question of whether or not interest was an element of cost! Wright seemed to have been considering here as a cost element the capital value of the land itself, that is, the amortization of its cost, instead of imputed interest on such cost.

In an unsigned article in *The Accountant*, 1894, there was also a reference to the topic under discussion. This unknown English authority handled the charging of interest in the same way as Norton. The interest on capital was treated as a charge to the profit and loss account, and thus served to reduce the amount of profit earned by the firm for the period.[105] It would not be correct to state that Norton, and more especially this anonymous author, considered that interest was an element of cost of production. Rather, they thought of it as a charge which had to be met before any "true" (their term) profit could be obtained. The truth of this assertion is borne out by the fact that in their "cost summaries" the interest does not appear; it is to be found only in the trading account. To express it in a different way, they looked upon interest on capital in somewhat the same way that modern accounting views interest on partner's capital; that is, as a scheme for dividing partnership profit or loss.[106]

A few years later, 1899, the American, Oberlin Smith, stated that it was the practice of his firm to include in its "expense account" interest on the "total capital" at a "fair" rate—say five or six per-cent.[107] (The percentages are Smith's.) H. M. Lane agreed with Smith but added that the interest charge should be based on "working" (his term) capital as well as "fixed" capital. Smith had meant by his term "total capital" only the valuation of the plant. It is not known whether the practice of the two firms represented by the speakers was in wide use. A questionnaire which was sent to some forty of the manufactories of the country about that time, revealed that a majority of the forty considered imputed interest a cost.

H. M. Norris included in his list of "general expenses" an item for interest and deterioration, which obviously meant that he desired depreciation and obsolescence to be mixed with the interest charge.[108] He recommended the use of a six percent rate, but did not state the reason for his preference. In the same year Henry Roland published an article in which he commented on the fact that several large United States firms of his knowledge did not include, in their cost estimates, any charge for interest on the value of their plant.[109] This practice, in his opinion, was a "most unwarrantable omission." His views are worth quoting as illustrative of the reasoning of the period:

> If the plant were rented, the rent would undoubtedly be included in the expenses account and duly distributed as a part of the total cost of the machines built. Again, if the plant were sold, and its value in cash loaned, the lender would expect to receive interest on the amount as a matter of course. Viewing the shop or plant as an individual entity transacting business for itself, the case is the same; the plant carries an indebtedness to someone equal to it cash value, present or original. This indebtedness is necessitated by the creation of the plant, and interest on this amount is certainly a part of the general expense account, so long as the indebtedness exists. This indebtedness can be cancelled only by the earnings of the shop above total expense. Profits of operating the plant might be credited to the shop, until this indebtedness and interest were cancelled and the original investors in the concern had their money back again. In this case, the shop would own itself and be in debt to no one, and the interest charge would rightly disappear from the general expense account, but, until this establishment cost is liquidated in some way, the interest charge in the expense account is certainly legitimate.[110]

Roland's idea that the plant was an individual entity was a bit original to say the least. As noted in the quotation, he did not seem to know for how many years the interest charge was to continue; it was to continue until "liquidated" (his term) in some way. His reasoning will serve to illustrate the limits to which some of the early exponents of the inclusion doctrine went in their search for adequate justification for their charge. The opponents of inclusion, on the other hand, did not seem to bother too much about giving substantial explanations for their opinions. They merely ignored the whole question of rationalization.

The English viewpoint around the turn of the century was completely expounded by F. G. Burton in his *Engineering Estimates and Cost Accounts*. First of all he admitted that the question of interest was a rather complex one, so complex in fact that he recommended that it *not* be included when an engineering firm was making tenders for projects.[111] When it came to the actual cost accounts, however, he thought it necessary that a charge for use of machinery, including interest on same, should be made on the records of the firm. Supposedly, the reason for not including it in estimating was the nonuniform practice of various competitors; and since some firms did not make any charge, it was necessary for all to omit it so as to make the bids comparable on this point at least.[112] There was one exception, however. He suggested that if the buildings of a firm were owned *in fee,* that firm should, in lieu of rent, include in its estimates interest at the rate of four or five percent per annum, on the actual cost of the buildings, less accrued depreciation. He was emphatic at that point, however, in stating that partners or stockholders should not be credited with interest on their capital. The computations for the imputed interest were to be based on the figures derived from a summary statement drawn up each month, listing the various plant assets one after the other. Furthermore, the amounts to be used were those as of the close of the previous month, and not those at the last balance sheet date. A column was also provided for "stock," which he said included work in progress. Evidently, then, the types of assets on which interest was to be debited comprised land, buildings, machinery, tools, and stock.[113] What was the rate to be used? On this point, Burton strayed farther from his contemporaries than at any other place, for upon close examination one finds that he was not thinking of imputed interest at all, but of sums which the firm might have paid out on notes, debentures, preferred stock dividends, or even common stock dividends. In fact, he reversed himself as to the matter of interest on partner's capital, in that he might even include it in the amount to be distributed. In regard to the dividends, he stated: "Now this interest [sic] has to be yielded by the various departments into which the works are divided, and therefore forms part of the cost of the work they execute."[114] Burton's reasoning in the light of present-day knowledge of the subject is so confusing to the reader that it is small wonder that he was led to state that "we admit readily that this question of interest is a difficult one . . . There is much reason in the contention that interest is no part of the direct cost of work."[115] As a matter of fact, the type of interest—dividends, etc.—of which he was thinking, had never been seriously suggested as forming an element of factory cost. In concluding, he stated that his only reason for mentioning it at length was that Lancashire engineering establishments had become so accustomed to considering "interest as earned anterior to profits, and as increasing cost," that it would be hazardous even to suggest that another method should be used. Finally, Burton asserted that whenever a firm decided to omit part of the interest charge from its account, it should omit all; he had no sympathy for the part-inclusion theory.[116]

The literature on the subject of interest as a cost increased rapidly after 1900. For example, in this country, A. Hamilton Church, in a series of significant articles which he wrote in 1901, included interest on the capital invested in the factory buildings, land, and machinery in his "production factors." This was, in fact, one of the first steps in compiling the overhead rates. He noted that special care had to be observed in deriving the basis for the interest charge, that is, whether differences in cost were significant or accidental.[117] Beyond a few more bare statements concerned with the necessity of including interest as a cost, this author did not give any more details as to his opinions at that time. As will be pointed out further on in this section, however, he did elaborate upon his views in later works.

The Canadian practice at that time was illustrated by the opinions of W. C. Eddis and W. B. Tindall. These authors stated that some factories included interest on capital invested in the plant as an element of cost, but they did not recommend that such a charge be made.[118] No reasons were given for their recommendation. H. L. C. Hall was just as brief, but advised that a charge should be made for interest on capital actually invested in each machine.[119] Both of these works typify the casual attitude with which a large number of authorities treated the question during the early years of this century. Another example is afforded by Sir John Mann's article in the *Encyclopaedia of Accounting*. Mann wrote that where a factory was owned instead of rented, an equivalent of the rental charge should be included in the cost of the product and credited to a rent account. The balance of the rent account was to be treated at the end of a fiscal period just as though it were an income from some outside investment. If money had been borrowed and interest paid, the rent account could be applied to reduce such a charge.[120] This was at least a fresh viewpoint on what was rapidly becoming an old subject. Although it does not strictly pertain to the topic under consideration, Mann also advocated that a charge be made as an element of cost for a "fair" (his term) working salary to any proprietor who managed his own business personally. It was evidently his opinion, then, that "true" (his term) profit did not appear until all entrepreneur items had been allowed. He said also that "interest on the general working capital of a business, calculated at a minimum rate, should be provided for as an item of cost."[121]

Mann's countryman, H. S. Garry, had considerably more to say on the question of inclusion and exclusion of interest. In the first place, he agreed with Burton that interest should not be considered in making estimates or placing bids for proposed projects.[122] But what about the cost accounts proper? Here he was more inclined to hedge. The gist of his discussion was that the efficiency of the factory management could not be effectively shown unless a charge was made for interest on plant under their control; that is to say, since nearly all factories utilized varying types of equipment, no comparisons could be made between them unless the interest charge was made. This reasoning is reminiscent of later trade association arguments to their members, and was the reason why provision for interest was incorporated in so many industry uniform accounting systems. Garry was not particularly concerned with that, however; his interest lay along the line of judging the results obtained by managers of factories which had been consolidated or merged under holding companies. Under the same argument, he insisted that interest should also be charged in a factory on the stock of raw material which it held on hand from time to time;[123] moreover, any "extra" capital which a factory might possibly use to advantage should appear as a charge against the efficiency of that factory. In addition, where the land on which the factory building was located was owned as a freehold, a rent equivalent should be created—just as Mann had suggested. It is interesting, however, that in spite of all the theoretical considerations brought out by Garry, he did not choose to include interest in the accounts of the hypothetical firm which he used as a model illustration. This omission perhaps showed his true sentiments.[124]

John Whitmore, writing in this country in 1906, made the statement that up to that time it had not been customary to include interest on capital in the cost of production, and that most manufacturers and accountants had been reluctant to adopt such a practice. Yet in his opinion, its inclusion was essential "to an accurate distinction between varying costs."[125]   His reasoning was based upon different rates of return derived from the several departments of a business. Occasionally, in the productive process, articles did not go through the entire routine before being sold.   In such a case the necessary profit could not be figured, according to this author, unless interest on the capital employed was included as a cost.   When he came, however, to the accounting for interest, Whitmore was somewhat more explicit. At the time interest was charged to the several departments as an "expense," an interest-credit account was credited.   He enumerated the items on which the charge was to be based as: buildings, land, machinery, power equipment, storeroom fixtures, and the "average" goods in process.[126]   Any interest paid out, say for borrowed money, was to be debited to this interest-credit account.   It is difficult to reconcile the above treatment with the statement later on that "the difference between the two is interest on the capital which we started out to provide in our cost figures."   It would seem that only the credit total would show the sum of the interest on capital.   But one did not need to take that inconsistency too seriously because "I think I ought to warn you that this is a method of my own, and that as far as I know, it is not used except where I have used it."[127]

During the next year, 1907, several English authorities added their opinions to the already long list.   Henry Spencer, for instance, reasoned that interest calculated at a predetermined percentage on the value of the plant, buildings, and internal fixtures should be listed among the various general establishment expenses.   His theory was that if the assets mentioned were sold and reacquired at a rental, such a rent payment would most assuredly need to be included in the cost of goods manufactured.   "In other words, the original investors in the real property of a company are entitled to a return on their investment before subsequent holdings can receive a share of profits that may be earned and declared."[128]   He did not define either "original investors" or "subsequent holdings."   G. A. Mitchell, in his *Single Cost Accounts*, figured interest on the capital account at five percent, and added the result into the total of his general charge."[129] H. S. Garry, on the other hand, used as a base for his calculations five percent on the net values of the different sections of his hypothetical chemical plant at the last balance sheet date.[130]   Again he argued, just as he had in *Multiple Cost Accounts,* that there was no better way to judge the relative efficiency of new equipment than to include interest on such new plant as a part of the process cost.[131]

Two years later, 1909, J. L. Nicholson wrote into his comprehensive *Factory Organization and Costs* his decision that interest on plant should always be included in cost of manufacture, even though at the time it was rather rare to find it thus handled. His reasons were twofold. In the first place, he gave the now familiar idea that the money invested in the plant could be earning interest elsewhere; and secondly, where interest was paid on mortgages or notes, such payments were practically the equivalent of rent, and therefore should be handled just as rent would be, that is, as an element in the cost of production. The second reason seems unrelated to the first, and this prominent American did not state whether he would include both the interest paid out and the imputed interest in his charge.[132] He did mention, however, that whatever the amount finally decided upon, it should be distributed between the several departments of the enterprise in proportion to the "present value" of the equipment in those different departments.[133] He did not define "present value."

By the end of the first decade of this century the various writers who had expressed themselves on the subject of interest as a cost seemed to be fairly unanimous in holding that it should thus be treated, but they were not agreed on the reasons for the inclusion, nor the method of carrying out their charging technique. Some interesting opinions had been expressed, but by and large no complete discussion had been attempted. The topic was absorbing more attention, however, and nearly every authority had something to say about it.[134]

Beginning with 1911, the discussion became more vituperative. In that year the prominent English and American accountant, Sir A. Lowes Dickinson, expressed the opinion that imputed interest and rent should never under any circumstances form any part of the cost of a product.[135] It did not matter, according to him, whether a factory was rented or owned; neither payments to the landlord nor the interest on borrowed capital should be allowed to increase cost. In other words, instead of holding as prior writers had done, that for the sake of uniform costs, interest should be allowed on capital, or imputed rent charged when property was owned, Dickinson stated that rent actually paid and interest actually paid should not be considered part of the cost of the product. They were both division of profits, even though they were paid to persons outside the organiation. In this way, Dickinson would secure comparable costs from various firms making similar products, not by including rent payments in burden, but by excluding them. This suggestion caused the exponents of the interest-as-a-cost doctrine to redouble their efforts to find more plausible reasons for their beliefs. It also led directly to the long discussions in *The Journal of Accountancy* a few years later.[136] In so far as the imputed interest on capital and interest paid on borrowed capital were concerned, Dickinson had an able supporter in the person of L. W. Hawkins. Hawkins did not consider either item a cost of manufacture.[137] E. P. Moxey disagreed with Dickinson and Hawkins. He concluded that the rent paid to a landlord should be considered a cost because it was "an amount paid to supply the necessary instruments [of production]."[138] If this were true, interest on investment should also be included. Moxey continued his discussion by stating that wherever a manufacturing firm owned its own buildings and equipment, without debt, it occupied a a dual role, that is, it was both landlord and tenant. (The same viewpoint had been expressed before.) If the company's roles could be divided in this fashion, interest on investment must by necessity, according to him, be added into the cost of the product turned out by a factory.

The American practicing accountant, F. E. Webner, while advocating the charging of interest as a cost, went on to point out quite specifically that in the final accounting no difference would result, if it were assumed that selling prices were the same in both instances.[139] Moreover, he disputed Dickinson's assertion that rent payments were a division of profits and not a cost. His rebuttal is worth quoting as Webner represented a trend of thinking which had great weight in later discussions:

> From the standpoint of practical costing Mr. Dickinson's logic is not satisfactory. The interest on an investment in plant and equipment, or rent paid for use of factory would seem to be almost as direct an incident of cost as labor, material, power, or incoming freight. It is obvious that the manufacturer cannot make his product without a plant, and its rental or interest charge is usually one of the first incurred manufacturing expenses. Why, then, should it be differentiated from all other manufacturing expenses and be excluded from the cost of the product? . . . From the practical standpoint any cost necessarily incurred in the production of goods is more conveniently and most safely included in production costs.[140]

The question had now become one of "practical considerations," and Webner continued his discussion by describing in detail the composition of the interest charge. It was to be made on an annual or semiannual basis, and credited to a reserve account, which, in reality was a sort of revenue account representing the earnings on the capital invested. In case interest was actually paid out, say to mortgage holders, such sums were to be direct charges to the so-called "reserve" accounts, thus reducing the interest earned credit. In order to emphasize the fact that the profit and loss account would show the same "net gain" (his term) under either the exclusion or inclusion theories, Webner gave two hypothetical illustrations.[141] In addition, he suggested that where interest was charged on unused or inactive equipment, it would be desirable to pass such a charge directly to the profit and loss account, instead of through cost of production. This was due to the fact that it was "manifestly unfair to burden the product of other departments with interest on the investment in inactive departments."[142]

The contenders were now getting down to particulars. A. Hamilton Church, for instance, discussed about that time the theoretical distinction which could be drawn in a case where a mortgage on a piece of land might be drawing a higher rate of interest than that allowed on the land if it had been bought and paid for with cash. He seemed to think that the allowed rate should be used under these circumstances and any interest paid in excess of that be treated, not as a cost of production but in some other way.[143] Webner in his *Factory Costs* pointed out that this sharp refinement had little practical value.[144] It was his opinion that the full amount of interest paid on the mortgage should be added into the burden charge, only in cases, however, where the mortgage was put on the property at the time of original purchase—a sort of purchase money instrument. If the loan happened to be floated subsequent to the original purchase, any interest paid was extraneous to the costing of the product. Church might well have replied that Webner's refinement was one of "somewhat doubtful utility"—an expression which Webner had used in regard to Church's idea. The author of *Factory Costs* also insisted that production costs in general should show the lack of ample capital for efficient operations, and that the manufacturer whose resources might not be comparable with other possible competitors really desired to know what his actual costs were and not what they might be under improved conditions. This statement, of course, contradicts somewhat the aim of present-day standard costing, but is illustrative of the thinking of the period.

The matter came to a crisis when both sides marshaled their best talent in a series of articles published in *The Journal of Accountancy* for 1913. The question as to the exclusion or inclusion of interest as a cost was argued exhaustively by the leading cost accounting authorities of the time. Their attention was centered, however, for the most part upon either the reasons for considering imputed interest and rent as an element in the cost of production, or the reasons for their entire exclusion. No effort was made by the "inclusionists" to develop any further refinements in the accounting techniques for handling the charge; too much was at stake to bother with such trivialities. There is no need to summarize here the views of the various writers. Some, who had already written on the subject, have been treated in the preceding pages, while the others added relatively little that was new. In fact, the question seemed to have degenerated into a "yes" and "no" proposition.[145] The note on page 368 gives the final conclusion of each author.[146]

What was the English viewpoint during the period immediately preceding the First World War? It will be remembered that, except for Hawkins, most of the prior English authorities were in favor of including interest in the items comprising the cost of an article. M. W. Jenkinson, however, in a lecture reported in *The Accountant* (April 18, 1914), admitted that there was a divergence of opinion on this topic, and that perhaps from an economic standpoint the charge was justified. It was, moreover, an essential item to be considered in making estimates for jobs. This last statement was in direct contradiction to the views espoused by some of his countrymen, who had maintained that it should not so be considered. When it came, though, to the computation of the profits legally available for dividend purposes, interest should be excluded. The reason for this, Jenkinson said, was that interest "being only a form of profit, the amount, if any, included in the work in progress must be written back for balance sheet purposes."[147] Incidentally, if interest were to be charged, it must be based, according to him, upon the whole of the assets employed in production excluding, however, goodwill and organization expenses.[148] Sums paid out on account of bonds or bank loans were to be omitted from the burden charge, and treated as a charge against profits, that is, closed directly to profit and loss. In summary, Jenkinson concluded that in most cases the attempt to allocate interest to each job was more trouble and caused more work than the results justified. His views in general, however, were so conflicting and vacillating that even after a thorough study of them one would be left wondering in just which direction his decision fell.

In the same year, 1914, the master printers of England drew up a cost finding system for their industry, in which they recommended that five percent interest on the capital employed in each business be included in the cost of orders and allocated over jobs along with other costs. In America, too, the printers were among the first to adopt a uniform system.[149]

The industrial management engineer, N. T. Ficker, criticized his fellow Americans who advocated inclusion on the grounds that they were not comprehensive enough in the base which they used for computing the charge. He found an inconsistency in the fact that accountants generally used only the investment in factory equipment instead of all the working assets of a firm. It was his opinion that imputed interest should be calculated, if at all, on not only the fixed assets but also the investment in raw material and that part used up by shop expenses.[150] He showed some hesitancy, however, in advocating the inclusion of interest as a cost of manufacture, and preferred that it be shown as a financial expense. It was not quite clear whether he was here speaking of interest paid out, or imputed interest. There was no doubt in his mind that if imputed interest was to be considered a cost, it should be based upon both fixed and working assets; there was no justification at all for the exclusion of the working assets. Incidentally, he made the statement that there was no case on record where a writer had argued that the current assets should be included in the base upon which the charge should be calculated. As a matter of record, both H. M. Lane in this country, and Sir John Mann in England, among others, expressed such a theory.[151]

By 1916, the literature on the subject of interest as a cost had reached such a stage that C. H. Scovell felt it necessary to devote a whole section of his *Cost Accounting and Burden Application* to the topic. His was perhaps the most thorough investigation that had been made up to the time. After prefacing his remarks with the statement that few managers or accountants had ever taken the trouble to think the problem through in a logical way,[152] he immediately

announced that he himself belonged to the inclusion school. If anyone disagreed with him, let him, he argued, go to the political
economists for final answer.[153] In order to get their opinion on interest as a cost, Scovell engaged a trained economist to search dili-
gently for the various views of that group.[154] The consulting
economist reported that the authorities on economic theory were
practically unanimous in holding that interest should be distinguished
from profits, being different in principle. The only exception among
the modern economists was Irving Fisher, and his dissenting view was
more a matter of terminology and classification than it was fundamental. Scovell seemed to place a great deal of emphasis upon this
unanimity in the economics group, even though he did not make
much use of their reasoning in his own discussion.[155] In it he first
marshaled all the benefits which could be derived from the inclusion,
such as more accurate fixing of selling pieces, determining efficiency
of varying equipment, the cost of carrying inventories, and closer
estimates on proposed jobs. Interest as a cost, according to him, was
absolutely essential for the successful accomplishment of these aims.
In regard to the rate to be used he turned for help to the studies
of the Harvard University Bureau of Business Research, which had
decided in favor of a rate which the capital invested in the particular enterprise would have earned if committed in high grade
securities (mainly bonds) where practically no risk was taken. The
investment thought of would be of a long-term nature, and located in
the same locality. Obviously, this rate would differ throughout the
country, but Scovell, following again the Harvard Bureau, decided
that this was of small importance. To quote: "As to the . . . interest
rate to be used in cost accounting, nothing more is required than
that it should be reasonable and *agreed upon* by the persons concerned."[156]

    The accounting technique that Scovell would employ was quite
similar to that of certain preceding authorities; that is, determine
the asset values "of all kinds,"[157] apply the rate current in the locality,
and distribute this amount over the product. The credit was to be
passed to an interest-charged-to-cost account, which in turn was to
be closed to profit and loss account periodically. Interest on borrowed money was not connected in any way with this problem; it
was simply a financial expense, and imputed interest had no relation to it. This particular treatment was opposed to that advocated
by some prior authorities, for example, F. E. Webner. Scovell in-

sisted that the cost of production of an article was neither larger nor
smaller just because interest happened to be paid out, say for bank
loans or bonds.

Scovell's extensive remarks on the subject of interest as a cost
served to intensify the argument. Some outstanding authorities,
however, were beginning to be rather cautious, and to be more inclined to present both viewpoints and let the reader decide which
method he preferred. Dogmatic statements of opinion became more
and more rare. For instance, A. Hamilton Church changed his earlier
views and stated in his 1917 work that it was optional whether or
not imputed interest needed to be included as a cost of production.[158]
He was sure, however, that interest payments to outsiders were not
proper cost items, since they were purely financial matters, unconnected with "the efficiency of manufacturing," as he called it. It
will be remembered that Scovell had the same viewpoint. As a
matter of fact, that point was becoming fairly well established by
the end of World War I. Church also thought that imputed interest
should be included as a cost wherever one wanted to contrast alternate methods of carrying out a process, for example, one using a great
deal of labor, and the other a small amount of hand labor. He disagreed with Scovell as to the basis for the charge, however. It was
his (Church's) opinion that only the buildings, land, and equipment should be used in the computation.[159] In summary, this
prominent cost authority did not consider the whole vexing question
of interest inclusion very important. This is evidenced by the fact
that he only devoted about two pages out of some 452 in his volume
to its treatment.

The English viewpoint began to change also. By 1918 the editor
of *The Accountant* began to question the then prevailing idea that
interest paid out was an element of cost. It was his theory that any
item of expense over which the factory manager had no control should
be omitted from the cost accounting.[160] He pointed out that since
there were so many instances where firms failed because of poor
financing, rather than inefficient manufacturing operations, that the
officials ought to distinguish between factory efficiency proper and
total company efficiency. This could not be done so long as interest
paid out for loans was considered an element of cost. Production
costs would be too capricious, and be liable to fluctuate because of
nonfactory conditions.

As for the question of imputed interest, the English editor was

not quite so sure of his ground. There was, he admitted, a great
deal to be said for it; but wherever interest on capital was considered
a cost, the basis for the computation should be limited to the investment in plant and equipment only. The reason for the limitation
was that there was so little similarity in the total book assets of firms
doing the same line of business.[161] Some had been purchased perhaps from former owners at inflated values, or the book values had
been written down because of overconservatism. All of these factors
would make for noncomparable results, and the editor doubted the
efficacy of the whole theory.

But the editor's views were not accepted unanimously in England.
A. E. Goodwin, for instance, had no doubt about the fact that imputed interest was a cost.[162] After stating that rent paid out to a
landlord was undoubtedly a cost to be distributed over product, he
continued by pointing out that if the factory were a freehold, a rent
equivalent should also be provided. It would be, in his opinion, inconsistent to hold otherwise. Then, too, cost comparisons could not
be made unless interest on the plant facilities used under each
technique was included. This was a theoretical advantage which
had been pointed out by several previous authorities. Also, the
working as well as fixed capital should be used in the computation of
the interest charge, especially where a process required an unusually
heavy stock of materials or supplies. Goodwin would not commit
himself upon the valuation base that should be used for deriving
the interest. He proposed that a vote be taken of the Institute of
Chartered Accountants members as to whether cost, present value,
or replacement value should be adopted as a standard; at least he
said that he would like to obtain the official view of the Institute.

In the same year, 1920, L. W. Hawkins, whose earlier views have
already been discussed,[163] agreed wholly with the editor of *The Accountant* in that interest paid out for borrowed money was really
a matter of finance rather than of cost of production,[164] and should
be kept entirely out of the cost accounts proper. This authority,
moreover, failed to see the advantage, logic, or justification for the
inclusion in cost of imputed interest on capital. He maintained this
position through at least five editions of his work, and was thus the
redoubtable opponent of the English inclusion group. His reasoning
was the same as before; that is, "the return produced by capital is
profit, whether it be the return of a sole trader, of a partnership, or
a company, and the case is not affected if part of the capital of a

company consists of preference shares."[165] In addition, he could not understand why some advocates of the interest-as-a-cost doctrine assumed that a rate of five percent was about right; that assumption in itself showed their position to be illogical, according to him. Incidentally, Hawkins placed himself on record as favoring the inclusion of rent payments as an element of factory cost, but not imputed rent.

By 1921, when E. T. Elbourne wrote his comprehensive *Factory Administration and Cost Accounts,* the English cost accounting authorities seemed to be about equally divided as to the advisability of including imputed interest and rent as cost elements. Elbourne admitted that the general practice among English firms was to omit such charges, but he felt that the issue should not be thus evaded.[166] A manufacturer deceived himself, it seemed, if he failed to provide for the rent equivalent in his accounts when he owned the property in which his factory equipment was located. Moreover, production burden rates would not be equitable to the different departments unless some recognition of the capital values involved was taken. This authority even reverted to the theory that interest paid out for long-term loans was a factor in cost of production. The efforts of the editor of *The Accountant* seemed to have no influence on Elbourne's opinion. Elbourne, however, recognized the fact that inventory values should be reduced at balance sheet dates because of the anticipation of profits caused by the inclusion of interest in cost of products inventoried. His reasoning here was somewhat inconsistent with his prior views. While there would be an inflation of inventory valuation under the circumstances mentioned, this English writer went on to state that "inasmuch as the payment of interest is contingent on profit, and in that sense a distribution of profit, to include any interest element in the stock values carried forward would be deceptive, seeing that the goods have not been sold within the year and, therefore, no opportunity afforded of reaping the profit wherewith to pay the interest."[167] But on a previous page he had stated that there was no profit until interest was paid. Supposedly he was referring to the same sort of interest in both places, although he was not specific on the point. Incidentally, Elbourne was one of the few English writers during this period who showed the accounting technique for making the interest charge. He did not, however, discuss the basis of valuation to be used nor the rate to be assumed.

As has already been intimated, the writers on industrial accounting in this country after the First World War were rather inclined to present both viewpoints, that is, both the exclusion and the inclusion theories, and let the reader determine which he preferred. In the last analysis, the question had narrowed down to a matter of cost interpretation and personal opinion. As examples, J. L. Nicholson and J. F. D. Rohrback held that imputed interest on land, buildings, machinery, and equipment should be counted as a cost,[168] while J. P. Jordan and G. L. Harris concluded that the preponderance of arguments against seemed to favor its entire exclusion.[169] The decision of Jordan and Harris was reached after a most searching and diligent inquiry into the merits and demerits of both viewpoints. In the meantime, the discussion had filtered into the meetings of the various accounting associations. The 1918 meeting of the American Association of University Instructors in Accounting (now the American Accounting Association) devoted one of its sessions to the topic. C. H. Scovell and L. H. Haney were the principal speakers.[170] The former defended the proposal, while Haney argued against it.

Also in 1918, the American Institute of Accountants took cognizance of the controversy. A special committee, consisting of five prominent members, was appointed to make a report on "interest in relation to cost." This report was later printed in the *Yearbook* of the Institute and presented the very definite opinion of the Committee that imputed interest should not be considered a cost. In a word, "the inclusion in production cost of interest on investment is unsound in theory and wrong, not to say absurd, in practice."[171] The Committee decided, however, that interest included in factory cost purely as a statistical device might be of some value to the managers of a firm, but each company would have to consider this possibility from its own point of view.

The, at that time, newly organized National Association of Cost Accountants also appointed at an early date a special committee to collect data and a bibliography on the subject. The report was later discussed at the 1921 annual convention,[172] and a questionnaire was prepared which was mailed to members of the Association, requesting their views on the important aspects of the controversy. Some 2,016 ballots were sent out, and 567 of them returned for tabulation.[173] Out of those tabulated, only 112 were absolutely convinced that interest was a "proper" element in the cost of production. It should be mentioned, however, that of the 455 who voted "no," some 252 gave no reasons in support of their view; while of the 112 who voted "yes," only two failed to substantiate their opinions. These results seem to indicate that the inclusionists felt that the burden of proof was on their side; this is an interesting sidelight upon the debate.

The disputation waxed warm during the entire early years of the 1920's, reaching a temporary climax with the publication of C. H. Scovell's *Interest As a Cost* in 1924—an entire volume devoted to the subject.[174] Since the individual firms or cost accountants must, in the last analysis, make their own decision, based upon their own requirements, a sensible note was struck in 1928 by G. H. Newlove in the following conclusion: "Since the primary purpose of cost accounting is to serve as a guide to the management, cost accountants . . . should include interest on investment as a cost element whenever such inclusion will make the cost statistics more valuable to the management."[175] This section may well end with that statement.

PART III. THE BURDEN CONTROL ACCOUNTS

As was typical of the accounting for manufacturing burden in general, the matter of burden control accounts received little attention prior to the twentieth century. There are at least two reasons for this neglect. In the first place it is more than likely that a great number of manufacturing firms before that time used a modified commercial (trading) accounting technique for what records they kept; that is to say, they adapted the mercantile systems in vogue to their own purposes. In this way they were able to derive a rough approximation of their costs and profits by taking an inventory occasionally of not only the articles made, but also of the equipment with which they were manufactured. If the factory books were handled in this way, and there is ample evidence (see Chapter II) that they often were, no control accounts would be necessary to handle the burden element of cost. For example, a very popular American author, J. H. Goodwin, mentioned in 1881 that it would be wise to keep separate accounts in the ledger to show the amounts consumed of the different items which went into the finished product.[176] These were periodically closed to a manufacturing account, which, in reality, was a sort of trading account. Other examples of the same technique could be cited, but it is sufficient to state here that so long as industrial accounting was thought of in that light, no need would arise for burden control accounts.

Nor, in the second place, was the development of the use of

control accounts assisted by the next stage in the evolution of modern costing techniques, that is, the use of independent, statistical "cost accounts," unconnected with the financial, or "counting house," books as they were called. The idea of extramural costing persisted for several decades, especially in England. (This topic is treated *in extenso* in the next chapter.) Obviously, so long as the factory cost elements themselves were not assembled completely on the commercial books, overhead accounting itself presented few problems, other than distribution and allocation. All that was called for under this type of industrial accounting was that accounts be maintained on the financial ledger for the various expenditures which were made on account of burden items. The departmentalization and distribution took place entirely in the "cost accounts," using the term in the sense of the statistical records of jobs performed, as it was in those early years. Incidentally, this practice caused several turn-of-the-century writers to deplore the fact that the cost records would never check absolutely with the counting house records. This error was sometimes reconciled by tracing the causes back to (1) the allocation of too much or too little overhead to jobs in comparison with that shown on the financial records, or (2) the incorrectness of the raw material and direct labor records. Obviously there would nearly always be a small difference between the total factory costs as shown by the ledger in the office and the costs as shown by the cost ledgers in the factory, so long as the two were unconnected or not tied together by means of reciprocal accounts. This problem bothered some of the early authorities, while others took the matter for granted. Occasionally one would attempt to reconcile the differences, or point out that a reconcilement should be made periodically as a sort of internal check on the factory superintendent. Incidentally, it is interesting to note that according to these writers any mistakes, frauds, errors, etc., would necessarily be found in the "cost accounts"; the counting house records could not be wrong because they were based on actual transactions with outsiders.

Henry Metcalfe, who wrote in 1885, and whose system of cost keeping contemplated a separate set of records, was especially downcast by the fact that the two sets of accounts would never balance. He stated: "I have vainly tried to find some simple current method of reconciling the cost sheet with the cash accounts [really the financial books], since this would establish the aggregate truth of the cost sheet before the highest court of audit. . . ."[177]

The late nineteenth century English ideas on the subject were similar. G. P. Norton, writing in the 1880's thought it very unwise to consolidate the cost records and commercial records, and as a result he showed on the financial ledger several accounts for burden expenditures.[178]

One of the earliest references to what might be called a "burden cost applied" account was contained in an 1897 address by President Broaker of the then prominent American Association of Public Accountants, the predecessor of the American Institute of Accountants. This authority stated that when a job or article was finished, the cost sheet should be closed out by adding to the direct labor and raw materials used an amount thought sufficient to cover the trading and management expenses, which sum was to be credited to a special account, entitled "estimated expenses."[179] The special account was later on closed out to revenue, and was "contra to the actual expense incurred." Broaker was rather hazy as to how the debit would be handled when this method was used, that is, when the estimated expenses account was credited. Supposedly, however, it would be debited to the manufacturing account, because he mentioned specifically that the labor and materials used would be charged to that account when an article (piano) was finished, and it was his opinion that the incidental expenditures were a part of the cost. One wishes that he had discussed his views and techniques more carefully; he gave no model journal or ledger entries, being content with mere explanatory material. Incidentally, he stated that his methodology had been in use several years.

J. Slater Lewis (1896) wrote in England of a "shop establishment charges account," which upon close inspection proved to be only a summary account on the financial ledger to which all of the miscellaneous items of expense were posted monthly from the "bought book," a sort of purchases journal with a column in which all such expenditures were entered.[180] In one place (page 386) he stated that the shop establishment expenses account was to be closed to profit and loss. This would indicate that he considered the account itself incidental to the actual costing of the jobs. But in another place (page 475) he advocated that the jobs be debited, through the journal, and the shop establishment charges account be credited. Then the shop establishment charges account was debited "each month with its proportion of the salaries, foremen's wages, fuel, lighting, heating, rent of shop, etc., all of which the establishment charge credits from the journal are supposed to wipe out."[181]   This statement would imply that the individual charges were first entered in separate accounts, and credits at intervals made to those accounts for charges on machine tools, which sum, as stated above, was charged to the shop establishment account.   Lewis thus described two techniques for handling the expense control accounts, neither one of which was very satisfactory, although there is evidence that his system was used not only in England, but even in this country.[182]

David Cowan, the next English authority to treat this particular topic with much care, showed a knowledge and understanding far in advance of his contemporaries. His technique for handling the burden element of cost, although lacking accuracy in certain respects, was distinctly superior to the then existing methods. More than likely, however, it was not used to any great extent at that time (1899).[183]   Like Norton, Cowan recommended that an account be set up on the commercial ledger, to which all the shop charges were posted in aggregate as they were incurred. It was to be called, however, "the compensating account," and was credited whenever jobs were completed for an amount predetermined in advance, depending upon the number of hours the job consumed. It was his idea that this account should remain unclosed, the balance swinging from debit to credit as the "representative cycle" (his term) of years passed by. Evidently he was thinking of a business cycle. In periods of good business the account would have a credit balance, while in periods of bad trade it would swing to a debit balance. A second account, to be maintained also on the commercial ledger, was called the "shop charges recoveries account." This account was to be debited with the credits from the compensating account. The recoveries account was a sort of work in progress burden account, since it was credited when jobs were completed for the amount of burden contained in the article made. The corresponding debit was to a "net cost account," which was an intermediate account between goods finished and the stock accounts.   The recoveries account would always have a debit balance, equal to the burden element in work in progress at any time. Incidentally, the general and selling expenses were to be handled by means of the same technique. Separate accounts were to be set up, however, in order to keep them distinct from the shop charge, a legitimate element of cost. In summary, Cowan would have used his compensating account as a device for allocating his charges on a normal business cycle basis; that is, he would have set burden rates keeping the cyclical swings in mind. This subject, however, will be discussed at greater length in a later section.

The burden control accounts introduced in 1901 by A. Hamilton Church are worthy of passing note. His technique involved the establishment of a "shop-charges account;" the debits to this account included the items which made up his machine rate.[184] The same account was credited with the so-called machine earnings, which together with the supplementary rate closed the account. In those early articles Church did not give entries and accounts, so the specific accounting which he recommended is not known. From what he wrote later (1909) one can ascertain that he would have set up accounts for the factory expenses, which in turn were closed to the profit and loss account at the end of a fiscal period. Thus he offered nothing new in regard to the topic under discussion.

Eddis and Tindall added a new idea.[185] They suggested that since the details of the factory expense expenditures would merely clutter up the general ledger, it might be wise to use a pure control account in that ledger to take care of the total of such items, while the particulars could be entered in an "expense detail book."[186] The detail book was distinctly modern in nature, being a columnar page with divisions headed with the names of usual factory charges. The "factory expenses" (control) account was credited for the estimated allocated burden when jobs were finished, while a "manufactured stock" account was debited. At the end of a financial period the factory expenses account would show whether or not all the burden had been allocated to orders. They did not discuss specifically what should be done with any balance in the factory expenses account, although it was implied that it would be closed to profit and loss. The most important aspect of their technique, however, lies in the fact that they had applied the control account principle to the burden element of cost, a very definite improvement.

In 1905, Glenn H. Frost reported and compiled some cost theories which had been propounded by H. C. M. Vedder, one of which was concerned with the present topic. It was Vedder's suggestion that an account called "accruing manufacturing expenses" be set up on the ledger to which would be posted all the various incidental costs concerned with manufacturing. Although he did not state it specifically, he implied that the account mentioned was to be used as a semi-control account. At any rate, it was to be debited with the total of the overhead items listed and recorded first in a "summary sheet of vouchers." Any necessary reserves, such as depreciation, were also to be debited to the account. At the end of a fiscal period, an entry was to be made charging a manufacturing account (really goods in process), and crediting the accruing manufacturing expense account. This last entry was for the purpose of allocating the burden to the jobs worked on or completed during the period and was in an amount sufficient to close the accruing manufacturing expense account completely. Vedder was sure that it would be enough because he suggested that the burden allocation be delayed until after the end of a fiscal period; that is, predetermined rates were not to be used. In spite of this last by then somewhat outmoded recommendation, this American accountant showed an unusual grasp of the flow of costs through the ledger, and offered some suggestions along other lines.[187]

In the same year H. Deighton, an American engineer, recommended that departmental expense accounts be set up on the general ledger, one for each major division of a firm's business. To these accounts was to be charged all the overhead or indirect burden properly attributable to that department alone.[188] He went on to suggest that individual accounts be established for burden items not assignable to any one division. These accounts were in turn to be closed monthly to the departmental accounts, through the journal, on some equitable basis. When jobs or orders were finished, the "manufacturing" account was debited and the proper departmental expense accounts credited. This step was also handled through the journal, and was usually at some predetermined rate. Although Deighton did not use Eddis and Tindall's idea of controlling accounts, he did illustrate the concept of productive departmental expense accounts on the general ledger. It would be an easy transition to use those accounts as controlling accounts if the need arose, as it did later on.

In fact, the very next year (1906) found C. E. Knoeppel adapting the control principle to expenses on a somewhat grand scale.[189] In an American organization with which he was familiar there were about 500 accounts on the general ledger, and he had found it desirable to establish seven expense controlling accounts thereon: namely, repairs; power, heat and light; stock room; general expense; labor and materials; supervision and records; and selling expenses. Each of these was given a code number, and the detailed items under each were lettered. As the charges accumulated during a month the sub-accounts were credited; the control accounts were debited for totals only at the end of the month. This technique, obviously, was contrary to later, more modern practice wherein the sub-accounts are also debited. Knoeppel did not make it clear why he followed such a practice. His reason was: "This is . . . not carrying out to the letter the principle of controlling accounts as applied to advanced accounting; in fact, the application of the rules of double entry bookkeeping to this system of cost comparison has not even been attempted; but inasmuch as the controlling accounts are charged for the expenditures, the amounts covering the sub-accounts must, of necessity, fall in the credit column."[190] What he was attempting to do, perhaps, was to use an opposing entry procedure; but, if so, it was needless for all practical purposes. The sub-accounts were to be kept on cards in a separate file. The posting to the expense controls was to be done only once a month, and a looseleaf "record book" was used. At the left side of this large sheet the various charges were summarized and apportioned over the columns representing each of the seven control accounts. On the last day of each month each column was totaled and posted to the proper control. This seems now a very cumbersome system. At the present time the control accounts are posted directly from the voucher register, journal, etc. But Knoeppel recommended that they first be carried through this intermediate record sheet. While his system gave rise to only one entry per month to each control, the disadvantages, as contrasted with modern practice, are obvious.[191]

The English cost experts contributed little during this period to the development of the use of control accounts for burden. Most of them clung to the extramural costing technique, that is, the separation of cost records from financial accounts. They were, therefore, not concerned with control accounts, being content to set up accounts for burden expenditures on the commercial ledger, and closing those accounts periodically to either a trading or profit and loss account, depending upon their individual preferences.

In an article which he wrote in 1908,[192] F. E. Webner stated that one of the control accounts which he would establish on the general records should be called "accruing manufacturing expense," but he did not explain its use. Supposedly it was a control account for burden.[193] The article was not particularly concerned with the topic under review; consequently this American authority said nothing further.

A writer in the *Cyclopedia of Commerce, Accountancy and Business Administration,* 1909, proposed that an expense ledger account be opened on the general ledger for each shop within the firm. (More than likely he was thinking of departments.) To these accounts would be posted as debits all the overhead items pertaining thereto. This was somewhat the same idea expounded by Deighton several years before; but the writer in the *Cyclopedia* elaborated upon Deighton's technique by first charging to individual expense accounts the items which were not applicable to the shop expense accounts, and then closing those individual accounts to a general expense distribution account each month. It is difficult to see the purpose of the last step, since the general expense distribution account was not used as a device for spreading its total over the different shop expense accounts, but rather was merely closed out monthly to the manufacturing (work in process) account *in toto.* This practice again appears to be an unnecessary bit of red tape comparable with Knoeppel's record sheet. One should not be too hasty, however, in criticizing those early technicians. Their objective was commendable even though they had not developed the polish and finesse of later practitioners.

By 1910, the idea of a burden control account was firmly established in this country, in spite of the fact that many authorities did not consider it a worthwhile device. A. Hamilton Church and J. L. Nicholson, to give two examples, continued to follow the individual expense account technique, with periodic closing to profit and loss. By then the procedure had been explained for using subsidiary burden expense accounts, controlled by one or more accounts on the general ledger, and one authority had even hinted at a burden applied account. The under or over absorbed burden account had not been invented, but Cowan with his compensating account had attained its basic advantages. Later experts now began to build onto the structure laid by the group discussed above.

B. A. Franklin, for example, suggested that all payments of money be made under a voucher system, in which a register was maintained with a column for "expenses."[194] The total of this column was posted to one expense account in the ledger. At the end of the month an analysis sheet for a report was drawn up, based upon this column; it divided the items into specific expenditures. On this same report the noncash costs, such as depreciation, were also entered. All burden items were then departmentalized. Since the report was designed expressly for the use of the management, the expenses were divided into what he called "controllable and non-controllable" expenses—one of the first uses of those terms which are now so familiar in flexible budget discussions.[195]

The well-known author of *The Science of Accounts*, H. C. Bentley of Boston, had somewhat the same idea on this subject as the writer in the *Cyclopedia of Accounting*. He suggested that individual burden expense accounts be maintained until the end of the month when they were all to be closed to a manufacturing expense account.[196] At the close of the same month, if profits were ascertained monthly, or at close of each fiscal period otherwise, the manufacturing expense account was closed to manufacturing account—a sort of work in process account. In addition, a comparative monthly analysis of the charges in the manufacturing expenses account was to be kept, on a cumulative as well as monthly basis. This analysis was to be presented to the management for inspection and control purposes. Bentley thus obtained, for all practical purposes, the same objective as a system of subsidiary accounts.

Although a number of authorities had (prior to 1910) touched on the technique of using controlling accounts in cost accounting, no one had given it a comprehensive treatment. This neglect was remedied in an article by L. H. Bosher which appeared in 1912. In evolving his system this American accountant first mentioned that, if desired, a separate expense account for each department could be set up on the ledger, to which would be posted all expenditures peculiar to that department. For those miscellaneous expenses not applicable to any certain division of the business, individual accounts should be established, which were, however, closed out monthly to the departmental accounts.[197] This treatment was comparable to that of Deighton, but Bosher made a suggested possible improvement which could be adopted to save some work. He recommended that a manufacturing expense control account be set up on the general ledger to which would be charged all the miscellaneous factory expenses mentioned above; a subsidiary expense ledger or book would show the sub-accounts, and give the required detail. In this way only one credit would have to be made when the miscellaneous control account was closed to the departmental accounts. In addition, if there were many departmental expenses, control accounts should be set up for the different departments, with subsidiary accounts in a separate ledger. The condensation could be carried still further; that is to say, just one expense control account could be established on the general ledger if desired, and all the details kept in a subsidiary ledger. Bosher stated that the last practice was perhaps best for general use.[198]   But this author was only partially satisfied with this clear-cut method of handling the actual burden costs.   He desired another technique for handling all the costs applied to the goods in process account.   For this purpose he suggested a "production account," for all intents and purposes an offsetting account to the goods in process account.   It was used not only for burden costs applied but also material and direct labor applied.   He thus came quite close to the idea of a burden applied account, the only difference being that his "production account" included the prime cost elements as well as burden.   It would at least be easy for later authorities to take his suggestion and add the necessary details.   Since it was his theory that the factory ledger should not be closed monthly, but that statements should be drawn up at monthly intervals, he felt it was necessary to have some procedure for making his manufacturing costs accounts balance within themselves; that is, to be able to draw off a monthly trial balance.   With this end in view he proposed, in case all the actual costs for a month were not applied in full, that the unapplied balance be carried forward to the next month by making a journal entry in which a deferred charges account was debited and expenses not applied account was credited.   Later, when the excess of costs was finally applied, the entry would be reversed.   He did not consider the possibility of overapplication, seeming to think that such a balance would never exist.   Again this came very close to the modern technique, lacking only the finer points.

In his 1913 work, J. L. Nicholson explained a technique for handling the burden element of cost very similar to that discussed by some of his United States predecessors, but differing in some respects.   It was his recommendation that individual indirect factory expenses be charged during a month to separate accounts set up for the purpose.   These postings would usually come from either the cash book or purchase journal.

> At the end of the month they are credited with the balance of the account, unless part of same is to be treated as a deferred charge. The overhead account is charged each month, through a journal entry, with the items composing the indirect expenses, and is credited through the fixed overhead percentage with the total amount applied to the various production orders and cost sheets.   The balance, if a debit, shows the undistributed portion of the overhead, which means that the fixed percentage added to the labor cost was not

sufficient to cover the indirect expenses. When there is a credit balance, however, it shows that the percentage allowed was more than sufficient. In either event, the percentage to be used for the next period should be adjusted in accordance with the information thus disclosed.[199]

Nicholson did not discuss at that time what should be done with the balance, if any.

Writing a few years later, C. H. Scovell was not so indefinite as Nicholson as to what should be done with the balance unapplied or overapplied. It was his theory that such a sum should be closed to the profit and loss account, since it usually represented a cost due to idle capacity.[200] A widely read bulletin of the Federal Trade Commission, published in the same year, expressed the same idea, but was much more explicit as to the technique for handling the under or over absorbed sum. After pointing out that the volume of business done by most firms fluctuated considerably as between the different months of a year, it suggested that burden rates be set which would be based on a year's volume instead of the next month. But this would cause the amount of burden absorbed to fluctuate also as between months. What should be done with the under or over applied figure each month? "The method of doing this is to establish a Reserve for Overhead, and credit this account with the reduction in cost during the busy season, and charge it with the increase in cost during the dull season."[201] While the exact technique for doing this was not illustrated, this reserve for overhead account seemed to contain the gist of an over and under absorbed burden account.

The next year, 1917, found C. E. Woods recommending that an "overhead account" be set up both as a control account for the various individual burden costs, which were detailed in a subsidiary record, and as an account which should be credited for burden applied. It was thus a combination account. If, at the end of a particular month, the amount of burden incurred were say $100,000, and the amount applied only $97,000, "there would be $3,000 to be disposed of in either of two ways; first it can be taken from this account and wiped out through profit and loss, or, second, a 'holding account' can be created under 'Assets-Inventory,' in order to allow time for showing whether or not the percentage basis for overhead would be undistributed expense that remained as an asset."[202] Woods thus secured the desired control over the burden element of cost through the use of just one mixed control account. He had also suggested at least two methods of handling the underapplied overhead. Later authorities added other suggestions to the two mentioned by this American.

In the same year, F. E. Webner elaborated upon his earlier "accruing manufacturing expense." It turned out to be merely a control account for burden expenditures, and charges from the journal. The details were kept on an "expense analysis" sheet which was subdivided into as many subsidiary divisions as required. The expense analysis sheet was in reality an expense ledger, but it was all on one page.[203]   Departmental distribution was carried out on another large columnar form.

Also in 1917, A. Hamilton Church, who had first given his views in 1901, summarized more completely his preferred method of handling the burden items. The charges were first to be debited to individual accounts, just as he had previously recommended; but periodically, through the means of a burden journal, they were to be transferred to departmental burden accounts, as debits in total. From the departmental burden accounts, which were not control accounts, the amounts applied to goods in process were to be transferred, this time through a manufacturing journal, to departmental manufacturing accounts, one for each department.[204]   Church thus used a rather roundabout device for securing the desired control over burden without actually using true control accounts at all. This might have proved more cumbersome in practice than some of the methods or techniques already recommended.

A use of a pure burden applied account was described by C. M. Bigelow the year after the First World War. This authority, writing on the accounting for woodworking shops, recommended that the actual burden items be individualized on the general ledger, just as so many writers before him had done. But in order to keep track of the amounts applied to work in process, he suggested that such credits be handled in a separate account called "reserve for factory burden." The total of this account from time to time could easily, according to him, be contrasted with the actual outlays as indicated by their respective amounts.[205]   Although Bigelow's reserve account was not in itself a control account, it served the same purpose as the now familiar burden costs applied account.

A somewhat unique technique for handling burden was provided in the uniform cost system devised for the cover paper manufacturers.[206]   Three accounts were particularly pertinent: (1) departmental burden accounts, (2) one overearned and unearned burden account, and (3) a burden variance account. The first named accounts were used to collect the departmental fixed charges, supplies, indirect labor, and various service department charges. A budgetary estimate of the amount that should be charged to the departmental account was then entered right under the title of the account. This step was taken, of course, at the beginning of a period. At the end of a period (length not specified) an inspection was made of the amount applied and the budget estimate. If the budgetary figure exceeded the amount applied, the difference was considered unearned, and was debited to the overearned and underearned burden account, while the departmental burden account was credited for the same difference. If, on the other hand, the amount applied exceeded the budget figure, the reverse of the preceding entry was made. After making whatever entry appropriate, the difference between the debit and credit sides of the departmental burden account was closed to the burden variance account. The balance of the burden variance account, as well as the balance remaining in the overearned and unearned burden account, (after all departmental burden accounts had been handled in the way described) were closed to profit and loss at the end of a period. Obviously the method described was useful not only for recording the actual burden incurred, but also in maintaining a sort of budgetary control over the various items.

While developing nothing new in regard to the control accounts for burden, D. C. Eggleston did make the point that whenever a firm came to the end of a fiscal period with a large amount of burden undistributed such a sum should not be closed directly to profit and loss, but should be allocated over work in process, finished goods on hand, and cost of sales account by means of some "flat rate."[207] Trifling amounts, on the other hand, could be carried forward from year to year without any sacrifice of accuracy. For this purpose he suggested the by then familiar reserve for overhead account.

In the same year, J. P. Jordan and G. L. Harris accurately described the philosophy underlying the use of what they called a "burden credit account."[208] While the idea of such an account was not new, they were the first to explain adequately the real reason for such accounts. Incidentally, their burden credit account was not a pure control account, since they recommended that one be set up for each department (productive) of the factory. In this way they could be used as opposites to the burden (actual) accounts. But why should they be adopted? It was the opinion of these Americans that if the burden accounts themselves were credited when burden was applied to cost of production, "all control for statement purposes would be lost, and a continuous comparison of burdens throughout the year would be impossible. . . . Therefore, the credits to each operating burden account should be placed in the Burden Credit account, in order to leave the Burden account free for adjustments only and to accumulate each month the actual burden incurred as the year goes by."[209] The burden credit accounts were to be posted only once a month, preferably through one compound journal entry. What about the probable differences between the burden accounts and the burden credit accounts during the year as profit and loss statements were prepared? On such statements the difference only was to be shown for each department, either as underapplied or overapplied. In cases where there were so many departments as to clutter up the statement with the individual balances, it would be satisfactory to prepare a schedule of them and show only the net difference on the face of the income statement itself, as an addition or subtraction from the gross profit shown thereon.[210]

Some time later (1921), the American authority, G. H. New-love, described a technique for maintaining budgetary control over burden costs, somewhat with the same purpose in mind as that developed by the paper cover manufacturers. It was his suggestion that after the indirect expense estimate had been compiled at the first of a period that the total be debited to a "manufacturing expense in goods in process" account, while the offsetting credit was to be made to a "factory expense" account, the latter being also used to accumulate the actual expenditures or charges during a period.[211] As the burden was applied, an entry was made charging the goods in process account, and crediting the manufacturing expense in goods in process account. Under or over absorption of burden would be shown very distinctly if the factory expense account showed either a debit or credit balance at the end of the period. On the other hand, if a balance existed in the manufacturing expense in goods in process account at the close of a period, it would reveal "that certain manufacturing expenses have been charged or are yet to be charged on the cost cards of the unfinished orders, jobs or contracts."[212]

Even as late as 1921, the English industrial accounting authorities were still stressing the idea of independent cost accounting arrangements,[213] although such writers as E. T. Elbourne had developed methods of interlocking the "works" accounts with the financial accounts.[214] These were cumbersome as compared with the American techniques. There was also a great deal of overlapping in the accounting entries although Elbourne considered that feature somewhat desirable, mainly because of internal control and convenience. The actual working of his burden control system was very complex; the essential elements, however, can be described without introducing too many details. A "works disbursement suspense account" was set up on the financial ledger, to which was posted all items pertaining to the burden expenditures, as well as a considerable number of other matters. On the works ledger there were, first, several works expenses allocation accounts corresponding to certain standing orders. The allocations called for in those accounts were transferred to a works expense distribution account as a debit. This account was in turn credited with the distributions as reported by an abstract of charges to production. Factory expenses incurred outside of standing orders (which were, it will be remembered, handled in the works expenses allocation accounts) were set up in separate accounts. Some of the items for which no standing orders were prepared were depreciation, interest on capital, loss of tools, material handling expenses, etc. The works ledger had its own sales account, profit and loss account, and many others. It should be mentioned, however, that the financial ledger accounts were rather condensed, even though the information carried there was duplicated to some extent in the works ledger.[215]

In the United States in the same year the authors of *Business Costs*[216] illustrated the coding of expense accounts where one control account was maintained, with departmental items individualized In addition, certain miscellaneous accounts which were periodically closed out to the manufacturing and selling expenses controls were also charted. This practically completed the development of the control aspect of actual burden expenditures or charges.[217]

By the middle of the 1920's, at least one American authority, J. L. Dohr, found it desirable to explain the use of a burden credit account and a burden adjustment account; the burden adjustment account was used to take care of any burden which had not by the end of the cost period been charged to cost of production.[218]

While all three of the necessary control accounts for burden (i.e., burden (actual), burden applied, and burden under or over applied) had been described here and there in cost literature before 1927, no one had given an adequate and careful combined exposition of the uses and advantages of the three. That deficiency was remedied by the American authority, G. H. Newlove, in his *Cost Accounting*, first published in 1927. In that work he recommended that three control accounts be established on the ledger, each supported by subsidiary accounts. The first was the actual burden control account; the second was called "burden-credit," and was used to record the totals of the monthly allocations of the burden element of cost to producing departments; the third was called "under and over-absorbed burden account," and in turn was used to control the monthly variations between burden incurred and burden applied. At the end of each month the burden credit account was closed to the under and over absorbed burden account. Proper supporting entries were to be made in the respective subsidiary ledgers. Provision was also made in the accounts for budgetary control over the fixed charges of the manufacturing establishment.[219] The structure for the control of burden was now complete; later authorities found it difficult to improve upon the flexibility and accurateness of this system.

PART IV. THE ALLOCATION OF BURDEN TO PRODUCT

The question of the allocation of burden has received perhaps more attention than any other single problem connected with cost accounting. C. B. Thompson, for example, in his *How to Find Factory Costs*, 1916, was led to state: "Indirect expense is one of the most important of all the accounts appearing on the books of the manufacturer. Methods of handling its distribution [he meant allocation] have given rise to more arguments than the problem of the descent of man. It is the rock upon which many a ship of industry has been wrecked. . . . "[220] Many writers, both practitioners and theorists, have had a part in keeping the flow of literature on the subject moving along at a fast pace. Beginning with the early 1870's, writers on industrial accounting began to take notice of the increasing importance which miscellaneous items of factory cost assumed in the computation of total cost. Up to that time, even though the burden element of cost had been mentioned (see Chapter II), it had not received adequate treatment. This apparent inadvertence began to be remedied by certain English accountants in the last quarter of the nineteenth century.

As far back as 1873, a Newcastle (England) accountant suggested that factory "establishment charges," as he called them, such as rent, taxes, and salaries should be allocated over the product turned out by a manufacturing firm in the ratio of "total cost"—meaning material, wages, and depreciation of tools.[221] Even before then, one authority had pointed out that the indirect costs should not be prorated at the same percentage over every department, since each division of a firm would not necessarily incur the same amount of those costs.[222]

Thomas Battersby made passing references to several methods of absorbing overhead.[223] First, it was his theory that practically every firm should be departmentalized.[224] For example, the power department accumulated its own charges, which in turn were apportioned over the product on the basis of indicated horsepower required in the different processes. Any costs which could not be departmentalized —now called "general burden items"—were to be applied to jobs by a uniform percentage based upon the amount of wages (direct and departmental) which had already been incurred. It is almost needless to mention that his entire system of costing was separate from the financial books. On these, the general expenses were transferred to the profit and loss account, as was customary in those early days. His discussion of allocation, therefore, was confined to the "cost ledger." This practice continued for several decades.

The unit of output method of allocating indirect expenses was foreshadowed by F. H. Carter's system, which he devised particularly for English mines and rock quarries.[225] Here the overhead items were collected on a separate cost sheet, one sheet for each month. These costs were then divided by the tons of rock or slate produced during the month; and the total cost of operating each level of the mine was obtained by adding to the wages a sum for general costs, in proportion to the tonnage taken out of each gallery or level. This method of costing was evidently in fairly wide use at the time, since several economic historians have referred to it.[226]

In America, Henry Metcalfe seems to have been one of the first authorities to treat this particular topic with much consideration. His costing arrangement was external to the financial books, but he suggested, nevertheless, several new aspects. After first observing that a great many firms at the time did not take any account at all of miscellaneous charges in their costing, he went on to explain that such a practice, in his judgment, generally caused much harm.[227] It was his opinion that the general burden items should be covered in costs by adding a certain percentage, and here he listed four methods. They were: (1) an arbitrary charge, depending on the circumstances of each case; (2) a percentage of the gross cost of the job; (3) a percentage on the value of the labor with or without an additional percentage on the value of the material; (4) a price, varying with the time actually employed on the job. The last method was his favorite, mainly because it was his theory that the miscellaneous costs bore a closer relationship to the time element than to the value of labor or materials or both. He mentioned that William Sellers and Company, a prominent firm, used the fourth method. In addition, he believed that the incidental expenses were mainly incurred for the purpose of making labor more effective, and had practically no connection with the amount or value of the material used on a job. Evidently it was common at the time to use the total of prime costs as a basis for allocation, and he wanted to end that practice.[228] It should be recalled, however, that Metcalfe was an army ordnance officer; he was interested primarily, therefore, in cost allocation situations in which general burden would be rather small in amount.

Metcalf continued with some additional details of his preferred method. A "cost factor" (his term) was to be determined for each department, made up of distributed general burden items, standing order charges, and each department's own individual expenses. This total, divided by the number of days each department worked the past year, gave the "factor" desired. This amount per day was then allocated over jobs passing through each department, on the basis of the number of days devoted to each job. This factor would not ordinarily vary much, according to Metcalfe; he compared it with the actuarial probability feature of life insurance, that is, over a period of time a reliable rate could be developed.[229] Incidentally, he also made the point that since low-priced labor usually cost more to watch and supervise than high-priced workmen, this was an additional reason why the quantity of labor should be used as the divisor instead of the cost of labor. The difference would be in the reverse direction if a firm used the cost of labor. As Metcalfe stated it: "you would have to charge more for dear labor than for cheap labor."[230]

In England, Emile Garcke and J. M. Fells were arguing about the same time along similar lines. They, too, observed that many factories did not make any attempt to allocate indirect costs over the jobs or product turned out,[231] preferring to ascertain prime costs only. This system, according to them, had only simplicity in its favor, and a more correct costing arrangement must necessarily provide for the apportionment of the incidental expenditures. These two authorities were rather hazy as to how such items were to be allocated on the books, even though it was their idea that the commercial and cost ledgers should be connected, or tied together. They recognized this deficiency in their discussion, however, and gave as their reason for the inadequacy of their treatment the fact that there was such a multiplicity of methods in vogue at the time. Evidently it was their theory, although they did not so state, that the factory overhead element was to be handled in the same fashion as materials and wages, so far as the ledger transactions were concerned. What methods of allocation could be used? They listed three: (1) cost of wages expended upon a job; (2) cost of wages and materials used on a job; or (3) the time of laborers spent upon a job. The third method was to be used only in certain instances, but in those cases it was the only correct one. Here, also, they made the same point that Metcalfe had, that is, that the indirect items incurred often were intimately related to the number of hours a job or process required. Garcke and Fells also made certain proposals as to a machine charge for depreciation and repairs to the equipment. It was suggested in this connection that the total working time of different pieces of machinery be estimated and as the machinery was used a debit was to be made to the works orders in accordance with the amount of time that expired. "Plant debit notes" were to be filled out daily by some responsible individual showing the number of the ma-chines, the orders employed on, and the time employed. These were summarized at the end of a week or month onto a "plant debit sum-mary." Again, the specified ledger technique was not noted. They did, however, mention that if this practice were followed, the depre-ciation would not appear, as such, on the profit and loss account, but would be included in the cost of goods manufactured. Incidentally, these authorities were here more concerned with the proper recording of plant assets than they were with the burden allocation problem. All of the preceding material was in their chapter on "Fixed Capital." In summary, it may be stated that these two authors did not devote any large amount of discussion to the problem of allocation; it seemed to be their opinion that the whole subject was more or less a matter for each firm to decide for itself, and they did not appear overanxious to get too involved in either the theoretical or practical aspects of burden application. The following is indicative of their views: "The principals of a business can always judge what percentage of gross profits upon cost is necessary to cover fixed establishment charges and interest on capital."[232]

The next year, 1888, G. L. Fowler, writing in this country on the cost records needed in a foundry, deplored the usual practice of adding an average percentage to the prime cost of castings to obtain the total cost.[233] Averages, according to him, could only be used where all the products turned out were uniform and standard; in all other cases, they should not be adopted. To avoid such an error, he recommended the use of certain formulas and ratios, which need not be elaborated here. It is sufficient to state that, in the final analysis, the ratios devolved to a percentage which was to be multiplied by the molders' wages. Adding this figure to the molders' wages and cost of iron gave the total cost of a particular casting. Fowler did not claim to be the originator of the plan; he attributed it to a German, A. Messerschmidt, who had been using it for some seventeen years. According to Fowler, it was the most accurate and flexible system that had been devised for costing foundry work. He gave, however, no information as to the ledger treatment of the burden element.

G. P. Norton, a prominent English textile mill accountant, gave the present subject only a passing notice. The reason is not difficult to find. Obviously, in a textile mill, the costing would be on a process basis rather than a job or production order basis. His problem would be centered, therefore, around the departmentalization of burden rather than its allocation to specific units of production. As will be discussed in more detail in a later section, he was unusually clear in his treatment of the latter subject. In certain instances, however, the plant might produce piece goods. Wherever that situation obtained it was Norton's suggestion that the nonmanufacturing charges (in the sense of nondepartmental items) be equally distributed over the work done in each division of the mill. He pointed out that some other base might be used, such as wages paid or cost of materials used, but that would necessitate additional calculations, and might not give any more accurate results. In summary, the equal basis "will be found the safest and most reliable method."[234]

In regard to engineering establishments, a man who described himself as "A General Manager" examined in 1890 the merits of a constant base for allocating indirect costs as contrasted with the direct labor cost base. The direct labor cost technique was better, in his opinion, taking all factors into consideration.[235] In the next year, 1891, the Englishman, Sir John Mann, published his significant pamphlet entitled *Notes on Cost Records*. In it the quantity or value of material basis for allocation was dismissed as being entirely inaccurate. The prime cost basis also generally proved fallacious, according to him. Incidentally, he gave some examples of the possible misconceptions which might result from the use of the prime cost base. Then, too, where workers were not paid the same rate of wages, and such instances were frequent, there would be considerable danger in using the direct labor cost as a basis. All in all, it was Mann's theory, just as it was that of Metcalfe and Garcke and Fells, that the labor time element was the most important factor. The indirect items, therefore, should be allocated on that basis. This authority also made some general comments on the possible desirability of using a machine hour rate for more correct results. This suggestion may be the first reference to that particular method, which later became so popular.[236] Mann also suggested the practice of making periodical credits to the "oncost" accounts and debiting the cost ledger account entitled "wages and materials."

Obviously, the subject of burden allocation had received quite a bit of emphasis in this relatively early period. Writers had begun to recognize the importance of its careful apportionment, but most of them really did not have an adequate grasp of the costing theory underlying such a division. They were positive that it needed allocation, but were not so sure of their reasoning, nor the method of handling it on the cost records. No one had explained clearly the ledger treatment, mainly because of the extramural costing arrangements which obtained in most instances. Beginning with the decade of the 1890's, however, the flow of literature quickened, and many thousands of pages have been written on the subject since then. A great majority of this material merely duplicated what had already been said many times. After a survey of a large part of this mass of theoretical and practical observations, one is forced to conclude that each speaker or writer felt it essential that he cover the subject as though no one had ever examined it before. This in part explains why there have been so many opinions handed down. In developing the thinking on this subject from 1890 on, then, the central aim here will be to point out only the major contributions, brushing aside practically all the extensive repetitive remarks which have been made from time to time by almost innumerable authorities.

An unsigned article in *The Accountant* recommended a few years later that the management expenses and depreciation be spread between the cost sheets either in proportion to a percentage of gross profit, or in proportion to the number of hours the job consumed.[237] The former was one of the very few suggestions of that sort. Obviously, the use of the gross profit,whatever that meant, would usually give entirely different results than the second base mentioned. This is again illustrative of the carelessness with which many early cost accountants treated the subject of allocation. Battersby had proposed a similar scheme several years before.[238]

The English author of *Commercial Organisation of Factories,* J. S. Lewis, expressed well the prevailing attitude of the cost writers of the 1890's. Lewis gave definite proof of the statement previously made above that cost theorists of the time were not interested in the ledger handling of the burden element of cost.[239] He stated: "For the mere purposes of commercial bookkeeping . . . it matters . . . little in which way the general and shop establishment charges are dealt with, so long as they are eventually paid for out of profits made on the work, that is to say—it matters little whether they appear in the books as chargeable to general revenue or are allocated to the several items of work in progress in the shops."[240] He thought very little of the latter idea, however. It was his main contention that the cost books should be kept purely on a prime cost basis, except at inventory dates, "so that the naked truth of the cost of operations which have taken place in the shops shall plainly appear on the face of the accounts." When making estimates for bids, however, the firm should have very elaborate figures as to overhead available, in order that the proper amount could be added to the direct wages which would be incurred on the proposed project. For this purpose, Lewis gave involved details concerning departmentalization, and the relative expensiveness of different types of machinery. In the foundry department, if there were one, the indirect charges should be based on the cost of the materials used, since that was such a large proportion of the total cost. Another possibility in this connection would be to use the output of cleaned castings as a basis. Under this system of prime costing it was necessary to add a percentage to the labor and material only when the inventory was taken at the end of a fiscal period. For this purpose Lewis suggested a "suspense" (his term) account arrangement, which after a new year had started, was reversed, and the books continued under the usual prime cost basis.

This noted English authority did not, however, entirely ignore the rival technique. He recognized that many large firms did allocate currently their shop expenses over the product or jobs finished. This was, according to him, an objectionable procedure, needlessly complicated and troublesome, and requiring entirely too much work. (As a matter of fact, it was much superior to Lewis' own preferred method.) But how was the "needlessly complicated" method to be carried out, in case a reader wanted to use it? The first step was to arrive at an approximate rate for establishment charges, based upon "each class of labor, until sufficient new data are forthcoming to fix the percentage of such charges definitely."[241] Certain special prime cost books would be needed also, in which there would be a column for establishment charges. At the end of each month, each job would be examined and a sum entered in the special column on account of the indirect items. This amount would vary according to the types of labor employed on the different jobs. All of this could not be done directly; it was necessary to have a charges journal as a book of original entry. An entry was made in that journal crediting an establishment charges account for each shop or division of the firm, and debiting the order sheets in the prime cost books. In this way all items finished would move into the warehouse at their total shop cost. It must be remembered, though, that all of this was external to the "counting house" (his term) records. The establishment charges accounts were debited with proportions of the actual expenditures, and thus if there were any balance at the end of a fiscal period it would indicate either under or over absorption. If they had debit balances they were to be treated as assets; if the reverse situation obtained, they were liabilities. Lewis did not explain, however, just what happened after that, being content with "what may be an asset in one year, as the result of the charges being fixed too low, may be transformed into a liability the next, as a result of their being fixed too high."[242] In case the establishment charges rate was changed, and Lewis seemed to think it very often would be, he thought it absolutely necessary to revalue all the goods in process and finished stock. Just why he did not state. Two other special journals were to be used for that purpose, called the "stock survey journal" and the "goods in process survey journal." Each of these had two sets of columns for material, labor, establishment charges, and miscellaneous. The first set was entitled "old value," and the second set was given the name "new value." The revaluation debit or credit, as the case might be, was carried through the profit and loss account. Only the totals of the different columns needed to be posted. Again Lewis was very indefinite about how this affected the stock ledgers, commercial ledger, etc.[243] In a concluding remark he mentioned that very few firms in his experience checked their so-called prime costs by a double entry system; most of them relied upon "figures arrived at by the highly objectionable system of single entry."[244] Whether Lewis realized it or not, neither of the techniques he himself described would be classified as double entry. Did he intend to include his own within the "highly objectionable" group?

A year after Lewis wrote, H. M. Lane, in this country, was arguing that burden should not be allocated *en bloc*, but should be divided into what he called a "plant charge," and ordinary items. The plant charge was an hourly or daily charge for the use of machine tools. It included interest on investment, depreciation, and the machine's share of the distributed power cost.[245] The figure derived in this way would necessarily vary for each item of equipment, but when once established, would not usually change very much. It was to be added on to the cost of a job in exactly the same way as workmen's pay, that is, at so much per hour or day. This idea clearly foreshadowed the later production factor method so ably expounded by A. Hamilton Church. The ordinary burden items were to be allocated on the by then familiar direct labor time basis.[246]

The idea of a plant or tool charge, although sound in principle, was not so easy to carry out as Lane had intimated. F. A. Halsey, the industrial engineer, questioned the divisor which was ordinarily used, namely, the number of hours a plant remained open in a year. It was his contention that large pieces of machinery were often idle, and that factor would have to be considered.[247] Also, Halsey felt it was "grotesque" to charge the same rate per hour on the labor of a fifty-dollar grinding machine, as on a fifty-thousand-dollar boring mill.[248] Lane's "plant charge" would remedy this defect to some extent, but Halsey was primarily criticizing all the many authorities who did not make any adjustment at all. In spite of the increased accuracy which a plant charge would allow, Halsey was not, in the end, convinced that the "formidable addition to the system of keeping books" was worth the effort. However, he seemed to reverse himself when he stated that "at the same time it is very easy to exaggerate the importance of these things. . . . I do not think they are of such vast importance as a good many people think."[249]

H. M. Norris also avoided a definite conclusion as to the advisability of making an individual tool charge.[250] Each firm would have to decide the matter for itself. He agreed with Halsey that it was rather important wherever a factory had considerable light and heavy machinery—he meant low priced and expensive tools. Otherwise he did not believe the extra cost of bookkeeping was worth the increased accuracy. Both he and Halsey had a tendency to overstate the degree of difficulty involved. According to the former it was "stupendous," and the latter's views have already been noted. In general, Norris contended that no method was perfect, and all gave only approximate results, so he did not favor the more elaborate techniques. This was somewhat a defeatist attitude, and cost accounting would still be in its former low state if all authorities had followed his thinking on the subject.

Some time later an English Chartered Accountant, E. Andrade, presented a new viewpoint as to the technique of allocating burden charges.[251] In order to arrive at a "fair and equitable basis" it was his suggestion that the different overhead items be statistically analyzed as to their relation to cost. For example, the superintending charge should be proportioned according to the direct labor time worked on a particular job or contract; the same basis should be used for depreciation, rent rates and taxes. Interest paid out and discounts allowed should be apportioned on the basis of turnover—he did not mention, however, what sort of turnover. The wages of pay roll employees varied with the amount of wages disbursed on any job; while salaries of storekeepers, and freight and cartage, were to be divided according to the amount of materials used. Any additional overhead items might be allocated by a similar analysis as to their true nature. This technique, although perhaps more accurate than a general averaging process, would require considerably more attention on the part of the cost clerks. Andrade did not discuss the ledger treatment of the overhead charges, but he did give an illustration of an "apportionment book" which was to be used for dividing the general expenditures.

Another Chartered Accountant, G. E. Goode, recommended that for a firm which conducted continuous processing operations, the manufacturing incidental costs might be apportioned according to the (1) money volume of sales or (2) the weight of the respective products which were sold.[252] The recording of the weight of sales was an integral part of his system; proper columns were provided on the books. This authority did not commit himself as to which of the two possibilities was the best, leaving the matter to be decided by each establishment. Incidentally, this is one of the first references to the fact that the allocation of burden for a processing firm might be different than that for a job order business. Previously, most of the discussion had centered around so-called engineering organizations.

Goode's countryman, J. MacNaughton, also dealt with a processing firm—paper mill accounting.[253] It had been his experience that the "fixed charges" (his term) formed a large part of the cost of production of paper, and also that such charges remained fairly constant no matter whether a large or small quantity of paper was made during a certain period. Since this fact was established, he recommended that the previous year's total fixed charges be divided by the number of days the machines were in operation the previous year, in order to arrive at a per-day charge for the current period. This would give, however, the amount per day to charge if only one machine was operated or one type of paper was made. If, as was usual, more than one machine was used, the fixed charge on a daily basis would have to be divided among them either on the basis of their relative output, or with regard to the expense of preparing the materials used. MacNaughton showed a clear understanding of the problem involved, although he was not very explicit as to details of his technique. It was his idea that the "index of a mill is the capacity of production of its machines in a given time, say per day or week, and hence the cost for fixed charges is based upon machine time." This is another fairly early reference to the use of the machine hour method for allocating overhead charges, with emphasis on the total practical capacity of the machines as a base. MacNaughton's method was obviously much more accurate than the ordinary averaging technique, and was in general superior to most of the discussions of the time.

In this country the machine tool charge principle continued to receive considerable attention. In a book which attempted to summarize the accounting methods used by prominent firms of a manufacturing nature, it was stated that each machine should be loaded with its own cost factors as well as an arbitrary sum for general factory charges and dieroom expenses.[254] In case, however, any particular tool or machine was subject to heavy repairs or breakage, its percentage or amount should be raised arbitrarily and some others reduced, so as to leave the same total. One accountant agreed that each work-producing tool had a certain charge standing against it, which it must necessarily earn if the firm were going to stay out of debt.[255] This authority went on to state, too, that if a tool was idle, "this indebtedness is cancelled or paid by the profits gained from work produced by other tools which are earning money while the idler is eating his head off."[256] The method advocated had proved entirely satisfactory, according to the writer, and was conducive to much greater accuracy than the common direct labor cost basis, even though both were still somewhat arbitrary. In another section of the same work it was mentioned that the Hyatt Roller Bearing Company used the number of employees working during a month as a basis for allocating the burden items.[257] Under this method the percentage would change practically every month, but even then the company found that the margin of error between the actual overhead and the amount applied to the "flat cost" (his term) figures was usually less than one percent; the estimates were thus surprisingly accurate.

In a series of articles which appeared in 1901, A. Hamilton Church developed his later famous "scientific production center" technique for allocating burden items. This noted authority first worked in England, but moved to the United States about 1900. He did not present an entirely new approach even though he called it the "ideal system." In fact, it was for the most part a great elaboration upon the machine hour method, which had been mentioned by several prior authorities. Church's procedure was so intimately bound up with the problem of handling idle time that only the strictly pertinent features will be discussed at this point, leaving to another section most of the details. In addition he devoted some space to a criticism of the prevailing allocation methods; these dyslogistic remarks, however, need not be examined here. The first interesting feature of Church's new technique was concerned with the proper incidence of shop charges. It was his idea that these could be narrowed down in large part to six or seven "factors," such as land, building, and power, to give three examples. That is to say, a large proportion of indirect charges were not so general as commonly believed. In fact, he would subdivide practically all these charges, leaving only a relatively small amount to be divided on a strictly arbitrary basis. This narrowing down was to be carried only so far as was profitable, and each firm would have to decide that for itself. After the "factors" had been determined, the plant was to be divided into what he called "production centers." These were not necessarily departments in the ordinary interpretation of the term; they might be a series of machines or workbenches. What they actually were did not matter so much. It was more important to make some separation of the producing units within the plant. After this had been done, the machines or centers were charged with their proper proportion of the "factors" and general items. The division was to be on the basis of floor space, number of employees, value of equipment, or some other logical base, depending upon the nature of the charge.

The machines or production centers were to be credited with work turned out or completed each month, based upon a "normal" number of hours for the month. Jobs were to be charged on the basis of machine hour time elapsing on each operation. Obviously, if a normal base were used and the machines were idle any part of the month, all the charges would not be absorbed. This difference was to be taken care of through a "supplementary rate" (his term), which will be explained in more detail in a later section of this chapter. In regard to the allocation of "unfactored" charges and the unallocated charges due to idle equipment, it was Church's suggestion that they be divided on an hour basis rather than an hour-value basis. The reason for this was that the "incidence of the charges cannot be considered as varying with the value of the different machines, but rather as pressing equally on all work done in the shop hour by hour, irrespective of whatever machine it may be done on."[258] Such was the essence of Church's system. It was soon hailed as the greatest step forward which had been taken up to the time, and many cost authorities later on drew heavily upon his suggestions. He himself added to the fine points of the technique in books and articles which he published in later years. As will be described in another section of this chapter, however, parts of his theory were subjected to considerable criticism beginning with the period around 1910-1912. But for the decade intervening, his work was looked upon as the last word on the problem. As a matter of record, though, it is doubtful whether many manufacturing firms actually adopted his system of apportioning burden charges; by and large many of them continued to use a percentage on wages technique, or perhaps labor time.[259] Church himself admitted that the former would often yield satisfactory results if proper precautions were taken to vary the incidence of the charges according to classes of work and types of employees. It had to be confined, however, to shops or plants which satisfied certain conditions. The scientific production center method was to be used where there were a great number of complex factors to be considered; no simple system could be devised to handle adequately an intricate situation, according to him.

David Cowan, writing in the same year, gave a good summary of the English thinking around the turn of the century.[260] He mentioned a "machine charge" and discussed some of the difficulties which would have to be handled in case it was used. In general, however, it was his opinion that there were few instances where it would be needed. "In an engineering shop making a variety of heavy products, in the

present state of the art of shop-management, such a state of accounting
is neither possible nor desirable. In the case where products are much
alike, and specialized, it is unnecessary."[261] This left out a few firms,
and Cowan was not convinced at all that machine charges should
form part of the technique of allocating overhead items. His view
should be contrasted with that in this country at about the same time;
it is a further illustration of the general attitude toward cost theory in
England as compared with the United States. Cowan listed and compared critically seven methods of allocation which he stated were in
general use in his country at the time. These were: (1) a percentage
on the prime cost of the work; (2) a percentage on the values of direct
labor, only, entering into the prime cost; (3) a percentage computed
on the values of direct labor, and a second percentage computed on the
values of materials; (4) averaging the rates paid for direct labor all
over the shop, this average rate being increased sufficiently to cover
the overhead; (5) a constant charge, at so much per hour, on the
quantities of direct labor, in addition to the rates actually paid to the
workers for such labor; (6) an average charge of so much per man
per day; (7) an arbitrary charge depending on the circumstances of
each case. It was his opinion that the labor quantities method
would prove most satisfactory. The general burden items should be
distributed to the producing departments on some equitable bases, and
then the whole of the overhead charges allocated to product turned out
on the basis of the hours spent by direct workers on each contract
or job. He called this charge a "factor," but it had no relation to
Church's "production factor." Cowan was considerably in advance of
his contemporaries in regard to the ledger treatment of burden, but
he added little new along the line of allocation procedures, contenting
himself with a summary of existing practices. He did mention, however, that each department of the firm should have an individual rate
per hour, unless the product was uniform or highly specialized. In
such cases a "consolidation" (his term) rate might be used without
great loss of accuracy. He made it clear, however, that there was always danger in such a practice. In connection with this topic, Cowan
mentioned a doubtful indirect advantage, which, so far as the present
writer can ascertain, was unique. To quote:

> By thus consolidating these charges [burden], and loading the
> products with oncost at one uniform all-round rate, a kind of natural
> selection is fostered [Darwinian influence on cost accounting?],
> which sifts out, from the work tendered for, that class for which

the establishment, as a whole, is most suited; since the orders for these products whereon the average load of oncost is an excessive burden will gradually gravitate to some other shop, whilst those that are undercharged will be placed with the concern tendering on these lines. This may at the outset be an apparent disadvantage for a time, but if the management is alive to the effects of such a policy, and if it devises special means for the more economical production of these special orders, the at one time small general engineering shop is now in a fair way of being transformed into a factory for special products, and where at least components and parts may to some extent be manufactured—not made.[262]

This viewpoint is contrary to practically every other authority who has written on the evils of averaging. Cowan did not mention the fact that while the evolution to a specialized plant was taking place the firm might fail on account of doing business perhaps for years at below cost. Then, too, when would the evolving process stop? Evidently not until the business was producing only one article, if it lasted that long. He did not describe the difference between "manufacture" and "made" as used in his last sentence. Ordinarily the two words are used synonymously.

Thus many authorities, before 1902, had decided that the direct labor time or quantity basis was the best all-round method to use for apportioning overhead items to product. On the other hand, the two Canadian writers, Eddis and Tindall, reached the conclusion that the cost of labor was the most logical and accurate method. Their reason was centered around the fact that the labor employed was generally not of the same class, and that it would have to be reduced to a comparable basis by taking, say, a beginner's time as standard for performing a certain job, and letting the time of the more experienced employees be a multiple of that base. But, according to the Canadian authorities this would lead to a number of complications, and so long as this situation obtained it would be better to use the relative value of the direct labor.[263] Although they did not mention the matter, the direct labor basis was, of course, subject to just as important a defect in that it assumed that most of the overhead varied with the labor cost of a job or process; numerous experts before them had pointed that out.

Sir John Mann, writing in 1903, was inclined to hedge on the question as to which technique of allocation was the more accurate. After listing and discussing each of the ordinarily used methods, he continued by pointing out that all of them were compromises, and that no technique should be arbitrarily selected without a thorough examination of the peculiarities and special circumstances which might exist within the plant.[264] He also made the entirely sensible suggestion that it might even be wise in some instances to adopt different procedures in the different departments of the same firm, or even to go a step further and distribute different classes of overhead items by different methods. The latter had already been recommended previously by several authorities. Mann was not at all inclined to be dogmatic about allocation procedures; this viewpoint is to be contrasted with that of prior cost accountants. This authority also mentioned the "tool basis or machine rate" method, which in general had not received so much support in the hands of the English as it had in this country.

Not long after Mann's article in the *Encyclopaedia of Accounting* was published, H. L. C. Hall, an American, brought out his *Manufacturing Costs*, in which he followed the same tactics as Mann, that is, he did not care to assume the responsibility of deciding just which method was the best for most cases.[265] It was fairly obvious, however, that he did not think the scientific machine hour method, developed by Church, was worthy of much consideration; it could be used only in isolated cases. The tool charge idea, on the other hand, was treated carefully by Hall; he even discussed the idle time problem involved. This authority also was quite interested in departmentalization and in the spreading of overhead items among departments. He illustrated two "expense distribution sheets" which would be helpful.[266] Taken as a whole, Hall's treatment of the topic was typical of the period. While developing nothing new, he did give his readers a practical insight into the problems involved in burden allocation, and stressed the importance of proper bases being used.

J. H. Whitmore took Church's scientific machine rate theory of allocation and worked out the details of its application to specific cases. This was something that Church had not done. Church was more interested in the theoretical aspects of the method, and neglected to give much attention to the ledger treatment. Whitmore, while adding relatively little that was new to Church's proposals, did render American industrial accountants of the time a signal service in the series of articles which he wrote in 1906,[267] in that he gave attention to the debits and credits which had to be made. He was also a little more explicit as to the departmentalization of the charges, and the organization of the production centers. This American author did not follow Church, however, when it came to the distribution to departments of the factory general expenses. Whitmore suggested that the factory general expenses be proportioned by means of a "percentage corresponding to the ratio between the total machine rates in the department plus the total direct labor to operate the machines fully, and the amount of the factory general expenses; and this percentage is added in the cost accounts to the direct labor and machine rates of that department." Church, it will be remembered, had recommended an hourly charge basis for these items. The general charges peculiar to a single department were to be handled the same way. Whitmore's discussion, in general, was superior to the typical cost writer of the period under review. He was a great deal more thorough, and represented an advanced viewpoint in regard to costing theory.

The apportionment of overhead charges in a foundry received careful attention in 1908. In that year C. E. Knoeppel, an American practicing accountant, discussed the various proposals which had been advocated in the past, and finally concluded that an allocation on the basis of both tonnage produced and direct labor was the best.[268] The easiest way of doing this was to use a formula:

$$C_3 = \frac{(W \times M) + L + (W \times B_3A) + (L \times B_3B)}{W}$$

In this formula:
W = Weight produced per man per day
M = Metal costs
L = Amount paid to moulder per day
B_3 = Burden on direct labor B and tonnage A
C_3 = Cost per 100 pounds on tonnage and direct labor appointment

Knoeppel gave some rather lengthy illustrations of the use of his favored method and of other prevalent techniques. Incidentally, foundry costing received considerable attention throughout the first decade of the present century. Up until Knoeppel's time, however, the general technique for allocation had been the tonnage of castings produced.

The allocation of burden items continued to receive more and more attention as the years passed by, but the authorities who treated the subject duplicated each other's efforts and theories to a large degree. Gershom Smith, for example, gave an unusually precise description of the machine hour method in 1909.[269] In the same year J. L. Nicholson, a Certified Public Accountant, published his *Factory Organization and Costs* in which he devoted many pages to a theoretical discussion of the merits and disadvantages of some seven prevailing allocation methods. One of his observations was that in spite of all the stress which had been put on the subject by various cost experts, it had been his experience to find hundreds of firms without an adequate method of collecting and apportioning burden charges. He emphasized, as did many other writers, the importance of the overhead element of cost, and proceeded to give his ideas as to when any certain technique should be used. One of the methods which he suggested might be used with advantage, and which had received little publicity, was called the "new pay rate." The indirect general expenses were departmentalized and added to the expenses peculiar to the departments. The former were to be distributed to the departments according to the ratio of direct labor cost of each department.[270] After this had been done, the departmental expense rates were added to the rates of pay of the employees within the department. This combined burden and labor cost rate was to be charged to the product passing through the department by a process of multiplication of the time consumed by each worker on the operation or job, by the new rate. The addition of the materials consumed would give the total factory cost of the process or order. This technique, according to Nicholson, was admirably adapted to plants which did not need the careful control of the overhead items provided by some of the more involved systems. It saved a considerable amount of the expense of maintaining and operating a complicated costing arrangement, but should only be adopted in a factory which did not care for a sharp analysis of the cost of its products. Nicholson also proposed what he called a "new machine rate." This was a combined direct labor per hour and machine hour expense basis of apportionment. Products passing through a department would be charged with this consolidated rate according to the number of hours the machines were occupied on them. Adding on the cost of the materials would give the total cost of the product. This method should be used, according to Nicholson, only where most of the processes were performed on machinery of comparable expensiveness and size. The employees should also be paid comparable wages.[271] In concluding his discussion, Nicholson made the statement that the practical solution to the whole problem was centered around the proper departmentalization of the factory's products and divisions of production. He thought that departmentalization was the most important contribution which had been made toward the solving of the age-old question. It allowed for a wider choice of methods and at the same time localized a large part of the overhead items, which under nondepartmental systems would be proportioned by some general overall averaging technique. As has been pointed out, however, some of the earliest references to factory overhead, as an element of cost, emphasized the strategic importance of its proper departmentalization as a prerequisite to its allocation. Nicholson, therefore, was emphasizing an old concept.

In the same year that Nicholson wrote, A. Hamilton Church published a series of articles in which he added considerable detail to his earlier scientific machine-hour-production-factor method of apportioning burden.[272] The production factors were again accumulated, and production centers were established. The charges from these were to be debited, on a monthly basis, to a waste or balance account. This balance account ascertained the amount of machine rates not distributed to product. The machine earnings were then credited to the balance account and charged to what he called a monthly summary of works orders. Any sum left in the balance account was later also cleared to the monthly summary by means of his supplementary rate, which will be discussed in another section.[273] Only the ordinary machine rate was to be allocated to individual production orders. It was Church's idea that there would be rarely, if ever, any occasion to charge the orders with the supplementary rate. It would be possible to do so if the information were necessary, but since all "the elements of actual cost are already represented when we know the wages and machine time; . . . the ratio of utilized to unutilized capacity has no connection with any purpose for which detail costs are commonly required."[274] The ratio referred to in the quotation was, of course, the supplementary rate, and it was only to be shown on the summary of works orders, and not on the orders themselves. He discussed also the possibility of carrying this unallocated sum forward from month to month. Incidentally, all of Church's costing was external to the financial or general ledger. On the general ledger the overhead items were closed directly to profit and loss at the end of the fiscal period. The above discussion, by the way, should not be taken as a complete analysis of Church's system; he himself devoted several scores of pages to his recommendations and suggestions; only the gist of his method has been presented here.

Somewhat later, F. E. Webner, an American practicing cost accountant, synthesized all the important allocation methods in his *Factory Costs*. In this work he not only described the pertinent features of each technique but correlated each into a costing "plan," each of which took the name of the apportioning method used. Nicholson had attempted to do this same thing several years before, but had used a different basis. Webner, moreover, did not hesitate to recommend the conditions under which each plan should be used. In addition, this authority suggested one or two rather new ways of allocating the burden charges. For example, he discussed the "list percentage plan." Under this method the burden rate was to be expressed as a percentage of the list price (supposedly the selling price) of the various products manufactured. The rate itself was to be determined either by a test, by estimate, or by checking through past production records.[275] The tests were to be continued from time to time so as to keep the various elements of cost of each particular article at a fairly correct ratio to its "list price." Webner also introduced what he called the "sold hour plan."[276] This was to all intents and purposes a combined direct labor and overhead charge per hour to be added to the cost of the material consumed on the job or in the process. It can be compared with the "new machine rate" proposed by Nicholson, except that Nicholson's scheme contemplated a consolidated machine and direct labor hour charge. The sold hour plan, on the other hand, was based upon an average cost per hour of direct labor in a department plus a charge per hour for overhead items. As products passed through each department, then, they were loaded with this combined hourly charge depending upon how long the goods remained in the department.[277] Again, it was a device for reducing the bookkeeping costs and was not very conducive to strict control of the cost elements.

In the years immediately preceding the First World War, burden application procedure had developed sufficiently to permit one practicing cost accountant to draw the following conclusion regarding the shoe industry: "The base which is generally accepted today is productive labor cost. If shoes are more or less difficult to manufacture, if they require a longer period of time in the processing, or if they require more or less machinery and equipment, these facts are reflected in an increased or decreased cost of productive labor. On the assumption that labor is paid on an exact basis of the value of the work which is performed, labor cost would be a very accurate basis upon which to pro-rate expense . . . there is no basis of pro-rating expense that is more accurate."[278]

English cost authorities during the period under review had a tendency to follow, instead of lead the procession, when it came to important contributions to the present topic. They did not neglect it, however, even though they originated no new theory. All of the English experts of the time devoted much discussion to the merits of each allocation method.[279]   Most of them concluded that either the direct labor cost or time was the best method, being simple at least. L. R. Dicksee, in 1911, made the rather significant suggestion that since the establishment charges must be allocated to the contracts or jobs before the end of a fiscal period, it would perhaps be a better procedure to carry out the apportionment at frequent intervals, say every week or so, even though the jobs might not be finished by that time.[280]   His "cost accounts" were extraneous to the financial ledger, so the "counting-house" clerks would need to supply for checking purposes the actual burden incurred figures to the costing department at the same frequent intervals. It was his opinion that the allocation would be more accurate under this technique, since inequitable results could more easily be detected and adjusted. Just to be on the safe side, however, he suggested that the amount allocated by estimate be raised a little above what would be a true figure, so that the results on the cost ledger would show a conservative estimate of the total cost of the jobs either in progress or finished. In addition, the same method of allocation should not be used for all sorts of overhead items; the charges should be subdivided and a "fair" method adopted for each group of items. Some should be applied on the direct wage hour basis, others by labor cost, and so on. Sir John Mann had made the same suggestion a decade before. In summary, Dicksee was typical of the English writers of the period around 1910. Several other books on general accounting also contained references to the needs of the manufacturers.[281]

F. W. Taylor, the famous American exponent of scientific management, worked out a few years later a modification of Church's production factor, machine hour method. It was called the "cost number or cost factor" basis.[282]   The machine rates were to be determined in a fashion somewhat similar to what Church had suggested, but the rates themselves were not to be considered a value figure. They were to be used to determine relative numbers called "relative cost numbers," or merely "cost numbers." If, for example, the cost of maintaining and operating two machines were four cents and four dollars per hour respectively, the cost numbers would be four and four hundred respectively. As each product was worked on by the machines the number of hours spent was multiplied by the cost number of the machines used. At the end of any certain period, "the total hours by cost numbers for each article or class of product on which it is desired to compute costs and also for the entire shop, are added together." This result was practically the same as the one Church had obtained from his system, with the exception, however, that the supplementary rate would no longer need to be used. Idle time would be handled in a way that will be discussed in another section of this chapter. It was Taylor's supposition that the cost number basis could be applied to most ordinary manufacturing establishments, but strictly speaking it should be used only where the machine process was highly important in the plant. Such was Taylor's contribution to the question of the allocation of burden.

Another American cost expert, C. H. Scovell, also had high regard for the scientific machine rate. It was, he stated in an important and widely read address in 1913, about the most significant development that had taken place in cost accounting technique in the generation. It might be noted, incidentally, that the period of time mentioned by Scovell would have taken in practically all the writing which had been done since the beginning of modern costing schemes. He insisted that the machine rates would allow for as much accuracy in the hitherto estimated burden element charge as formerly had obtained in regard to direct labor cost. This, of course, was obviously an overstatement of its accuracy; no system would do that. In addition, it required, according to him, no more costing effort; yet it offered the further advantage of an exact measure of the reduced cost which might result from improved manufacturing techniques or processes. He continued by emphasizing the fact that when a new and improved method of performing some operation was devised, it not only reduced the labor cost of the factory but had usually a tremendous effect on the factory overhead costs. For burden allocation under conditions where automatic machines were employed in large number, Scovell mentioned that one firm had solved the problem by a plan of efficiency charts, which made possible the charging of burden to the jobs performed according to the cost of the effective operation of each machine. When this plan was used the cost records provided considerable precision in measuring the loss which could be attributed to low production, or the inattention of the operator. Scovell did not give, however, any specific details as to this technique. He contented himself with the following sage remarks:

Whatever the effect on sales policy, good cost accounting, including correct burden distribution, is a matter of enduring importance from the point of view of manufacturing. Changes in volume may completely obscure gains or losses in efficiency, and render comparative costs of similar jobs impossible from season to season, solely because of the variations in the amount of business done. Exact costs, comparable under all conditions, are not to be secured unless the burden charged to production is only that appertaining to the equipment that is actually at work. From the manager's point of view, the significant fact is that the burden which it is proposed to apply through a series of equipment rates is not appreciably less when the operating schedule of the plant is reduced. It is true that power charges may be slightly less, but the fixed charges for building space, interest, insurance, taxes, depreciation, and in some circumstances for repairs also, are no less when the machines are idle. The manager of a machine shop cannot make a greater mistake in figuring costs than to charge a higher burden in any form whatsoever for the operation of part of his equipment, because the rest of it is temporarily idle, or a higher rate for a smaller labor force because the plant is working on part time. These differences which have always attracted the attention of observing managers are almost entirely clear loss or waste, and should be recognized as such and charged directly to the profit and loss account. It is essential to distinguish clearly between losses or gains on machines actually made and sold, and losses due to slack production or inefficient use of equipment. It must be borne in mind that the finished product has absorbed only the burden of the equipment actually used in its manufacture. It has not absorbed the burden of unused equipment or idle machinery. If the plant includes a foundry and the management decides to purchase castings, the idle foundry has contributed nothing to the product. It is obviously unfair to charge into the cost of goods the burden charges on the automatic machinery that may be idle because the management is buying and not making machine screws. If only three quarters of the lathes run, the idle remainder have not helped machine parts actually manufactured, and although the plant may go into bankruptcy if it cannot utilize its equipment, the cost of the work actually done is not greater on that account.[283]

For "process" industries, F. E. Webner, also in America, suggested in 1917 an application of departmental overhead on the basis of a constant per ton, pound, yard, gallon, or whatever unit was customarily used.[284] This method considered the departmental burden charges as a unit, and allocated them over the product going through each department on the basis mentioned in the previous sentence. If the firm made several different grades of finished products which could not be satisfactorily averaged to a common denominator, Webner recommended that a so-called "point system" reminiscent of Taylor's "cost number" method be adopted. According to this technique the time required to produce the grade consuming the greatest amount of time was given a certain point value. say ten or a hundred. Then the other grades were given lesser numbers, comparable to the time required for them. This system could be used also to allocate the labor cost of employees to products of varying nature. Webner suggested that tests be made from time to time to check on the points previously determined. According to him, the method could be used in a large variety of industries.

Webner's countryman, William Kent, treated a year later a special problem which often arose when the scientific machine hour method was adopted. It was concerned with the case where a larger machine than absolutely necessary was used on a certain job or operation just because the correct size machine was too busy to handle the work. Obviously where a higher burden rate was in effect for the larger machine the job or process would be charged with an extra amount merely because of the substitution, unless some allowance was made on the cost sheets. Kent recommended that the job be charged only with the amount which would have been applied if the correct size machine had been used. The difference supposedly would be left unapplied although he did not mention the exact technique to be followed. A notation was to be made on the records that the larger machine had been used, so that the cost clerks could make the proper allocation.[285]

The allocation of factory overhead in a textile mill was handled rather carefully by D. C. Eggleston in his work published in this country in 1918.[286] He suggested the same procedure as that used by the United States Tariff Commission in its comparison studies. The burden items were applied in a spinning mill to the different yarns produced, on the basis of the number of spindles used in each count. This could be readily done since it cost generally about the same to operate each spindle. In a weaving mill a so-called "loom day" system was to be used. Under this method the costs of operating one loom one day was ascertained and each fabric or type of cloth which was woven on any loom was assessed according to the number of days it was on the loom. Again, this method could be adopted since there was such a small variation in the costs of operating looms of comparable capacity. Eggleston also discussed the "average number" method of determining conversion costs of plain cotton goods,

but since that is not altogether peculiar to the topic under consideration, it will be omitted here.[287]

The most important contributions to burden allocation theory,
after 1915, were concerned with the discussion of refinements in existing well-known methods. This has been typical of the period from
that time to the present. Authorities began to deal more with the
problem of idle time and capacity and less with apportionment
methods *per se*. This is not to say that there were fewer pages devoted to the question. On the contrary all the authorities felt impelled to deal with the problem, even though they added little new.
Some, however, began to question the desirability of devoting so much
attention to detailed allocating techniques within a manufacturing
establishment. G. Charter Harrison, for instance, as early as 1919,
wondered "whether the cost accountant after laboriously atomizing
and allocating every item of expense and exercising considerable ingenuity has evolved in the name of costs and in the shape of sheaves
of looseleaf sheets, among which every dollar has been painstakingly
spread, a result any more accurate or correct than the most simple and
summarized statement for expense would afford. . . . There is a
limit beyond which further degrees of refinement of burden distribution in many cases will not yield advantages to warrant the effort."[288]
In some instances he had observed situations where the allocation efforts came close to being ridiculous. It should be remembered,
however, that Harrison was a strong advocate of the standard costing
technique, and while that type of costing involves dealing with details,
they (the details) are not strictly comparable with those found under
so-called "actual costing" schemes. This particular authority continued
his criticism of current practices a few years later. At that time he
made the outright statement that it was absurd for a firm to try to
keep track of its incurred manufacturing costs for the same article
month after month.[289] and go through the elaborate distributions,
which according to him, were mostly useless rituals. The best way
to handle the problem of burden distribution and allocation was to
make one careful and accurate analysis of the costs and then use
that as a basis for future comparisons. Some "simple" (his term)
way of recording the variations from the once established figures
would be required, but the original cost estimates would not need to
be changed unless the manufacturing techniques became outmoded.
All complex distributions would be avoided except a single proration
each month at predetermined amounts.[290]

By 1921, some of the more advanced allocation theories and techniques had permeated the English literature on costing. In one of the most comprehensive reviews of current methods published during the 1920's, E. T. Elbourne developed what he called a "production service" and "producing units" system. These were synonymous with Church's production factors and production centers, but his application of the ideas was somewhat different.[291] After grouping the major burden items into some eight production service classes, he discussed the division of the overhead charges among them quite carefully. The service accounts—external to the financial ledger—were in turn transferred to departmental oncost accounts and some process summary accounts which indicated whether or not all the oncost had been allocated to product. Normal rates were used in spreading the burden costs to the departmental accounts. Elbourne gave a very thorough theoretical discussion of the technique to be employed. His system in general, however, was top-heavy with allocations and reallocations—exactly the sort of thing toward which Harrison had addressed his previously mentioned vitriolic remarks. In spite of this, it may be said that Elbourne's treatment remained standard for a number of years; other English authorities did not even approach the completeness of his work.[292]

Such has been the evolution of burden allocation techniques— from the crude, rough methods of the nineteenth century to the highly complex systems of the last few decades, the latter sometimes so involved that there was serious questioning of their efficacy. And the contrast is even more striking when one compares the brief remarks of the authorities of the 1880's with the weighty tomes of A. Hamilton Church or J. M. Clark[293] (both written in the 1920's)—entire volumes devoted to the various practical and theoretical considerations involved in the problem of apportionment. At least no one can say that the subject has been neglected either by the practitioners or the academicians. In recent years, however, much attention has been centered on the apportionment of distribution costs, and the administering of normal burden rates, with little new being proposed in regard to the allocation of manufacturing burden, *per se*.

PART V. PREDETERMINED BURDEN AND THE PROBLEM OF IDLE TIME

Although the advantage of costing jobs and processes before the end of a fiscal period has been recognized now for several decades, the practice has not always been observed. In this connection it should be noted that there were, in the early development of the art of costing, two somewhat different concepts of the nature of costing in general. One might be called the strictly historical basis, which contemplated delaying the costing of jobs until perhaps months had elapsed. The second was concerned with costing on a part historical and part predetermined basis; the material and labor elements were historical in nature, while the burden or overhead element was predetermined in advance of the time when its exact total would become known. Both of these bases assume, of course, that the total manufacturing cost was to be ascertained. A considerable number of factories used only a prime costing system in the last century; in fact, the practice is still prevalent in small establishments. So long, then, as the prime cost theory was held by industrial accountants and manufacturers, the overhead problem could be ignored, and there was no need for any discussion as to the merits of the two bases of costing outlined above. Neither would the matter of predetermined burden rates be pertinent. The present discussion will naturally be limited, therefore, to those authorities who did expect to arrive at total factory costs from their records; they might, incidentally, either be merged with the financial ledger or be extramural to it. The consolidation or nonconsolidation has of course no import at this point.

With the subject matter of the first part of this section thus narrowed down to relevant details, attention should be given to certain early aspects of the problem of idle time, which will be considered simultaneously with predetermined burden rates. A few words should be said, perhaps, as to why these two topics are so related that they may be discussed alongside of each other. Upon first glance they do not seem to have much in common. Yet upon closer inspection it will be seen that if it were not necessary, in a great number of instances, to use predetermined burden rates, (that is, if the costing could be delayed for several years, or at least a year) the problem of idle time in a factory or plant would be comparatively easy to handle. Thus, it is recognized that the determination of burden rates in advance is indissolubly bound up with the theories underlying the techniques for handling idle time and capacity. In the 1890's, the matter of predetermined burden rates received considerable attention; this was before the question of idle time became important. Then, too, while there are a few scattered references[294] to idle time before the beginning of the present century, the subject had not assumed the tremendous significance which it later acquired. The main purposes of this section, therefore, are first to trace the development of the idea of predetermined burden rates, and then to show how the techniques for handling idle time gradually evolved out of the earlier practices connected therewith.

Practically all of the cost authorities before 1885 thought of the burden problem as purely historical in nature. Some of these writers could be enumerated, but that would be superfluous here. Even though the preceding conclusion holds true so far as costing practices *per se* are concerned, there is no doubt that many engineering firms made estimates for bids or tenders in which they had of necessity to guess or forecast what the burden would be on the prospective job or contract. More than likely these were only very rough, arbitrary, approximations, which they hoped would be enough to cover all the expenditures incurred on the job. As was intimated in Chapter II, job costing itself grew out of such needs. Thomas Battersby, the Manchester (England) public accountant, implied that even where overhead rates were established, they were pure guesses, and often were without any relation to the actual "working" (his term) expenses themselves.[295] Emile Garcke and J. M. Fells, a few years later, discussed "factory charges," but, by implication, these charges would be loaded onto the jobs, if at all, at the end of a certain period. It should be mentioned, however, that they did not treat the main topic very carefully, preferring rather to describe a methodology for comparing estimated costs and actual costs. Since this description was distinctly ahead of anything that had been given before, it is quoted at length below:

Before any order to manufacture is given it is advisable, as tending to produce greater economy in cost of production, that the designer, draughtsman, or other person best acquainted with its processes and details, should, on a properly ruled and headed form, estimate the probable cost to be incurred in wages and materials in the production of the articles in question. This estimate should be a minimum rather than a maximum one. The works manager or foreman should be supplied with a complete specification of all material and parts included in the estimate. The storekeeper should also be furnished with the same particulars, and should not without special authority issue more material for the order than is estimated.

To ensure consideration of the question of what economies are practicable in construction or manufacture, the heads of the designing and manufacturing departments should be advised of the cost of each order when it is completed in such detail as permits of a comparison being instituted between the actual and estimated cost. As a matter of convenience the estimate forms may include columns for the actual costs to be inserted when known. The employer should be advised of the differences between actual and estimated cost in such detail as he may require. It is also desirable that a comparative cost register should be compiled showing the difference in cost of making the same or similar articles under differing conditions of time, material, parts, or quantities. This register will be specially serviceable in preparing estimates and quoting for orders, and permits of the necessary adjustments in quotations consequent upon the increase or decrease in the market price of material.[296]

G. P. Norton, a fellow countryman of Garcke and Fells who wrote in 1889, was equally brief on the subject of predetermined rates, but in connection with a summary of work done by departments, a column was provided for "average of standing expenses." In regard to the filling in of this column, Norton stated: "The average of standing expenses is based upon the departmental accounts prepared in previous years."[297] This early cost authority did not elaborate upon this mere hint of a predetermined burden rate, leaving his reader to derive for himself any of the additional details. There is some reason to believe, however, that the text writers were behind the times in respect to this matter since Alphonse Perren has stated unequivocally that normal burden rates "were used in England as early as 1886 in the Atlas works of John Brown and Co., Ltd."[298]

In this country the subject was treated with a little more consideration during that early period. Henry Metcalfe, for example, in the year 1885 made the point that overhead items were never exactly known until after the year was past.[299] Since this was true, it was logical, according to him, to assume that there would be no large variation in such charges from year to year; and thus in order to obtain a loading factor for the current year, one should take the total charge for last year and divide it by the total number of hours of shop work done last year. This would give a figure, expressed in dollars and cents, which could be used during the present year for each hour worked on a job. A little farther on, however, he stated that after a firm had been in business three years, an average of those years should be taken to obtain the overhead rate, and so on. He never did mention what was to be done during the first year of a firm's life.

Writing a few years later on the cost accounting for a foundry, G. L. Fowler made an unusually clear statement of how the problem should be handled, and incidentally made a passing reference to a simple way of handling idle time.[300]   First, all the indirect costs—he called them "expenses"—should be estimated as of the first of a year. (He did not explicitly state the first, however.)   Then:

> When this is done, it is best to make a studied review of the business for several years, learn what has been done, what was the average of the pay-roll for brisk times, dull times, and when only a fair or medium business was being done.   Take these three items and compare them with the present status, and the probable total pay-roll for the coming year; this will give a ratio or percentage to be added to each and every dollar paid to the moulders. . . . To be sure to establish this ratio and make it exact is a work which should be thoroughly done, but when once accomplished, it should be in such shape that a simple reference to our pay-roll, which will show whether we are doing a brisk, medium, or dull business, will determine which coefficient should be used for the month.[301]

As noted, Fowler, did not definitely state that the "coefficient" was to be applied when a certain casting was finished, or at the end of a month, but it is the opinion of the present writer that it was to be used as a predetermined figure.   Evidently, also, all of his real costing was external to the financial books.   In addition, he neglected to mention, just as Metcalfe had, what would be done in a company which had just been organized and which had no previous experience. Fowler gave credit for the plan to A. Messerschmidt, of Essen (Germany), who had been using it for seventeen years.   In that case, it predated any of the so-called modern cost systems, in so far as the handling of burden was concerned, and was also one of the earliest recognitions of the problem of idle time.

An unsigned English article in *The Accountant*, 1894, discussed the topic under review, but was limited to the determination of burden rates in advance.   The anonymous authority boldly pointed out, however, that the burden percentage was an estimate based upon past experience, which should, however, be as carefully compiled as any estimate could be.[302]   At about the same time F. G. Burton, the manager of a large British engineering establishment, discussed the problem of idle time when it came to making bids or tenders for large contracts, such as building a ship.[303]   The usual method for estimating the burden element, according to him, was to take a percentage of wages on jobs expected to be accepted during the next six months. But what should be done in case the "year" was, say, only half full of work, and was expected thus to continue?   Obviously, the percentage would be higher under such circumstances.[304]   Could this larger proportion be collected from customers? Burton did not think so, the reason being centered around the fact that the competition of rival firms would tend to keep bids down to what they would be if all the firms were operating at near capacity. The extra cost, then, would have to come out of profits. Burton also made the observation that many contracting engineers tendered their bids just as though their plant was operating at full speed. This practice did not, however, meet with Burton's approval, although it did have the advantage "of bringing the estimate nearer to the amount at which the tender can be rendered, but it has the disadvantage—and it is a grave one—of not showing the nearest possible approach to expected cost of the contract."[305] How could it be overcome? At this point Burton became very indefinite. He referred, for example, to a total estimated net cost with an addition for use of machinery and tools at a "fixed proportion" at—[per cent], and a "fixed proportion" for management charges, which included rent, rates, insurance, coal, gas and water, and superintendence, also at an unknown percentage. The total of these three plus a profit figure would give the amount of the bid. Strangely enough, he did not indicate how all this would solve the question of idle time, unless the fixed proportion mentioned was a sort of normal burden percentage; he gave, however, no clues as to what he meant by his terminology, nor how his technique would help in estimating.

Although Burton at least recognized that there was a problem of idle capacity when it came to making tenders, he did not hold to the same idea in his "cost accounts," which, as usual at the time, were not integrated with the financial records. In the cost accounts, every item of cost had to be apportioned to the product or jobs each month, and what was more, all the overhead charges were proper costs in the month in which they occurred. The costings were to be completed each month, "as longer periods would involve much complication, and it is essential for correct results that the establishment charges for any one month be distributed over the direct wages for that month."[306]

Burton's viewpoint may be taken as somewhat representative of that group of cost accountants who insist that the manufacturing cost of a product or job is that total which will be incurred at the time the job or article goes through the plant, no matter whether the factory is operating at full capacity or partial capacity. To express it more succinctly, if only one article were made during a period, that article would be assigned all the factory overhead incurred during the period. The contrasting viewpoint, that is, normal burden rates, will be discussed subsequently. The issue was thrown into sharp relief a few years later, but that controversy is also treated later.

Around the turn of the century, accountants and engineers began to consider quite seriously the matter of predetermined burden rates. The American engineer, Oberlin Smith, for example, in an address suggested that the "theoretical way" to determine an "expense" rate was to take last year's rate, adjust it in the light of actual expenditures during that year, and use this figure for the current year.[307] But H. M. Lane and H. M. Norris, who spoke at the same meeting, did not agree with Smith; these two authorities thought the costing should be done at the end of each month or period.[308] Idle time, where a machine charge was included in burden, was also mentioned. H. L. Gantt, the industrial engineer, propounded the question as to what should be done in case a machine tool was run only, say, one-tenth of the time, and then gave an answer to his own question. It was his opinion that the previous year's total running time divided into the cost of maintaining the tool the last year should be used as a basis for fixing the rate for the current year. "This is probably as accurate as any other method," was his observation.[309] Oberlin Smith, however, did not agree with him; he insisted that the machine would be accumulating charges at practically the same rate as if it were running full time. He would, then, "average things up all round and take one uniform rate, thus having the accounts as simple as possible."[310] F. A. Halsey also recognized the difficulty brought on by large machines being unused a considerable part of the year, and, too, often being used for work below their capacity. According to him, the problem could not be solved by any means compatible with the extra records which would be necessitated. The tool time might be kept, but was the additional accuracy worth the labor involved? Halsey did not think so.[311]

Such was the state of costing around 1900, at least among the industrial engineers. Very few accountants, in this country, had taken any interest in costing topics. Matters such as idle time seem to have been mere trifles. This neglect, on the surface, appears to be rather singular. The usual explanation is centered around the fact that up to that time there were few large-scale industrial units with their enormous overhead costs.[312] Yet periods of prosperity and depression—the business cycle—had been known and recognized for decades before a thorough treatment of the idle time problem appeared. This circumstance makes the neglect all the more strange. And, as a matter of fact, there were quite a number of large manufacturing establishments before 1900. The contributing factors, then, were all present long before the turn of the century; nevertheless, no comprehensive examination of the problem had been written.[313] The usual explanation for the remissness seems, therefore, only partially satisfactory. What were some other contributing causes for the negligence? At least one may be discussed here. It is concerned with the revitalized interest in all aspects of factory management which took place around the turn of the century. The period after the War Between the States had been one of rapid internal development along commercial, transportation, and agricultural lines. Exports were largely products of the mines or soil, and since there was an abundance of both, no special efficiency or waste-saving devices were needed on a large scale. Industrial accounting refinements were not called for so long as economic development in this country continued along the lines indicated. Even England, which had already seen a phenomenal expansion of its factory system, had the field almost to herself until the early 1900's. Again, there was no special need there for refined techniques, one example of which was the handling of idle time. As long as she had no strong competitors, she could still retain her markets without the advantages of scientific management; there was no incentive, then, to spend very much energy or time in working out better cost practices or theories in that country.

But beginning about 1898, there came a surging American interest in factory improvements and betterments of all kinds. Even though the industrialists of this country hardly knew it, they had placed themselves in a position to capture a considerable portion of the commercial trade of the world. The War with Spain showed the European nations that the United States was again united in spite of the effects of the War Between the States. If nothing else, her easy victory over the Spaniards demonstrated not only her military might, but also her large fuel and steel resources—sinews of any industrial struggle. It was at about that time, then, that Americans (as well as Europeans) became vitally conscious of the power of their coal, iron, copper, food products, and a capable labor supply, which, taken together, were enough to assure them of a share of the expanding world market for manufactured goods—if these natural resources were properly handled and combined. And at this juncture, the American factory manager, already endowed with the native traits which made him a natural opportunist, began to see the prime importance of more accurate cost accounting. Costs of production, both in periods of prosperity and depression, became an absolute necessity. The skillful manager needed to know the factory cost of his product, first in order to set selling prices on a world market, and, second, to keep those prices lower than competing nations. Details became much more significant than they had previously been. Desirable articles had to be made at low prices, and in order to do this, production costs had to be more and more minutely divided. Vigilance would be unavailing if the proper control factors were missing; corrections could not be applied unless the facts had been definitely ascertained. The facts had to be compiled in such a way that they could be relied upon. In a word, accuracy in costing became a requisite rather than a luxury.

Not all firms, of course, appreciated the improved costing techniques which appeared around the turn of the century. For example, one careful student of a textile machinery manufacturer (The Saco-Lowell Company) has drawn the following interesting conclusions:

> The accounting system of the company grew out of contemporary small business practice and was formalized in a set of detailed instructions drawn up by a committee of two directors in November, 1841. Both these men were bankers, and this fact may account for the relatively unspecialized nature of the accounts. Records of the company are not complete, but the fragments indicate a lack of detailed costing procedure, which contrasts strongly with the accounting methods employed by the Boston Manufacturing Company twenty years before. Direct and overhead costs were allocated to the various types of machines and to the various activities of the company, but not, as at Waltham, to the component parts and processes. This came later, and may not have been considered necessary when only one contract was on the books and activities were on a limited scale. . . .

> Accounting practices evolved little in the years from 1897 to 1912. Indeed, a simplicity is evidenced in company bookkeeping methods which was reminiscent of the early days of the Boston Manufacturing Company and was not at all typical of the complex concepts which were beginning to form elsewhere in the field of corporate cost and financial accounting. This simplicity appears to have been characteristic of much of the textile machinery industry, which as late as 1916 was said to have neglected cost accounting to a great extent. At least one large firm at that date was still using a single entry system for its general books. A smaller firm until 1912 had not taken an inventory of stock on hand for twenty-

five or thirty years.   Two other large concerns recorded expenditures in detail but had no unit-cost system.   The Saco and Pettee
Machine Shops had an excellent and detailed unit-cost system in
the factory, but there was no distribution of the items of general
expenses, taxes, insurance, and other overhead expenses by the general office; thus, while the factory unit costs were complete, a total
unit cost could not be shown.[314]

But a few industrialists took a different view.   Alfred P. Sloan,
Jr., who started his career with the Hyatt Roller Bearing Company,
and later joined General Motors Corporation, has told in a most interesting way of his turn-of-the-century thinking regarding fixed and
variable costs.   These costs are, of course, closely related to the
question of predetermined burden rates and the handling of idle time
losses.   To quote:

> In my early contacts with the Ford organization I met C. Harold
> Wills.   Seemingly, no one had any title in the Ford organization,
> but Mr. Couzens and Mr. Wills both had important jobs.   Mr. Ford
> had determined that he had to have better steel in order to make
> stronger cars, at the same time avoiding the tendency to make them
> heavier and heavier.   As a result of Mr. Wills' efforts, the answer
> was found in vanadium steel.   When Mr. Ford prepared to intro-
> duce this new material into his Model T, I did the same at Hyatt.
>
> This man Wills had started in overalls as an apprentice in the
> shop of the Detroit Lubricating Company.   After four years he was
> a journeyman toolmaker.   Thereafter he studied at night, taking
> correspondence courses in engineering, industry, metallurgy.   To-
> day many big steel companies pay license fees to him for the
> privilege of making steels according to formulae of his.
>
> Although Harold Wills was the one I usually dealt with when
> I had business in the Ford Motor Company plant at Highland Park,
> I was never there without sensing the presence of Mr. Ford, with-
> out knowing that Mr. Ford was the initial force.   Each successive
> visit revealed growth and efficiency.   They were gaining volume.
>
> Volume justifies machinery and methods otherwise impossible.
> Volume makes possible a better relationship between what we call
> variable and fixed expense, reducing costs and justifying lower sell-
> ing prices.   I had been so busy trying to make more and better Hyatt
> roller bearings that I had had little time to consider the economics
> of Hyatt's position.   I remember there was a period of four con-
> secutive years when I was at the Hyatt factory every day from 8:30
> to 6:00, except Sundays and holidays.   No five-day week.   No extra
> holidays.   No eight-hour day.   But my first realization of the im-
> portance of price as affecting volume was taught to me by Henry
> Ford.   He had the vision to see that lower prices would increase
> volume up to the point that would justify such lower prices through

reduced costs. This great idea has dominated the automotive industry ever since Mr. Ford had the courage to put his belief into practical effect.

One day when I entered the Highland Park plant to discuss the Hyatt production of bearings for the future, Mr. Wills interrupted me to say, "Maybe I'd better talk first." Then he proceeded to tell me that Mr. Ford had determined to make a drastic reduction in the price of the Ford car. They were going to make only one chassis. It was the time of famous decision: "The customer can have a car of any color he likes so long as it's black." Everything was being predicated upon the increased volume that Mr. Ford expected; this would justify the lowered price.

Hyatt was in a stronger position than most of Mr. Ford's suppliers. Our product was a patented article. We might have argued he could not easily dispense with us. Yet I knew we needed him more than he needed us.

I knew my cost system was sound. But Mr. Wills was telling me that a due proportion of lower costs of our bearing resulting from the increased volume of Ford cars ought to be reflected in reduced prices for bearings.

"Look," said Mr. Wills, "We'll be taking the equivalent of 65 per cent of your last year's production. Don't you want to figure again?"

"Come down to Harrison, Mr. Wills. I'll show you everything."

The result of going over our books together was that Mr. Wills pointed out some debatable items outside the question of volume.

"Mr. Sloan, the only way we figure in your sales overhead is for a two-cent stamp when you mail us a bill." He grinned because this was an exaggeration, but he had a point. "Are you advertising in order to sell us? Why should you charge us for any of the selling overhead of the remaining 35 per cent of your business?"

A week or ten days later, after days and nights of figuring and planning, I went back to Detroit. I think we were getting sixty or seventy cents for our bearings. When I walked in, I proposed a substantial reduction.

Mr. Wills rubbed his hands together and said, "That's a boy!"

Now I have forgotten just what specific changes in our factory procedure were adopted to justify the lower selling prices that I made on this bigger order for Ford. One thing we did not do was to reduce wages; that was done too often in such cases in those days. But I had learned that increased productivity would support higher wages.

Primarily the automobile industry in early days was ruled by its production men, by engineers and master craftsmen. The demand for cars was so great the insistent problem was production. Ford was growing as no industrial enterprise had ever grown before. Hyatt Roller Bearing Company was obliged to grow with Ford, or else give way to some other supplier who would keep pace.

The whole trick of that growth was to keep improving the technique of manufacture and to keep lowering the price of the car to reach an even bigger market.[315]

In view of the above, the subject of predetermined burden rates and the problem of idle time began to assume more importance in the literature of cost accounting around 1900. In fact, it was about that time that the noted accountant and engineer, A. Hamilton Church, first made public his famous "scientific" machine hour method of distributing burden, the broad outlines of which have already been discussed in the previous section. In order to simplify the problem of dealing with idle time, Church used the now classic illustration concerned with "little shops." Let us examine, he said, the nature of the charges which would be assessed against each of the so-called little independent shops.[316] The rent would go on whether it was idle or busy, while the power charge might be cut off completely if the shop were entirely inactive. But if the shop were running say at half capacity the power required would not be just half as much, it would be something over that figure. "Now if the mechanic in one of these shops is only working half his time it is pretty clear that he must double his rate of distribution on such work as he does, if he is to distribute his month's rent and power over his month's work. But instead of doubling his rate, he might continue to charge at the normal rate, and then at the month end find out how much he was yet in arrears, and distribute this undistributed amount only as a supplementary rate."[317] According to Church, this technique of charging the normal rate—which was, incidentally, the predetermined rate which would have been charged to the little shop or department if it had been operating at practical capacity—would offer two distinct advantages. First, the manager would be able to obtain comparable costs of like articles at different periods of time, since the normal burden rate would be about the same each period; and, second, the amount of the supplementary rate, or its ratio to the normal rate, would serve as a sort of barometer as to how much the idle time was really costing the firm in the way of wasted capacity. This latter advantage would be of great assistance in a large plant, where the manager or superintendent could not keep all the details well in hand. Thus, the use of the supplementary rate distinguished Church's system from the ordinary machine hour system. He defined it as "the undistributed balance of shop charges due to idleness of productive centres."[318]

As was mentioned in the previous section, Church advocated the allocation of the supplementary charge, and the unallocated general burden items, to products on the basis of direct labor hours. This method was preferred "because the incidence of the unallocated charges cannot be considered as varying with the value of the different machines, but rather as pressing equally on all work done in the shop hour by hour, irrespective of whatever machine it may be done on."[319] But what about the possibility of spreading the idle machine time, not as a part of the general expense rate per hour, but as a kind of extra supplementary rate to the machine at fault, that is, the one that was idle? This particular technique would have the tendency to confine the cost of idleness to the machine that caused the trouble. Church thought that this would be the ideal method, but hardly the practicable one. His reasoning should be noted carefully, as it gave rise a few years later to a veritable storm of criticism and argument, which, incidentally, is still quite prominent in cost literature. To quote:

> The machine at fault cannot alone be charged with the cost of idle time because if a machine were to be at work only one hour in a given month, all the burden of the other two hundred and odd hours would be discharged on the unfortunate job done in that one hour. And worse still, if no work at all were done in the month the unallocated rate would either be lost altogether or else thrown into the supplementary shop rate after all. We are obliged, therefore, from motives of expediency, to look upon idle time as a kind of visitation of Providence which the whole shop ought to bear.[320]

Since there were these objections to the alternate method, it is rather difficult to see why Church should call it the "ideal" method; an ideal technique, *ipso facto*, should have no disadvantages.

The issue had at least now been clearly differentiated. Church, who was an electrical engineer with much experience in both England and the United States, had treated the subject more adequately and comprehensively than any preceding authority. The English cost experts began to investigate the problem at about the same time.[321] David Cowan, a short time later, for example, spoke of a "shop hour-factor," which was a sort of consolidated direct labor time unit charge.[322] It was not to be just a predetermined average burden rate for any certain year, but rather a "cumulative average" over a series of past years, covering a complete business cycle, or "trade cycle" as he called it. It was, moreover, to be modified from time to time in accordance with improved efficiency, machinery, and the like. His idea, then, contemplated the establishment of a rate which would have the tendency to be too much in some years and not enough in others, but over a period of ten years or so would be just about right. The factors were to be checked with the "outlay registers" from time to time. Cowan advocated also the setting up of certain compensating accounts and recoveries accounts, which would assist in carrying the under or over absorbed burden from one year to another. Since all of his costing was external to the financial ledger, from which would be prepared the annual balance sheet, he had to provide a method for showing the under or over applied burden. But in regard to the latter he became rather indefinite; he spoke of carrying the balances to an account in the commercial books, "when it is desired that the true condition of the business should be shown."[323] He did not, however, explain just how this was to be done. This oversight or neglect was especially confusing in the light of the nonintegration of the cost and the commercial books. All he indicated was that "when there is a surplus credit balance in both accounts [compensating and recoveries], it should be allowed to remain therein as an equaliser of profits in future years of bad trade. Prudent business men are never likely to treat as an asset any debit balance that may arise in the compensating accounts; these should be cleared off as they arise by credits derived from profit and loss."[324] While there was thus much that was confusing in Cowan's technique, it was at least an early noteworthy attempt to solve an important problem which existed with many firms, that is, the handling of idle time.

Two or three years later, H. S. Garry, also an Englishman, in an address before the Society of Chemical Industry, advanced the theory that wherever an industry was of such a nature that its wages bill remained fairly constant in spite of fluctuations of output, that firm should treat the difference in costs between full capacity operations and partial capacity operations as a "dead charge."[325] He did not expand upon his brief statement, but it is to be understood that he advocated that the loss due to idle capacity be handled, not as a part of the cost of product, but as a sort of waste. On his cost summary he showed the total cost of his processed goods on a unit basis; then he deducted the "excess of cost due to partial output" to arrive at the "standard cost" per unit.[326] The increase, over standard, of the price of materials used was treated as a separate item. He thus had three figures available: (1) the actual cost; (2) the standard cost; and (3) the total of standard cost, excess cost due to idle plant, and the increase in the cost of material. As was usual with the early English writers, he gave neither entries nor ledger treatment. Supposedly, however, all of his costing was extramural to the commercial ledger. This, incidentally, was one of the several early attempts to obtain the advantages of a standard cost system. Garry's "excess cost due to partial capacity" was attributed to the fact that most firms found themselves unable to reduce capacities to output fluctuations, and some firms required a certain minimum bulk for operating at all. Both of these causes were to be found particularly in the chemical industry and similar processing businesses.

In the same year that Garry wrote, Sir John Mann contributed an article on "Oncost" to the *Encyclopaedia of Accounting*, in which he made the point that wherever the total hours worked did not remain steady, no simple burden allocation method would give satisfactory results.[327] One method of making an adjustment to compensate for varying hours was to change the percentage charged as burden in accordance with the number of employees at work day by day. While this method had some advantages, according to Mann, the value of possible comparisons of costs would be eliminated. The cost of products produced in slack times could not be contrasted with those produced in a busy season. The best way to avoid this difficulty was to set "normal" (his term) burden rates, determined from the "normal output or turnover." Mann admitted that "the calculation of these two factors, and the relation between them, demands the earnest attention of the highest skill in any establishment—and not merely at long and irregular intervals, but on each occasion on which the commercial books are balanced and the trading results brought out. At such times the cost books should also be balanced and the results compared and reconciled with the commercial books, and the expense ratios adjusted if necessary."[328] In estimating, or drawing up bids for proposed jobs, the manager of the firm would have to rely heavily upon the normal rate to guide him as to the amount to add for burden. In regard to the normal rates Mann made the significant observation that if the firm had a "lean order book" and few inquiries, it might wish to bid at a price which would cover materials and labor plus an extra amount which would cover only part of the normal overhead. In this way the plant could stay busier than if it refused to accept the offer at all, even though it would still show a net loss if the full amount of overhead had been charged on the job. As he stated it "the prudence of taking such work must be judged by the difference between these losses and the normal oncost apportioned to each item. These considerations lead to the conclusion that the difficulty of a changing volume of trade may be overcome in any of the methods described by separating the expense rates into normal and abnormal, and adopting the former only in estimating and costing."[329] This practice would later have been called "cutthroat" competition, and of course was one of the contributing causes of such a type of rivalry. Mann also described a method of computing machine hour rates which was practically the same as that suggested by the American authority, A. Hamilton Church. The gist of Mann's system was the separation of normal and abnormal overhead charges, the normal being allocated by the regular machine hour rate, while the abnormal were to be apportioned by an "adjustment" rate which fluctuated with the state of business activity. Copious illustrations were given in Mann's article, even though his explanations were often too generalized for specific reference purposes.

In the same article Mann suggested that the factory overhead estimates should be revised at short intervals, and compared with the actual burden items. This was to be done without waiting until the annual balance sheet date. The information obtained would be used to adjust the estimate of "oncost" adopted in the costing. This seems, however, to be contrary to his previous view that burden rates should not be changed too often lest the comparison advantage be lost. Even though Mann was one of the eminent cost authorities of the day there was some vagueness in his work.[330]

The idea of a predetermined burden rate had its opponents, however. S. Pedder, who wrote in England in 1905, advocated the by that time usual practice of charging a job with its estimated amount of overhead when it was finished, instead of waiting until the end of a period. Pedder made a technical distinction between estimates based upon past results on the one hand, and expected performance estimates on the other hand. He preferred the former since it would allow for more frequent revision. The latter had a semblance of what should be attained, while the former was bound up with what actually had been attained in past years or periods.[331] In a sharp criticism of Pedder, the editor of *The Accountant*, who of course spoke for many English cost accountants, examined the whole fundamental basis of burden accounting, and took issue with all of those authorities who advocated predetermined, normal, or estimated overhead rates. He insisted that only an old, established, and practically static firm could adopt such a technique, implying also that that type of firm was greatly in the minority. For all others, the practice was neither reliable nor scientific. The editor, however, somewhat begrudgingly admitted that it would have to be used for making bids or tenders, but that was absolutely the only exception. As for the cost records themselves, nothing would do except actual costs, and these could not be determined until the end of an accounting period, when the overhead was assembled. The primary purpose of the cost accounts, according to him, was to verify the estimates and that purpose could not be satisfactorily met so long as predetermined burden rates were used. He did point out, however, that it was his opinion that the accounting period should not be so long as six months or a year; the costing certainly could not be delayed that length of time. Further, he saw no "insuperable difficulty" (his term) in ascertaining the total amount of factory overhead items every week or two weeks, and allocating them at that time. He did not mention, though, the difficult problem of seasonal variation, idle time, or other types of fluctuations. All he had to say on this was that "these weekly or fortnightly totals may, of course, have to be subject to final adjustment, but such adjustments ought to be capable of being kept within very narrow limits, so as to not materially disturb the accuracy of the results."[332] No details were given as to the nature of those adjustments nor how they were to be handled in the cost accounts. This, incidentally, constituted the real crux of the problem.

The editor also had little use for an idea like Cowan's, that is, the establishment of a normal rate for an entire business cycle. This seemed to him particularly dangerous since it had the tendency to cover up the fact that the actual costs were much higher or lower than the normal rate suggested. If the burden cost items were averaged over the output for a long period, the management would never know just how much profit was made on any certain job. In addition, he could not understand the necessity for maintaining cost accounts at all if they did not explain the poor results which might obtain in periods of depression. But why had the predetermined burden rate theory gained such a strong foothold in costing practice? This authority thought that it was due to the desire to justify estimates which had been made on jobs; "but, if the matter be rightly viewed, it must, we think, be admitted that there is nothing essentially wrong in the estimates not being borne out by the costing if the period when the work was actually performed was one of exceptional pressure or unusual slackness."[333]   The issue was thus clearly drawn, even though very few cost authorities followed the editor's viewpoint in the years to come.   There is no doubt, however, that many factories maintained their records along the lines suggested.   (It is not an easy matter to compile predetermined burden rates, and where up-to-date costing is not necessary, it is obvious that purely historical costs can be more readily ascertained.)   The point may be raised, though, that one of the most important advantages of costing would be lost, that is, the possibility of quick action in case of changing conditions.   Before passing over to what was taking place in this country it might be noted that most of the English cost experts of the period around 1905 did not agree with the editor of *The Accountant*.   The specific references are given in a reference note.[334]

In this country most of the authorities, during the period 1902-1910, were elaborating on A. Hamilton Church's scientific machine hour method; predetermined burden rates were also being stressed. For example, O. N. Manners recommended that an average be taken over a period of many months or years, and used as the overhead rate for the current month.   According to him, it would be entirely "unfair" to any one month's output to charge it with the burden items incurred in that month.   The reason for this was that the items during a month might vary because of extraneous factors not connected with the costs for that period.   For such cases he proposed the long-term average.[335]   Incidentally, he favored the direct labor cost basis of burden allocation.

In 1906, John Whitmore, an American accountant, made several refinements in Church's system, as well as elaborating upon the basic technique.   First, as Church had said, the total of the machine rate cost was to be derived, and then divided by the total reasonable working hours to arrive at the rate per hour to be charged for the time the machines were in operation.   Obviously, then, any idle time not allowed for in the total working hours would remain unallocated at the end of a period.   Church, it will be remembered, suggested that this unapplied amount be added to the factory general charges and distributed upon a direct labor hour basis.   Whitmore did not think that particular method the best, although it was his opinion that it would be satisfactory under some circumstances.[336]   In developing his own technique for handling the idle time element, Whitmore first made the significant observations (1) that in reality no method would be ideal that provided for charging into cost of production the "expense" of factory idle capacity; and (2) that the cost of any article was somewhat dependent upon the arbitrary division of the time element. For example, "if the distribution is made monthly an article produced in the first week of the month will have its cost increased by the machinery being idle in the last week."[337] If the allocation, on the other hand, were made every two weeks, an inequitable allotment such as this could not take place. This factor, however, would not be very important if every plant produced only for order, and never to build up stocks. In the latter event, when the articles were finally assembled and sold, some might have been produced in a busy month and others in a month of slack production. According to Whitmore, "the cost of the assembled article is not of a known character," under circumstances such as those mentioned. That in essence was his main criticism of Church's supplementary rate technique. How could the problem be avoided? In answer, Whitmore recommended that a separate account be set up on the ledger entitled "factory capacity idle." To this account would be charged all the cost not absorbed into product by the regular normal machine rate. Whitmore would not admit, however, that idle capacity was not a cost at all, but an outright loss, as later authorities did. He insisted that it should be absorbed into cost of product, but "the costs of the products of the factory operated and the cost of the factory idle" should be kept separate from each other.[338] Obviously, this was somewhat similar to Church's proposals, but it did have the merit of separately showing the idle capacity item so it could be studied by the management, and kept as low as possible.

In regard to the computation of the machine rates, Whitmore suggested at least nine charges which would necessarily have to be included. In addition, he made a distinction between types of machines. Church had neglected to do this. Three classes of machines would usually be necessary. The first group would include those "of full efficiency, whose use is general, and whose full capacity should under proper conditions be constantly used. The second class will consist of machines of full efficiency, installed for special and occasional use, and not upon a calculation of continuous operation. The third class is for machines which are not for the highest efficiency, but which are maintained and used when other machines which could do the work more economically are busy."[339] Hourly rates would be derived for each group separately, taking into consideration all the pertinent factors, such as possible idleness. Whitmore did not think that the procedure suggested would prove unusually difficult, even though it was not just a simple arithmetical calculation. A table was to be prepared at the end of each four weeks' period showing the amount of machine time absorbed into product and the loss on account of idle time for the period. This would serve to focus the attention of the management upon the importance of keeping the machines busy. The idle capacity account was on the general books and was debited at the time the machines rates account was credited. Incidentally, as noted above, Whitmore had advocated the considering of the idle capacity item as a part of the cost of the product, but on another page he almost changed his opinion when he stated that the

> cost figures are thus freed from the fluctuating and confusing element of the expense of capacity idle that ought to be operated; and profits are determined on the basis of these cost figures; but against these profits is always set out the idle capacity expense that has to be deducted from them, giving thus the net result of the operations, subject always to certain adjustments of values that have to be made in respect of any shrinkages from the book value of the current assets.[340]

This seemed to imply that the idle capacity "expense" was not to be spread over product at all, but used as an adjustment item on the annual statements. If so, Whitmore was one of the first Americans to advocate such a practice. This authority was not, however, consistent throughout his discussion, mentioning both techniques as being preferable.

A. A. Murdoch, a practicing public accountant, took Whitmore severely to task, a short while later, for proposing the division of the machines in a plant into three groups. It was his idea that such a proposal would really involve setting up an individual performance standard for every machine in the factory, giving rise to endless "hairsplitting" (his term) and quibbling. It would destroy, moreover, a great part of the utility of the records of unused machinery for comparison purposes. To summarize: "A machine shop that installs special machines without being in a position to use their full capacity wants particularly to have the idle time shown upon the same basis as other machines, so as to get a line on the loss resulting from their installation."[341]

Murdoch also thought that costs should always be quoted to the sales department at what they would be if the factory were operating at practical capacity all the time, leaving it to the management to add enough "loading" (his term) to cover the idle time charge. It would also be a duty of the executives to keep the idle time at the very minimum. Murdoch evidently had the idea of a normal cost of production, especially the burden element, which was to be contrasted with actual costs only for the sake of comparison.[342]

In the same year, 1906, D. C. Eggleston noted that the unallocated charges due to idle time, which would inevitably arise under the machine rate system, should be applied to product according to the percentage which the unallocated charges bore to those already proportioned by the machine unit system. For current costing purposes, then, he would add to the "standard cost" (his term) the supplementary rate. The most important advantage of this method lay in the fact that cost comparisons would be more scientific, since they would be based upon similar conditions.[343] Evidently he was thinking of comparing only the standard costs, as the addition of the supplementary rate would render the data nonhomogeneous.

The problem of dealing with cases where work was done on machines of larger size than absolutely required engaged the attention of cost experts in those early years also. For example, P. J. Darlington in this country thought the machine rate should be applied based upon the rate for a machine of just the proper size to do the job correctly and efficiently. If a larger one were used, for the sake of expediency or because it was idle, the job should only be charged with the rate normal to that type of work. He did not mention just what should be done with the difference, but supposedly it would become part of the idle time loss. It was also one of his fundamental principles that the machine rates should be based upon expected normal activity instead of actual activity. The actual activity plan had the tendency to drive work away from the factory in dull times, and, in addition, was impractical and illogical. He recognized also the possibility that the time required to perform the job might be longer or shorter when a larger machine was used than if the regular machine were used. Ordinarily, however, according to him, the difference would be slight, and not enough to warrant any adjustment.[344]

Darlington did not hesitate, as Whitmore had done, to advocate that the idle time or capacity balance of unabsorbed machine rates be charged directly to profit and loss. He insisted that if the plant were partially idle during a period such charges as were due to the lack of production did not form any part of the factory cost of the product. He took direct issue with Church, therefore, and was one of the first of a long line of cost authorities to recommend such a procedure. In addition, he had little patience with such proposals as that made previously by the editor of *The Accountant*,[345] that is, to change the overhead rates very often. Darlington could see no reason for varying the rate with activity, his main point being that such a practice would destroy all comparative figures; and, as so many persons since have pointed out, the changing burden rate would tend to raise cost in the face of declining output, when reduced selling prices might help regain business for the firm. It is interesting to note, however, that the advocates of so-called actual costs used exactly the same argument in support of their thesis; the matter had by now developed into a battle between the relative advantages of the two theories. Obviously, what was needed was both sorts of cost figures; in fact, standard costing was already beginning to be advocated as a device for accomplishing that particular result. C. E. Knoeppel, for example, in this country, used a so-called standard burden rate as early as 1908. The work in process account was charged with actual burden and credited with standard. Any difference which might result from this practice was carried to departmental burden adjustment account. It was Knoeppel's idea that a firm could make the most profit when it was operating at near normal levels. The burden rates should be handled, therefore, so that no business would be lost just because the plant happened to be working at less than a normal rate of operations. While Knoeppel did not elaborate upon how the standard rates were to be ascertained, it is evident that he was applying a technique very similar to later practices.[346]

Gershom Smith, the American industrial engineer, stated a few years later that his firm had used a modified scientific machine hour rate system ever since 1902. The normal number of hours expected of each group of machines was estimated as of the first of a year and divided into the estimated cost. This gave the hourly rate. But Smith recognized the impracticability of doing this for each machine, so he grouped his into some ten classes. Each class, then, had a different rate, and all the individual machines were assigned to the class nearest their exact rate. This procedure, according to him, saved a lot of bookkeeping. Because he felt that there should be a safety factor, he always set the machine class rate just a little higher than what would be strictly called for. The effect of this was also seen in his idea of accumulating a reserve in busy years, which could be used in subnormal periods to keep the burden charge more or less stable. In this way the rate would not have to be raised "at a time when cost can least afford the additional burden."[347] This feature of his system, however, did not have to be adopted unless the management desired it; the excess charge could be disposed of monthly by dividing it by the direct labor hours and applying it to the orders in process for the time under consideration. What would be the procedure if, in case of a depression, the reserve established by an overcharge in normal periods was all consumed by an excess of idle time which had not been anticipated? In such an event, he would charge the idle time loss directly to the profit and loss account, and thus maintain his so-called normal costs. This recommendation was the same as that made by Darlington a couple of years prior.[348] It will also be remembered that David Cowan, the Englishman, as early as 1901, had suggested the adopting of a rate which would be uniform throughout a business cycle. As a matter of fact, Smith's idea seemed directly descended from that proposal. It is not known just how many firms actually used these "long period" burden rates. It may be concluded, however, from the little attention they merited, that they were rarely adopted.

As has been noted, Church's famous machine hour system was already being modified and criticized in several respects. By 1909 J. L. Nicholson was pointing out a basic defeat in the reasoning underlying the use of the supplementary rate. It was his opinion that no matter in which direction the discrepancy between the normal burden applied and the actual incurred burden might fall it was still added or deducted from the machine rate amount already allocated to the product. Of course this criticism would not apply to those who advocated charging the excess amount to profit and loss, but it would apply to Church's procedure. According to Nicholson, the trouble lay in the fact that an ideally normal number of hours was used when estimating the machine hours; this was essentially too arbitrary. In view of this, Nicholson suggested that the average or actual running time be used as a divisor. It was his opinion that this was a more logical technique, and would give rise to much less excess or deficiency to be handled through the supplementary rate. To sum up: "It is not a question of what a machine can do but what it does do, day in and day out, even if this represents only forty per cent efficiency."[349] Nicholson's procedure, however, would defeat one of the basic advantages of Church's system, that is, the separation of the idle time "cost" (losses) from the normal costs.

All of the American authorities were not at this time recommending the use of yearly predetermined rates. A writer in the *Cyclopedia of Accounting*, for instance, suggested the adoption of an interval of one month. This could be easily carried out, he stated, if proper control accounts were set up for the individual items making up the overhead element of cost. It was his idea that a period of a year was too long a time interval, and that large discrepancies between burden applied and burden incurred always resulted when that period was adopted. By selecting a shorter interval, the burden application rate could currently be adjusted to conform with the actual expenditures, and thus avoid such errors of allocation. Even though this authority pointed out that certain items, such as taxes or insurance, would be paid perhaps all in one month and must therefore be divided between the months, he did not mention the seasonal fluctuations in cost which would result from his technique. It would seem that he had in mind the approximation of actual costs each month, and not the smoothing out of the burden cost of production over an entire year.[350] If this supposition be true he was following the same practice the editor of *The Accountant* had recommended a few years before. The writer in the *Cyclopedia*, however, was so interested in his control accounts that he may have advocated the above technique in order to emphasize their general usefulness and advantages.

The controversy between the advocates of historical incurred burden application rates and predetermined rates spread into the accounting literature of a more general nature. Henry R. Hatfield, for example, discussed, in 1909, the conflicting viewpoints in his *Modern Accounting*. Terming it a "vital difference in method," this well-known American authority presented several of the cogent reasons which had been advanced by each group of participants. The group which advocated the monthly period of costing, he stated, certainly had the benefit of greater accuracy on their side; Hatfield, however, seemed to have contemplated here the delaying of the burden charge until after a month had elapsed. His view, then, should be contrasted with those who, like the writer in the *Cyclopedia*, advocated the predetermination of rates for one month only instead of a year. The second group, according to Hatfield, also had a strong argument; that is, the costing would not have to be delayed, but could be completed just as soon as the job or process was finished. He would not state just which method was most desirable as a general practice, preferring to leave the question for each firm to decide, taking into consideration its own peculiar needs. But in regard to the predetermined rate technique he did state that "it should be remembered that for certain purposes what is desired is not so much the actual amount which it cost to produce a certain commodity, as an estimate of what it will cost to produce more of the same kind of goods. This is especially true where special contracts are undertaken."[351] And in connection with the controversy as to whether the past month should be taken as a basis for predetermining the burden rate, or whether the past year or series of years should be taken, he was also rather noncommittal. "Just what experience will give the best indication of future costs may be debatable. It does not necessarily follow that the experience of the present month is any better criterion than that of last year."[352]

The method employed by Church for the disposition of his supplementary rate was also sharply criticized by William Kent, an American consulting engineer, at about this same time. Darlington and Greshom Smith had already suggested that the idle time factor was not a part of the cost of the product, as Church had advocated, but Kent elaborated upon their viewpoints considerably. He insisted that the supplementary rate was not really, as Church had written, an index of the efficiency of the factory; but rather it was a measure of the condition of the business in general, and particularly of the efficiency of the selling division of the firm.[353] It was also his idea that the efficiency of the plant could only be tested by comparing the labor costs of doing a certain piece of work at two different periods, leaving the machine burden rate fixed throughout the year. Proposals, such as Church's, which would have added the idle time charge to the cost of the product, would not allow the effectiveness of the shop to be estimated accurately; and, moreover, gave rise to an extraordinarily complicated accounting system. All of these defects could be remedied, he stated, by clearing the idle time charge through profit and loss instead of through the cost of goods produced. Incidentally, Kent claimed that he had applied the same idea as early as 1887, but that it had been in connection with the percentage of direct labor cost method of allocating overhead. At that time an account called "factory expense" was charged on the "factory ledger" (he did not elaborate upon the nature of this ledger) for the amount of burden incurred. The same account was credited with the amount allocated to product. If, at the end of a year, any balance remained in the account, it was closed to profit and loss.[354] Kent did not state definitely whether the percentage was predetermined or not, but evidently it was, or else there would not have been any unabsorbed balance at the end of the period.

All of the various criticisms of the scientific machine rate plan began to cause Church himself to become rather doubtful of the efficacy of considering the idle time charge as a cost. In one of his major books published in 1910, he stated that the relation of the supplementary rate to the "normal cost" was rather arbitrary and that in reality the former was not a cost at all, "but merely the ratio of wasted capacity to utilized capacity."[355] In spite of this theory he went on to give the method of allocating it to products or jobs—usually by a direct labor hour charge—but insisted all the time that it was in no sense a cost, "since it can afford no information of service either for estimating or for comparison with past or future jobs of the same kind. It merely represents the accidental circumstances of the shop during the period, and to that extent is a barometer of conditions."[356] If all this were true, why allocate the supplementary charge at all? Church admitted that there was no real practical advantage in doing so, and all the merits of the system could be obtained by merely presenting the total to the management in a single monthly figure. But for the sake of those managers and accountants who desired to see "every item of expense" allocated over the product produced, he suggested that it be applied to the work actually turned out. It should be noted that he still called the idle time charge an "expense," and that he at this point made it clear that the desirable practice was to apportion the "idle time expense" to processed goods, and not to close it out to profit and loss as an outright loss.

Yet in another place in the same book he recommended that the individual job orders not be charged with any portion of the supplementary rate, stating that all the elements of factory cost were already represented by the total of materials, labor, and the predetermined machine rate.[357] What should be done with the supplementary charge if this procedure were followed? Church advocated that it be shown only on each "works order as a whole on its monthly total and not upon its constituent jobs."[358] This seemed to conflict with the procedure described above, unless he had in mind a similar idea at that point also. At any rate, the occasions would be very rare, according to him, where the idle time charge, as represented by the supplementary rate, would be needed for specific jobs. If, however, any circumstances developed where it was desired, it could be easily obtained by merely turning to the month in which the job was done, and finding the necessary rate. As previously stated, he could not think of any instances where such data would be of service. As he put it, "the ratio of utilized to unutilized capacity has no connection with any purpose for which detail costs are commonly required."[359] In summary, it is evident that Church came very close in 1910 to being converted to the doctrine of his critics, but that he was not yet entirely convinced of the validity of their thesis. The efforts of the opposition, however, became stronger and more potent as the years passed by, and Church again modified his views in his later works.[360]

A popular American author, H. M. Rowe, who wrote in the same year, was likewise unwilling to commit himself definitely as to what should be done with the supplementary rate charge. After first stating that it must be allocated to the product produced during the current period, he reversed himself when he suggested that it might be carried into the next period, and used there as an increase in the burden rate. If the latter technique were adopted, it would result in a larger cost figure for the second year; if not handled in either of the ways mentioned, it became a "dead loss" (his term) to the firm. But what about the case where an overestimate of the machine rate had been made? Rowe thought that this situation would have the advantage of creating a reserve which could be carried forward to the next year and used as a reduction of the burden rate at that time. In general, each extreme should be avoided, wherever possible; he would not state just which was the better practice.[361] Incidentally, the burden rate was to be set by drawing up a budget of manufacturing expenses, and then dividing the total by the number of monthly periods included in the budgeted period. Supposedly, the monthly figures would then have to be divided again by the estimated number of hours that the machines were to work each month. He was not, however, very specific on this point.

Another American authority, John R. Wildman, followed Rowe. To him the final decision was a matter of "desire," or preference, for the most part, although as a general rule he felt that the idle time factor should be included in the cost of production. In cases, however, where laborers were paid during the period of a strike or other enforced inactivity, such amounts should be charged to profit and loss.[362] It should be noted that in the preceding sentence Wildman primarily had reference to direct wages. As for the idle time loss due to the underabsorption of the burden element, he thought that it should be distributed to the product by the usual supplementary rate procedure, which Church had explained. Wildman also took cognizance of the often confused thinking as to the difference between predetermined burden rates and estimated burden rates. It was his idea that the former were to be "constructed from predetermined standards scientifically obtained, whereas estimated costs are purely hypothetical and are founded on the assumption that the costs for the current period will be the same as those of the next preceding period."[363] He hoped this definition would clear up any possible misunderstanding as to the nature of the two concepts. As a matter of fact, they had been used more or less as synonymous terms up to that time.

H. C. Bentley, the prominent American accountant, added a further thought in his *Science of Accounts*. What should be done with the expenditures incurred by a plant in case it was closed down for several weeks? Bentley suggested that such items were proper profit and loss charges, being in the nature of an extraordinary "expense." In case just a few jobs were in progress during a period of considerable inactivity, he would apportion to those jobs only the burden portion applicable to them. He did not state, however, how such a "portion" was to be determined, nor what degree of idleness was necessary for such a procedure to be adopted.[364]

Beginning about 1911 a period of more intense controversy as to the nature of the idle time charge was inaugurated in this country. Some authorities advocated that it be included in the cost of the product, along the lines of Church's revision system, while others were equally emphatic in recommending that it be charged directly to the profit and loss account. One of the strongest exponents of the profit and loss doctrine was the well-known accountant, C. H. Scovell. Although he did not publish his idea until 1913, he used his preferred technique in the early part of 1911. There was no doubting his opinion on the subject:[365]

> The burden on idle machinery is no more a part of the cost of manufacture—unless due to enforced seasonal variation—than the burden on a shop owned by another corporation. When there is a proper distribution and application of expense burden only the burden is charged to cost which represents the equipment utilized in manufacture, and burden not applied remains as a balance to be charged direct to the loss and gain account at the end of the month, six months, or a year. This is readily accomplished through the means of burden accounts which collect by a very simple bookkeeping practice all of the charges in a given class, and receive credits as burden rates of the same kind as charged to the cost of product going through the works. The unearned burden in some cases may indicate an error which is to be corrected by using a more accurate rate in a subsequent period, but when proper records have been

established, the unearned burden is a clear loss, and the balances of the burden accounts should be transferred directly to the profit and loss account. If the distinction is maintained between losses or gains on goods made and sold, and losses due to restricted output, the management will consider sales policies in a much more certain way than is possible when the facts are obscured in the haze of average costs, calculated on varying volumes of product. In respect to burden, it is frequently true that costs figured as averages vary beyond all hope of comparison as the volume of output goes up or down. When a cost accounting practice is maintained that distinguishes carefully between prime costs for material and labor, (which vary almost directly with the volume) and overhead charges or burden, the managers can see exactly in times of slack production at what price they can take any work that is offered and get something to carry the burden of the shop, in addition to the direct cost of labor and material. This, it must be admitted, is to some extent a matter of policy, for it may be better to hold a price and restrict output, rather than break the market by quoting prices that will give temporarily a little additional profit.

Scovell reiterated this view at every opportunity during the succeeding decade.[366]

F. E. Webner, a practicing Certified Public Accountant, on the other hand, thought that the loss should be absorbed in the product cost in some way. One method would be to establish a reserve account which, at periodic intervals, would be closed out to the cost of the product. Another method, not recommended, was to leave off the reserve and divide the total burden element due to idle time by the actual number of hours applied to product, and add this on to the jobs. The second procedure, if used at all, was only adaptable to the direct labor hour basis of allocating overhead. As for the seasonal fluctuation within a company's business, Webner recommended that the overhead rate be set at least with a year's activity in mind, so that the seasonal influence would be smoothed out. A reserve account was to be used to record the over and under applied amounts as between the different months of the year.[367] He recognized that this method had some relation to the undesirable practice of "averaging," but it was proposed because of the advantageous result obtained; that is, the uniformity of costs at least within the current year. It was his idea, also, that after a few years, the firm could determine a rate which would leave only a small amount under or over applied at the end of the period, except for pure idle time. Idle time would have to be handled in a different way.

Webner and Scovell, therefore, were quite opposed in their views.

Both recommended predetermined rates, but were entirely at odds as to the handling of idle time. H. A. Evans, in the same year, reverted to the opinion that costing should be done on the basis of actual rates determined at the end of each month. It had many advantages, according to him, at least from the standpoint of the bookkeeping involved. The entire "expense" would be allocated each month, and there would be no need for any "loss and gain expense" account, as he called it.[368] But like several authorities before him, Evans thought it desirable to use average rates, based upon previous years, when making an estimate for a prospective contract. The average rates might even be adjusted in the light of prospective future conditions, if necessary, in order to obtain a more accurate basis for the bid. Evans was almost alone, however, in his proposal to retain the distinctly historical burden rates; nearly all the other authorities were by this time on the other side of the question.

The English cost experts were also quibbling over details in those early years of the twentieth century. L. W. Hawkins, for example, although recommending the predetermining of the burden element so that it could be charged to jobs when they were completed, had some trouble in reconciling his "cost accounts" as such, with the general accounts. Then, too, he suggested a suspense account arrangement for handling the factory burden which had not been apportioned to work in process, uncompleted as of the end of a period.[369] In the case of a new firm, the estimate would have to be based upon the experience of others, modified to some extent in accordance with any peculiar conditions which might exist within the individual plant. Even though it was an estimated figure, it ought to be adjusted, he stated, every time the general accounts were closed, so as not to become too fixed in the minds of the managers. Hawkins' views were somewhat beclouded by the fact that he advocated the charging of all types of expense items to jobs, no matter whether they did or did not pertain to the factory. Incidentally, he did not mention the idle time problem.

The English author of *Advanced Accounting*, Dicksee, however, did not prefer the predetermined plan. He admitted that it was in popular use, but called it a makeshift method of handling burden. He said that it was adopted only because the "counting house," as he called the accounting office, did not usually find itself able to supply the cost clerks with frequent totals of the "oncost" items. It was his idea that if oncost items could be accumulated, say on a weekly basis, the apportionment could be carried out more accurately.[370]   In addition, he followed the editor of *The Accountant* in insisting that actual costs should be derived, varying with the state of activity of the plant. This was entirely in accordance with his idea of delayed costings. To express his theory in a different way, the cost accounts should show that the cost of an identical job or a product was a larger figure in time of slack business than in a period of brisk business; averaging techniques and predetermined normal rates, therefore, should not be adopted. All such practices, according to Dicksee, had the tendency of destroying the real usefulness of the results. In contrast to Hawkins, he thought the better precedure was to assign the burden to jobs or processes every week, if possible, instead of waiting until the product was finished. This would allow the work to be done more accurately, as inequitable results could be corrected before it was too late. Dicksee seemed to have forgotten that the shorter the time interval employed the more complex and difficult the allocation problem became. In summary, he thought that no matter what system might be used within a plant for recording burden costs, unsatisfactory results and errors would be obtained at least occasionally. These errors could be detected more easily, he stated, if the overhead application took place by continuous installments; nothing was said, however, about the increased bookkeeping which would be involved.

From the above, it can be seen that English accountants were contributing little to the theory underlying the accounting for idle time during the period immediately preceding the First World War. But in this country the controversy continued. S. H. Bunnell, for example, in 1912, advocated the accumulation of a surplus appropriation, in a period of good business, to take care of the added costs in depression years. He compared it with the stabilization of dividends, and the ledger accounts were to be handled the same way. Another of his rather novel suggestions was that the sales department should be charged with the costs of maintaining seasonally-used equipment when it was idle through no fault of the factory. It was his theory that it was up to the selling division to keep such machinery busy, and if it did not supply the orders, it ought to be charged with its failure. It is very doubtful, however, if many sales forces or managers would have been convinced of the merit of his plan. It should be remembered, though, that his proposal was only concerned with that type of equipment purchased or built purely to satisfy some seasonal demand.[371] In a previous work Bunnell had advocated the charging of idle time losses to profit and loss, in line with Scovell and others and for exactly the same reasons,[372] although he stated that they represented "trade" (his term) gains or losses, and not operating costs. It was his opinion, also, that after the machine burden rates had been carefully determined, they should remain fixed until some permanent alteration in operating conditions, not caused by idle time or capacity. This was a point that most of the authorities of the period neglected to mention, perhaps because they were not so sure of their ground. They implied, however, that a new set of rates should be compiled at least once a year. Bunnell was much more definite; he also stressed the importance of examining with a critical eye the differences between predetermined figures and actual costs. Such differences were indexes of efficiency, in his opinion.

J. L. Nicholson, whose earlier views have been discussed, added a refinement to the calculation of the machine rates when he published his *Cost Accounting* in 1913. It was intimately related to his method of handling the idle time problem. His idea, in essence, was that the rate for each group of machines should be divided into at least three separate parts: the first part was to include the operating charges only, while another represented the annual fixed charges allocated to the particular department or group of machines. The third section of the rate structure was the department's prorata share of the estimated general overhead items. The use to be made of these three distinct classes was described by him as follows:

Allowances for idle time would now be made . . . . The maximum number of the operating hours is multiplied by the total rate for each machine, which gives the total amount charged against that machine. The sum of all these charges constitutes the total estimated factory charge. The number of idle hours for each machine is then multiplied by the operating expense rate only, which represents the expense charged against the machine but not actually incurred. When the sum of all allowances for idle time is subtracted from the total estimated factory charge, the result is the net estimate and the actual expense is then adjusted through the supplementary rate. In such case the supplementary rate becomes far more important, because it is no longer limited only to adjusting mistakes in the estimates, but also becomes the indicator of idleness in the factory, and provides the means for distributing the resulting burden over the whole product manufactured. The supplementary rate, which distributed these expenses, reflects in actual figure the fact that idleness in one part of the plant is a burden on the rest of it.[373]

His theory, therefore, contemplated the inclusion of idle time in cost of product, but his separation of the machine rate charges allowed the amount of idle time losses to stand out sharply in relief. As a matter of fact, however, his refinement was not followed by most later authorities, and was of doubtful practical advantage. Nicholson's contemporary E. P. Moxey, for instance, considered that idle time losses were no part of manufacturing cost, and should be closed out as a direct charge to profit and loss. Moxey also advocated that an account called "idle capacity" be set up on the ledger, and used to collect all such charges. In regard to the use of the supplementary rate, advocated by A. Hamilton Church, Moxey stated:

> The distribution of indirect expense upon the supplementary rate plan is exceedingly unjust and generally unsatisfactory. The calculations are based, in the first place, upon the ability of the company to gauge in advance the number of hours during which the plant is likely to be operated. Under conditions of uncertain demand this is almost impossible. A better method is to provide for the charging of idle time to an Idle Capacity account, whose balance at the end of the year is charged to profit and loss . . . . One of the best indicia of the efficiency of a plant is the comparative size of the Idle Capacity account; for its ratio to the total amount of indirect expenses is an index of the manager's success in keeping his machinery employed.[374]

This suggestion was the same as that made by John Whitmore, some seven years before, although Whitmore was rather indefinite as to what should be done with the balance of the account.[375]

Even as late as 1913, the English editor of *The Accountant* was still insisting in his editorials that all costing should be purely historical, and that the burden element of cost could not be applied to product until after the end of a certain time period. One editorial in 1913 was written as a commentary on the uniform cost system which had just been drawn up for the Master Printers of England. This system contained a recommendation to the effect that the overhead of the previous year should be used as a guide for allocating the current year's figure, or if the last year were unusual in any respect, an average of several previous years should be taken. This practice, according to the editor, resulted in a system which was not costing, but estimating, and was "hardly the last word on the subject. . . . We cannot regard it as more than an instalment on account of a complete costing system."[376] This authority, then, did not trust predetermined burden rates, and what was more, any industry that used them was treading on dangerous ground. All the contrary opinions expressed since 1905 had made no impression on the editor; his position on the subject was still firm.

The editor's viewpoint should not be considered as representative of the majority of English cost accountants during that period. More than likely a large number disagreed with him. For example, M. W. Jenkinson recommended in no uncertain terms that the burden be estimated in advance, and expressed in the form of a percentage of the annual turnover, also estimated. He did not state just what sort of turnover he had in mind,[377] but did point out that the whole problem was one that required very careful attention and calculation, especially where a firm made several different kinds of commodities in several departments. After the above estimates had been made, the superintendent of the factory would know that he must add to the cost of each job a percentage large enough to absorb all the overhead. There might be, incidentally, two reasons for underallocation at the end of any certain year. One would be due to the fact that orders from customers did not reach the estimated total, in which instance the factory manager would be absolved of any blame. The other was concerned with the insufficiency of the overhead percentage (assuming that the estimated turnover had been reached). This insufficiency would indicate that profits which supposedly existed on "certain jobs" were overstated.[378] Jenkinson did not point out just how the likely discrepancy was to be handled, preferring to leave the matter unsettled; his treatment of the subject was typical of the English attitude before World War I.

Beginning about 1915 the view that idle time was not a proper part of cost of production but an outright loss began to be advocated with increasing vehemence. Not a new idea, it came into particular prominence in the early years of the First World War. Several authorities also began to argue about credit for the concept and some obvious ill will resulted because of claims made by different parties. As a matter of fact, the development of the theory, as is usual with most new ideas, cannot be attributed to any one person. It was probably first hinted at by one expert, then suggested by another, and finally advocated by a third or fourth individual. But the period around 1915-20 proved to be a turning point. In 1915, for example, H. L. Gantt, the famous American industrial engineer, examined critically the fundamental bases of cost theory, with special reference to the matter of idle time and capacity. He concluded that most cost accounting systems were much more beneficial to the group he called "financiers" than they were to the factory superintendent or manager. The methods in use at the time, moreover, had the tendency of focusing attention upon the factory for every shortcoming of the entire firm. In his opinion this was unfair, and not very conducive to the greatest all-round plant efficiency. Costing should be more attuned, he said, to the needs of the factory proper, and to do this the system must give the plant manager data as to whether he was doing his work economically as circumstances would permit; this aim, according to Gantt, had been seriously neglected in cost procedures in use up to that time. In order to attain that objective it was necessary to approach the problem in a different way, especially with reference to idle time. How could this perplexing question be solved? Gantt's answer was to state that "the indirect expenses chargeable to the output of a factory should bear the same ratio to the indirect expenses necessary to run the factory at normal capacity as the output in question bears to the normal output of the factory."[379] There was really nothing original in this theory; it was in essence the same one that Scovell and others had advocated several years before. But Gantt's pronouncement of it seemed to have borne more weight; at any rate it received more publicity at the time. Gantt pointed out also that most firms did not follow his suggestion, but charged to cost of production the entire expenditures of a period, no matter at what rate the factory may have been operating. In his opinion, many entirely unsound business policies could be directly attributed to this false concept. In summary, what he proposed was that the factory cost of an article was not what it had actually cost in the past, "but what it should cost if the proper manufacturing methods were used and the shop were run at full capacity. This might be called the ideal cost, and toward its attainment all efforts should be directed."[380] With this declaration the stage was set for the fierce struggle between the supporters of different ideas which took place in the next decade.

In the same year, N. T. Ficker elaborated upon the concept of "normal" burden rates in *The Engineering Magazine*. The term, he pointed out, was often used in different senses; to him it represented the amount of burden "which past experience and present knowledge of future conditions would warrant as being applicable under normal shop activity."[381] Obviously, the determination of the normal shop activity was one of the important aspects of the problem, but Ficker did not dwell on it. In case there was doubt, however, as to the estimate of the overhead amount, it was better to be conservative. As he put it, "the normal expense should be neither high nor low, but a safe basis on which costs can be computed."[382] He continued his discussion by examining the supplementary rate technique which had been so strongly advocated by Church. According to Ficker, the theory was almost useless as a practical device for controlling costs; the loss due to idle time should not under any circumstances be considered an element of cost. The management should be made aware of any variations in cost due to fluctuating output not attributable to factory conditions. This could be done by establishing a separate account on the books, where the idle time charges would remain until offset by over-normal activity credits, or until they were cleared through profit and loss. In determining the amount of costs to allot to the factory, this authority suggested that "the expense chargeable against the shop should be that portion of the constant expense which the current activity is of the normal activity, plus the actual current variable expense. That is, if the activity for a certain year was found to be sixty per cent of the normal activity, then the expense chargeable against the shop for that year would be 60 per cent of the constant expense plus the actual variable expense incurred during the period."[383] Ficker did not state definitely whether he recommended the carrying forward of unabsorbed or overabsorbed idle time charges,[384] but even if they were not, the amounts involved during a series of years could be used as an indication of the efficiency of the management. In order to carry out his idea of fixed and variable costs it was necessary for him to give elaborate details as to their compilation. In addition, he devoted several paragraphs to a criticism of contemporary cost practices.

In the same issue of *The Engineering Magazine*, H. L. Gantt again put forward his proposals for a more careful analysis of idle time losses. In essence his ideas as expressed here were practically the same as those described previously, except that he seemed more certain of his reasoning. He tried to convince his readers that no cost plan worthy of the name would treat idle time as an element of cost of production. It was his belief, moreover, that such a practice had been one of the most fruitful sources of causes for the failure of firms; that is to say, firms which did not properly account for idle capacity continued to exist, not because of their costing arrangements, but in spite of them. In addition, Gantt took considerable care to emphasize the tremendous amount of loss caused by idle plant and equipment. In fact, he stated it to be "absolutely unbelievable."[385] It will be remembered in this connection that the United States was beginning to come out of the depression of 1913-14 about that time, and Gantt's personal observations were probably still fresh in his memory. The problem of idle time, therefore, needed a more accurate accounting treatment,[386] according to him. Cost techniques and theories required a new viewpoint which would emphasize the normal burden incurred in the manufacture of a given amount of product instead of the actual burden. To express it in a different way, the output of the plant should not bear all the overhead items and amounts, but only that portion needed to produce it. If a statement were drawn up regularly showing the loss involved in maintaining idle facilities the management could do one or both of two things. It could ask itself the question: can some work be obtained for the idle machines that will bring in the regular profit? If this were answered in the negative, then it could ask itself whether it could find some jobs for the machines which would result in less loss than to allow the equipment to remain idle. In other words, the management would have something tangible upon which to base its decisions. Even though Gantt was proposing nothing new in the way of theory, he did deserve some credit for emphasizing the importance of idle time losses.

Gantt's theories, however, (and for that matter those of a whole group of authorities) were criticized at some length by R. E. Flanders a short while later. Flanders was entirely in sympathy with the final aim of those fellow Americans who advocated that idle capacity losses should be closed directly to the profit and loss account; but he insisted that comparable costs and effective control could be obtained by the old device of setting the burden rates with an entire business cycle in mind, and clearing all burden items through product costs. He called it the "average rate plan," while Gantt's system was entitled the "proportional rate plan."[387] Flanders' scheme was practically the same as that advocated by several previous writers, dating as far back as 1903. It contemplated the setting up of an overhead account the balance of which would be carried forward from year to year, the theory being that the debits and credits would offset each other after a complete business cycle. The rate was not to be changed very often, if at all, and this was one of the advantages he claimed over the proportional rate plan which was supposedly changed at least every year. Flanders contended that there was "good reason for absorbing this periodically recurring expense in costs [idle time items], rather than in profit and loss. This charge has not the nature of an extraneous calamity . . . . We are forced, unfortunately, to reckon with cycles . . . as one of the conditions of doing business and this condition therefore is a regular factor in the cost of production, and should be so treated."[388] Here was, then, a clear statement of the idle-time-a-cost-of-production concept. Yet Flanders recognized the merit of a stable overhead rate, and deserved credit for reemphasizing the two methods of attaining it. It was his opinion that his technique was more logical in that "all costs" were finally distributed. As a matter of fact, the final decision rested on the individual preference of the firm desiring to adopt one of the methods; both of them had the same end in view, but they used different means to attain it.

Even though Flanders had insisted that the difference between his method and others was based upon the concept of what was cost of production and what was not, he was only partially correct. What Gantt, Scovell, and others were struggling for was a standard burden cost, rather than the use of any sort of averaging scheme. While they only hinted at the real theoretical bases for their technique, later authorities were much more explicit. It soon became common knowledge that no system of averaging the overhead rates over a period of years would perform all that was required of an adequate costing arrangement. W. E. McHenry, for instance, pointed out a short while later that only predetermined normal (he called them "standard") burden rates would give satisfactory results under conditions of varying production. This was especially true where there were several products in varying stages of completion as of the close of any certain cost period. McHenry also disputed the contention of those authorities, such as Flanders, who insisted that a long-term average rate was practically the same thing. According to McHenry there was no comparison between the two.[389] Variations in costs could be scientifically accumulated only by setting up predetermined standards of comparisons; this theme, incidentally, was to be repeated continually in the years to come. McHenry, however, was not by any means the originator of the idea. Its essential features can be traced at least as far back as 1889 and perhaps further. Several authorities had even given fairly comprehensive descriptions of the fundamental details.[390]

The idea of normal burden rates was being advocated so strenuously by their protagonists that the Federal Trade Commission recommended their adoption in its widely read pamphlet on costing published in 1916. In that work it was stated that the overhead items should be estimated or budgeted as of the first of a year and divided by the expected yearly normal output in hours of the factory machines; this rate was not to be changed at any time during the current year. Any unabsorbed or overabsorbed amount was to be closed to the profit and loss account[391] at the end of the fiscal period (one year).

At about the same time D. S. Kimball, the American engineer, counseled caution in adopting the plan which charged all losses due to idle time to the loss and gain account. While he did not desire to condemn it completely, he did point out an assumption which was fundamental to the system and which had been recognized by others as well, namely that all the machines in the factory would operate at full capacity during the year. This assumption, according to him, might not necessarily be altogether logical. There were, he stated, some pieces of equipment in most plants which, while indispensable, were not used all the time. A false rate would be obtained, therefore, if it were assumed that they were to operate all the time. As a matter of fact, however, most of the schemes which had been proposed had recommended "practical" capacity as a basis, and if this were adopted, Kimball's objection[392] would be obviated.

Kimball also criticized the so-called "average rate" plan on the grounds that it was an averaging scheme and was subject to all the hazards of any plan based on such a technique. If both of the by then usual systems of handling idle time were unsatisfactory, what method could be adopted which would at the same time be accurate and scientific? The answer was that no one method would ever give desired results under all circumstances, but it seemed to Kimball that the machine rate plan used "in connection with a supplementary rate based on a long period of time would do much to solve the perplexing problem."[393] This plan would at least, according to him, correctly allocate the burden to the product that was completed, and except in periods of very great depression would prove satisfactory. By using a long-period supplementary rate the losses due to idle capacity would be equalized over the entire business cycle, and the extreme danger of allocating too much overhead during a period of depression would be anticipated. Kimball did not know whether his proposal had ever been tried or not. As a matter of interest it would appear that it was subject to the defects of the long-term averaging technique, which he had just dismissed as being entirely inadequate. In fact, it was similar, although Kimball did not give any details as to the compilation of his "long-term supplementary rate." He concluded that "the entire question of expense burden with change in volume of product is interesting, though com-

plex. It is unwise to make sweeping generalizations regarding a solution. . . . This phase of cost finding . . . will bear close inspection
by managers whose volume of production varies markedly."[394]

By 1917 the advocates of the idle-time-a-loss concept had argued
so well that A. Hamilton Church dwelt upon both the cost and the
loss views in his comprehensive work published in that year.[395] He
again summarized the supplementary rate technique and then explained that the balance of burden unabsorbed and shown in the
burden account represented a pure waste. He still recommended
the practice, however, of allocating such amounts over the production orders. In a separate section, though, Church discussed the
idle-time-a-loss viewpoint, and stated that in the last analysis all losses
would have to come out of profits, if any. The closing of the idle
time to profit and loss, he admitted, was a much simpler method,
and in certain cases it could be perhaps recommended, say in a firm
which had only a few departments containing large machines regularly operated. In general, however, it was more desirable to express
this loss as a percentage of actual cost; there was, in his opinion,
comparatively less danger of factory managers being deceived as to
operating efficiency. He admitted also that the supplementary percentage was only a partial barometer of idle equipment, while previously he had viewed this point much more specifically. His position
on the whole subject was thus rather wavering; as will be seen later
in this section, he modified his theory still further in later works.

The idea of a predetermined overhead rate, therefore, was fairly
well established by 1918; only a few authorities here and there still
advocated waiting until the end of a month or year to allocate the
burden element of cost. Most of those who did restricted their
recommendation to so-called process cost situations. But the controversy over the idle time or capacity problem continued even during the First World War prosperity period. Apparently the cost
accountants who wrote on the subject during that period thought that
near-capacity production would not last very long and wanted to
have their position on the subject ready for the expected depression
of the postwar years. At any rate there was little abatement during
the period in the variety of opinions expressed on the topic. William
Kent, for instance, advocated that the burden element of cost should
be that amount which would be incurred to reproduce the article
within the near future under normal conditions. This was, in his
opinion, essentially a standard burden rate, and had the important

advantage of saving a great deal of the clerical work ordinarily required. [396] In addition, the cost of maintaining machines which were essential but not used regularly should be included in the machine burden rate even though they were idle. This would answer the criticism advanced by D. S. Kimball, even though such an idea would have been more or less arbitrary in its application. Kent continued by advocating the usual profit and loss treatment of any burden excess not apportioned to the cost of product during any certain year.

The English authorities also returned to the problem after World War I. For example, in 1920, A. Cathles recommended that since it was generally impracticable to wait until the end of a fiscal period to allocate burden, the total should be compiled on a budget at least once a year and used as a basis for making the apportionments. The budget was to be drawn up in detail in order to keep a proper control over the estimated, actual, and allocated figures for each item. In addition, the different departments of the firm were to be kept in mind, since they provided a means of ascertaining properly the incidence of some of the charges.[397] In general, Cathles showed considerably familiarity with the modern machine hour method of handling the overhead problem; his discussion of idle time, however, and its accounting treatment, left a great deal to be desired. G. S. Hattersley, who followed Cathles, was much more explicit. He recognized the work which had been done in the United States and seems to have been influenced by such writers as Scovell, Gantt, Ficker and others. The usual concept of cost of production gave highly fluctuating costs because all the burden incurred during a period was included in cost no matter at what rate of capacity the plant operated. Hattersley criticized this method and then gave the same formula for the accepted determination of factory overhead cost as had been given by several of the Americans. That is to say, in periods of curtailed production, the burden chargeable to cost was the same percentage of the total overhead, as the curtailed production was of the so-called "standard production." This concept was described as that level of production which would give the lowest consistent cost figures. If the technique mentioned were not adopted the costs would "appear highest when the trade is most needed, a condition of affairs which will certainly not popularize costing with the practical manufacturers."[398] Hattersley then went on to recommend that the loss due to idle time be deducted from profits. He had reached the same conclusion as many experts in this country.

Another English cost authority, E. T. Elbourne, also had the concept of "normal burden" included in his elaborate costing arrangement.   He did not advocate the usual preëstimate of the overhead items which would probably be incurred during the coming period.   A preëstimate would, he thought, cause the rates to fluctuate widely in periods of varying production.   The better technique was "to base the oncost rates on the expense figures which will obtain when the factory is working efficiently as regards the volume of output.   Such expenses may be considered as the normal, and the oncost rates based on same may also be termed normal."[399]   How were the normal rates to be derived?   The answer was that they were the lowest that could be safely adopted in making estimates of costs which would allow a profit to be derived from the product or job.   Since Elbourne probably represented the more advanced English viewpoint in regard to this problem, his remarks should be quoted in extenso:

> If the contention can be admitted that commercial estimates of cost should always be prepared on normal lines as regards the provision for oncosts . . . it will give much more value to the actual cost figures if the production oncosts are applied at normal rates in the cost allocation accounts.   There is another and perhaps more important reason for using normal oncost rates in works accounts, and that is to set up some standard by which the departmental production may be compared.   If the oncosts as applied to the production of any department for a given period, amount to a less total than the actual expenses apportioned to that department, it may be assumed that the volume of production is below the normal or accepted efficiency level. . . . Opinions will differ as to what is to be considered the normal output for a given factory, and three-fourth of the factory's full capacity is suggested as a suitable standard.   The decision must depend on local factors.[400]

If there were any over or under allocated burden after carrying out this technique, it would be handled on what he called a "works accounts annual abstract."   This abstract was a sort of clearing or balancing statement for the "works" books, which were, incidentally, entirely separate under his system.   As can be easily seen, Elbourne was following in the steps of those cost experts in this country who were beginning to advocate with some fervor normal (standard) costing arrangements, with particular emphasis in that period to the burden element of cost.   After all, the burden element (or cost component) was the one that had caused comparatively the most trouble in the past, so it was natural that they should start with it.[401]

In the United States the trend seemed more and more towards the normal predetermined burden rate plan. Several authorities advocated its use in the early 1920's, sometimes with a slight modification, but generally about the same.[402] The practice gradually worked into complete standard costing systems. More and more attention began to be given also to the determination of the normal percentage of capacity and all the attendant problems connected therewith. Certain authorities again occasionally recommended the establishment of overhead reserves in periods of good business which were to be drawn upon, somewhat as an earned surplus reserve, during slack production years.[403] The controversy after a few years became to some extent a matter of disagreement over the finer points involved, rather than broad principles, although occasionally some authority would revert to older concepts. In addition, the technique of flexible budgeting for controlling and accounting for burden came to the forefront.[404] This technique was, of course, merely an extension of the long recognized fixed and variable overhead grouping, which can be traced back at least to the 1880's.

This section cannot end without reference to the fact that by 1930, A. Hamilton Church, who had, some 29 years before, so strongly advocated the supplementary-rate-a-measure-of-idle-time-cost theory, was at last won over to the opposing viewpoint. In his comprehensive *Overhead Expense*, published in that year, the loss due to idle capacity was recognized as such and closed to profit and loss. Church still recommended, however, the use of the supplementary rate technique in a few isolated instances.[405]

PART VI. DEPARTMENTALIZATION AND DISTRIBUTION OF BURDEN

Departmentalization was one of the topics that received early attention from costing authorities; its companion subject, distribution, was also handled with some care by industrial accountants. Since the two are so obviously related, they will be treated simultaneously in the present discussion. The term "distribution" is here used in its technical sense, that is, the spreading or dividing of manufacturing overhead costs between the departments of a factory.

One of the first references to the problem in modern times was that contained in a correspondence given in the *Engineer*, an English publication, in 1870. After mentioning that the burden cost items usually caused the most trouble in costing, the writer insisted that "general" (his term) overhead rates would be insufficient to solve the problem. What was needed, he said, was a special rate for each department of the firm. In order to derive these rates he recommended that the accounts of each division be distinguished on the ledgers; and, furthermore, the totals of all the departmental items should, in the end, agree with the costs in total.[406] Thomas Battersby, another English accountant, also advocated the departmentalization of the factory; he even divided the factory overhead items on the basis of whether or not they were peculiar to the departments involved in his system. Several which he included are now called service departments. He listed: the steam power department, the power department—lathes and tools, and the smith's department. The costs from each of these were accumulated on a daily basis, and were to be added to the workmen's wages in order to arrive at the cost of a job passing through a department. Machine repairs and upkeep were divided in accordance with the capital value of each, while the power was divided on the basis of horsepower required.[407] While Battersby's ideas were somewhat confused, he did show considerable originality in handling the problems involved in departmentalization.[408]

By 1886, then, the need for departments had been recognized, but the treatment of the subject in general had been rather superficial, especially in regard to the distribution of overhead to the divisions. In that year Henry Metcalfe, an American Army ordnance officer, read a paper on the "The Shop-Order System of Accounts" before the American Society of Mechanical Engineers in which he referred to "departmental cost factors." This early authority did not give any general discussion of the basis for departmentalization, but did mention that in a foundry there should be at least five departments, namely, pattern shop, molding, melting, mounting, and unclassified. The cost factors were to be determined by (1) distributing such items as rent, taxes, and insurance "among the departments profiting by them according to the most probable hypothesis";[409] (2) distributing various incidental items among the departments on the basis of the total day's work done in each one; (3) adding to the preceding two items the total of each department's own peculiar costs; and (4) dividing the total of the three by the number of direct days' work done in each department during the past year. These factors were then used to determine the cost of making any article or job which passed through the department. Metcalfe also gave a schedule for making the distribution of the indirect burden items among the departments. It was the simplest sort of statement; all the indirect items were distributed in proportion to the days worked in each division of the firm. It will be remembered that Metcalfe had recommended the use of the previous year's figure for the determination of the cost factor, or, as an alternate, an average of two or three years;[410] the schedule, therefore, was worked out on that basis. Incidentally, in the melting department of the foundry, the output of good castings in pounds was to be used as a basis of distribution instead of the number of days worked. This was due to the fact that the cost of iron was much more important in that work than the labor involved. In summary, it might be said that Metcalfe saw more completely the problem of departmentalization than either of the authorities who have been examined; yet his treatment left much to be desired.

On the other hand, the Englishman G. P. Norton, who wrote in the late 1880's on the accounting for textile mills, gave a great deal of attention to the topic of departmentalization. In fact, it was an integral part of his system and requires a rather lengthy review at this point. The number and variety of departments were matters that each firm had to decide for itself. Norton, however, recommended at least six. These were: woolen carding and spinning, worsted combing and spinning, weaving, dyeing, finishing, and stores. Each of these had a separate column provided in the purchases daybook to facilitate the collection of the expenditures peculiar to them. At the end of each quarter the total of each of the columns was posted to individual accounts in the "nominal ledger." Sales and sales returns of both yarn and cloth were to be differentiated, and after all the miscellaneous expenses had been apportioned, the profit on each line of goods could be derived. In order to distribute the "standing expenses" (his term) to the several departments, Norton advocated the use of an analysis statement. This had columns for a total, then one for each department, and one for patterns (an asset). How were the miscellaneous items to be distributed? Norton was unusually explicit on this point. First he mentioned that there was no necessity of distributing the warehouse and office expenses since they were unconnected with the manufacturing departments; as for the factory overhead, there were various bases which could be used. The storeroom supplies used by each department would be kept separate by the storekeeper. The cost of mechanics, joiners, and plumbers would be ascertained by recording the time they worked in each department. The power cost was to be apportioned in accordance with the machinery turned in each department. Rent and taxes were to be divided on the basis of floor space occupied, or else combined with the power cost in one charge. Lighting would be distributed on the basis of the number of gas lights used, or separate meters might be installed in each department, if desired. Fire insurance was usually found already distributed in the policies themselves, while the repairs and renewals of equipment were usually separated in the purchases book. Repairs to the building, on the other hand, should be distributed on the basis of the invoices received from the people who did the work. Depreciation was allotted on the basis of the value of the machinery in each department.[411] Incidentally, Norton noted that a great part of departmentalization could be carried out by the vendors of the firm in question, if they were given proper instructions. In addition, he warned his readers that the whole matter of distribution could be easily carried to absurd limits, and that substantial accuracy was all that was required; minute details, which would perhaps require the services of several extra clerks, were not worth the added expense. Norton thought that "the ordinary staff of a well-organized mill, if properly directed, can do all that is essential for the preparation of departmental accounts on the principle here described."[412] Taken as a whole, then, Norton's system would have been surprisingly effective for the type of enterprise that he had in mind. He even made some proposals for testing the efficiency of the manufacturing division of the business by charging each department of the firm with its proportion of the expenditures incurred, as outlined above, and crediting it at "standard" (his term) prices for the work which it completed. The standard referred to was a sort of trade price for that particular process. This suggestion may be considered one of the first intimations of the essential aim of present-day standard costing arrangements; it at least had the same purpose in view. Norton stated, too, that he had found it to be reliable and satisfactory in practice.[413] In summary, it may be concluded that this authority's technique as to departmentalization was not improved upon for more than a decade; in fact, it held a place of its own for some fifteen years.[414]

F. G. Burton, another Englishman writing a few years later, referred to the departmentalization problems within an engineering establishment. While Burton's treatment was not so complete as Norton's it is deserving of notice at this point. His first observation was that the firm should be divided into departments, each one having an account (separate from financial books) for each month. (See the accompanying illustration.)

FITTERS—JANUARY 1895[415]

Debits

	Quanti-ties	Materi-ials and expenses	Salaries and wages	Trade Debits
Stock Jan. 1:				
Parts				
Work-in-Progress				
Purchases				
Wages				
Transfer from Departments-Process				
Transfers from Departments-Establishment Charges				
Interest				
Depreciation				
Total				

Credits

	Quanti-ties	Materi-ials and expenses	Salaries and wages	Trade Credits
Estimated Charges				
Transfers to Departments				
Transfers to "B" and "C" sheets				
Stock January 31:				
Parts				
Work-in-Progress				
Total				

These accounts were not designed to show the departmental profit and loss, as was typical during that time; rather, they were used particularly as a method of deriving accurate costs. The "estimated charges" referred to on the credit side of the account were those expenditures which had been made for the department which had not been paid for at the end of the previous month, and which were included in the "purchases" on the debit side for the current month. The "transfers" listed in the account on both sides were to be handled according to the best ability of the accountant. In regard to these transfers, only the actual costs were to be included, but Burton was not very specific as to the exact technique to be employed. He stated merely that the technical officials of the firm were to be consulted as to the progress of the work, and that the cost clerk was to make his entries accordingly. Burton did not elaborate upon this most important point. All the transfers from the various departments were to be summarized on a separate statement, called "Sheet B." This was used to collect, month by month, the departmental charges against any particular section of a job. When Sheet "B" had been filled out it was in turn transferred to Sheet "C," which was a sort of cost sheet for each job; Sheet "C" was not closed, then, until the job was completed. Burton's scheme contemplated, therefore, (1) departmental cost statements, (2) contract divisional statements, and, finally, (3) contract or job cost statements. The columns entitled "trade debits" and "trade credits" on the example were used for the possible occasions when a firm desired to record what it *would have cost* to get the work done outside of its own shops (trade debits) and for what the *work which was done* would be worth if it had been executed for outside firms (trade credits). It was, therefore, a device like Norton's for testing the efficiency of the departments, remotely similar to a standard cost system of the present time. It was crude, of course, but no more could have been expected in view of the state of costing in general around the time Burton wrote. Interestingly enough, Burton did not mention this device in his *Engineers' and Shipbuilders' Accounts* published several years later.[416] Did he consider it, at that time, impractical? While there is no answer to this, Norton and Burton were two of the very few who ever advocated such a scheme; present day standard costs are correlated to a different sort of base.

Both of the preceding authorities showed a tendency to gloss over the difficulties inherent in departmentalization; that is, they assumed the problem to be relatively simple in nature. J. S. Lewis, their countryman, was less optimistic. It was Lewis' opinion that there was considerable doubt as to the extent to which all the general establishment expenses could be distributed; it varied with the circumstances peculiar to each firm. Lewis pointed out, however, the various possible bases which might be used, say for repairs, gas, water, power, and the like.[417] He spoke frequently of "fair" methods and "equitable results," phrases which had been typical of previous authorities; but, in general, Lewis was somewhat more thorough than his contemporaries. His ideas, however, were not so succinctly stated as those of Norton's.

In the United States the problem began to receive much more attention around the turn of the century. H. L. Arnold, for example, in 1899, illustrated a ledger for a foundry with seven different departments. Each one of these had its own loss and gain account; the balance was closed to a sort of general profit and loss account at the end of the year in order to arrive at the net loss or profit for the period. To give one example, the boiler shop account had the following debits posted to it throughout the year: departmental purchases of productive materials, transfer of productive material from other departments, departmental purchases of productive labor, transfer of productive labor from other departments, departmental purchases of unproductive material, transfer of unproductive material from other departments, departmental purchases of unproductive labor, transfer of unproductive labor from other departments, and the department's proportion of general burden items (on basis of material and labor incurred in the department). On the credit side there were the sales from the sales account and the transfers to other departments. The result gave the departmental profit. Each of the seven departments was handled similarly. Arnold's system was an obvious improvement over the usual profit and loss account technique; he neglected to mention, however, the crux of the problem: How were all the interdepartmental transfers to be priced?[418] What Arnold evidently had in mind was a departmentalized profit and loss statement, but he omitted some of the more controversial distribution points connected therewith.

The departmentalization procedure advocated around the turn of the century by A. Hamilton Church should be discussed briefly in this section, even though his views have already been presented at length in previous sections of this chapter. It will be remembered that he proposed a "production center" theory which would be used to localize the overhead as much as possible. In reference to the "centers," certain "production factors" would have to be assembled. These were the land factor, the building factor, the power factor, and so on. All the possible burden items which could be debited to the factor accounts were charged thereto; these accounts were in turn closed out to the shop-charges account on some "fair" bases. All the general burden items were distributed to the shop-charges accounts on the basis of direct labor cost or time, preferably time. Church gave also considerable detail as to the method of dividing the factor accounts among the shop-charges accounts. These, incidentally, were cleared by the machine earnings (a machine hour rate) plus the "supplementary" rate if necessary[419] Taken as a whole, Church's system of departmentalization and distribution was the best that had been proposed up to that time; in fact, it served as a model for a great number of cost authorities in later years. He continued to improve and elaborate upon his technique for nearly thirty years, finally reaching the culmination of his discussion in *Overhead Expense* (1930), a book consisting of several hundred pages.

By 1901, therefore, a fairly comprehensive examination of the problem of the departmental distribution of burden had been given; the need for departmentalization itself was emphasized more and more, and special distribution questions soon began to receive consideration. For example, H. S. Garry, the Englishman, wrote a book on process cost accounts in 1908 in which he showed particularly the methods of dividing and accounting for the departments of a chemical plant. Various other English authorities devoted a few pages to the problem as it existed in engineering establishments.[420]

In America the topic received careful consideration in the writings of John Whitmore who followed Church's suggestions for the most part, although he did give a few more details.[421] Clarence Day, a short while later, discussed the departmentalization of a cotton mill in his *Accounting Practice.* There were to be at least five departments, and the labor and incidental costs peculiar to each were to be distinguished in the accounts. General burden items were to be divided by some "equitable" procedure, the exact technique being dependent upon the nature of the charge. In this way a departmental cost statement could be prepared readily from the records maintained throughout the year.[422] Day did not add much that was new to the theory of the subject; he merely emphasized the process costing approach to the problem. His contemporary, J. L. Nicholson, on the other hand, gave a more generalized discussion. He pointed out that the operating departments would vary between different firms, and according to the nature of the product manufactured. To quote: "It should be the aim, in making these divisions, to limit each department to as simple and uniform operations as possible. Where the processes in the same department differ in any appreciable degree, the same difficulty arises that existed before the classification was made, and to avoid which it was undertaken at all."[423] Costs were to be recorded in the individual departments under the three main elements which, taken together, made up the total. Nicholson advocated the use of the direct labor cost basis of distributing the general burden items to the departments; according to him, that procedure would give the percentage of indirect costs which each department should bear. He differed, therefore, from certain previous authorities who had suggested "more equitable" bases for the charges. In addition, Nicholson provided a system of distinguishing the sales of each department so that, in the end, the firm could ascertain the gross profit for each of its divisions.

By 1911, the art of departmentalization had reached the point where F. E. Webner thought it desirable to devote a whole chapter of his *Factory Costs* to the subject. After first emphasizing the fact that in practice the cost apportionment could hardly be carried too far, Webner stated that there was an irreducible minimum beyond which the departmentalization could not be definitely determined; no matter to what extent the process was carried, therefore, there would always be a few items which would have to be averaged. These should be as few as possible, even though "no amount of detective work economically possible will trace down and definitely place every item."[424] With these introductory remarks out of the way, Webner next recommended that the different burden costs be separated under various headings; at the end of a month all of them were to be entered on what he called a "distribution sheet." This had columns for account, number, amount (total), basis for prorating, department 1, department 2, department 3, and recapitulation. The distributed proportions of each overhead item were entered in the proper departmental columns. The amounts included in the first column totaled, of course, the same as all the departmental columns taken together. Webner was unusually specific in his discussion of the bases for the distribution of the various costs to the departments. Rent, for example, was to be distributed according to the space occupied. Engineering costs were to be subdivided into three component elements and distributed accordingly. Many other types of expenditures and charges were likewise analyzed by Webner and a plan of distribution proposed for each. Certain "safety reservations" were also mentioned, such as the over, short, and damage account, variation in weights and measures, and a "factor of safety." Taken as a whole, this treatment was as complete as would have been expected at that time, and has, as a matter of fact, been improved on very little since then.

In his 1913 work J. L. Nicholson, whose earlier views have been mentioned previously, emphasized the importance of making a fundamental distinction between operating departments and indirect or service departments. The reason for this emphasis was that the service group had to accumulate their charges for a period, the charges later being spread over the operating departments along the lines that Webner had suggested.[425] For each department accounts were to be maintained which would show the material, labor, and overhead pertaining to its operations.

In connection with the departmentalization of the charges for depreciation, interest on investment, fire insurance, and taxes, F. J. Knoeppel recommended a monthly schedule of fixed charges. On that schedule, the productive and service departments were separated as in the accompanying example.

MONTHLY SCHEDULE OF FIXED CHARGES

To be applied against	1 Valuation	2 Depreciation	3 Interest	4 Fire Insurance	5 Taxes
Operation A	xx	xx	xx	xx	xx
Operation B	xx	xx	xx	xx	xx
Operation C	xx	xx	xx	xx	xx
Etc.					
Service G a	xx	xx	xx	xx	xx
Service G b	xx	xx	xx	xx	xx
Etc.					
Total	xx	xx	xx	xx	xx

"The accounting department will periodically—in this case every month—incorporate the costs appearing under operations in columns 2, 3, 4, 5, into the proper group . . . and the costs appearing under services in columns 2, 3, 4, 5, into the proper group. . . . "[426]   In addition, a journal entry was to be made each month summarizing the schedule totals. The scheme illustrated, therefore, was essentially a device for collecting the departmental allotments of the items enumerated on the schedule; it was not the entire distribution procedure.

In his 1917 work, F. E. Webner introduced a more elaborate

"expense distribution sheet" than had appeared up to that time. Columns were provided for suspense and reserve credits, manufacturing expense analysis credit, symbol number, expense classification, suspense debit, reserve debit, symbol number again, assets debit, commercial costs debits, producing departments (as many as necessary), plant factor, works management, engineering, purchasing, stores and stocks, power, patterns, time and cost, tool making, and test and inspection. The direct burden charges to each of the preceding accounts were to be entered on the first line of the sheet, and the various general burden items immediately below. General burden items were apportioned to the producing and service departments on various equitable bases which he discussed completely. When the last step had been carried out the various service department totals were re-allocated to the producing departments, commercial costs, assets, reserves, and suspense columns. In this way the entire procedure was concentrated on one large sheet, and a great number of journal entries could be avoided. For a fair-sized firm the technique would prove of particular advantage, even though it could be used in any case wherever several departments were involved.[427]

In contrast with Webner, some authorities recommended the use of so-called "apportionment journals" as a method of departmentalizing the burden element of cost. This was to all intents and purposes a book of original entry which took the place of the distribution sheet as well as the journal entries which arose from it. One authority, for example, illustrated an apportionment journal (really a large sheet) with credit columns for prepaid expenses and unapportioned expenses, and debit columns for building expenses, power department, drafting department, production departments (as many as necessary), and commercial expenses. The items of expense were first entered, one under the other, on the journal, and apportioned to the columns mentioned. At the bottom the building and power costs were re-allocated to the producing departments and commercial expenses.[428] As can be easily seen, this was essentially the same as Webner's distribution sheet, except that it was used as a journal as well as a distribution schedule.

By the early 1920's the English cost authorities were also discussing the departmentalization problem in a more thorough manner. E. T. Elbourne, for example, recommended at least eight service groups, somewhat similar to A. Hamilton Church's production factors. These were: building service, power service, producing unit service, tool service, material service, departmental service, administration service, and contingency service. Each of these was subdivided and the individual items examined as to the "formula" (his term) to be used for apportionment to departments of the firm; several pages were devoted to this topic. As for the necessary accounting, Elbourne suggested a "production oncost book" which contained accounts for each of the above eight services, a depreciation account, an interest on capital account, departmental oncosts accounts (as many as needed), departmental process summary account, stock production differences account, production oncosts supplementary account, and several others. All of these were used to record (1) the burden incurred, (2) the distribution to departments, and (3) the allocation to product, This authority, therefore, did not recommend the use of distribution sheets. Incidentally, he noted that the entries in the accounts mentioned were memorandum entries only; his costing was extramural to the financial ledger.[429]   Elbourne's system involved an unusual amount of red tape. Interestingly enough, L. W. Hawkins, another English cost writer of the period, did not even discuss the departmentalization problem; yet his work was fairly complete in other respects.[430]

The basic theory underlying the division of a factory into departments, and the distribution of overhead, was about complete; relatively few improvements have been made since the early 1920's. Machine methods of keeping the details have been introduced, but these involve no change in fundamental techniques. At about the same time, G. Charter Harrison, the famous exponent of standard costing arrangements, began to criticize what he called the "elaborate rituals" which took place each month when burden items were distributed. It was his idea that the essential product cost data should be gathered only once; then, "instead of making elaborate burden distributions every month, and in the majority of cases . . . these are absolutely necessary if we are going to get even approximately correct costs, we make a most careful distribution of burden to producing departments once, and use these results as a basis for the monthly figures."[431]   This practice would obviously reduce considerably the number of distributions. A vital part of Harrison's technique also contemplated introducing a method of keeping track of the variations from the predetermined standard costs. This whole procedure was a somewhat different approach to the problem of burden distribution, and has been expanded and elaborated upon by numerous authorities in recent years.[432]

CHAPTER VI

EVOLUTION OF THE INTEGRATION
OF THE
COST AND FINANCIAL RECORDS

THE COST DEVELOPMENT DISCUSSED IN THIS CHAPTER HAS PROVED OVER the past decades to be one of the more dramatic phases of the evolution of modern costing techniques. The transition from the accounting for merchandising concerns to that for factories was slow in taking place; and when it did come, the records devised for costing in manufactories were, for the most part, extramural to the financial or commercial books. Even then they were often crude and unsatisfactory, mainly because few factory managers would trust them implicitly, since (1) they were not coördinated in any way with the general accounts, and (2) only the roughest sort of internal check was possible. In addition, many plants used modified trading concern books, with the addition of an account for "manufacturing." The various reasons for this slow development were considered in detail in Chapters II and V, and need not be reiterated here. It is sufficient at this point to state that even after 1885, when modern costing really began, numerous authorities who delved into the subject often succeeded in leaving it more confused than before they had attempted their exposition. Gradually, however, over a fairly long period of time, there emerged more and more specific techniques until at the present time the ideas are considerably more uniform, often differing only in particulars.

Up until the early 1880's very little had been done in regard to the consolidation of the factory and general accounts. Wherever a factory opened up two or three accounts on its financial or trading ledger—one of which was usually "manufacturing"—such a scheme within itself had some of the features of a merger of the cost and general records. In the true sense of the word, however, one should not call such a technique actual costing of the product; it was rather a record of expenditures, and only a very crude estimate could be derived as to the cost of the manufactured articles. Even to obtain these guesses, inventories had to be taken at periodic intervals, the intervals often covering a year or more in time. More than likely, however, when later cost authorities began to consider methods for tying in cost accounts with the financial ledger, they drew heavily upon the earlier attempts at ascertaining costs along these lines.

By 1885, the idea that ordinary commercial records were not satisfactory for factory account keeping was fairly well established, even though no one had presented a thorough description of an improved system. In that year an American Army officer, Henry Metcalfe, published his *Cost of Manufactures,* which, while not pertaining directly to industrial plants, was devoted in part to the present subject. His system of costing involved the use of cost sheets on which would be accumulated all the elements going into the product. The cost sheets, labor records, and stores ledgers were not tied in with his "cash accounts," which were separate and distinct; but a partial reconciliation of the two could be made at the end of each month. For instance, the labor element of cost as shown on the cost sheets was supposed to reconcile with the aggregate disbursements for services on the abstract of disbursements, as he called it. The material element was checked "by two necessities: First, of accounting for all material received, whether paid for or not; and, second, of charging to some shop order all material expended or subject to expenditure, whether by accident or design."[1] The third element of cost, overhead, was almost impossible to reconcile, according to Metcalfe; at any rate, the technique which would be required would be so comprehensive and difficult to carry out that the results would not be worth the extra trouble. In connection with this problem, Metcalfe admitted that he had tried in vain "to find some simple current method" of making the reconciliation, but was convinced that, not only was that impossible, but that "substantial truth" would be "neglected for the sake of striking a balance."[2] His reasons for the failure to reconcile the items were: (1) that the shop was always paying out in one month for material which was used in another; (2) that the shop did not necessarily use at once all that was paid for; and (3) one could not always ascertain whether "what we are expending has been paid for or not, still less whether it has been for the time covered jointly by the two sets of accounts or previously."[3] These reasons are interesting as indicating the state of cost thinking during the period under consideration. Metcalfe concluded that even if the reconcilement could be carried out completely it would more than likely "paralyze the manufacturing." He seemed to think, also, that the three elements could never be proved independently, but only in aggregate, which, obviously, would be of small benefit so far as their control was concerned. All in all, he made a rather hopeless case out of the proposition of consolidating the cost with the financial records and of showing the flow of costs through the accounts. It was not long, however, before other cost experts began to inquire into the nature of the problem.

In fact, just two years later, the English practicing cost authorities, Emile Garcke and J. M. Fells, wrote into their *Factory Accounts* the, at that time, extremely novel suggestion that the factory books should never be considered as mere "memoranda, which are not necessarily required to balance."[4] There was not the slightest hint that the factory accounts should ever be outside of the regular double entry framework. Their scheme provided for a number of modern features. A goods in process account (they called it a "manufacturing account," but the context implies the other concept) was to be set up on the commercial ledger, to which would be charged (1) all the material consumed from the raw materials account, and (2) the labor from the wages account. In addition, although they were not very specific on the point, the overhead element of cost was also to be charged to that account. As goods were completed, they were to be taken out of the "manufacturing" (goods in process) account and transferred to finished stock account. Except for their hazy details as to the handling of the establishment charges (burden), this procedure was the same as that often used today. A major hurdle had been taken, therefore, when this treatment appeared; furthermore, the internal transactions, showing the flow of costs through the ledger, had been partially developed. As was common, however, among the English

cost authorities of the time, Garcke and Fells continued to refer to
the prime cost books and all the paraphernalia connected therewith.
It is probable that their technique represented the more advanced
ideas of the period, even though the system described was evidently
in current use, especially since these two practical cost experts were
not given to theorizing or philosophizing to any great extent.[5] According to Garcke and Fells, the tie-in was not to be sacrificed or
neglected just because the plant happened to have a large number of
departments, or a number of subsidiary ledgers; these factors only
made the coördination more imperative. As a matter of fact, one of
the important advantages would lie in the close check which could
be maintained, to give one example, over the stores ledger and the
storekeeper. For instance, the physical inventory would prove the
stores sheets, while the total of the stores sheets would check with
the stores account on the commercial ledger. Incidentally, Garcke and
Fells referred to the "commercial ledger"; their system did not con-
template the use of what is at present called a "factory ledger," which
is, in turn, tied in with the "general ledger" by means of a reciprocal
account. This technique did not appear until somewhat later, as will
be explained on subsequent pages.

It should be emphasized, however, that the procedure advocated
by the preceding English authorities was not adopted immediately
by other English factory cost accountants. In fact, it was around
1910 before the English began to use the type of coördination provided by the Garcke and Fells arrangement. As will be developed in
later pages of this chapter, the American writers on the topic soon
took up the idea, but the English insisted on independent "cost accounts" until well into the twentieth century. Even in the same year
that Garcke and Fells wrote, another English accountant made the
statement that the "cost books, being supplemental to, and outside of,
the commercial books, cannot be used for the purpose of embezzling."[6]
This viewpoint of the advantage of distinct cost books permeated
the arguments of several later authorities, especially those outside of
this country. Two years later, the immediately preceding theory
of non-adunation was again expounded by G. P. Norton, a practicing
accountant in northern England. Norton referred to the idea of
merging the cost records and the financial or counting house records
as being entirely unfeasible and undesirable, stating that the inten-
tion of such a plan was "perfectly right, but the method is altogether
injudicious."[7] Norton went on to provide a rather complicated, al-

though workable, system of costing in the departments and processes of a textile mill, claiming, however, that the accounts required therefor should be separate and distinct from the trading account and the ordinary accounting transactions and records. His concluding statement left no doubt as to his position on the matter: "Much unnecessary complication is introduced into a comparatively simple operation when the details of the departmental accounts are mixed up with the books of the counting house."[8] Even though Norton thus dismissed the idea of consolidating the cost accounts with the general accounts, he showed, nevertheless, on his commercial ledger some accounts which contained the germ of later developments. For example, the stable account collected all the charges pertaining to the hauling and drayage expense of the mill; and was credited for (1) any balance which might be carried forward as an asset to the next period, (2) the amount that was transferred to the mill account for services rendered thereto, and (3) an amount that was transferred to the warehouse account for the expenses of delivering the finished product. This procedure is carried out today through the medium of a burden distribution sheet. Incidentally, this description was quite advanced for that period, which makes his ideas on the "merging" all the more surprising; it is not definitely known why he was so utterly opposed to the tie-in. It may be surmised, however, that he felt that the necessary details were better handled, and a more adequate control provided, if the two ledgers were kept distinct. An integral part of Norton's costing presupposed that the results of operations would be contrasted and compared with what it would have cost to obtain the products from some outside firm—the basic advantage of imputed costing arrangements—and this procedure may have been one of the contributing causes of his preference for separate cost books, unconnected with the counting house accounts.

A few years later, in an unsigned article in *The Accountant,* an English publication, a statement was made that formerly the cost accounts of a factory "were invariably quite distinct from the books of account proper."[9] This unknown authority continued by pointing out that in view of this, professional auditors rarely, if ever, investigated the nature of those records, the reason being that they (the auditors) were disinclined to "embark upon a line of action that necessitated a more or less intimate acquaintance with the technique of each different class of business whose accounts they were called upon to verify."[10] After a further discussion of the relation of auditors to the cost accounting of a firm, this expert specifically recommended that the cost accounts be kept entirely separate from the financial books, just as Norton had suggested. His reason for adopting such a procedure was the later familiar argument that if the two were separate, any errors or fraudulent items would show up at the end of the period, especially in the inventories. In other words, the two sets of accounts would give a mutual check on each other. He did not discuss, however, just how a reconcilement was to be made; it is evident that he had some sort of checking scheme in mind or else he would not have been so definite in his insistence that the accounts be uncoördinated. It should be remembered, though, that Garcke and Fells had given the same reasoning in support of the adunation arrangement. Obviously, the latter was preferable, at least in the light of later developments; but at that time this unknown writer concluded that "those who prefer that the two sets of accounts shall form a complete and scientifically constructed whole may readily modify our system to this end by means of adjustment accounts."[11] Nothing was said, however, as to how the adjusting was to be carried out; that was something outside the bounds of practicality. Incidentally, the books required under his system of cost accounts were: wages book, stock book, cost book, summary of cost accounts, and a reference index. Such was the force of precedence, and the power of the status quo, that even though this authority admitted that the integrated scheme was the one that was "complete and scientifically constructed, and theoretically preferable," he chose the other possibility as the one which should be ordinarily adopted.

Even though the English cost authorities around the turn of the century were thus almost unanimously agreed that the cost accounts as such should be separate from the general financial records, they continued to search for some simple method of reconciling the two. For example, although he was quite specific in holding that the factory records should not be coördinated with the others,[12] F. G. Burton thought it desirable to have some means of checking the special cost accounts. His scheme was rather naïve; a monthly "approximate" profit and loss statement was to be compiled from the shop accounts, somewhat like the accompanying illustration on page 261.

The figures for the statement were to be derived for the most part from the regular commercial ledger, and Burton pointed out that the stock accounts would have to agree or check with "the total stock of the cost sheets"—this last being a rather hazy description

Approximate Profit and Loss Account for Month of March, 1895[13]

Debit		Credit	
To Stock March 1	xxx	By Sales	xxx
Purchases	xxx	Additions to Plant:	
Salaries	xxx	Material	xxx
Etc.	xxx	Wages	xxx
Estimated Charges, viz:		Estimated Charges:	
Rents, Rates, Taxes	xxx	Work in Progress	xxx
Interest, Gross	xxx	Stock March 31, viz.	xxx
Depreciation, Gross	xxx		
By Profit	xxx		
	xxx		xxx

of the method of proving that important item of cost. He continued by suggesting that the costs of an establishment be collected by the use of three groups of "sheets," namely, sheet "A" for departmental accounts; sheet "B" for process accounts; and sheet "C" for contract or job accounts. The method of operating these "sheets" was discussed in the previous chapter. It is sufficient to state at this point that a summary of the balances of the three groups of sheets was to be drawn up each month, and, as he described it, "we shall find that we obtain exactly the same profit or loss"[14] as shown by the approximate profit and loss account illustrated. The reason why this agreement could be effected was that the cost accounts were a complete duplication of the financial records; the sales were even recorded in both sets. This idea of a duplicate set of independent accounts was elaborated upon at length by later English cost experts, culminating in the extraordinarily complex system devised by E. T. Elbourne in 1921, which will be described at the end of this chapter.

The partially integrated technique employed by J. S. Lewis, 1896, should be treated at this point. Lewis' costing contemplated the use of a "manufacturing" account on the ledger (he recommended just one ledger) to which would be posted the "prime costs" (his term) of a period. The stores used, for example, would be debited to the manufacturing account and credited to stores, while the wages incurred would be debited to manufacturing and credited to wages account. The products completed at prime cost would be taken out of the manufacturing account and debited to finished stock account. Thus, as can be easily seen, the manufacturing account was really a work in progress account except that prime costs only were recorded in it. At a balance sheet date, however, this British accountant advocated the addition of the factory overhead items, properly allocable to both the work in process and the finished goods, to the prime costs of those still on hand. This was to be done through a rather cumbersome suspense account arrangement, and was the principal defect in his otherwise admirable system. Lewis was not willing, or perhaps did not know how, to show not only the flow of prime costs through the ledger, but also the burden element of cost. He discussed the handling of "establishment and shop charges," as he called them, at length, but did not present a procedure for carrying them along with the prime costs; the prime cost precedent seemed too strong for him to entirely overcome. He at least did not advocate separate and distinct factory ledgers and accounts uncoördinated and not tied in with the general or commercial accounts in any way. Incidentally, he was one of the first, after Garcke and Fells, to advocate the integration of the accounts; his place in the history of the subject would have been much more secure, however, if he had not refused, or failed, to provide for the flow of total costs through the accounts. His work was unusually thorough and complete in other respects; charts of accounts and illustrations were given in profusion to help the reader in understanding his preferred procedures.[15]

One of the earliest American authorities to consider this topic, after Metcalfe, was President Frank Broaker of the American Association of Public Accountants (later The American Institute of Accountants). In an address which he gave before the Association in 1897,[16] he chose as his subject the organization of cost accounts. While his remarks were not very detailed, he did describe a procedure for coördinating the cost and the financial records. The tie-in was to be handled through what he called a "consumption journal," the exact purpose of which he did not make clear. It was, however, a book which connected the various costing sheets and other detailed labor and material data with the financial ledger. In addition, it served as a check upon the manufactured articles "as received and the raw material and labor as consumed, proving not only the labor charges upon the costing slips and other dockets, but controlling the labor pay rolls in aggregate and bringing the entire factory working . . . under the crucial test of double entry in every particular."[17] Here was indeed the semblance of a new idea and it is unfortunate that he did not dwell more upon the uses of the consumption journal. Beyond some generalized remarks, which are given in the reference notes, he gave no further information about the nature of his integration scheme.[18] Evidently, however, he had in mind a type of double entry technique which would serve to bring together the costing and the commercial ledgers.

H. L. Arnold, a few years later, while discussing the cost records maintained by some fifteen prominent American firms of that period, mentioned that the common practice of the time was to keep inviolate the distinction between the financial and the cost books. One firm,[19] for instance, had adopted an accounting arrangement in which the two had no relation or connection or modifying influence whatever on each other. A few concerns, however, according to Arnold, did attempt to carry some of the factory accounts on the commercial books; this idea, though, in his opinion served no real need. Absolutely no advantages, it seemed, would be obtained thereby which could not be gained by the complete independence of the cost accounting. Arnold concluded by stating emphatically that the factory accounting should be as separate as though the manufacturing division and the sales division were in wholly different hands, that is, independent corporations.

The most prevalent doctrine around the turn of the century, therefore, did not provide for the integration of the cost and general records. There were a few dissenters among the authorities, but their views did not carry much weight. The consensus among the manufacturing firms, as well as among those who wrote on the topic, was that there should be a distinction made between cost accounts as such and the financial record keeping. Some authorities, however, saw the necessity for their reconcilement; yet their methods, on the whole, for carrying it out were crude and generally unsatisfactory.

One of the first authorities to suggest the use of a separate factory ledger tied in with the general ledger by means of reciprocal accounts was E. Andrade, an English Chartered Accountant, who wrote in 1899.[20] This was almost an entirely new idea, although various experts had been hunting for such a scheme for some time. In fact, his discussion probably grew out of the work which had been done by his predecessors, such as Broaker in this country. In essence his scheme was rather simple. A "connecting account" was to be opened in each ledger (cost and general), to which, at closing date, all the accounts in each ledger which pertained to the other, were to be closed. The balances of the two accounts would then agree, according to Andrade, thus affording a definite proof of the accuracy of the respective accounts and the postings therein. The scheme would also allow the cost accounts, so-called, to be balanced independently on the double entry principle. Except for the fact that his procedure contemplated the delaying of the postings to the connecting accounts until the end of a fiscal period, the system described would still be standard. Andrade did not give any illustrations of how it would be handled in actual practice, nor did he mention just what accounts would appear on each ledger. The big hurdle, though, had been taken; later authorities did not have too much difficulty in filling in the details of the technique.

Since Andrade had brought the issue to a critical point, the controversy between the integrationists and the nonintegrationists soon began to wax warm. In 1900, the editor of *The Accountant*, an influential English publication, took cognizance of the problem and devoted several editorials to a discussion of the matter. It was his conclusion that only in quite rare, exceptional cases, would it be practicable to incorporate the cost accounts with the financial books; in most instances it would be better to leave them entirely independent. He at least admitted, though, that their consolidation was not an impossibility. Incidentally, his rationalization on this point was somewhat unusual. The two sets of accounts should not be coördinated because, in his own words, "costing clerks belong to a somewhat different category to ordinary bookkeepers; and it is desirable that the two . . . should be kept separate, for this reason if for no other."[21] He did not state wherein this difference was to be found, nor whether his remarks were designed as dyslogistic to the cost group or to the other accountants. During the next several years, four or five additional articles were published in the same magazine, arguing the question at length. The main point involved seems to have been the proposition that if the cost books were kept entirely separate, there could be exercised over the factory superintendent and foremen a modicum of internal control which would be lost if the integration plan were adopted. As a matter of fact, later developments proved that the consolidation scheme gave more audit assistance along these lines than any noncoördinated system ever devised.

Around this time, also, the matter of reconciling the results of operations as shown by the cost books and the general accounts came back into prominence. Sir John Mann, for example, in his article contributed to the *Encyclopaedia of Accounting* in 1903, while recommending that the nonintegration plan be adopted, did stress the importance of comparing the results. In fact, he made the specific point that the cost system should be framed in such a way as to allow for the comparison. The reasons for such a necessity were, in his opinion, quite obvious. One was that any erroneous "guess work" in connection with the allocation of factory overhead might be corrected; or, again, if any omissions of sales data, or other errors, had crept into the commercial records, they could be found by the reconciliation. His procedure for making the contrast, however, was rather hazy as to details. Summaries were to be prepared from time to time; the wages charged in the cost books were to be reconciled with the wages paid out; the materials consumed, "after adjustment of increase or decrease in stocks, will disclose either a surplus or a deficiency when compared with the actual inventory"; and the overhead was to be examined, and adjustments made, if necessary, in the future rates.[22]

Cost accountants in England during the next two decades followed, for the most part, Mann's treatment of the subject; that is to say, they recommended that the factory records remain uncoördinated with the general accounts, with perhaps a partial reconciliation being made at intervals. As a matter of fact, the very names of their published works gave an indication of their feeling on the matter. Practically all of their important contributions included the words "cost accounts" in their titles, implying to some extent at least that the factory records were more or less a separate entity. Some examples are given in the reference notes.[23] The philosophy underlying the English viewpoint was very well expressed by Stanley Pedder in 1905, when, after indicating that he preferred the extramural costing arrangements, he pointed out that, in his opinion, the essential difference between the financial or commercial accounts and the cost accounts proper lay in the fact that the latter were analytic, while the former were mostly synthetic. As he stated it:

> Cost accounts endeavor to arrive at the net result of manufacturing by an analysis—a separating of all details and particulars of costs—showing in the end, as it were, a *series of small trading or profit and loss accounts*. Commercial accounts aim at grouping together the results, not of each item of work, but each class of expenditure.[24]

It might be noted, in connection with the "small" profit and loss accounts mentioned by Pedder, that the entering of sales and returns in the cost records was almost invariably a feature of those English cost systems which were being described during the decade under discussion. In essence, then, those authorities really recommended the use of two sets of books, each containing somewhat the same information, except as to details. This last conclusion is borne out by Pedder's remarks that both systems (cost and general records) should arrive at the same results, except for such minor inaccuracies as the difference between overhead allocated and incurred.

While the preceding statements and conclusions hold true so far as the English techniques in general are concerned, one other development in that country should not be overlooked. This was the gradual evolution of a distinction between costing arrangements based on the job cost principle and those based on process cost systems. (See Chapter XI.) Several English authorities in the period under review began to treat rather extensively process cost accounting, and wherever that distinction was made there was more tendency to merge the cost and the financial records and accounts. Following this trend, there were, during the first decade of this century, several references to the use of a "manufacturing" account on the general books, which served for all essential purposes the same function as a work in process account.[25] The conclusion is that it seemed easier for the English cost experts to recognize the advantages and techniques of coördinating the accounts under process cost conditions than under other circumstances.

The Canadian viewpoint around the turn of the century was given by Eddis and Tindall in 1902. It was their opinion that although the cost accounts themselves should be kept apart, they should, nevertheless, form an integral division of the ordinary commercial books. In addition, they should be so designed as to permit their balancing in conjunction with the commercial accounts. Following the English practice of the period, they divided the general costing systems into what are now called job costs and process costs arrangements. In order to obtain the tie-in, they recommended the use of a cost ledger account on the general ledger; the general ledger was merely a summary record of all the details which had previously been entered on the cost ledger itself. As each job was finished a separate record was kept for it in the cost ledger, and at periodic intervals, say a week or month, all the completed jobs were summarized on a schedule, and manufactured stock was debited while the cost ledger account was credited. The cost ledger account was thus a sort of work in process account. On the debit side it had columns for date, particulars, folio, factory wages, material, direct expenses, factory expenses, and total; while on the credit side were to be found columns for date, particulars, wages, material, direct expenses, estimated factory expenses, and total. The use of this scheme permitted, then, the subdivision of the jobs into their cost components.[26] The debit side was posted from the purchases journal and the cash payments book, in total, each six months. The uncompleted work was carried forward in this cost ledger account, by elements of cost; these two authorities, however, were indefinite as to how the amount of goods in process was to be determined. Supposedly, though, the totals of the job accounts in the cost ledger itself would give the desired information. Incidentally, the difference between the amount of the factory expenses column of the cost ledger (which showed the total overhead incurred) and the estimated expenses (credit) column (which showed the amount allocated to jobs) was closed out to the "trading"[27] account at the close of the fiscal period of six months. In general, therefore, the conclusion must be drawn that the Canadian authorities dismissed as being entirely inadequate the nonintegrated systems which had been advocated so strenuously by the English.

Attention should be turned now to developments in the United States. The various American authorities were somewhat divided as to the procedures to be employed; that is to say, some advocated the coördination and some opposed it and there was less uniformity of opinion than in England. A few experts soon began to break away from the two-sets-of-accounts idea, but the trend took place comparatively slowly. The views of J. E. Sterritt might be cited as an illustration of the non-integrationists group. In an address before the Pennsylvania Institute of Certified Public Accountants in 1903, he argued along practically the same lines as Stanley Pedder.[28] Sterritt, however, preceded Pedder by two years, and recommended the maintenance of two entirely distinct systems of books. He did mention that in a few instances ("almost unworthy of consideration")[29] the cost books could be coördinated with the financial ledger. The financial ledger accounts were to be arranged, however, so as to facilitate the collection of data which would be needed by the cost clerks; the two were to work along together "as a harmonious whole." In summary, it was Sterritt's opinion that the ideal system of cost accounts, even though separate, should "use the checks and balances of double entry, and reassemble the totals shown by the financial books in such a plan as will show the cost of the article produced, not only in total, but in its constituent elements."[30] Unfortunately, he did not give any other details about the topic under discussion.

H. L. C. Hall was even more certain that the cost system should be extramural to the commercial ledger or accounts. In fact, according to him, the functions of the former usually ended where those of the latter started. To quote: "The cost accounts are in no wise a part of general accounts,"[31] and no complex set of books was usually required to ascertain costs.

At about that same period, the integration ideas of the Canadians, Eddis and Tindall, began to filter into this country. H. C. M. Vedder, for instance, described a coördination system similar to theirs. On the main ledger an account called "manufacturing" was to be established which controlled the cost ledger; it was thus a work in process account, and was handled in exactly the same way as that account is handled at the present time. Vedder's discussion was rather general in scope, but a person with some prior knowledge of what he was attempting to do would not have had much difficulty in understanding his exact procedure.[32]

Other American authorities soon began to build on, or to adopt in toto, the ideas of Vedder. John Whitmore, who elaborated upon and explained in considerable detail the costing system advanced by A. Hamilton Church, adopted the manufacturing account (work in process) arrangement for controlling the factory cost sheets.[33] Church had neglected to discuss this important subject when he wrote his earlier series of articles in 1901.[34] Since there was little that was new in Whitmore's contribution it may be passed over briefly at this time. It is sufficient to point out that he emphasized the importance of synthesizing the cost and the general accounts, as well as providing for the flow of costs through the ledger, through a series of journal entries and the maintenance of the necessary detailed subsidiary ledgers.

By 1908 cost experts in this country were referring to the "production ledger" and the "general ledger," not definitely tied in, however, with each other, even though the germ of the idea was present. One authority, C. M. Day, for example, in discussing the nature of the production ledger, listed the following accounts which might be maintained on it: general ledger account, work in process account, material account, labor account, and production expenses. The general ledger account was to have whatever balance was necessary to establish a self-balancing "production ledger."[35] So far as the general ledger itself was concerned, no details were supplied as to the nature of the offsetting accounts, if any, which might be opened. While there was thus much that was vague and obscure about this accountant's explanations, he did add a further notion in connection with the development of the coördination technique.

By the end of the first decade of this century, therefore, cost accountants in this country were generally recommending for factories the adoption of an integrated system of accounts in which the flow of costs would be shown on the ledger.[36] In spite of this advanced procedure, however, the various authorities who treated the subject had considerable difficulty in devising a system of interlocking ledgers for use in case, for some reason or another, the factory ledger was to be kept in a separate place or in different hands. C. M. Day had hinted at the matter but his technique was defective in several respects. One of the best statements made before World War I regarding the advantages of integration was given by F. S. Small in 1914: "The system herein described and illustrated does not separate the regular bookkeeping from the cost work, but inaugurates the cost work as a part of the general accounting. The reason for so doing is that the profit and loss figures shown in reports of costs and the balance sheet of the same date must correspond, whereas in other systems not so combined, the accuracy of the cost accounting reports cannot be proved, there being no balance sheets made at corresponding dates."[37]

The viewpoint of the English authorities in the period immediately before the First World War was somewhat the same as that described for the years around the turn of the century, except that there was more emphasis on the reconciliation of the cost accounts as such and the financial books. Moreover, a deflective note began to appear in some of their discussions. W. Strachan, for instance, although recommending the avoidance of the procedures which intermingled cost accounts with the general financial records, emphasized the "blending and the proving" of the results, as well as the comparison of the total costs as shown by each system.[38] L. W. Hawkins, on the other hand, frankly recognized the advantages to be derived from the integration technique; but he overstated the difficulties involved, and as a result, in the end, concluded that a dual system was the best.[39] He seemed to think, too, that the coördination would require a triple entry procedure. As a matter of fact, his own suggested accounting involved more entries than the later popular, fully-articulated method; but he would not recommend the use of the latter, preferring rather to devote several pages to a discussion of reconciliation schedules and all the elucidation necessary in connection therewith. Historically speaking, the comparison-and-reconciliation-technique of costing reached perhaps its finest development in the hands of Hawkins; he made provision for the determination and investigation of all the possible reasons why the costs accounts (separate) did not show the same details, totals, and results as the financial, or "general books," as he called them.[40] No stone was left unturned; his discussion of this topic alone covered some forty pages.

It should not be assumed that all English accountants during this period recommended the use of entirely separate factory accounts. L. R. Dicksee, for example, while concluding that a reciprocal account arrangement should not be adopted, did suggest that a tabulated adjustment account be set up on the cost ledger, ruled with distinctive columns for each separate class of items dealt with in the cost ledger. The advantage of such a scheme, according to Dicksee, was that the cost ledger could be very simply balanced, independently of the financial books, and the totals of the columns in the adjustment account reconciled with the general ledger. In addition, on the general ledger books, there was to be a work in process account, which would be used, however, only as an inventory account for balance sheet and profit and loss purposes; that is, at the end of a fiscal period, it would be closed to "trading" account, and the new inventory of unfinished goods debited to it, while the credit for the final inventory would go to "trading" account. Entries would be made in the work in progress account, therefore, only at the close of each fiscal period, and not continuously during the period, as is often done today, and as had been recommended by the integrationists. Dicksee's deflection, in the last analysis then, was more nominal than real; his views were not very different from those of Hawkins and other Englishmen of the period, especially in view of his statement that "the cost records are, as a rule, best kept quite separate from the financial books."[41] A few years later M. W. Jenkinson, a Chartered Accountant, made an effort to describe two types of work in progress accounts, which could be used, he insisted, for proving the clerical accuracy of the entries in the cost books. One of these was for the direct labor in process, and the other was for materials in process; both were to be handled somewhat as they would be handled today. This authority neglected to mention the third account of that sort which is sometimes used at the present time, that is, the burden in process; the nearest he came to it was in advocating the valuation of manufactured goods on hand at a balance sheet date at the total cost of manufacture. He was consistent, however, with his accounting procedure, when he suggested that partially completed goods should be valued at prime costs only, omitting the burden charge which might have been incurred. His system, then, contemplated the integration of the cost and the commercial records so far as prime costs were concerned, which step, in general, went much farther than most of the English cost authorities of the period. He deserves credit, therefore, for that development if for no other.[42]

American authorities, by the time the First World War started, were for the most part adopting the theory and practice of articulated costing arrangement along the same lines as are in general use today.[43] Statements were being made such as the following: "It must be borne in mind that, generally speaking, a system of factory accounting does not reach its highest efficiency unless there is this control exercised by the general ledger over the balances of the subsidiary ledgers."[44]

At about the same time, J. Lee Nicholson, in his *Cost Accounting* (1913), described a procedure for coördinating the cost and financial ledgers, allowing the two to be separate in a physical sense, yet tied together by means of reciprocal accounts, one on each ledger. The reciprocal accounts were the now familiar "factory ledger" and "general ledger" accounts. The use of these two accounts permitted each ledger to be independently balanced without destroying in any way the integration of the accounts involved. Nicholson recommended that the following accounts be established on the factory ledger: raw materials and supplies, labor, indirect expense, work in process, part-finished stock, finished stock, and general ledger. The flow of costs from the materials, labor, and indirect expense accounts was accurately described and illustrative journal entries were given. Costs allocated to goods finished were transferred from work in process to finished stock, and, finally, the cost-of-goods-sold entry was made. When he came to the description of the financial or general ledger, Nicholson mentioned that either of two techniques might be employed for articulating the accounts of a factory. One was along the line of the recommendations which had previously been made, that is, the use of just one ledger containing accounts with material, labor, indirect expenses, work in process, and finished stock. The second method, on the other hand, was the reciprocal account arrangement, which called for a factory ledger account on the general ledger. If the second procedure were adopted the details of the costs would be found in the factory ledger, but the factory ledger was fully controlled by the general accounting office.[45] This last point, then, was the essential difference (although there were others) between the technique recommended by this American authority and that which had been almost continuously proposed by the English cost experts.

It was not very long, after Nicholson's exposition, before other writers began to consider various refinements in his technique. Stephen Gilman, for example, recommended the use of three work in process accounts instead of the usual one. Jenkinson, the Englishman, had suggested this some two years before; but Gilman decided that if three were used—one for each element of cost—more data would be currently available regarding the profits and financial condition of a firm. Each one of them, too, would act somewhat as a control, and mistakes or errors could be found with greater ease.[46] Other than these last advantages, Gilman's technique was similar to that of Nicholson.[47]

William Kent, in 1918, proposed a rather novel control account arrangement which might be considered at this point, although it is not of any great historical importance. It was his suggestion that not one, but two control accounts be opened on the "general books." The first was to be called "factory plant," and was to be used to record the company's investment in the permanent equipment of the factory, such as the land, buildings, and machinery. In reality, this appeared to be merely a control account for the factory fixed assets, the details of which would be kept at the factory itself. The second of the control accounts on the general books was given the name "factory operations," and it would be charged with all the cash sent to the factory for pay rolls, incidental costs, and other charges which the factory had to bear. The factory operations account would be credited (and here is where Kent differed to some extent from Nicholson) with the "value" of the products shipped from the plant. According to Kent, there were several sorts of "values" which might be adopted;[48] either the so-called "factory cost or the cost of sales"[49] might be used, depending upon the desire of the management. There were, he stated, three types of factory costs, namely, actual, recorded, and normal; he did not explain, however, just exactly what he meant by the terms. As for the cost of sales, there were also several possibilities. For example, the catalogue list price could be used, less an estimated percentage to cover trade discounts and selling and administrative expenses. A second possibility was the use of actual selling prices less a fixed percentage, or a percentage varying with business conditions (prosperity and depression); while still a third "value" might be the total of the charges against the factory operations account "during a month, or other fiscal period, plus the decrease, or minus the increase, of the inventory during that period."[50] Although Kent did not discuss the matter of "values" further, it was not so easy a problem as he implied. In fact, the use of any of the "values" except factory cost would have caused a considerable number of complications which he slighted entirely. Evidently what he had in mind in this connection was to charge the factory operations account with all the costs incurred at the factory, and to credit it for the output on one of the several bases listed above. But what was to happen to the account at the end of a period? Where were the factory inventory accounts to be located? Kent did not answer either of these two questions, even though they were vital to the problem.

The English cost authorities after the First World War still recommended the disadunation of the cost and general books. Their ideas reached perhaps their finest development in E. T. Elbourne's *Factory Administration and Cost Accounts*. His system not only contemplated the separation of the factory records, but also was so independent and self-contained that balance sheets, profit and loss statements and financial accounts could be compiled from them. In a word, he advocated the use of a dual set of accounts. He was aware that such a procedure would take more work and be more expensive, but he thought that the overlapping and duplication was well worth any additional trouble. His reasoning was interesting, even though partially fallacious:

> Such duplication or overlapping that may seem to exist is justified on the two grounds of (1) independence of each set of accounts—cost and financial; (2) the summarizing effected by the manufacturing ledger involves practically no more work than if the cost ledger were developed to provide the condensed information required for the financial accounts.[51]

He did not think it possible, it appears, to maintain an integrated system of accounts; his cost records, moreover, were so complete that he did not bother very much about reconciling any differences between the two sets of books. In fact, the financial or commercial records would be quite incidental under his scheme; he did not even discuss them at any length. In summary, it was his opinion that the interlocking technique was too difficult to carry out in practice, even though perhaps the more desirable procedure in theory, and, as he stated it: "The difficulties are all dissolved by having a self-contained cost accounting system."[52] Interestingly enough, however, his discussion was strikingly more complex than that of his American contemporaries.

By 1924, so much progress had been made that one American authority, James L. Dohr, was able to state:[53] ". . . some cases will be met in which the cost accounts are not only kept in a separate ledger from the general accounts, but in addition are not in any way connected with, or controlled by, the general accounts. . . . This scheme has very little to commend it, in that the costs so determined do not have the advantage of being verified by the general accounts and are consequently less apt to be accurate."

The mechanisms and the techniques for the adunation of the cost and financial books were now complete, at least in so far as this country was concerned; few important developments have taken place since the early 1920's. Various statistical costing devices have been perfected, especially in connection with the use of tabulating machines, but these involved no new principles. In addition, certain supplementary accounting arrangements have been advocated from time to time, such as the handling of the imputed interest on investment charge, external to the main cost books, and not integrated with them.[54] All of these more recent trends are interesting developments, but are not of any great importance in connection with the subject matter of the present chapter.[55]

Before concluding this chapter it might be appropriate to quote from the works of one of the modern observers of the integration problem, Katsuji Yamashita; he called his technique the "Third Form of the Profit and Loss System":

> Through this last form of bookkeeping system, that is, by the complete whole incorporation of cost accounting to the financial accounting of the manufacturing enterprise, it became possible for us to calculate industrial income accurately, which method is no

other than the individualized accounting of industrial accounting. It is neither the system of simple periodic profit and loss accounting nor the system of individual profit and loss accounting. It rejects both systems, but it is a new system of profit and loss accounting incorporating both systems into one organic whole. This we may characterize as the third form of the profit and loss accounting system. The periodic profit and loss accounting system that first developed as the calculation of commercial income is now assuming, from the necessity of meeting the demands of calculating the industrial income, a form commensurate with the calculation of modern industrial income, and the over-all periodic profit and loss accounting system is assuming an individualized acounting method. This is the present tendency of development of the profit and loss accounting system.[56]

CHAPTER VII

EVOLUTION OF THE ACCOUNTING FOR INTERDEPARTMENTAL TRANSFERS OF PRODUCT

BY ITS VERY NATURE, THE TOPIC DISCUSSED IN THIS CHAPTER MIGHT BE expected to receive more attention in processing industries than in engineering, or job costing, establishments. As a matter of fact, this expectation has been fully realized in the development of present-day ideas and theories on the subject. G. P. Norton, the English process costing authority, treated the matter at least in a casual manner in his work published in 1889.[1] He regarded it as useless and a waste of effort to attempt to charge each department through which a product went with the cost of the goods supplied to it by other departments. How were the interdepartmental transfers to be priced, then, if the costs were not to be accumulated? In answering the problem, Norton proposed an arrangement whereby the foreman of each department was to keep a record of the work done on the product in his division of the firm. A so-called "profit or loss" was to be ascertained for each department by comparing the departmental costs with the trade prices (value) of the product which had been turned out for the week or month. In other words, there was no necessity for pricing interdepartmental transfers under his system; each department was handled as a separate entity, and a proportion of the total cost of running the whole factory distributed to it, with a credit being given for the output at what it would have cost the firm to get the work done elsewhere. As was noted in Chapter V, this technique was one of the earliest attempts to obtain an important advantage of present-day standard costing procedures.[2]

Norton's treatment of the subject seems to have remained the best authority on the matter of interdepartmental transfers until well after the turn of the century; in fact, there was apparently very little interest in the subject. By 1903, however, other cost accountants began to consider the problem, even though their suggestions at that time were really not altogether pertinent to the main point. For example, one anonymous English authority, in connection with his treatment of factory accounts, made a distinction between the truly manufacturing operations of a firm and its trading or selling operations.[3] Following this distinction, it was his idea that, in order to determine whether or not the company should continue its manufacturing, the managers would want to know what profit, if any, it made on the factory operations, as contrasted with the profit on sales. That is to say, this authority treated the factory as a distinct branch of the business, which would "sell" its products to the selling division. Through the adoption of this fiction, the firm's managers were supposed to be able to determine whether or not to continue operations of the factory, and if they decided in the negative, the firm would buy its products ready-made from some other manufacturer. All this assumed, however, that the same products were being turned out by some other plant, although this last point was not mentioned by the authority under discussion. The methods which he suggested would help attain the desired results are shown in the accompanying illustrations.

Under the first method the manufacturing division of the company showed a so-called "profit" of 2,640 because it was assumed that if the selling department had been forced to buy the articles it sold, it would have had to pay 21,840 for them. The "trade price," therefore, which was given in the account, was that price which the products would have cost if purchased from some competitor. This unknown authority, however, did not enlarge upon this matter; he seemed to think that the ascertaining of the trade price would be quite simple. He did, though, point out that if any difficulty arose, the manufacturer could solve the problem by adding on a certain percentage to cost, according to the usual gross profit figures in the

First Method[4]
Manufacturing Account

January 1:		December 31:	
To Stock Raw		By Trading Account	
Material (cost)	3,000	(below):	
To Stock Goods		Trade Price of Goods	
in Process (cost)	500	Manufactured	21,840
		Stock on Hand:	
	3,500	Raw Material (cost)	1,900
December 31:		Stock on Hand:	
Purchases (period)	10,000	Goods in Pro-	
Wages	2,500	cess (cost)	900
Expenses of			
Manufacture	6,000		
Profit on Manufacture			
to Profit and Loss			
Account	2,640		
	24,640		24,640

Trading Account

January 1:		December 31:	
Stock of Manufac-		By Sales	30,000
tured Goods at		By Stock of Manufac-	
Trade Prices	8,000	tured Goods at	
December 31:		Trade Prices	2,650
From Manufacturing			
Account (above)	21,840		
General Expenses	1,000		
Gross Profit on			
Trading to Profit			
and Loss	1,810		
	32,650		32,650

Profit and Loss Account

December 31:	
By Profit on Manufacture	2,640
By Gross Profit on Trading	1,810
Total	4,450

Second Method

Manufacturing Cost Account

January 1:		December 31:	
To Stock Raw		By Stock Raw	
Materials (cost)	3,000	Material (cost)	1,900
To Stock Goods in		By Stock Goods in	
Process (cost)	500	Process (cost)	900
	3,500		2,800
December 31:		By Trading Account	
Purchases	10,000	(below) for Cost	
Wages	2,500	of Goods Made	19,200
Expenses of			
Manufacture	6,000		
	22,000		22,000

Trading Account

January 1:		December 31:	
Stock Manufactured		By Sales	30,000
Goods (cost)	6,000	By Stock Manufac-	
December 31:		tured Goods at Cost	2,000
From Manufacturing			
Cost Account			
(above)	19,200		
General Expenses	1,000		
Profit and Loss			
(below)	5,800		
	32,000		32,000

Profit and Loss Account

December 31:	
By Profit from Trading Account	5,800

trade. As for the second method, he stated: "No account is taken of the trade price at all and the goods are valued at cost throughout."[5] This, incidentally, is the method often used at the present time; the selling department takes the finished goods from the factory at cost. In this way no profit or loss is shown on manufacture. If this no-profit-on-manufacture method were adopted, an overall firm profit of 5,800 would be shown for the period; this is evidenced by the example given on page 279. As can be easily seen, the reason for the difference between the two profit figures lies in the valuation of the inventories. In contrast with the usual decision as to which would be the preferable technique, this authority selected the first, and even recommended the use of the "trade price" of the "stock" on the balance sheet. It was his opinion that the advantage of having the manufacturing profit figure available offset the possible over-valuation of the inventories. He did point out, however, that care should be taken not to add to the inventory value unduly; if necessary a reserve could be set up on the balance sheet to reduce the inventory to "cost." If the trade price, on the other hand, were less than the cost price, the former would be the correct price to place on the statement of financial position.

The principal idea expressed by this unknown writer was, to some extent, the prevalent doctrine or theory held by English cost authorities during the period immediately under review. To say the least, their aim was meritorious; that is, they were striving for a method with which the general efficiency of the factory operations could be measured. G. P. Norton had a similar end in view, and his system was even more sharply developed than that discussed on the past few pages.[6]

It was not until around 1908 than any material contributions were made to the subject of interdepartmental transfers of products. From the evidence available, the various processing firms which had to deal with the problem used the cumulative technique; that is, they accumulated the costs as the product went from one department to another, in such a way that, by the time it reached a finished item, ready to sell, it had been fully costed. This last conclusion is borne out by some illustrations given in England in Stanley Garry's *Process Cost Accounts*, in which the product, as it flowed from department to department, was transferred at a continually increasing cost figure.[7] Other references might be cited also, but they would show few differences from Garry's procedures.[8]

Some English authorities of this period, although they recommended the accumulation of costs as Garry had suggested, reverted to the ideas of Norton in that they proposed that each department of a processing plant be considered more or less a separate entity, which earned its profit when the goods which it happened to process had passed on to the next department. L. R. Dicksee, for instance, strongly urged this practice for use under certain circumstances.[9]

A definite prearranged scale of prices was to be compiled, and referred to from time to time as the flow of products was entered on the ledgers. Curiously enough, the advantage of this novel arrangement was that it "lends itself readily to the preparation of *detailed and accurate* accounts, and speaking generally, *infringes no* fundamental *principle of accounting.*"[10] Dicksee, however, recognized that this procedure could easily lead to the overvaluation of inventories for balance sheet purposes. He suggested, therefore, that at the close of each fiscal period, a general review be made of the goods in process to guard against their being taken into the inventory figures at a higher-than-cost value. There was one exception, however, which would allow a higher-than-cost price to be used; that is, if there were no reason to suppose that the unfinished goods would not be completed in the usual course of manufacture and be sold at the regular price, they might be valued at the gross interdepartmental transfer value on the balance sheet. If, on the other hand, there were any doubt under either of the two possibilities, a reserve for inventory valuation should be established on the financial statement. All of these last propositions, however, were somewhat contradictory to the italicized portions of the quoted statement above; that is to say, the technique either infringed the fundamentals of accounting or it did not. Incidentally, his suggested procedure as to the handling of interdepartmental transfers has some standing in modern cost circles, especially in cases where divisions of manufacturing establishments are scattered, each using the products turned out by the others. The interdepartmental profit is now practically always eliminated, however, for purposes of annual net income determination, even though the procedure is sometimes a very difficult, if not impossible, proposition.

Dicksee's departmental profit idea was subjected to considerable criticism in this country. F. E. Webner, for example, after giving an *in extenso* quotation from Dicksee's work, proceeded to state that "there would seem to be little to commend such a plan. No profits are made until goods are sold, nor can either the factory as a whole, or any department therein be consistently considered as making a profit. The factory delivers its products at cost to the commercial department, and it is the function of this department to realize profits for the entire establishment. . . . The departmental cost figures cease to be cost figures when they include an element of profit."[11] His viewpoint was typical of the authorities in this country throughout the period under review, and should be contrasted with that of Dicksee and the other English cost experts. Webner, incidentally, was interested in this matter only in so far as it affected the accounting required under his so-called "list-percentage" plan of costing, which involved departments. It was his concluding opinion that the "process charges to each succeeding department are the actual costs of the labor, material, and expense incurred in the preceding departments."[12]

By 1913, cost accountants in this country (J. L. Nicholson, for example) were making references not only to the cumulative (at actual cost) technique for pricing the interderpartmental transfers, but also to the noncumulative procedure.[13] Under the noncumulative method the quantities transferred would be shown, but the accrued costs would not be given after the first department; the unit cost of each operation (department) would, however, be emphasized and clearly shown. Obviously, so far as the total cost of the finished product was concerned, there would be no difference in the result; and, as a matter of fact, the second method might involve more effort than the first. It did have certain advantages, though, which caused it to be adopted in some instances. Nicholson also recognized the proposals which had been put forward for pricing the output of the factory at a "standard price" (his term) so that the superintendent of the plant would be given credit for work turned out on that basis. In essence, it would be considered that the sales department "bought" the product from the factory. In this way the management would "be put in the position of being able to hold each department responsible for results." Nicholson did not state whether or not he recommended such a practice, but he gave an illustration of a sales sheet which might be used in connection with it.

The following is representative of the views of a practicing cost accountant in the years immediately preceding the First World War: "If a stock shoe department is run in connection with a manufacturing business, it should be treated as a separate business, being charged with rent for the space it occupies to carry on its affairs and also with the capital used in its operation as well as insurance, taxes, interest, etc. It should not be charged with shoes at cost plus a profit, but the factory would be credited and the stock shoe department charged with goods at total manufacturing cost."[14]

The trend of opinion in England in the period immediately before the First World War was inclined to follow, for the most part, the American viewpoint (pricing at cost)[15] although there were certain exceptions which dealt with special cases. As an illustration there might be cited the technique recommended by M. W. Jenkinson, which was particularly designed to be employed where a salable product was obtained at each stage of the processing of the material; that is to say, some of the departmental output might be sold while some of it was passed on to other divisions for further processing. In the event that this situation obtained, Jenkinson recommended the adoption of an interdepartmental pricing scheme which would allow each department to show a profit. Jenkinson seemed unfamiliar, however, with other logical possibilities for handling such transactions since he stated that if the cost prices were used "not only would one department show a profit at the expense of another department, but so far as the cost accounts are concerned, the results would be misleading, the materials being charged out at less than the actual cost if bought on the open market."[16] This theory was quite similar to the views of other cost accountants in England a few years earlier. Jenkinson went on to recommend the use of reserves for interdepartmental profits at balance sheet dates, unless the firm dealt only with what he called "contract work," in which event no reserves were necessary. In addition, the articles were to be priced (for the interdepartmental transfers) at the regular selling prices, less only the sales expenses. Proper books had to be provided for recording the transfers, and he suggested that these be reconciled at least monthly.

Although the consensus in this country and in England in the period during and after the First World War seemed to favor the pricing of interdepartmental transfers at cost,[17] either on a cumulative or noncumulative basis, it was recognized that in a few rare cases other techniques might be employed. In the meat packing industry, for instance, several possibilities were open to the manufacturer as the product went from department to department. He might sell the meat after it had been partially processed, or he might send it on to other divisions.[18] In such cases it was recommended by several authorities that the market price be used for pricing the interdepartmental transfers. James H. Bliss was one of the American costing experts who developed the finer points of this procedure.[19] He referred to the technique as the "opportunity cost" transfer theory, which meant that the product was "worth to a department of an organization what the preceding department had the opportunity to get for it were it to sell it in the outside market."[20] Each department, under this plan, would stand on its own feet; individual profit and loss statements could, if necessary, be prepared to show the results of the efforts of the departmental managers. Bliss seemed to think this was essential. In connection with the use of the technique, however, he recognized that the inventories might be inflated with the unrealized profits shown by the various departments. It was his opinion, though, that such overstatements would be of little consequence, especially in view of the fact that the same basis was used both at the beginning and end of a fiscal period.

By 1924, several authorities were referring to opportunity costs in their discussions of the problem of interdepartmental transfers. J. L. Dohr, for example, stated that "as a matter of internal accounting the theory has some advantages . . . From the external viewpoint, however, the method is open to objection in that the profit so shown is not a realized one . . . Generally, the method of transferring forward at cost will be found the most satisfactory."[21]

Very few proposals of an original nature have been made within recent years in connection with the topic developed in this chapter. Refinements in the accounting for the elimination of the interdepartmental profits have been suggested, but these involve no new theory. It is generally agreed now that the preferable procedure is to show the transfers between departments at actual cost either on a cumulative or noncumulative basis, unless some other plan is peculiarly useful in the firm. The evolution of the subject by 1925, then, was fairly complete.

CHAPTER VIII

EVOLUTION OF THE ACCOUNTING FOR BY-PRODUCTS

THE DEVELOPMENT OF THE ACCOUNTING FOR BY-PRODUCTS,[1] ONE OF THE more specialized topics connected with the evolution of cost theories and techniques, has not had a long history. In fact, it was hardly considered a problem worthy of attention by the early cost theorists. As has been described at length in the preceding chapters most of the energy of the authorities who wrote on costing up to about the turn of the present century was devoted to the proper handling and costing of material and labor elements. Obviously, then, little was done about such a technical problem as the costing of by-products. More than likely, the comparatively few manufactories which were confronted with by-products[2] in any of their processes merely treated them as incidental sales, and did not bother too much about their accounting requirements. There were many large firms already in existence, however, before cost authorities began to treat the subject in their published works. An exception was one early writer who suggested in 1886 that the cost of the main product should be reduced by the full selling price of the by-product.[3]

Since flour mills present a rather interesting by-product problem (main product—fine or patent flour; by-products—bran, screenings, etc.), it is not at all surprising to find that one of the first references to the topic should be in connection with their costing. Interestingly enough, this reference used the term "by-product" to refer to the bran and screening. S. S. Dawson, an Englishman, writing in 1897 on the "Stock and Cost Accounts of a Flour Miller,"[4] gave a short description of the accounting methods which he recommended for the manufacturer in question. When wheat of various qualities was bought it was debited to a wheat stock account by grades. A type of perpetual inventory (by quantities only) was provided. Each day, the amount

Grinding Account Week ending 8th January 1896[5]

Debit

Centals	Description Type of Wheat	Price	Amount			Sacks
			£.	s.	d.	
900	Californian	7/–	315	0	0	7
400	Ditto	7/2	143	6	8	804
775	Walla Walla	7/4	284	3	4	41
425	River Plate	6/5	136	7	1	
275	Ditto	6/2	84	15	10	82
550	American Winter	6/4	174	3	4	126
255	Canadian	6/7	83	18	9	255
358,000	(lbs.)		1221	15	0	247
3,556	(889 sacks at 4 lbs. each)	5d	18	10	5	179
361,556			1240	5	5	

Credit

Capacity Sacks Pounds	Description	Price		Amount			Weight of Produce in Pounds
				£.	s.	d.	
200	Screenings		5/6	1	18	6	1,400
120	Bran		4/–	160	16	0	96,480
280	Low Grade Flour		12/–	24	12	0	11,480
				187	6	6	109,360
280	5 Diamonds Brand	27/7	1/3	113	3	7	22,960
do	4 ″ ″	25/11	1/3	163	9	0	35,280
do	3 ″ ″	24/3	1/3	309	10	10	71,400
do	2 ″ ″	22/7	1/3	279	4	11	69,160
do	1 ″ ″	20/11	1/3	187	9	0	50,120
	Differences				1	7	
	Loss in weight						3,276
				1240	5	5	361,556

of wheat put into process (by grades also) was recorded on the credit side of the wheat stock account, and debited to the grinding account. (See the accompanying illustration.)

The debits to the grinding account were supposedly priced on a first-in, first-out basis, although Dawson did not mention what method was used.[6] The credits to the account, however, were the most interesting. First, the by-products (screenings, bran, and low grade flour) were credited both as to production and as to price. Unfortunately, Dawson did not state just exactly what scheme he used for pricing them. Evidently, though, he adopted some type of a market price. At any event, the so-called "by-product offset" method was recommended. Next, on the credit side, appeared the main product—five different grades of patent flour, referred to as the "Diamond Brand." In this connection, the miller had to decide the value of the difference between the grades. "In this case it has been taken at 1s. 8d. per sack, and it is a simple calculation to arrive at the exact price [cost] of each different class, once the difference in price has been decided upon."[7] Obviously, the margin would be a matter of judgment, but Dawson did not think it would prove unusually difficult. After extending the product of the sacks times the price, the totals of the amount and the weight columns on each side were contrasted, to determine any differences; if there were any, he suggested that they be entered as indicated in the illustration. After the grinding account had been summarized for each week, the individual wheat-plus-sack costs per grade were entered on a summary report. This summary report showed not only the cost per grade of the raw material and sacks but also any grinding expenses. As a matter of interest, the grinding expenses were totaled on a schedule, somewhat as follows:

Grinding Expenses, for Week ending 8th January 1896[8]

	£	s.	d.
Wages of Mill Hands	46	10	0
Rent, Rates, and Taxes (1/52 of year's total)	15	5	0
Office Salaries and Expenses	24	8	0
Cartage Outwards	14	5	0
Repairs and Depreciation (1/52 of year's total)	8	0	0
Sundry Expenses	11	5	0
889 sacks at 2/8 1/6 =	119	13	0

Several interesting features were exhibited in the schedule. First it will be noted that the divisor used for ascertaining the grinding cost per sack included only the main product—the five grades of patent flour. This meant, therefore, that no part of these costs were considered as applying to the by-products. Second, *all* the incidental costs incurred during the week were apportioned to the flour, including the office salaries.[9] Third, the grinding costs were considered as applying in equal force upon each grade of patent flour. The last point was emphasized in the following summary schedule:

Schedule of the Cost and Sale Price of Flour
Week Ending 8th January 1896

	Cost of Wheat and Sacks (as above)		Grinding Expenses per Sack (as above)		Total Cost		Selling Price Quotations
5 Diamonds Brand	27/7	1/3	2/8	1/6	30/3	1/2	33/6 to 34/−
4 do	25/11	1/3	do		28/7	1/2	32/− to 33/−
3 do	24/3	1/3	do		26/11	1/2	30/− to 31/−
2 do	22/7	1/3	do		25/3	1/2	27/9 to 28/6
1 do	20/11	1/3	do		23/7	1/2	26/− to 27/−

Dawson's work may be summarized by stating that while there was much that was vague in his explanations, he did exhibit considerable familiarity with later, more modern techniques for handling the by-product problem. In addition, his methods were probably entirely adequate for the purpose he had in mind; it is extremely doubtful, though, whether a majority of the flour milling enterprises of the time used as accurate a system as he suggested.

In regard to a purely job cost establishment, one of the first references to the handling of by-products was contained in Lewis' *The Commercial Organisation of Factories.* This English authority referred to the small pieces of metal which often were left when stamping work was done, and which were used as raw material for a smaller article.[10] It was his conclusion that no general rules could be laid down for the proper handling of such cases. In general, however, the small pieces were to be taken back into the raw material storeroom, and reissued for the small article process "at a price intermediate between the value of raw material and ordinary waste, in order that neither process shall unfairly benefit by using up metal in this way."[11] Lewis was thus not very specific as to the exact details of his proposal although the "intermediate price" basis did have some merit. As was typical of most of the authorities during the period, he did not, in reality, think the problem very important, and dismissed it with the brief remarks just reviewed.

Lewis' countryman, J. MacNaughton, writing on the accounting for a paper mill (essentially a processing industry) was a little more explicit. The broke which was produced in connection with the paper manufacturing was to be carefully recorded in a broke book, which had columns for amount of broke coming from each machine, and from each calender, or the cutting, ripping or sorting departments. The total for each day was extended at the right side of the page. Of what importance was this in relation to the costing? The answer was that the broke had a certain value, not only for sale as such, but for processing into certain types of by-products.[12] Because of this fact, therefore, the broke had to be credited to the cost of each "make" of fine paper at such a "nominal value as may be thought sufficient."[13] In case the broke was used again in the making of fine paper instead of certain by-products, it was to be charged to the second lot of fine paper at the same rate at which it had been previously recorded (credited) to the first lot. MacNaughton did not indicate the price which would be adopted for the broke used in the by-products, but supposedly it would be the "nominal" price.

By the turn of the century, therefore, at least three methods of dealing with by-products had been suggested, namely, the market price principle, the "intermediate value" principle, and the nominal value principle. Later authorities now began to build upon these theories. A few years later, for example, Stanley Garry proposed for the British chemical industry,[14] the deduction of the sale value of the by-products[15] (less a deduction for the costs of processing) from the cost of the material which went into the principal products of the plant. There were two by-products and four principal products involved in his illustration. As a matter of interest, even though it is not pertinent at this point, Garry suggested that the raw material cost (after the by-product deduction) should be divided between the four main products on the basis of their relative sales values (there was just one raw material). In addition to these modern features of his discussion, he continued by explaining that one of the by-products was "neat"[16] while the other was "manufactured." Both of them, however, required certain processing before they could be sold. In summary, while Garry's treatment of this subject was only incidental to his main topic, that is, the setting out of the standard costs and excess of the products,[17] he did show considerable originality on the by-products problem, and thus deserves credit for his work.

In addition to the preceding English authorities, G. A. Mitchell suggested, in 1907, that the by-products of the malting industry, combing and culms, be credited to the "malting account" (an account which collected the costs involved in the malting process), and debited to the trading account at an arbitrary price. As he stated it: "In the present accounts culms always pass at a uniform interdepartmental price of £3 per ton. This average price simplifies the costing work, and any margin above this price realised on the sales falls to the credit of the trading account. A by-product must be priced in relation to its selling value, but it is only fair to the trading department that some balance of profit should be shown over the price at which it is taken from the malting account. The interdepartmental price is fixed on this principle."[18]

Although in England at the turn of the century cost authorities were discussing with some care the handling and costing of by-products, in the United States the matter was hardly mentioned until after 1900. The prevalent practice seems to have been to treat the sale of by-products in somewhat the same light as scrap, that is, as miscellaneous income[19] which, however, was to be credited to the departmental costs. No such distinction as is made at present between by-products and waste was made then. One American authority, for example, made the statement in 1904 that there were various practices followed, but that the scrap technique was the "correct" one.[20]

By 1909, however, cost authorities in this country had begun to make important contributions to the problem; some even devoted special sections of their works to a discussion of peculiar cases. For instance, J. B. Griffith recommended in that year that a separate department be organized to handle the processing of the by-products.[21] The scrap value of the material cast aside in one of the regular departments was to be credited to the cost incurred in that regular department and charged to the by-products department (also at scrap value). Other costs would then be applied to the by-products department, and its by-products sold in the regular course of business. Griffith recognized, on the other hand, that where the value of the by-products was small, any profit on its sale (less cost of production),[22] might be credited to the cost of the main product, but, in general, "it is not a safe rule to follow."[23] In addition, under most circumstances, it was his conclusion that the manufacture and sale of the by-products of a factory should be treated as an individual division of the business. His reason was that if this were not done, the by-product income in some instances (such as the making of soap or artificial gas) would amount to so large a figure as to show the principal product as having no cost; this result would be absurd.

A few years later, 1911, F. E. Webner argued exhaustively the question of whether the small items of scrap (subsequently made into rather inexpensive articles) should be charged to the by-products[24] at the original cost of the material, or at its scrap value. After considering the problem at length from both viewpoints, he concluded that "logically it would seem that the actual cost to the concern per foot or unit of material should apply to each and every article produced from that material. . . . Certainly this gives the most equitable basis on which to calculate the cost of the several articles of product, whether this product be made from scrap or from material in its original condition."[25]   According to Webner, also, the principal danger in not using the full material price lay in the fact that at some future date a reference might be made to the costs of a job involving by-products, and misinterpretation of their meaning be made, since not all the costs would be present on the cost sheet. (He meant that the material element might not be as large as necessary.)   This authority also made passing reference to the accounting required under his recommended plan. It was his suggestion that the difference between the scrap value of the material used in the by-products, and the regular valuation, be credited to what he called a "variation in weights and measures" account or the "over, short, and damage" account, especially since one of the two accounts had already been charged with the expected scrap values to be derived from the waste material, now converted into by-products. If the accountant did not care to credit one of these accounts, he might credit one of the corresponding reserves.[26] Webner was rather noncommittal as to which procedure was the better practice. The reason given for this particular technique of handling the difference was that a greater material cost would be charged into the regular product than was called for by the records unless the accounting was handled along the lines suggested. As a matter of fact, it would seem that an adjustment of the amount charged each month to the variations in weights and measures account[27] would also be necessary, but Webner did not mention such an adjustment.

At about the same time, the well-known accountant, H. C.

Bentley, in his *Science of Accounts*, also considered various methods of handling the by-products of a factory,[28] somewhat differently, however, from Webner. Bentley first gave an example of a by-products account (see illustration).

By-Products[29]

Debit: With the cost of productive labor, material, and manufacturing expense, used in preparing by-products for market.	Credit: At the close of each month with the cost of by-products sold, or otherwise disposed of. [See Sales of By-Products Account, *post.*]

This account was to be used only if the by-products had to be processed in any way after being split off from the main product. In cases where they did not require any additional work, but could be sold just as they were, Bentley advocated that they be given no value, and that no entry be made, until such a time as they were sold. When they were sold, an entry would be made crediting an account called "sales of by-product" (see accompanying illustration), and debiting cash or accounts receivable. If the by-products account were set up on the books, its balance at the end of the month would represent, of course, the asset value of the articles on hand at that date. Incidentally, this authority would not commit himself definitely on whether or not the cost of the main product should be credited with the value of the by-products produced.[30] In fact, he insisted at one point that no fixed rule could be adopted; the matter was one that the management had to decide. Yet at another place[31] his conclusion was that the revenue derived from the sale of a by-product (which required no processing), should be treated as miscellaneous income. In a word, "the cost of producing the regular product is not lessened by the amount realized from its by-product."[32] Again, however, he pointed out that any costs incurred in turning the by-product into a salable article should be charged against the income derived from the sale.[33] The costs here were to include factory overhead. Bentley also made a distinction between those by-products which required only incidental processing, and those which were entirely remade, perhaps mixed with raw materials of another type. In this instance, it was his recommendation that the cost of the principal product should receive credit for an arbitrary valuation to be placed on the by-product material. It might be noted here, however, that Bentley's distinction was very rarely followed by later authorities. His sales of by-products account is illustrated to bring out the differentiation which he had in mind.

Sales of By-Products[34]

Debit: At close of each month with the cost of by-products sold [see the by-products account, *supra*] provided the by-products have to be worked over in order to be made salable; otherwise there would be no debit to this account unless the management wished to carry the by-products at an arbitrary cost value.	Credit: At close of each month with the total sales of by-products (at selling prices).

The balance of the account, whether the debit was made or not, would be closed to profit or loss at the end of each month. In general, while Bentley's by-product discussion was somewhat more specific than that of his predecessors, it suffered because of his neglect in not illustrating the exact technique to be followed in carrying out the by-product-value-to-be-credited-to-cost theory. Although he did casually mention the latter procedure, a reader would have had considerable difficulty in determining just what entries to make in order to show the offset.

The practice in this country, in the period immediately preceding the First World War, was briefly summarized by J. Lee Nicholson in 1913: "The custom is to determine the per cent of the original product material used in the making of the by-product, and consider its cost as the material cost of the by-product, this being deducted from the cost of the primary product."[35] He mentioned, however, that if the determination of the percentage referred to was unusually complex, no deduction was to be made from the main product cost. Under these circumstances the sale price of the by-product was to be treated as a sundry income item. Supposedly, too, any labor and factory overhead costs incurred in manufacturing the by-products would be offset, in the last instance, against the revenue derived from them. Nicholson, however, did not discuss this point, preferring to leave the matter unsettled at that time.

By 1917, cost authorities in this country were treating the subject of by-products with considerable care and preciseness. For example, in that year, A. Hamilton Church devoted several pages to the problem in his *Manufacturing Costs and Accounts,* using the soap industry as an illustration. After giving the several viewpoints which might be taken, Church concluded that the fundamental matter to be decided was the price or value at which the "reject" was to be charged to the by-products processing account, and credited to the manufacturing account. His theory was that the by-products reduced the cost of the primary product. There were at least three bases, either one of which might be adopted:

1. Manufacturing account can be credited with the sale price of the by-product, less cost of recovery.
2. No price, or a merely nominal price can be placed on the reject, which is equivalent to making a present of its raw material to the by-product department, and enabling it to show a profit. . . .
3. When the amount of the by-product content in the original raw material can be calculated . . . then a fair price can be put on the reject, based on the relative weight of the materials divided between main and by-products.[36]

Church seemed to prefer the last plan, although the first had, in his opinion, considerable merit. In any event, a separate division of the plant should be established to handle the by-products processing, and as accurate cost and production records as possible be maintained for this division.

The English cost authorities, in the period of the early 1920's, continued to neglect this particular topic. Experts in England, while they contributed some of the most important early analyses of the problem, relinquished their commanding lead in this respect in the decade immediately after the turn of the century, and they never recovered it. In order to contrast their treatments with that of authorities in America, some remarks of M. W. Jenkinson might be summarized at this point.[37] At the conclusion of an address which he made before the Bristol Society of Chartered Accountants, Jenkinson was asked which was the "correct" way to deal with by-products, so far as the amount to be used for crediting the cost of the main product was concerned. Jenkinson replied that there were two possibilities: A standard price could be used, or as an alternate, actual market prices of the by-products. The determination of the standard price was not given. He implied that it was a sort of "normal" price which was not changed very often. He favored the standard price method if this price were changed at fairly long intervals in accordance with market fluctuations. It was his opinion that under this plan the cost of the primary product would not be made noncomparable except at the year end, when adjustments would be necessary to bring the cost books into agreement with the financial books (the two were to be kept distinct). At that time the average price for the year (of by-products) was to be ascertained, and proper adjustments (the nature of these was not indicated) made on the cost records. It seemed to be Jenkinson's main purpose, although he was not very specific in his discussion, to keep the fluctuating by-product prices from influencing the cost of the main product; that was in essence the reason why he suggested that a standard price be adopted.

The brief treatment accorded the topic by one other English cost authority might be cited. E. T. Elbourne, in 1921, stated that "in case of . . . swarf or cuttings, which are in the nature of by-products, the credit should pass, so far as possible, to the account to which the original material was debited, and the untraceable items ultimately credited to the . . . profit and loss account."[38]

In general, then, the English cost accountants of the early 1920's were treating by-products values as offsets to the principal product, but there was some disagreement as to the price to be used.[39]

In contrast with the general neglect of this subject in England, the expositions of practitioners and theoreticians in this country became more comprehensive and thorough. The research staff of the newly organized National Association of Cost Accountants, for instance, compiled a bulletin on the various methods of dealing with the problem which were in use in 1920. This report concluded with a general caution against needless "hairsplitting" (their term) devices which were not worth the additional costs involved.[40] In the same year, Jordan and Harris considered the subject of sufficient importance to devote a whole chapter of their *Cost Accounting* to it. Three methods of accounting for by-products were summarized, together with their advantages and disadvantages.[41] There was nothing particularly original in their description, yet it did serve to emphasize the importance of the proper handling of the problem.[42] By 1922, expositions of specialized techniques began to appear more frequently. C. C. Sheppard, for instance, discussed a "weight basis" for apportioning the cost of products (main and by-products) derived from a ton of coal, which, he insisted, would yield comparable costs for all practical purposes.[43] The wasted units were to be distributed to the main product (coke) and the four by-products on the basis of the amount of recovered products obtained from each ton of coal. After this adjustment had been made, the material cost was apportioned on the basis of the revised weights in pounds[44]

In the latter years of the 1920's the accounting for by-products continued to receive more and more adequate attention. Several authorities devoted scores of pages to this one topic,[45] giving not only the basic theory underlying the problem, but also many illustrations of the actual practices followed by leading industries. Little that is new has been added since that time.

CHAPTER IX

EVOLUTION OF THE ACCOUNTING FOR WASTE MATERIAL AND SCRAP

THE DEVELOPMENT OF THE COST IDEAS CONCERNED WITH THE PROPER accounting for waste materials and scrap* proceeded at a rather slow pace in the early history of costing; little interest was taken in the matter until some time after the turn of the century. The most important reason for this general neglect of the subject is not difficult to ascertain. It was not until around 1900 that much thought was given to the general importance of waste in industry, or to the accounting for such waste. More than likely some of the progressive firms of that time had given the topic serious consideration, but by and large there was little regard for the problem until the administration of President Theodore Roosevelt. Under his aggressive leadership various bodies and institutions initiated studies relating to conservation; and following that lead, cost authorities began to treat the

---

* Some of the more modern cost authorities draw a distinction between scrap and waste which is not of any great importance in connection with the development of the subject matter of this chapter. The distinction is as follows: Scrap has some of the qualities of a low grade by-product; it is made at the same time that the main product is made and in most instances can be sold at some price, even though a very low one. Waste, on the other hand, arises also from the process of manufacture, but generally has no value on the market. It may also be the loss due to shrinkage or evaporation. Cf. for the distinction, A. Hamilton Church, *Manufacturing Costs and Accounts*, (New York: McGraw-Hill Book Company, 1917), p. 86.

subject with more respect and consideration, paying special attention to the cost accounting arrangements which were required.

All of the above does not mean, however, that the early authorities neglected entirely the problem under discussion; it does mean that their techniques were usually rather vague or superficial. The English cost experts, Emile Garcke and J. M. Fells, for example, mentioned that factories did have scrap to be dealt with in some instances; they implied that it would be handled in the same way as surplus material returned to the storeroom. A "stores debit note" was to be filled in, but Garcke and Fells were absolutely silent on these important points: the valuation of the scrap; whether the job was to be credited, and, if so, at what amount; and what was to become of the scrap after it was split off. The illustrated stores debit note had columns for weight and amount, but it was not filled in; thus their readers had to supply their own details.[1]

In order to emphasize the general neglect of the topic during the early stages of the development of modern cost techniques, the treatment accorded it by G. P. Norton might be cited.[2] This English authority was especially concerned with the accounting for an industry in which considerable waste would be expected, and as a matter of fact he recognized that there would be a problem involved therein. Yet, when he came to the actual procedure to be employed, the best that he could offer was a mill sales daybook in which would be entered the sales of the waste and several other miscellaneous items, such as old machinery. The entries recorded in this book, so far as the waste was concerned, would be posted at the end of each day to the debit of some customer's account (assumed on credit) and credited to materials account in the "nominal ledger." This entry was made for the selling price of the waste and it was credited to the materials account on the same basis. Norton thus had in the materials account the purchases of materials at cost, and the sale of waste at whatever it brought. No entry was to be made for the waste until it was sold. As one can easily perceive, this was indeed a very loose method for handling this important matter, yet it was the best that had been suggested up to that time,[3] even though, as mentioned in Chapter II, one or two of the early French experts had briefly referred to the matter.

By 1898, when J. Slater Lewis wrote his *Commercial Organisation of Factories*, the accounting for scrap or waste had progressed to such a point as to cause him to pause and examine the problem with a little more care than had been considered necessary up to that time. Lewis was primarily concerned with English engineering shops, which would obviously almost always have some scrap or waste material. It was his recommendation, therefore, that the waste metal be taken back into the storeroom at a price just a shade less than the market value of the scrap material, and credited to the production order from which the item came. A stores return note was to be the authority for the entry on the stores card, and a less-than-normal price was adopted "in order that constant readjustment may not be necessary."[4] For the scrap that could not easily be traced to its proper production order, Lewis provided a standing order sheet which would be credited. At periodic intervals the scrap would be transferred to the warehouse and sold; this transaction would be handled through a sales daybook, just as Norton had suggested. Since Lewis' cost records were only partially integrated with the financial ledger, the sales daybook entry was really the only one that ever appeared on the "counting house books," as he called them. The technique employed by this authority was more specific than any that had previously appeared, but perhaps no more accurate. Lewis did emphasize, however, the importance of crediting the job which caused the scrap or waste. This, then, was his most important contribution to the required accounting procedure.

By 1903, some cost authorities were making a distinction between waste or scrap on the one hand, and spoiled work on the other. Spoiled work was not, of course, an anticipated sort of waste; it was due to the fault of some workman, machine, or material. An illustration given by John Mann[5] was concerned with a spoiled casting in a foundry. It was his recommendation that the excess cost of a job, due to the spoiled casting, should not be charged to the original job, but to a special account which was one of the oncost or burden accounts. This interpretation, or theory, was somewhat different from what had been previously advanced, although few authorities had bothered with such technicalities. It indicated, too, the increasing interest and respect with which the topic was treated after the turn of the century.

In this country the spoiled castings in a foundry also excited some attention at about the same time. H. L. C. Hall, for example, in 1904, made the statement that the cost of a casting was made up of raw materials (iron), labor, and expense (overhead). He continued his analysis by insisting that an imperfect casting had to be returned to the cupola as a "remelt" at the cost of the iron used in it, plus any overhead which had been incurred; the labor element was omitted on his assumption that the worker would not be paid for spoiled work. This was all he had to say at that point,[6] but later on it was his suggestion that spoiled materials, especially those in a process industry, should be charged to a waste account at the raw material cost plus the cost of labor.[7] He did not mention the overhead element in connection with this procedure, nor did he state what was to become of the waste account. His theory, therefore, was somewhat dissimilar to the opinion expressed by preceding authorities, in that the waste was priced into the waste account at a much higher figure than had previously been the custom. B. C. Bean, another American cost authority, decided that the scrap which came from the different jobs might well be handled in large lump amounts and "prorated to the material from which it came."[8] This particular procedure, of course, was rather vague, but Bean continued by stating that the credit involved in the proration was the amount at which the scrap was sold. If, however, the scrap were not sold, but *held* for sale, a "fair" (his term) price would be taken, the fair price being the mean market price. If returned to the works for remelting it would be considered worth the "scrap price."[9] This viewpoint was similar to that given by Lewis some years before and indicates the general neglect of the subject in this country during the period under review, as well as the hazy techniques recommended.

Another instance of the small importance of the subject during that time is afforded by C. M. Day's *Accounting Practice,* 1908. Day briefly stated that the "sales of waste are an offset to the material consumption and should be deducted from the material consumption to determine the cost of material."[10]

The paucity of material on the proper accounting for scrap and waste began to be remedied by the end of the first decade of the twentieth century, especially in the United States. This was undoubtedly a reflection of the increasing interest in all topics concerned with conservation and lower costs of production,[11] as well as of the renewed interest in costing matters in general. Up to 1909, the consensus seems to have been to treat the scrap or waste as a reduction of the cost of a job, although there had been some dispute in regard to this method. There was also little agreement on the pricing scheme to be adopted. In the year mentioned, however, J. L. Nicholson summarized the techniques which he considered to be standard practice, and later authorities soon began to elaborate upon his treatment. Nicholson first divided the waste or scrap into two classes, depending upon whether it was or was not worthless. The worthless items could be charged directly (at the cost of the original material) to the production order or to a defective work account, the defective work account being included in the "general expenses" of the firm in question. Obviously, the first technique would increase the cost of the articles called for by the order number. This authority did not state which method was to be preferred, merely mentioning that the net effect of each, generally speaking, was about the same. It is difficult to understand Nicholson's reasoning on that point. How could the net effect be the same?

The items of scrap or waste which were not worthless, according to Nicholson, were to be taken back into the raw materials storeroom at a "reduced rate, to be agreed upon, and the difference between the cost and this reduced rate should be charged" either to the order number, or to the defective work account.[12] If part of this reclaimed scrap could be used again in some manufacturing process, it was to be charged to the second process at the same price for which it had been debited into stores. While Nicholson was thus rather indefinite as to the better practice, and also as to some of the details involved, he did summarize more completely than had any previous American authority the various possibilities open to the factory accountant.

Two years later, the New York accountant, John R. Wildman, did not hesitate to suggest the method which, in his opinion, was the more accurate.[13] First, he outlined the following three possible procedures: (1) divide the cost of the job or lot by the number of good articles produced in the lot; (2) divide the cost of the entire lot or job by the number of good items, after deducting the scrap value of the defective articles; and (3) set up the defective work at its "actual cost" (nature not given) and carry it to a defective work account. Wildman implied, but did not state definitely, that under the third plan the credit would be to the original job or articles. His preferred technique, however, was the second one. Pure waste, on the other hand, was to be loaded on to the cost of the finished product; that is, no deduction on account of waste was to be made in the cost of the material which was charged into the final article or articles. Wildman, then, not only was quite specific as to his recommended plans, but he also gave some illustrations of how they would be applied under certain hypothetical instances.

S. H. Bunnell, who wrote about the same time, was less concerned with the practical details, but he did philosophize as to the nature of the scrap item to a greater extent than either Nicholson or
Wildman. It was his opinion that wherever defects occurred
which were not expected as a usual part of the manufacturing process,
such scrapped articles should be charged to an account called "defective material and labor" for the net loss involved. This loss was
to be computed by taking the difference between the scrap value
of the spoiled article and its prime cost at that time. Although he
did not so state, he implied that if the spoilage were a regular, expected matter, then the job responsible was to be charged for the
spoiled work by reason of the failure to give it any credit on account of the scrap value. As he stated it:[14] "Proper cost keeping
does not load the effect of occasional misfortunes upon single orders,
but spreads the expense of mischances as a light tax over the whole
product." This same concept had been hinted at by several of Bunnell's predecessors, but none of them had so clearly stated the issue.

Other American authorities also soon took up the problem of the
proper accounting for waste and scrap. F. E. Webner, for instance,
emphasized the importance of making timely reports of spoiled work,
waste, and scrap, and he gave some illustrations of forms which
might be adopted for that purpose.[15] The attention of the management was to be called to such matters, and a record of the efficiency
of each employee also maintained. Webner's system of accounting
for expected waste and spoilage was also worthy of note. He
recommended the establishment of an account on the general ledger
entitled "reserve for over, short, and damage," to which would be
credited each month a budgeted sum large enough to take care of
possible losses in connection with the manufacturing operations. The
debit would be to a factory overhead account with the same name
except for the omission of the word "reserve." As losses (waste,
damage, or shortage) actually took place, day by day, the reserve
account would be charged and work in process credited. His plan
thus provided for a type of budgetary control over this item and allowed the charge to be spread out over the entire accounting period.

The English cost authorities, during the period immediately preceding the First World War, also showed a renewed interest in the
problem involved in the handling of scrap and waste. L. W. Hawkins,
for instance, devoted several pages to the problem in the second
edition of his *Cost Accounts*.[16] He made a distinction, in his discus-

sion, between different types of scrap or waste. One type included filings, turnings, and other minute articles which, in his opinion, were not worth the trouble of apportioning between jobs. Such items, therefore, were to be sold for what they would bring and the "works expenses" (burden) account credited for the total cash received. This technique reduced the amount of the factory overhead, but did not deduct any sum from the cost of the individual jobs. Spoiled or defective castings, on the other hand, were to be handled along practically the same lines as those suggested by Bunnell in this country; that is, if the spoilage were a usual consequence of the job, it was to be treated as part of the regular cost of such orders, but where it was occasional or rare, the extra cost (or loss) incurred was not to be charged to the job but charged into an overhead account. In the latter event, only the prime cost of the casting was to be taken into account.[17] Hawkins also gave an illustration of how this would be carried out, both on the financial ledger and on the cost ledger, which, under his system, were not integrated with each other.

Another English authority, E. T. Elbourne, followed the theories and techniques advocated by Hawkins, except that he would not commit himself upon the specific plans to be employed. It was his opinion, too, that the type of industry played a large part in determining the method to be adopted for handling scrap and defective work. In some firms, he stated, it was probably the best plan to treat the cost of all the defective work as a burden item to be spread over all the output of the factory by some "average formula."[18] In others, it might be preferable to penalize the job responsible for the spoiled work. In spite of these details, Elbourne was much less thorough than Hawkins as to the nature of the problem involved and as to its handling. It can be readily seen, however, that the English cost experts were again seriously examining the subject. In spite of the fact that they had given it considerable attention in the earlier developmental period, their contributions lagged behind those of their American contemporaries until the First World War. Even then the authorities in this country continued to forge ahead; ideas inaugurated here, for instance, generally required several years to appear in English literature on the subject. This is illustrative of the neglect of the problem in that country after the first decade of this century.

Cost accountants in the United States, on the other hand, devoted more and more attention to refinements in the required tech-

niques as the years passed by. By 1917, for example, A. Hamilton
Church felt it necessary to make a most careful distinction as to the
difference between waste, spoilage, scrap, and by-products, as a prerequisite to their correct handling on the books of the factory. While
adding very little that was new to the subject, Church's discussion
was perhaps the clearest exposition of the problems involved that
had appeared up to that time. He concluded that waste should be
treated by dividing the cost of the material between the good articles
which were made; spoilage was best handled by setting up a spoiled
work account to which it would be charged, with full factory cost,
up to the time the item was spoiled; scrap had to have a value put
on it, and this value was credited to the job or department from which
it came, if this could be easily ascertained—otherwise it was to be
credited to profit and loss when sold.[19]

N. T. Ficker, in the same year, suggested the establishment of
a shop scrap account, to which would be credited, throughout the
year, the amounts received from the sale of scrap. On the debit
side would appear all the expenditures and charges incurred in handling it. These included the cost of the labor involved in converting
the scrap into a shape ready for sale, boxing, weighing, and various
other debits. While there seemed nothing unusual about such an
account up to that point, its disposition at the end of the fiscal
period was somewhat different from what was being proposed during those years. Any balance in the account was to be closed to the
shop raw material account, either as a debit or as a credit depending upon the circumstances. This particular treatment had not been
advocated for several years.[20]

A short while later, F. W. Kilduff suggested a rather original
distinction, which might be applied to the different types of spoiled
work in order to determine how it should be treated in the accounts.[21]
He too divided the spoilage into normal and abnormal, which several
authorities had previously advocated, but went on to insist that while
the normal spoilage was a proper addition to the factory overhead costs
for a period, the abnormal spoilage was not. Up to that time most of
the cost experts who had considered the matter had decided that
the unusual or rare spoilage should be handled as a burden item,
while the regular, expected spoilage articles should be included
in the direct cost of the jobs.[22] Kilduff's theory was almost the
antithesis of this prevailing doctrine. In addition, the so-called
abnormal spoilage was to be divided into two groups, depending upon

whether the business or firm was on what he called a "cost-plus-fixed-profit" basis or on an ordinary sales basis. In the first instance, the abnormal spoilage was to be shown on the income statement in the "profit and loss section;" in the second case, the amount would be shown on that same statement in the cost of goods sold section, as a "fourth factor of cost."[23] It was this second suggestion that was so novel. Kilduff thought of the abnormal spoilage (under the ordinary sales basis) as a part of the firm's cost of production, but absolutely distinct from material, labor, or burden. It was, in a word, a "fourth element of cost." As he explained his theory, the fourth element was to be shown on the income statement, but on the ledger it was never to "pass into the goods in process account. Instead, it should go directly to the profit and loss account, for there is no reason for deferring the charge to a later period. The loss—the measure of inefficiency—should penalize the period. The entire balance should be absorbed."[24] Even though Kilduff's suggestion seemed to have had considerable theoretical merit, it was slow to attain recognition. It will serve to indicate, however, the refinements in the accounting for scrap, waste, and spoiled material which were being advocated in this country during the period under review.[25]

By the early 1920's, therefore, the prevailing opinions in this country in regard to the subject may be summarized as follows: (1) Outright waste which had no recoverable value, and which was anticipated as a part of the job or process, was to be handled as an increased cost of material consumed; that is, the cost of the finished units was to include the unavoidable waste.[26] (2) Scrap, which of course had a salable value, was best handled as an offset (at what it was worth on the market, or at a nominal price) to the cost of the job or process which was responsible for it.[27] One authority, however, recommended that the amount received from the sale of the scrap be credited to a sundry account, or if the amount were small, it might be credited to the overhead.[28] If the plan for the small amount were followed, the cost of the original job or process would be the same regardless of the amount of scrap recovered; this viewpoint seemed to have been in the minority during the period under discussion.[29] (3) Spoiled work continued to be divided into abnormal (unexpected) and normal (usual) classes. The abnormal was to be handled as a part of the cost of the job or process, while the normal was to be treated as an element of overhead or burden to be spread over the entire output of the factory.[30] Some authorities distinguished between the types of defective or spoiled work by inquiring as to whether the production order, "on which the defective units were made," was one that would be repeated at frequent intervals, or was a rare, special type that probably would not be duplicated for many years.[31]   The accounting treatment required, however, was very similar to the other distinction which was being made; no change of theory was involved in this newer classification.

One further development in connection with this topic might be briefly discussed here; that is, during the decade of the 1920's some suggestions were made for establishing a standard unit raw material quantity charge for each item or article which a factory produced, and also a standard salvage or scrap credit. C. B. Williams, for example, proposed such a plan as early as 1921.[32]   Williams recognized that the determination of the standard unit quantities was probably the most difficult phase of the problem, mentioning that in most instances "this has involved a careful compilation of records and painstaking consideration of a large amount of detail."[33]   Records of previous periods and pertinent current data would need to be examined. Even though the problem might be tedious in a large number of cases, Williams thought that the results would fully justify the trouble. How would the proposed plan be carried out, assuming that the standard units had been established? First, each production order or process would be charged as usual with all the raw material requisitioned for it. Second, each order or process would be credited with its proportion of salvaged material as determined from the standard unit quantity credit; and finally the salvage account would be debited with the amount of this adjustment. The value to be assigned to the standard unit quantity credit (per unit) was to be determined in accordance with the use to which the salvage material would be put; that is, whether it was sold, or used in some by-product. If the salvage (scrap) were used in making some by-product, it would be priced into the by-product at the same value at which it stood in the salvage account. It would seem, then, that this plan took care of the perplexing problem of pricing the scrap, or salvage, as Williams called it. It had some advantage in those cases where it was difficult to determine the individual production order or article to which items of scrap were to be credited.

This idea, as proposed by Williams, was merely, of course, an extension of the by then familiar standard costing arrangements.

Williams, however, emphasized the handling of scrap to a greater extent than was customary in that period.

Various other proposals, like Williams', continued to be made as the years passed by. For the most part, however, they involved no new theory or change in fundamental techniques; comparatively few contributions have been made since the early 1920's. This conclusion is borne out by at least one fact; that is, when A. Hamilton Church revised his *Manufacturing Costs and Accounts* in 1929 (first edition, 1917), the comprehensive and carefully written sections devoted to the subject matter of this chapter were almost unchanged from the edition published some twelve years before. He evidently thought, therefore, that the basic theories underlying the proper accounting for scrap and waste required no modifications, in spite of the fact that a dozen years had passed by.

CHAPTER X

EVOLUTION
OF THE METHODS AND THEORIES
EMPLOYED FOR VALUING
FACTORY INVENTORIES

THE INVENTORY VALUATION PROBLEM WAS RELATIVELY UNIMPORTANT IN the early stages of the evolution of modern costing.[1] Emphasis was not placed upon it until almost the end of the last century. This neglect may be attributed to the fact that carefully and accurately compiled financial statements for factories were not deemed very essential until that date. The attention of the authorities seemed centered on other matters, some of which have been discussed in previous chapters of this volume. The accounting for materials and labor, for example, naturally assumed a prime importance in the early treatises on costing subjects; it was needed every day, whereas the valuing of inventories was thought of only once a year, if that often. In addition, competition between manufactories was not so keen as it was later; there was thus less incentive for comparable and accurate profit or loss figures. A firm might even exist for years without reliable cost records. All of this was not very conducive to strict or careful thinking on the inventory valuation problem.

In view of the above, it is not surprising to discover that one of the earliest [2] modern references to the problem of valuing inven-

tories in a factory appeared in 1862. J. Sawyer, writing in that year
on the accounting for the English tanning industry, remarked that
the contemporary practice was to value the finished goods and work
in process at cost, unless depreciated in value. In addition, "no profit
should be estimated unless realised . . . and subject further to the contingency of a falling market."[3] This doctrine had all the essential
features of a lower of cost or market theory, although he did not,
of course, refer to it as such. In spite of the fact that Sawyer considered this technique the better practice, he finally decided that in
the tanning trade there would be no fundamental objection to adding
on to the cost of the goods in process of manufacture (for statement
purposes) an estimated profit percentage, based upon the "time,
skill, capital, and labour" which were involved. Sawyer, however,
felt that there would be "insuperable difficulties" in connection with
this method. He did not indicate the real nature of the difficulties.[4]
His work was noteworthy, then, in that he did not adhere to the cost
principle with its attendant, no-anticipation-of-profit consequence. He
recognized, however, that the cost method was the prevailing theory at
the time. (The Pepperell Manufacturing Company, textile makers of
New England, for example was using the cost method all during the
middle 1800's.)[5] Incidentally, the cost of the partially manufactured
items was to include the cost of the hides, tanning material consumed,
labor, and a sum for rent and other expenses (costs). The full
factory cost was to be used, instead of the prime cost which some later
authorities advocated.[6]

By 1887, therefore, when the next English reference was published,[7] the cost valuation plan had already been questioned, but
not very seriously. In that year, Emile Garcke and J. M. Fells, whose
work was the first to examine comprehensively the industrial cost
problems of the time, devoted a whole chapter to the matter of
"surveys."[8] First, they insisted that the ordinary raw materials should
be valued at the net cost or invoice price. If, however, any items were
out of date or obsolescent, they were priced somewhat as junk, that
is, at the market value of such items.[9] In addition, the old material
required a special ledger account, distinct from the newer items.
These authorities neglected to give any illustrations of the accounting
required to carry out their preferred techniques; they contented themselves with mere descriptive matter. They also passed over almost
completely the work in process items. It may be understood, though,
that they recommended a cost valuation for that group of articles.

When they came to the valuation of finished goods, however, Garcke and Fells were much more specific, treating the matter with considerable care. It was their observation, first, that most of the better manufacturing firms used the cost of production plan, without any profit percentage added on, and without any so-called "standing charges," which included interest on capital and selling and administrative expenses. Factory charges (manufacturing burden), on the other hand, were to be included in the valuation base. They gave a rather lengthy explanation as to the reason for omitting the standing charges. Very briefly it was due to the fact that a factory might show a sizable profit for several years by building up larger and larger stocks of finished goods, which might or might not be salable. Such a practice, moreover, would tend to inflate the balance sheet with perhaps unrealizable assets. To quote: "The right principle undoubtedly is that in a manufacturing business a profit should not be considered to have been made until a sale has been effected, or until a contract for the delivery at a future date of goods already manufactured is entered into."[10] Again, like Sawyer, they anticipated exceptions under certain circumstances. For instance, if a firm were engaged in making a product which at all times could be sold at some stable, normal price (they did not, however, mention the names of any such products), it might be a perfectly correct practice to consider that the profit was earned on production and not on sale. Even in those rare cases, they concluded, it would probably be "more judicious" to adopt the "conservative" cost principle. Their reasoning on this point was also interesting. It was their opinion that if the cost, rather than market, prices were used, they would hold good for fiscal period after fiscal period, so long as the finished goods held their "pristine" (their term) condition or until an improved process caused the cost to be lowered. If this were true, no adjustments to record any market fluctuations would need to be made when financial statements were compiled. This, then, was the essential advantage of the cost valuation rule. Incidentally, Garcke and Fells made it perfectly clear that if this principle were followed, absolutely no account needed to be taken of purely market price movements; they might be entirely ignored. In case, however, of outright losses of value, through obsolescence or damage, the finished goods were to be reduced in value by debiting either the trading account or the profit and loss account (they would not commit themselves definitely), and crediting the finished stock account. Proper entries also had to be made on the stock sheets, since these contained the details which supported the control account on the ledger. Taken as a whole, therefore, and overlooking their neglect of the valuation of the work in process, the treatment accorded the topic by these two authorities was particularly noteworthy for such an early date. In fact, their exposition was not improved upon for more than a decade.

The valuation theories expounded by the English Chartered Accountant, G. P. Norton, should be briefly examined at this point especially since he was concerned with a processing industry—a textile mill.[11] According to him, the raw materials of the factory, mainly cotton and wool, were to be priced for statement purposes at cost plus transportation and buying charges. If any discounts[12] were allowed by the vendor they were to be deducted in obtaining the net amount to be adopted for the statements. This raw material valuation rule would still be standard practice except for the proviso concerning the lower of cost or market which is widely followed today; Norton, however, did not mention this point, which had been hinted at by J. Sawyer some thirty years before. When he came to the valuation technique to be employed for the goods in process and finished articles, Norton departed from the usual practices which had been advocated up to that time. For example, in connection with the unfinished items, he insisted that they be priced at the cost of the material consumed in them, plus "the *usual trade price* for the process or processes through which the goods have passed."[13] This technique, however, was entirely consistent with the unusual cost accounting arrangement which he recommended.[14]

Turning now to the valuation of finished stock, Norton divided it into two distinct groups,[15] the first being the goods on order, and the second, those not on order. Taking the goods on order first, he advocated that they be valued at selling price, subject, however, to a percentage deduction on account of the following items:

1. Interest for the term of credit.
2. The usual discount.
3. Possible claims, damages, and shortages.
4. Losses which might be incurred on goods returned.
5. Agents' commissions.
6. Freight-out if not paid by customer.
7. Cost of packing and delivery.
8. Average losses due to bad debts.[16]

If the goods were not made to order, all of the above deductions were to apply, plus a percentage for the following:

1. Interest on the probable term that the goods would remain in stock.
2. The tendency of the goods to depreciate.
3. Warehouse and office expenses.
4. Selling expenses.
5. Selling profit.

It is interesting to note that he did not discuss at all the problem of estimating all of the above deductions. As a matter of fact, it is quite probable that he merely desired the percentage deduction to be fully large enough to cover all the items *in toto;* individual percentage deductions would have been practically impossible. Norton observed, too, that the percentage should be the same at each inventory date; this was evidently an attempt to secure a comparable and uniform valuation scheme, but, of course, it was much more defective than the ordinary factory cost technique which had been advocated by Garcke and Fells[17] some years before. It should be pointed out, also, that Norton's proposed procedure moved in reverse order to that which is generally adopted today. That is to say, he recommended the plan of determining cost by taking the selling price and deducting all the items which had been added on to the cost to obtain such a selling price. At the present time the cost price is often adopted, based upon the cost records. Obviously, Norton's technique would be much more difficult to carry out, if not impossible. He evidently did not trust his cost figures implicitly, or else he would not have advocated such a unique method of inventory valuation. In addition to the preceding recommendations, this authority, following Garcke and Fells, mentioned that old or damaged stock should be reduced in value by a special adjustment. In the end, Norton again showed his inherent conservatism by stating that there was a general tendency in factories to overvalue goods ready for sale and that it must be "remembered that a profit is not made until the sale has been effected."[18]

In order to illustrate the valuation of inventories under the prime costing systems widely used in the 1890's, the elaborate technique employed by J. Slater Lewis[19] may be cited. Under his plan, only the material and labor costs per job would be accumulated on the "cost ledger"; the burden, or shop establishment charges, would be ascertained *in toto* separately and not applied to the orders as they were completed. Yet Lewis recognized that such a scheme would not be conducive to accurate valuations of finished and unfinished goods at "stocktaking" dates. He felt it necessary, therefore, to provide some arrangement whereby the factory overhead items could be added on to the prime costs at the end of each fiscal period. It might be noted that this particular procedure was to be followed only if the business were of a "thoroughly sound and non-speculative nature, and where a safe market were known to exist" for the goods.[20] Although he did not definitely point this out, it was his opinion that if the preceding requirements were not satisfied, the conservative doctrine to follow would be to omit any addition on account of establishment or shop charges. But in case the addition was called for, how was it to be handled? His method was very simple, although its actual application might not be so easy. An establishment charges suspense account was to be set up on the regular general ledger, and credited (at a balance sheet date) with the calculated percentage of overhead items which might be properly considered applicable to the work in process and finished goods. The debits were to the finished stock account and the manufacturing (prime cost of work in progress) account. Obviously, the computation of these figures was really the crux of the problem, but Lewis did not elaborate upon that phase of the subject.[21] After that journal entry was made, another one was necessary which debited the suspense account and credited profit and loss. The profit and loss ledger account had already been debited, supposedly, with all the actual burden incurred during the fiscal period. Neither of the preceding two entries affected in the slightest the job cost sheets themselves on which only the prime costs were entered. In view of the nature of the adjustments (they were merely for statement purposes and not part of the costing arrangement) it was necessary to reverse the first entry by debiting the suspense account and crediting the finished stock and manufacturing accounts before any entries were made in the next fiscal period. During the second fiscal period, the suspense account would be gradually absorbed in the cost of the goods sold which had remained on hand at the last balance sheet date and for which the suspense account had been established. Lewis was vague as to how this would be handled, merely stating that the "amounts thus allocated to goods in stock become chargeable to revenue when the goods are sold."[22] While his plan undoubtedly had considerable merit, it probably would have proved only moderately advantageous in practice, perhaps even less so than the altogether extramural costing arrangements advocated by a majority of the cost authorities of the time. There is, nevertheless, considerable evidence that his plan was adopted by some prominent firms of the time, not only in England, but in this country as well.[23]

In the United States, the problem of the valuation of factory inventories excited very little discussion or attention until around the turn of the century. The few authorities who touched on the matter dismissed it with only the briefest of remarks, and these few paragraphs were for the most part concerned with whether or not the factory overhead element to be added on (if at all) should include selling and administrative expenses (see Chapter V). One example, followed by an actual company, the Whitin Machine Works, will suffice to show the "rough and ready" methods then in use:

> Inventories in the 1880's were valued by a process no longer remembered. Perhaps the procedure was not dissimilar to that in effect at least as early as 1900 (and not abandoned until 1938). If so, the physical volume of inventory was determined as much by weight as by count. Poundage figures were computed by whatever method seemed simplest. The company always kept in mind that it was making only an approximation and so wasted no time on elaborate refinements. At the end of each year all foremen submitted to the front office an estimate of the pounds of castings on hand in their departments. The weight of finished castings was lumped with the weight of castings not yet machined. Loss of weight resulting from machining was approximated. The front office then multiplied the foreman's weight figures by the dollar costs of the raw materials involved. The value added by labor was also guessed at. Since the shop was so organized that a machine part was generally converted from the raw material (or casting) stage into a finished piece within one and the same department, the foreman of that department had a fairly clear idea of the value of the labor involved in the process. The front office then added raw material and labor values together to get a figure for in-process inventory. No overhead was included. The completed inventory report was then handed to Marston Whitin, who proceeded to adjust the final sum by whatever amount he thought current business conditions justified—and perhaps to whatever extent he wished to influence his final profit calculations. Not infrequently his write-downs amounted to 20 to 30 per cent. In fact, everything in Whitin's annual statements reflected his constant effort to view profits as conservatively as possible.[24]

In America the nineteenth century textbook contributions to the theory and practice of factory inventory valuation were conspicuous by their absence. One exception, however, requires attention. In 1897, F. A. Halsey, the engineer, in some criticisms of a paper delivered by H. M. Norris before the American Society of Mechanical Engineers in that year, insisted that the selling and general administrative expenses had no place in the group of items making up the burden charge which was to be allocated to the cost of the jobs. Norris had stated in his address that the "general expense is meant to include every outlay of whatever nature which is not chargeable to some specific order number."[25] It was this last statement which caused Halsey to take issue with Norris, and led him to state that

> my contention is that the items which are included in the cost of production include only those incurred inside the shop door and not those outside. The expenses incurred outside the shop door are properly considered cost of distribution and not of production. . . . This may seem at first like a distinction without a difference; but in point of fact the difference is more important than the distinction is plain, although, like everything else connected with the subject the distinction is one whose importance depends on circumstances. In the case of a factory producing goods solely on order, where no stock is carried on hand, except what is actually in progress, the distinction would be of small importance, but in the case of a factory producing goods without regard to the state of the market, large stocks being carried, *it becomes of very decided importance*. The reason is this: when the *annual inventory* is taken for *use* in the *balance sheet*, an *important item* of the balance sheet, in the case of works which carry heavy stocks of goods, is of course the value of those goods. . . . If they are *overvalued*, it simply *inflates* the business; and that is the *direct tendency* of including these office and sales expenses in the *cost of production*. . . . In other words, it inventories the expenses and *makes them* show as an asset, a condition of things that cannot be defended. I know this is *a common plan*, but it is as *wrong in principle* as it is common, although, of course where goods are made solely on order, it becomes of small importance.[26]

This statement indicates that Halsey was a rather careful student of cost theory; in fact, he was distinctly in advance of his contemporaries. His discussion, however, seems to have excited very little attention in this country. It might be noted also that his reasoning concerning the valuation problem was somewhat reminiscent of the English theorists of the period; he appeared especially familiar with the work of Garcke and Fells, although he did not refer to them. As was indicated in Chapter V, Halsey's distinction between the items properly composing the factory burden charge was accepted only in part by the cost authorities of the time. Norris himself, in rebuttal, stated that

> if one wishes to know the actual cost of an article . . . nothing should be included in the cost of production except hours, wages, and materials, but if we want to learn the whole cost of anything for the purpose . . . *of preparing an inventory,* the cost of production should include a part of the president's salary, as well as that of the superintendent or foremen. . . . There is no question but that the *inventory, based on these figures, would show an inflated value* . . . but . . . if the books show that the general expense for a certain month is $5,000—$5,000 no more, or less—is distributed amongst all the orders worked on during that month, and it matters not, so far as the cost goes, whether the product is sold immediately or lies in the storehouse for a year.[27]

Norris, then, remained in the end unconvinced of the validity of Halsey's contention, and felt that it was an unjustified distinction which had no place in connection with the problem of valuing factory inventories.

Beginning with 1901, however, the subject (and problems) began to be treated with more respect. In that year, A. Hamilton Church took cognizance of the question, particularly in relation to his scientific machine hour method of allocating the burden element of cost. After making the statement that all valuation was merely the attempt to represent certain facts, he went on to emphasize the "immense importance" of using a correct and accurate plan of apportioning the burden costs so that the inventory figures (he implied that total factory cost would be used) would be reliably and conservatively stated. No general averaging technique should be employed if the desired results were to be attained; most of the systems in use at the time, then, were extremely unsatisfactory, according to him. In addition, no arbitrary addition on account of factory overhead would ever give a balance sheet or profit and loss figure which could be relied upon. Rather, it was necessary to discriminate between the various classes of manufacturers and adopt a scientific burden application arrangement, which, of course, meant that he recommended the use of the method which he originated at about that time, the scientific machine hour technique.[28] This contribution was discussed in Chapter V.

With Church's attention thus focused on the problem, it was not long before other American authorities began to deal with the subject. John Whitmore, for example, in 1906, considered rather carefully the valuation and control of raw materials. He provided regular stores cards showing both the quantity and the value of the articles on hand. He observed that as the items were counted and inspected from time to time, variations would probably appear not only in the quantities but also in the valuation. Occasions for adjustments in the valuation, he stated, would arise particularly at balance sheet dates and would be due generally to deterioration or obsolescence. Two accounts on the general ledger would therefore be necessary under his arrangement, one to care for the adjustments in quantities and the other to take care of the decreases in values. He did not mention, however, what would eventually become of the two accounts. Evidently the cost price was to be adopted for raw materials, subject only to reduction for inactive or depreciated items.[29] This view seems, incidentally, to have been the prevailing opinion in this country during the early years of this century, although the matter was not touched on by very many authorities. It has been noted, also, that some theorists were advocating the total factory cost basis for valuing the unfinished and finished goods.

The valuation problem continued to receive more and more careful treatment in the hands of the English cost accountants and auditors, but American experts did not take much interest in the matter until around 1910. By that time, however, the English had made important contributions which were quickly adopted by the authorities in this country and elaborated upon at length. Perhaps the requirements of The Companies Acts[30] and the widespread adoption of independent audits induced this earlier interest in the matter in Great Britain. In connection with independent audits, it might be noted here that several of the better discussions and treatments accorded the topic by Englishmen concluded with the auditing procedure to be followed in verifying and establishing the inventory valuation to be used for a balance sheet of an industrial concern. John A. Walbank's article in the *Encyclopaedia of Accounting* is an illustration in point.[31] His work may be considered typical of the thoroughness with which the valuation problem was handled in England in the first decade of this century. It was, he stated, the general rule to value raw material at the lower of cost or market[32] since profits must not be anticipated. There were, however, certain exceptions and he discussed those with some care; they were for the most part concerned with material which had to be seasoned or stored for a time before use, such as timber or lead. Interest on the money tied up in such stored items might be charged if the matter were "carefully gone into, and it is seen that there is an actual permanent increase in value."[33] The work in progress, on the other hand, required even more careful valuation; in general, it was to be valued at cost, including both the prime cost and the factory overhead. If, however, the prime cost had fallen to such a point as to be below the market quotations, then the market figure was to be adopted. Walbank concluded with a discussion of the valuation of construction work in progress, and the auditor's responsibilities for inventory verification. He did not handle, as a separate problem, the question of finished goods; they would be treated in a manner similar to the work in process. In summary, his valuation procedures and rules would still be acceptable today, and his article reflects the advanced English thinking of the period under review.

In contrast, however, George Lisle, in his *Accounting in Theory and Practice*, 1899, stated that "all goods in stock which are partially manufactured or are completed should be valued at the prime cost of the raw material, *plus* the freight, duty, and other direct charges, together with the cost of any direct labour. Sometimes a percentage is added for general management expenses so far as they have been expended in the manufacture of the goods, but it is safer not to do this, as when it is done there is a risk of the profit from the selling of the goods being anticipated."[34] According to Lisle, the raw material on hand was to be valued at cost, the figure to include any freight or duty paid. Like previous authorities, he recommended that market prices be used if they were lower than cost. Lisle was a noted English Chartered Accountant and author. His views were probably representative of the more conservative British accountants and auditors around the turn of the century. He also had a section on "stocktaking" in his book. The term was defined as "the examining, finding the value, and preparing a priced inventory, of goods or merchandise on hand at a particular moment of time." The revised edition of his text was published in 1909, and contained the same views as those given above. By that time, however, the inclusion of the burden element in factory cost was being recommended by most authorities.

By 1907 the English authorities were dealing even more completely with the problems involved in "stocktaking," as they called it. G. A. Mitchell, in his *Single Cost Accounts*, for instance, devoted a whole chapter to the questions involved.[35] The raw material was to be taken at cost price (invoice price) plus the freight and buying charges, and less the trade discounts; the cash discounts were a financial matter, according to Mitchell, and need not be considered.[36] The work in progress was to be valued at cost including shop charges up to the point to which the work had progressed. As for the finished items, Mitchell, following Norton, recommended that they be divided into those which had a ready sale, such as ale in a brewery, and those which were more limited in their appeal. Strangely enough, this authority reverted to the practice, also suggested by Norton, of working back from the selling price to the cost price instead of in the other order. Various deductions were provided, therefore, for carrying out the plan. In addition to his other proposals, Mitchell suggested a reserve for inventory fluctuation in case the market price of raw material was lower than cost, somewhat like the reserve used at the present time. The debit was to either manufacturing or trading; he would not state definitely which one should be charged. Mitchell also stressed another matter which had received very little attention up to that time, that is, the importance of adopting a consistent basis for inventory valuation and retaining it as long as possible. As he stated it: "A bad basis, if it were consistently followed, would probably afford more correct results as between fiscal periods than would a scientifically correct survey, if the latter were not rigidly adhered to."[37]

The English authorities continued to recommend the cost or market, whichever is lower, rule for raw material valuation; and the cost, with some adjustments, for the other two factory inventories, up until the period of the First World War. Minor variations appeared from time to time, but these were of small significance. An illustration is afforded by L. W. Hawkins' suggestion that the lower of "average cost" or market should be used for material. The average cost was defined as the weighted average price of the quantities on hand at a statement date. Hawkins was a strong supporter of the "prudent" value theory as indicated in the following excerpt from his work:

> For stocktaking purposes the price should be the average cost price of the remaining stock or the then market price, whichever is the lower. To arrive at the average cost price, it may be assumed that what remains represents the most recent purchases. Whether cost price or market price is used for charging out ma-

terials to jobs, it should be remembered that those charged to work in progress and finished stock may have been charged at a price which differs from the market price at the date of the balance sheet. In the case of a falling market some provision for the consequent depreciation in value of those assets may prudently be made in the general accounts. In the case of a rising market, however, they should not be written up. This is in accordance with the sound accountancy maxim that all losses which can be foreseen should be provided for, but unrealised profits should not be anticipated.[38]

Cost accountants in the United States, taking their cue perhaps from their contemporaries in England, began to treat with more respect and care the factory inventory problem in the years immediately preceding the First World War. Their work, in general, however, lagged behind that of the British until around 1919. The authorities who considered the question generally adopted the same conclusions, with modifications in only a few instances. S. H. Bunnell, for example, while recommending that finished goods be valued at their direct cost (prime cost) plus their "share" of the overhead, suggested that the material, "if equal to new," should be priced at market value.[39] He did not elaborate upon these brief conclusions, preferring rather to discuss at length the most efficient procedures to be employed in counting and sorting all the various items, that is, "taking inventory."[40] In another place he mentioned that if the finished articles had already been sold, a percentage should be added to their balance sheet valuation because of selling expenses; otherwise the factory cost was to be used. The work in process, incidentally, was always to be priced on the factory cost basis. Bunnell was one of the few writers in this period who stressed the importance of careful consideration of the items to be included in inventory prices. As he stated it: "There is no justification for charging the cost of product with selling expense which has not been incurred. Product placed in stock is not yet sold, and the cost of selling it is yet to be paid from the profits realized from its sale. Product in stock should carry manufacturing cost only, and this should not be inflated by adding the loss due to slack production when under unfortunate conditions the shop must be run at short capacity."[41]

Both F. E. Webner and J. Lee Nicholson,[42] although they did not consider the matter worthy of much note, implied also that cost prices were to be adopted.[43] For factory inventories, therefore, the lower of cost or market rule had not attained much popularity in this country by 1915. In England, it will be remembered, that technique was being recommended by practically all the authorities.[44]

Before World War I few writers on cost accounting made anything more than a passing reference to the cost problems involved in reconciling book inventories with physical counts. An exception was E. P. Moxey. Writing in 1913, he made the pointed comment that it was quite customary for differences to arise between the physical and perpetual inventories.[45] If the difference happened to be small he recommended that the quantity shown on the stores card be changed to the correct amount; the adjustment in the money amount would be accomplished by changing the average per unit cost of those items actually on hand. As he explained it: Suppose a firm showed a book inventory of 100 bolts with a book value of $100, the actual number on hand being 99. The requisitions in the future would be priced at $1.01, rather than $1.00 (the former average unit price). If the amount of the discrepancy were large, Moxey recommended (1) that the cause therefor be investigated, (2) that the stores ledger cards be corrected, and (3) that the dollar amount of the discrepancy be charged to an inventory adjustment account and credited to raw materials account. The inventory adjustment account, he emphasized, should be closed at the end of the fiscal period, not to cost of product made, but rather to profit and loss. "If it were to be considered as a cost . . . it would be as if we took stock, and charged the difference between purchases plus previous inventory, and the results disclosed by subsequent stock taking, as the cost of materials consumed, with no assurance that such really had been the case."[46]

In 1918, William Kent summarized the various theories which had been suggested by American cost experts under the following headings:

1. At cost as shown by the books.
2. At the probable cost of reproduction.
3. At the standard cost of a normal or average of a five-year period, called record costs or five-year standard costs.
4. At the preceding standard cost plus or minus a percentage to cover advance or reduction in costs of labor, material, or burden since the standard cost was recorded.
5. At the market or selling price less a percentage estimated to cover normal selling costs and normal profit.[47]

It will be noted that Kent did not state what type of factory inventory he had in mind, although from the ideas contained within the various proposals it would be assumed that he was thinking primarily of the partially completed and the finished goods. According to him, method number five would ordinarily be very difficult to carry out, especially where the firm produced and sold several varieties of products. The essence of this difficulty lay in the fact that he considered it practically impossible to apportion the selling expenses and profit in such cases. As to which one of the first four should be adopted, he was somewhat vague, merely stating that the final decision rested mainly upon the burden allocation method which was in use in the plant. Kent did not dwell upon any of the complexities which would arise in connection with the actual application of the inventory valuation bases which he had listed. He neglected this, moreover, in spite of the fact that he had summarized more completely than any of his contemporaries the various theories which had been recommended up to that time.

In the early 1920's, in this country, attention began to be given to the so-called "normal or base stock" method of pricing those factory inventories which were rather uniform in quality and whose quantities did not vary materially from year to year. This was an attempt to avoid the large inventory losses and gains which were shown in some instances at year-end closing dates under the cost or market whichever is lower basis. The National Lead Company began to use the method as early as 1913, and various other firms adopted it from time to time. The essential feature of the method was that a certain large percentage of the products of some industries must remain on hand from year to year, if the company is to be successful. In the case of lead companies, for example, there must be kept in reserve an immense quantity of pig lead, which does not differ from year to year in quality, merely to be able to fulfill the contracts and sales which may take place. That particular portion of the inventory, therefore, takes on the nature of a fixed asset, which may be valued at a "normal" price, unchanged from fiscal period to fiscal period. Any excess quantity above the "base stock" would be valued according to the familiar lower of cost or market rule.[48]

Also during the early 1920's, some cost authorities began to inquire about possible revision of accepted principles to comply with the growing use of standard or normal overhead rates. One authority, for example, who examined the problem concluded that if the normal burden application theory were adopted, the inventory valuations given to goods in process and finished articles should be in conformity thereto; no "unearned overhead" should be included in such inventories.[49] The valuation of inventories at "standard prices" also began to receive some support in this period. Obviously, this plan was merely the logical outgrowth of the standard costing arrangements which received considerable impetus from the writings and work of G. Charter Harrison, C. E. Knoeppel, and others in the years after 1918. In addition, both English and American experts continued to devote considerable attention, in their treatises on costing matters, to the more general aspects of the problem of the valuation of factory inventories,[50] such as the merits of first-in, first-out versus last-in, first-out. They made, however, few significant contributions to the subject; the most important developments continued to be supplied by specialized articles and bulletins, which likely followed rather than preceded, the more advanced industrial practices.

EVOLUTION OF THE PROCESS AND JOB ORDER COST METHODS

THE SUBJECT MATTER OF THIS CHAPTER HAS BEEN TOUCHED UPON IN some of the prior discussions. It is desirable, however, to review in broad outline the principal developments in the evolution of the two prominent methods of cost finding.

Even though a few writers on, and practitioners of, cost accounting had something to say about the present topic before 1885, there were no well-defined, clear-cut expositions available to the general public. There is little doubt that these two methods of costing "grew up" together. With the advent of the Industrial Revolution, two types of factory activity soon became paramount, namely, (1) the continuous process, large-scale, uniform product type; and (2) the machine shop, specialized, made-to-order type. The term "engineering works" was often associated with the second type, both in this country and England. Some examples of the techniques and forms used in these early engineering works before 1885 were presented in Chapter II of this volume. These examples show that their sponsors possessed a keen appreciation of the need for factory product cost data. Nevertheless the accountants had difficulty when it came to presenting the integration of the cost sheets with the financial records. Their contributions should not be taken lightly, however; they gave a definite impetus to the writing and thinking of their successors.

The earlier nineteenth century authorities had laid the foundations so well that in 1885 Henry Metcalfe could give a rather thorough explanation, complete with forms, of what he called the "shop order" method. This was essentially the job order technique, and the American Army Officer proved to be an enthusiastic supporter of this plan of costing. After first recommending that a shop order book be set up, he suggested that all orders for work be noted in this book. The "work" to which he referred consisted not only of items which would today be called "finished stock," but also of jobs involving maintenance and new construction around the plant. An alternate name for the maintenance orders was "standing" orders, so named because they were originally stuck on a post in the factory and "stood" there as a constant reminder to the employees. As Metcalfe explained it: "A standing order is given for each of as many sources of general expense as it is desirable to know the cost of. These may be analyzed more or less closely at pleasure. It is well to start with a thorough analysis, remembering that while charges can always be combined, it is always difficult and sometimes impossible to resolve them into their component parts."[1] This was an admonition which would be equally apropos today.

It will be recalled from the discussion in Chapter III that Metcalfe's system of costing involved the use of many cards and tickets. These slips of paper were to be used quite freely within the plant to record material, labor, and burden costs, subdivided into types of jobs, materials, and employees. The tickets were also used as authority to get work done. They followed the work through the various operations, and after a job had been started the tickets were used each day to post to what Metcalfe called a "cost sheet." The cost sheet was in columnar form and space was provided for: shop order number; appropriation; objects to be made; services—time and dollars; material dollars; shop expenses; gross cost; total credits; net cost; total cost per last report; and balance available. The "total credits" column represented (1) material which had been excessively withdrawn from the storeroom and not used on the jobs, or (2) shop expense which had in error been charged to a job.

Metcalfe also recommended the use of three other forms entitled (1) "Analysis of service performed on components of shop order number—;" this had columns for nature of services, charged to, rate per unit, number of units, cost, total time units, amounts, and remarks; (2) "analysis of material expended on components of shop order number—;" this had columns for charged to, name, quantity, unit,

unit price, and remarks; (3) "consolidated analysis of cost of shop order number—;" this had columns for services—nature of; days worked—rate per day and total; amounts for—plant attendance, tools, work, total, and remarks. It was Metcalfe's opinion that the analysis should only be carried as far as the "circumstances" of each case required. The "consolidated" analysis was designed to give the factory manager an overall summary of the quantity and kind of labor required for similar future work. Incidentally, the data for filling in the three analyses were to come from the cards previously referred to, sorted according to the departments of the shop, the nature of the material used, and the type of service being performed.[3]

In regard to the monthly summaries of work performed, Metcalfe was concise and to the point: "Completed fabrications are compiled from material cards. The prices are to be obtained from the analysis of cost. Incomplete fabrications are reported by the cost clerk, who adds up the days' work done on them from the service cards found in the corresponding pigeon holes. Work done under standing orders is reported in the same way. . . . Orders on which no work has been done are reported by simply enumerating the empty pigeon holes for service cards."[2]

Within a short time after Metcalfe wrote his *Cost of Manufactures* S. A. Hand, an American engineer, explained that he used a form for costing jobs having columns for date, number of hours worked during the week, shop expenses for the week, average rate of expense per hour, number of hours worked on this job during the week, amount of wages for the week's work on this job, and cost of the week's work on this job. Each of these columns was totaled each week and an average obtained, "which will in the course of time show the percentage of full time made by the men, the average expenses per hour, the average of wages paid for each hour worked, and the average value of work turned out per dollar paid in wages. Below the average space is a blank left for cost of material used on the job, which, added to the total cost of machine work, gives the total cost of the job. If the shop owner has a certain charge per hour for work he can soon tell whether that amount is paying him or not."[3] Even though Hand stated that his "blank" was "very useful," he neglected to present the relationships which would have to be handled on the ledger in order to assemble the data with which to fill in the form.

Two years passed before the next major contribution was made to the subject. Garcke and Fells gave their readers in 1887 a fairly clear picture of their recommended "prime cost ledger" system. Although these prominent English cost experts made several distinct contributions to the theory and practice of cost accounting in the latter part of the nineteenth century, their prime cost methodology was notably weak in respect to the integration of the factory overhead cost with the material and labor elements. They also neglected to differentiate between the job cost and the process cost methods. Supposedly, however, their plan of costing would operate equally well under either set of conditions. The prime cost ledger was used to summarize the wages and stores assignable to each product. Provision was also made for a column to handle the "sundry disbursements" coming from the "petty cash book or its equivalent."[4] In addition to the preceding details the prime cost ledger system contemplated a separate sheet for each so-called "order;" this sheet had columns on the debit side for date, particulars, warrant number, number and weight, rate, material, other disbursements, and total; on the credit side were: date, particulars, debit note number, number or weight, rate, and amount. The total of the debits of all the sheets was periodically taken and compared with the amounts shown in the "commercial ledger." Completed jobs were entered on a "stock debit note," which in turn served as the authority for entries in the finished goods account and the stock received book.

Several other details could be given, but enough has been said to indicate the rough outline of the system advocated by Garcke and Fells. Even though their techniques were not too well polished they were generally superior to prior treatments. Further, the groundwork had been laid for other authorities.

G. P. Norton, who began to write on textile costing in England in the late 1880's, recommended a system which was in many respects similar to the procedures followed by authorities in the early part of the twentieth century. He illustrated a very comprehensive piecemaking or bulk book having the following 35 columns: date, piece serial number; folio or order number; description; range number or mark; pattern number; customer's number; date of delivery; strings; cuts; reed or stay; width; porties; plan number; warp—shade or stock number, counts or skeins, pounds, total pounds, average price per pound; weft—shade or stock number, counts or skeins, pounds, total pounds, average price per pound; picks; shuttles; loom number; weaver's name; date—on loom, out of loom; out of loom—yards, pounds; finished—yards, pounds; calculation number in piece cost book.[5] This was one of the most elaborate production cost sheets ever invented. It was supported in turn with what Norton called a "piece cost book," shown in the accompanying illustration.

Piece Cost Book

Calculation No. _____

Piece Nos.   _____

Description

Cost of material, viz.:		
_____ lbs. warp @	XX	
_____ lbs. weft @	XX	XX
Trade charges for processes, viz.:		
Sizing	XX	
Winding	XX	
Warping	XX	
Weaving	XX	
Scouring and Milling	XX	
Mending	XX	
Finishing	XX	
Dying	XX	XX
Total Cost		XX
_____ % for pattern making	XX	
Allowance for discount	XX	
_____ % for warehouse expense	XX	
_____ % general charge	XX	
_____ % for profit	XX	XX
Selling value		XX

Norton suggested that the piece cost book would be useful for "costing ranges and for checking the actual cost of the pieces after they are made. The percentages for pattern making and warehouse expenses and general charges may be determined, with the help of the manufacturing account, by the following method: Compare the aggregate of the work done in those processes mentioned in the piece cost book (1) with the aggregate cost of pattern making, and (2) with the aggregate of the warehouse expenses and general charges; and according to the proportion which these bear in the aggregate, so should be the ratio of charge in the individual calculations."[6] As a further implementation of his costing routine, Norton presented a form for reporting weekly or monthly the work accomplished in each department of the plant. The several departments, such as combing, woolen, worsted, winding, etc., were listed at the left. In succeeding columns (to the right) space was provided for (1) wages, (2) materials used, (3) average of standing expenses, (4) total cost, (5) trade charges for work done, (6) percentage of wages on work done, (7) profit, and (8) loss; the two last columns were used to distinguish his so-called "machinery or manufacturing" profit from the "net profit" in his "trading" account. Norton had the idea that the factory manager should be presented periodically with a comparison between the cost of the product turned out by the plant and what it would have cost to get the same work done by another (competing) firm. This was his method of determining the overall plant efficiency (costwise); it thus had some of the earmarks of the later popular standard cost method.

A few years after Norton wrote on textile costing an anonymous English author developed a "tabular ledger" plan of costing.[7] His cost book was divided into two sections. The first had columns for date, particulars, number of workers, hours, total hours, rate, total wages and stock (in money), management and establishment expenses, depreciation, and departmental totals. The second section had columns for cost of goods and work completed, and sundries. After the sums of the cost of each job had been ascertained on the tabular ledger, they were transferred to the "cost account summary." Somewhat like Norton's, this summary had columns for date, name, folio, cost, management charges, depreciation, departments—Number 1, 2, 3, etc., total cost, folio, contract price, profit, loss. A separate line was to be used for each contract. Since the total cost and contract price figures were adjacent to each other, the profit or loss on the individual jobs could be readily derived. The conclusion of this unknown author, in the light of the argument which was then going on as to the integration of the cost and financial records, was especially revealing: "The difference between the total of the profit column and the total of the loss column should agree with the balance of the profit and loss account for the corresponding period; but in practice—partly on account of clerical inaccuracies, and partly because the management expenses and depreciation, etc., employed in the cost accounts are only estimated amounts and not actual facts—there is usually a small difference. The clerical differences, unless of trifling amount, should be sought for and eliminated; while, if the percentages of management expenses and depreciation, etc., have been carefully fixed, the difference between the estimates and the actual results will not be large."[8] The difference was shown as an adjustment in the so-called "trial balance" of the cost accounts, in order to make that trial balance total the same as the financial books insofar as the management expense, depreciation, and interest on capital were concerned.

Later English authorities were more technical in their discussions. J. S. Lewis, for example, made a distinction between works orders and job orders, the works orders being the manager's approval of a new job, while the job orders were used (1) to give specific instructions to the employees and (2) to keep track of labor and material costs. No work was to be started until the job orders had been issued. Lewis came to grips with the details underlying the job cost method when he stated that "before commencing work the job order is taken to the job office by the workman, its number registered by the job clerk who at the same time enters the time upon it."[9] Lewis further explained that no worker should have more than one job order sheet in his possession at a time; material costs also were to be entered on the job sheet by the storekeeper. An internal check feature was provided in that occasional examinations were to be made to determine if all material in the custody of the employee was correctly recorded on his order sheet.

Lewis provided for other details. When the job was completed satisfactorily, the foreman initialed the order and sent it to the job office. This office in turn compared the data on the cost sheet with similar information kept on the job-order ledger. If the comparison revealed no major differences, the corresponding leaves in the job-order ledger were torn out and placed in a separately numbered envelope in the permanent office file.

In view of the description above and much more that has been omitted here, it can be said that Lewis covered the subject of job costs more fully than anyone who had preceded him. Except for some gaps in his treatment of factory burden, his system was substantially the same as that recommended by authorities thirty years later. It was comparatively easy for subsequent writers to supply the other details which are found today under job costs.

In fact, just two years later, H. M. Norris, an American engineer, brought out the specific uses to be made of what he called "piece orders." These orders were filled out by the job clerk immediately after a customer's order was received. Copies were forwarded to the material stock clerk who checked them against the stores inventory cards to see if the items needed were on hand. If the material was in the inventory the piece orders were transferred to the "general foreman" who kept them in his file until the work was assigned to some employee. Subsequently, they were forwarded again to the storeroom where they served as the authority to issue the material. At a later date they were returned to the job clerk. Norris very carefully defined the seven distinct purposes served by his piece orders: "(1) They furnish the necessary authority to the stock clerk to order material. (2) Their receipt by the general foreman tells him that the work is in the house, ready for assignment. (3) Their delivery to a department foreman indicates the order in which the work is to be gotten out. (4) Their stay in the hands of the department foreman shows him just what work he has ahead. (5) Their return to the stock clerk authorizes him to issue the material to the shop. (6) Their appearance in the drawing room shows that the work has been taken out of stores. (7) And their location in the job clerk's file signifies whether or not the work is actually in hand. The stock clerk files them by symbol, the foreman by operation, and the job clerk by the printed piece order numbers."[10] Norris described also the use of the time-slip which like that of J. S. Lewis, served as the authority for workers to change jobs and kept track of their time. A "time book" was recommended for summarizing the data shown on the slips. An interesting standard cost note was struck when Norris stated that "by looking at the time book, the job clerk can tell what work is being done by every man in the shop, and, after a little experience becomes so familiar with the length of time required to perform a certain operation that the workmen are likely to hear from the foreman whenever they begin to drop behind on their work."[11]

The American developments around the turn of the century were indicated in an important work by H. L. Arnold, published in 1899.[12] Arnold presented the actual cost systems in use in several prominent industrial concerns with which he was familiar. In one of these he illustrated a so-called "prime cost record." This sheet had columns for order number, catalogue number, description, quantity, weight, dimensions, the material used, nonproductive material, nonproductive labor, royalty, other disbursements, total expenditure, average cost of each, and date finished.[13] The process cost method was touched upon when Arnold described his departmental cost sheet. It had columns for date, direct labor, hours, proportion of general administration charges, superintendence, foremen, other indirect labor, power, heat, light, factory supplies, repairs to buildings, repairs to machinery, repairs to small tools, and depreciation.[14] This practicing cost accountant recommended that one of these sheets be used in each department; it would be "of great value to the general factory manager, because of the manner in which it presents the statistics of the entire plant, and of the separate departments as different members of the one producing unit."[15]

Arnold became specific in his discussion of the system used at the Hyatt Roller Bearing Company. A so-called "collective production order card" was first authorized by the general manager, addressed to the factory superintendent; this card requested that certain work be done. On the front of the card there were spaces to show the various factory cost items and number of hours of tool time. After the product had been completed and inspected, the production order was sent to the office for filing and indexing. The clerk also transferred the data concerning the items to a flat cost record book, having columns for each order with subdivisions for pattern making costs. Other columns were provided for labor, sundry, and unclassified items. The final line on the sheet presented the "flat cost" items, to which the "percentages" for shop expenses and office expenses were added. "These percentages are calculated from previous experience," was the comment made by Arnold.[16]

In the same work Arnold described a job order procedure in use in one of the plants with which he was acquainted.[17] The firm had developed an analysis (or distribution) sheet carrying the job order numbers in sequence. The sheets served a dual purpose in that they provided for weekly records of both labor and material. Time cards were kept during the week by the factory employees, collected at the end, sorted by order number, priced in terms of dollars expended on the order, and entered on the distribution sheet. The total labor cost reported on the time tickets was compared at the end of the week with the payroll total; this was a method of internal check. A similar procedure was followed for the material requisitions chargeable to the jobs. Again, at the end of the week the sum of the material used on any one order was derived and entered on the analysis sheet. The grand total of all the job material cost was then compared with the store room issues of material for the purpose of furnishing a degree of internal check.

While it is probable that Arnold described cost methodologies used in the more progressive industrial establishments of the time, his remarks and comments are indicative of the rapid growth in cost accounting in the early part of the twentieth century. By 1900 both the job order and the process cost methods had been pretty well described by several authorities on both sides of the Atlantic. Much of the later evolution was centered around the development of combination cost methods involving some of the features of both the job and process cost techniques. Some other authorities, following Arnold, began to describe actual procedures in use. J. Mac-Naughton, for instance, wrote around the turn of the century on paper mill costing.[18] This English accountant presented a methodology complete with an elaborate cost sheet giving full data on the unit cost of paper. One of these sheets was filled out for each "making" in the "production book." The production book had columns for date; making number; description; size; weight; order; price; machine—weight made, shift, total hours, sheet; finished—reams, weight; broke; weekly totals—tons, hundredweight, pounds. In order to show the care with which this writer approached his subject, the following description is presented: "A production book is required for each machine. The cost clerk each morning enters in it the details of the work done by the machine during the previous day and night shift, which he ascertains from the machine work book; and besides recording the date, he has a column for the number of the making of each different kind or quality of paper made. . . . The price of the paper is obtained from the original order book in the office. The outturn of the making is obtained from the finishing house book, and the weight from the invoice book, if the paper is dispatched as soon as made, or from the forwarding note if it is put into stock. The broke on the making is ascertained from the broke book. From these figures the value of the paper is calculated on the cost sheet."[19]

About the same time that MacNaughton described the details of paper mill costing, H. Diemer presented a comprehensive procedure for ascertaining the cost of tools, jigs, dies, patterns, and drawings made for use within the plant and not to be sold to customers.[20] He suggested that these internal orders be designated as Order E (for tools), Order F (for jigs and dies), etc. It was his further suggestion that after the cost of special (for some particular customer's order) tools, jigs, etc., had been ascertained, this cost should in turn be assigned to the production order for which it was intended, "so that the cost of the special job will include the cost of the special drawings, patterns, and tools."[21] Standing job orders were to be set up for work of a nonspecial nature, as well as for run-of-the-mill maintenance and repairs. Each foreman was supposed to keep a sheet covering a month's time, having columns for date, standing order number, type of material, quantity called for, quantity delivered, weight, and cost. Diemer wisely observed that the "list of standing orders will vary widely, depending upon the conditions in the particular shop. . . . A careful classification of the particular items constituting the expense account under separate standing order numbers will enable the management to compare them from month to month from the cost department's summary of such orders."[22]

Diemer also explained in a concise fashion a system of production sub-orders which would serve to support the "general orders" or "bill of material." Each of the sub-orders covered only the product that could efficiently be performed by one machine tool or one small group of equally skilled workers. As soon as a sub-order was complete, the data on it were totaled and entered on a card index having the following headings: drawing number, pattern number, article, material, weight, cost of material. The columns below the headings were: order number, sub-order number, operation, number of pieces, employee number, time, rate, and total labor cost. Diemer again showed his interest in the usefulness of costing when he stated that "it will be at once apparent that a card record such as this affords a most reliable basis, not only for the cost of each operation, but for establishing piece work and premium rates where such systems are in vogue in the shop."[23]

Around 1900 several prominent authorities began to correlate and integrate the job order and process cost methods with the newly developed machine hour technique of burden application. Both A. Hamilton Church in this country and Sir John Mann in England presented descriptions of this supposedly more accurate costing procedure. Several different forms were recommended for aid in keeping track of the details of chargeable and nonchargeable hours, as well as the burden costs assignable to the machines. While these developments, *per se,* did not contribute to the basic procedures underlying the job order and process cost systems, they nevertheless are indicative of the general flexibility of the cost theories of the time.

By 1904, writers on cost accounting were giving general descriptions of both the process and job order procedures in their published works. H. L. C. Hall, for example, referred to the job method as "Class I" costing and the process technique as "Class II."[24] This American authority quite carefully described the manufacturing conditions under which each class should be adopted. His treatment was both thorough and explicit, and even today would be considered satisfactory. His discussion gave particular emphasis to the shop orders, cost summaries, and other forms necessary for the implementation of the basic methodologies.

Within a year or so after Hall wrote, references began to appear dealing with the many details of the forms which were needed to integrate the machine hour method into the job order and process cost methods. Previous authorities had generally neglected this matter. H. Deighton, in an article which he wrote in 1905,[25] recommended that separate cost ledgers be set up for each of the three types of shop orders, namely, personal, stock, and plant shop orders. These ledgers were to include sheets having columns for date, particulars, direct material, direct sundries, direct labor, machine tolls, indirect manufacturing expense percentage, total—debit and credit. The machine tolls column was to be filled in from data kept on daily time slips, while the indirect manufacturing expense was based on a percentage of the amount of combined direct labor and machine tolls. At about the same time, Stanley Pedder in England illustrated the typical non-machine-hour cost sheet form with columns for date, special materials, stores, castings made in own foundry, shop wages, shop charges, outdoor wages, petty cash items, salaries, sundry, and total.[26] Clarence Day, however, writing in this country, stressed the "machine cost system," as he called it.[27] He first made the point that the cost sheets should be kept (1) by individual machines or (2) by groups of similar machines. This same sheet would be used to show the number of hours the machines operated. Of course, the burden was applied to product based on the number of hours the machines operated. Day also emphasized the fact that the details of cost shown on the cost sheets should be kept under accounting control through the media of general ledger control accounts. In a word, "the cost sheets in operation will be considered always as a unit. . . . If the cost sheets in operation are scheduled for any given time, the total of same should be the equivalent of the balance of the ledger account for work in process."[28] Work orders were to be issued weekly for finished product as well as for remodeling or rebuilding of machinery and buildings, or for any factory activity for which costs were desired; the work orders also served the purpose of obtaining a basis or rate which would be of aid in the setting of selling prices.

By 1909 so much progress had been made in the development of the fundamentals underlying the job order and process cost methods that several authorities felt it necessary to devote whole chapters of their works to the description of the techniques. One outstanding American practitioner, J. Lee Nicholson, was unusually thorough in his treatment of the subject.[29] He first explained the proper use of production orders by stressing the fact that only one order (with carbon copies) was needed when the product was to be made in consecutive departments. If, however, the same order was to be "prosecuted" (his term) in several producing departments simultaneously, sub-production orders should be issued covering the work to be performed in each individual department. Copies of the orders were to be sent to the shipping clerk, the stores clerk, and other interested officials. Nicholson wisely pointed out that the design of the production order form would have to depend upon the "conditions of manufacture." For example, "if it is desired to use the form purely for the purpose of regulating production, only the necessary explanatory matter need appear; but if, on the other hand, it is considered advisable to utilize a copy of the form for cost keeping purposes, separate columns with the proper headings printed therein should be added and so arranged as to facilitate posting from employees' time reports and reports of material delivered. Where it is desirable to keep the cost of operation, proper columns should be provided for each operation, and the form so ruled and designed as to enable the cost clerk to add overhead charges and ascertain the total cost of the order."[30]

Nicholson was even more explicit when he described the circumstances under which the job order and process cost methods should be used. He emphasized the fact that the job cost technique was most effective when goods were being made according to customer specification, or where the units were dissimilar. The process cost method, on the other hand, was frequently adopted in those instances where the products were uniform and made without a customer's order in hand at the time of production. This authority seemed to think that the process cost method ordinarily offered more opportunity for accuracy in reporting; it was also better adapted to those firms which employed trained cost accountants who could "bring to the attention of the management all the statistics incident to the operation" of the several departments.[31]

In explaining the use of the cost sheet in the process method, Nicholson mentioned first that a separate sheet should be set up for each article manufactured. The labor costs were entered on the cost sheet from the time reports kept by the timekeepers or foremen of the departments. Material cost could be taken from the material requisition or the summary report of material delivered out of stores. Burden was to be applied on the ratio of direct labor cost. Total factory cost was obtained monthly by totaling these three elements. While Nicholson was rather hazy as to the determination of unit costs when goods were only partially completed, he did state that the cost sheet should show both the quantity produced and the quantity unfinished. The total dollar cost charged on the sheet would be reduced by the amount finished. As he stated it: "The balance, representing goods in process of manufacture, is brought down for the beginning of the next month, and this balance should indicate the quantities and costs in the various operations."[32]   He thus ignored the delicate questions (and the difficulties) associated with the calculation of equivalent production and its concomitant, departmental unit cost data.

Nicholson should also be given credit for one of the earliest statements of the techniques and relative advantages underlying what were later to be called the "pyramided" and the "non-pyramided" departmental process cost methods. His comments were so pointed that they are quoted in full:

> If desired, the production and cost of each operation may be transferred from one operation to the other, until the last operation of finished product has been determined. This involves deducting from each of these operations the cost and the quantity transferred from operation no. 1 to operation no. 2, etc.; which means that the amount by which operation no. 1 would be decreased would at the same time increase both the quantity and cost of operation no. 2, and so on. As a result, the inventory, in quantity and cost, would appear in each of these operations together with the accumulated cost; whereas according to the other method the quantities would appear, but the accrued cost in each

operation after the first would not appear. The unit cost according to the operation of the article would, however, be more clearly shown than in the method just mentioned. In either case, so far as the cost is concerned, the result will be the same, but the second method involves more work than the first.[33]

Developments in England during the early 1900's were centered around the establishment of techniques for specific lines of manufacturing. The authorities who wrote on costing methods frequently gave clues in the titles of their works as to the nature of the firm contemplated. It was about this time also that several British authorities published a series of relatively small handbooks dealing with such topics as engineers' and shipbuilders' accounts, multiple cost accounts, single cost accounts, and terminal cost accounts. These handbooks had a large distribution; they constituted a distinctive contribution to the rapidly growing body of cost accounting literature. While space does not permit a full description of this material, the work of W. Strachan cannot be overlooked. Writing in 1909, he gave an unusually clear and lucid treatment of both the details as well as the overall view of the job order and process cost methods.[34] His illustrations of the forms used in costing systems would do credit to a modern text; the discussion was equally explicit. As brought out in Chapter VI, Strachan recommended that the cost and financial accounts not be intermingled. This recommendation forced him to give more information than would normally be the case regarding the "blending and proving" (his term) of the results of the cost and financial transactions. Strachan also favored the use of the current sales value method of reporting the completion of finished goods; that is, the stockroom should be charged with the amount in money which would approximate the sales realization figure, "thus showing the profit on manufacture."[35] All of this, of course, was to be done on the cost accounts. The financial accounts would show only the so-called actual cost data. It is interesting to observe, too, that this English authority urged that manufacturing firms use the looseleaf or "perpetual ledger" (his term) sheets for all accounting journals, ledgers, and supporting schedules.

Strachan's process cost methodology was reminiscent of that described by Nicholson in this country. After first explaining that the cost ledger would have accounts for each stage or operation and that all costs would be charged to such operations, he next emphasized that the various elements of cost should be kept separate on the cost ledger sheets. It was normal, according to him, for the cost ledger subdivision to vary in columnar arrangement. Quantities of product turned out would be placed at the extreme right side of the cost ledger sheet and the cost per unit determined. The old adage of "keeping things to oneself" crept into his discussion when he stated that "if deemed desirable for the purpose of secrecy these quantities of production and cost per unit could be shown on a separate cost sheet instead of in the cost ledger."[36] His normally used cost ledger account had columns for material—date, requisition number or credit note number, particulars, quantity, rate, amount, credits; wages— date, particulars, folio, amount; indirect charges—particulars, amount; total; quantity produced; and rate per unit.

By the time World War I started cost accounting authorities, both in this country and England, had worked out practically all the techniques necessary for the effective use of the process and job order methods. F. E. Webner, for example, devoted several dozen pages to a description of the "plans" of costing, as he called them. This distinguished American practitioner classified the methods as follows: specific cost plan, sold hour plan, and list percentage plan.[37] The last two procedures had some features of both the process and job cost techniques.

Later developments (from 1911 on) centered around the sharpening of unit cost calculations under the process method, and the adoption of normal burden rates under the job order procedure. The question of normal burden rates was treated in Chapter V, and thus need not be reviewed here. An example of the sharpening of unit cost determinations is afforded by H. C. Bentley's discussion. As early as 1911, this American accountant gave an illustration of the technique of figuring the cost of goods transferred from the plant to the finished product stockroom under both the first-in, first-out and the average cost methods. On a subsequent page he stated: "There is no question but that the former method is the correct one, but if the labor costs did not vary much from month to month, the average cost method would involve a little less detailed work, and the result would be close enough for monthly showing. . . . If no weight were lost, it would be a simple matter to compute the cost of raw materials included in the . . . tons finished. In almost every case, there is either a shrinkage, or the product runs over on account of taking up dampness, etc. It is necessary, therefore, to ascertain by inventory the raw materials represented in the goods in process, or estimate the shrinkage or increase as the case may be, as accurately as possible."[38]   Later authorities had difficulty in improving upon Bentley's general conclusion.

CHAPTER XII

IN THE LIGHT OF
THE PAST

THE BROAD ASPECTS OF THE EVOLUTION OF SOME OF THE MORE BASIC COST accounting theories and techniques have now been developed. With this task completed, certain rather general observations and inductions are permitted, based in part upon material presented in this study and in part upon the investigation into cost accounting literature which accompanied it. Keeping in mind, therefore, the natural limitation to which all statements of the present type are subject,[1] the following seem justified:

1. Although there was some interest in cost theories and practices before 1885, few authorities prior to that time had considered the subject worthy of their undivided attention.

2. English cost accountants contributed a large proportion of the original ideas and procedures before 1900. After that date the American theorists and practitioners forged ahead of their British contemporaries, the latter never regaining their relative standing.

3. Prime cost systems came into use much sooner than the more complete factory costing arrangements.

4. The third element of cost (factory overhead) was comparatively neglected in the period before 1900, but after that date more attention was devoted to it than to the other two elements of cost combined.

5. Subject to considerable qualification and opinion, it seems from the evidence available that so-called "depression years" in industrial activity have been especially fruitful periods for introducing and developing new cost techniques and procedures.

6. Industrial engineers, rather than cost or general accountants, took a more active interest in costing problems in the early development of the subject in this country.

7. Theories and methods for valuing factory inventories did not attract as much attention in the early American cost discussions as in the English.

8. The integration of the factory and financial records proceeded at a very slow pace until well after the turn of the century, all of the details not being worked out until around 1920.

9. Cost theories and techniques have evolved as a product of their industrial environment, and their rapid development has been necessitated by the continually increasing complexity of manufacturing processes.

The remaining pages of this concluding chapter are devoted to a brief exposition of the foregoing inductions.

1. Interest in cost theories and practices first began to be evidenced in the mediaeval era. Attention during that period was centered, however, upon the accounting for the flow of materials through small workshops which had been established as a result of the increased interchange of goods accompanying the Renaissance and exploration epochs. Records seemed to have been maintained at that time almost altogether for the purpose of accumulating the expenditures made on account of the material and labor used in the product. In addition, while there is some indication that the concept of "cost of production" was recognized, the various guild regulations probably prevented its effective adoption as a means of determining the short or long term selling price of the articles made. As the domestic and handicraft systems gave way gradually, however, to the more impersonal factory system, based upon production for a market, increased opportunity was afforded for individual competition between establishments turning out similar types of goods. Accordingly, factory cost of production became more significant, and various authorities began to consider with a little more care the records and accounts required for industrial firms. These pioneers, as it were, generally merely modified their commercial or trading bookkeeping arrangements in order to care for the needs of manufactories. While

there are a few exceptions (as detailed in Chapter II), most of the costing procedures advanced before 1885 were very crude, and perhaps should not be called "cost systems." Further, in spite of the fact that factory technology in general was making rapid progress, the period from 1820 to 1885 was particularly barren in regard to contributions to cost accounting. It is possible, however, that the records of industrial establishments, as actually maintained, showed a little more progress than that evidenced by the published material.[2] Be that as it may, the conclusion must nevertheless be drawn that modern costing procedures really date from the 1880's. The preceding statement holds true even though some of the practices and theories elaborated upon after that decade are much older. A few examples of these are: departmentalization of a factory, the continuous inventory technique, and certain rather simple methods of applying the overhead or burden costs.[3]

2. English authorities made most of the basic contributions to cost accounting in the period prior to the turn of the century, and more especially between 1885 and 1900. During those fifteen years at least three noteworthy works appeared in that country, all being devoted to an exposition of costing theories and techniques.[4] The first of these was the now classic *Factory Accounts,* by Emile Garcke and J. M. Fells, which ran through four editions by 1893. The preface to the second edition of this work stated that it was "the first attempt to place before English readers a systematised statement of the principles relating to factory accounts, and of the methods by which those principles can be put into practice and made to serve important purposes in the economy of manufacture."[5] A second important English work published during the period was G. P. Norton's *Textile Manufacturers' Bookkeeping* (four editions were issued before 1900), while a third was J. Slater Lewis' *Commercial Organisation of Factories* (first edition, 1896). In addition, a few authoritative monographs appeared. Nothing comparable to these treatises was written in the United States until the latter part of the first decade of the twentieth century. Several contributions of note, however, were made by experts in this country around 1900, notably A. Hamilton Church's series of articles on "The Proper Distribution of Expense Burden,"[6] and John Whitmore's series on "Factory Accounting as Applied to Machine Shops."[7] The conclusion remains, though, that the English costing authorities had the field almost to themselves until the turn of the century. After that date, American contributions be-

gan to come to the forefront; and, before many years had passed, the Americans had forged ahead of their British contemporaries. Except in a few isolated instances, such as in regard to the theories to be employed in valuing factory inventories, the English never regained their relative standing. Moreover, ideas and procedures inaugurated in this country generally required several years before they filtered into the writings of authorities in other nations. The reasons for this are inextricably bound up with the leadership which the United States assumed in world trade and commerce in the period after the Spanish-American War. This matter, however, was detailed in Chapter V, and thus need not be elaborated upon at this point.

3. Prime cost systems (that is, accounting for the cost of raw materials and direct labor included in the finished product) ante-dated complete costing arrangements by several decades. To express it differently, after cost accounts had begun to be distinguished from the regular financial accounts, they were first designed to ac-cumulate the prime cost of the completed articles. The incidental expenditures and charges were partially recognized, but most of the authorities hesitated to consider them as applied costs. More often they were thought of as expenses, rather than costs; and even in those cases where burden allocation schemes were provided, the technique employed was so crude and inequitable that unsatisfactory data as to total manufacturing costs were probably drawn in most instances. In fact, several writers in the period before 1900 frankly admitted their inability to cope with other than prime costs, and de-veloped rather comprehensive plans which dealt with only the first two elements of cost.[8] The factory overhead element, under these systems, was grouped with the "expenses" of the establishment, and thus was never attributed to "cost," except occasionally for balance sheet inventory values. Considerable progress had been made, though, by the time this particular type of cost arrangement came into general use. It was not an easy or simple task to add in the overhead element, but prime cost systems obviously cleared the path of a great many obstacles which would have delayed still further the introduction of modern practices. As a matter of fact, the cost accounting for raw material consumed and the labor incur-red was only a natural outgrowth of the rough memoranda which engineering machinery manufacturing firms must have maintained beginning with the early years of the Industrial Revolution. It was entirely logical that these firms should desire approximations of the

total expenditures on the contracts which they undertook, and prime cost systems developed out of those crude cost sheets. Major assistance was given, of course, by adapting the principles of double entry bookkeeping to the problem at hand; but for the most part cost techniques *per se* were innovations rather than adaptations.

4. The handling of factory overhead cost was neglected almost entirely before the turn of the century. There had been some discussion of the subject, but no comprehensive examination of the problem had appeared. Idle time and the concept of normal capacity had received almost no attention. A few English and American cost authorities had outlined some of the simpler schemes for allocating the burden costs of an industrial plant, especially under job order conditions. In the main, however, there was little interest in the matter.[9] But the period around 1900 brought to the forefront the importance of a more careful accounting for burden costs. Before many years had passed, this topic was receiving as much attention as the other two elements of cost combined. No phase of the problem was neglected. The items to be included in the burden charge were carefully examined; the ones which were non-manufacturing in nature were cast aside. The question of imputed interest and rent as costs was analyzed from several viewpoints, the controversy waxing warmer as the years passed by. The technique involved in burden control accounts began to receive considerable notice; and various procedures gradually evolved, not only for the actual burden incurred, but also for the burden applied to product and the burden under or over applied. The methods advocated for the allocation (or application) of burden, even though they had already received considerable attention, were elaborated upon, and several new ones were originated.[10] Predetermined burden rates and the problem of plant capacity became increasingly important; some authorities even began to consider the problems involved therein as worthy of their undivided attention. And lastly, the departmentalization of factories, with particular emphasis upon overhead costs, was thoroughly treated by various cost experts. In addition to the preceding factors, the period around 1900 brought an increasing recognition of the fact that the miscellaneous manufacturing expenditures and charges of an industrial establishment were costs rather than expenses, and there was also more tendency to consider them as applying to the products produced. Better and more accurate techniques were devised for handling the flow of those

costs through the ledger. In summary, it may be concluded that the accounting for manufacturing burden did receive the attention it merited in the period after the turn of the century, and that the neglect which it suffered in the years prior to 1900 has long since been remedied.

5. Depression years in industrial activity have proved to be rather fruitful periods for introducing and developing new cost techniques and procedures. This conclusion, as a matter of fact, seems only logical. Obviously, data on cost of production have greater importance when expenditures must be pared, and more attention would also be devoted to improved costing practices during such periods. In order to indicate the basis for this conclusion a few illustrations may be cited (all are concerned with material previously presented in this volume): The more refined methods of allocating the burden element of cost were developed in the latter part of the 1890's; the years around 1907 brought even more careful analyses of the problem involved. Both of these periods coincided with years of comparatively moderate business activity in this country. The concept of idle-time-a-loss began to be advocated with increasing vehemence in the depression years before World War I, and many cost authorities were converted to that doctrine. The period 1913-15 also brought to the forefront a renewed interest in the proper accounting for waste, scrap, and by-products. In addition, the postwar depression years caused cost accountants to inquire more carefully into the different methods of pricing material requisitions and valuing factory inventories. Finally, standard costing arrangements were perfected, and so-called "normal burden rate" plans gained many adherents during that same period.

6. Industrial engineers, rather than cost or general accountants, took a more active interest in costing problems in the early development of the subject in this country and England. This is borne out by the numerous references which have been cited to their work in previous pages of this volume. In fact, it may be safely stated that the profession of cost accounting developed out of the attention which was shown in the subject by early industrial engineers, if that term is used to refer to the group of engineers who showed interest not only in the technical engineering problems of industry, but also in the more skillful management of manufacturing enterprises. The dividing line between the two professions is not

finely drawn even at present. There is no need, however, for a careful delineation of their respective spheres of work. It is sufficient to note here that the industrial engineers made many important contributions to costing theory before 1900; and, even after that date, their discussions were significant. The following is a remarkable commentary, for the time at which it was written (1893), of the relationships between costing and engineering:

> While on the one hand, it may be argued that there are a large number of remunerative appointments open to competent engineers in which their lack of commercial knowledge does not entail any very serious drawback, on the other hand it must not be forgotten that what may be termed the manufacturing section of engineering offers the largest number of such appointments. It must not be supposed that the commercial knowledge here referred to is limited to what is commonly known as bookkeeping; it also includes a thorough grasp of the principles and practice of prime costing, depreciation, and so on. In this age of keen competition and finely cut profits, it is needless to say that an engineer who possesses a sound knowledge of such matters is much more likely—other things being equal—to rise to the top rung of the ladder than one who does not. What chart and compass are to the captain of the ship, the costs department is to the manufacturing engineer of a works. It is the most infallible guide he can have, not only in showing him the true financial value of his present arrangements but also in shaping his plans for the future. That the value of a sound knowledge of the commercial principles of an engineering business has not been over-estimated will soon be apparent to anyone who has taken the trouble to analyse the qualifications of many of our successful engineers, so-called. In the great majority of cases it will be found that the predominent qualification is that of the successful business man, while the engineering ability is frequently of a very secondary order and, in some instances, almost entirely supplied by subordinates. The rigid precautions adopted by manufacturing engineers to confine all knowledge of the costs department to the staff of clerks engaged in the work renders it impossible for the young engineer to learn anything of the system during his apprenticeship. The natural result is that the great majority of young engineers are always entirely ignorant of a very essential part of their training.[11]

7. Inventory valuation theories attracted more attention in England than in the United States in those years preceding World War I. The reason for this is not difficult to surmise or determine. Professional auditing experienced a more rapid growth in England, and the Companies Acts there were also conducive to greater ac-

curacy in this important matter. Both of these factors caused costing authorities in Great Britain to notice and discuss problems
connected with the proper valuation of factory inventories several
years before Americans investigated the subject.

8. The technique for articulating the cost and the financial
records and accounts proved a stumbling block of considerable
magnitude in the systems advocated by most of the early cost authorities. Further, the transition from the accounting for merchandising firms to that required for manufactories was slow in evolving.
Even when it did take place the plans advocated very often contemplated the establishment of independent "cost accounts." By
1887, however, the broad outlines of an integrated scheme had been
suggested.[12] Progress was slow even after that date; very few improvements were made until around 1910. Beginning about that
time the details were supplied for not only the coördinated (one
ledger) plan, but also for the two ledger (reciprocal account) arrangement. Incidentally, this development in itself was no small
accomplishment. In fact, one authority has gone so far as to state that
"it is not too much to say that the formulation of cost accounting
procedure can be ranked as an achievement second only to the
original development of bookkeeping according to double entry
principles."[13]

9. Cost theories and procedures have evolved as a natural
corollary of their industrial environment. The expansion of the factory system during the last hundred years, the immense improvement in manufacturing methods and techniques, and the keener
competition brought on by widening markets all combined to cause
the manufacturer to appreciate more fully the necessity for adequate
information as to his cost of production. Cost accounting as a
managerial instrument was the most significant method of obtaining desired results. The problems associated with product costing
have thus become important factors in the efficient administration
of industrial establishments.

❋   ❋   ❋

Like all accounting, industrial costing had its origin in very
humble surroundings. Conditions were propitious, however, for its
rapid development, especially after the middle of the nineteenth
century. Spurred on by the demands of plant managers, who of
course had a keen interest in the matter, cost authorities after 1885
originated comprehensive systems for recording and controlling the

output of factories. The purpose of this study has been to highlight the development of the theories and procedures upon which those systems were based.

An appropriate concluding note to this volume has been suggested by that outstanding scholar of accounting development, A. C. Littleton, who has stated that "the evolution of accounting . . . is another cross section of the unending stream of history wherein 'all events, conditions, institutions, and personalities come from immediately preceding events, conditions, institutions, and personalities'."[14]

REFERENCE
NOTES

CHAPTER I

1. A. C. Littleton, *Accounting Evolution to 1900* (New York: American Institute Publishing Company, 1933), pp. 320-321. David Solomons does not altogether share this view. He thinks that the Industrial Revolution caused factory overhead to come to the forefront; material and labor costs were already problems. See *Studies in Costing* (London: Sweet and Maxwell, 1952), p. 2.
2. DR Scott, *The Cultural Significance of Accounts* (New York: Henry Holt and Company, 1931), p. 143.
3. Walter Scott, *The Principles and Practice of Cost Accounting* (Sydney, Australia: Law Book Company of Australasia Pty., Ltd., 1947), p. 7.
4. Cf. Basil S. Yamey, "Scientific Bookkeeping and the Rise of Capitalism," *Economic History Review*, Second Series, 1 1949, 110-113. Cf., also, Federigo Melis, *Storia della Ragioneria* (Bologna: Dott. Cesare Zuffi, 1950) p. 540, where he states: "The second subject, worthy of the greatest attention in connection with the origin of capitalism and its spreading . . . is the emergence of cost accounting. . . . The capitalist, with the help of good cost accounting is able to predict the future." (Free translation.)
5. The following is an interesting quotation bearing upon this conclusion (two reference footnotes omitted):

> Cost accounting is probably as old as financial accounting. Its origin harks back to the first forms of social life. The great trading people of antiquity, the Chinese, the Egyptians, and the Phoenicians, and the Arabs had accountants in the service of the royal courts, some of whom specialized in the determination of costs. In Egypt, 3,000 years before Christ, these accountants had to present to the Pharaohs each year a detailed report on the net cost of the harvest, so that just taxes on wheat could be levied. The ancient Code of Manu made obligatory the periodical auditing of trading profits by court auditors, called Kayasthas, a caste still in existence today in the province of Bengal, India. These audits were made for fiscal reasons and for the purpose of regulating the sales price of essential agricultural products and other manufactured or imported commodities. In Books VII and VIII of these

sacred Laws we find the following two passages: "Merchandising experts will establish the sales price of goods, so that the king may levy 1/20 of the profit thereon" . . . "the sales price of merchandise shall be evaluated according to the distance it has traveled, the time it is kept in storage, the expenses connected with it, the time it has to travel to reach its final destination, and the profit that can be anticipated."

Other instances of primitive forms of cost-keeping could be cited, but in antiquity, as well as under the Greek and Roman Empires, the main purpose of the estimation of costs was to create a basis for taxes, and the work was always carried out by salaried court officials. Alphonse Perren, "The Development of Cost Accounting in Europe," *N. A. C. A. Bulletin*, XXIV (1944), 1059.

6. John Manger Fells, "Cost Accounting; Its Evolution and Its Trend," *The Accountant* (England), LX (1919), 550. The same suggestion has also been made by Abbott Payson Usher in his *Industrial History of England* (Boston: Houghton Mifflin Company, 1920), pp. 190-191.

7. Cf. Perren, *N.A.C.A. Bulletin*, XXIV, 1060.

8. E. H. Byrne, *Genoese Shipping in the Twelfth and Thirteenth Centuries*, Publication No. 5, Monograph No. 1 (Cambridge, Massachussetts: Mediaeval Academy, 1930), pp. 59-61.

9. Byrne, p. 59.

10. See H. Pirenne, "L'Instruction des Merchands au Moyen Age," *Annales d'Histoire économique et sociale*, (1929), 13-28.

11. *Ibid.*, p. 61.

12. Cf. Richard Ehrenberg, *Das Zeitalter der Fugger*, 2 vols. (Jena, 1896), Vol. II.

13. Ludwig Scheuermann, *Die Fugger als Montanindustrielle in Tirol und Karnten*, a monograph (Munich: Duncker and Humblot, 1929).

14. *Ibid.*, pp. 229-230.

15. Scheuermann offered no specific information as to why these particular valuations were adopted in the accounts.

16. Scheuermann, pp. 260-264.

17. Raymond de Roover, *The Medici Bank* (New York: New York University Press, 1948).

18. Florence Edler (Mrs. Raymond de Roover) has done an excellent job of describing these operations. See especially her *Glossary of Mediaeval Terms in Business, Italian Series, 1200-1600* (Cambridge: The Mediaeval Academy of America, 1934), pp. 335-426. Her husband, Raymond de Roover, has also made a noteworthy contribution in "A Florentine Firm of Cloth Manufacturers," *Speculum*, XVI (January, 1941), 3-33.

19. Letter from Raymond de Roover to the author, Nov. 8, 1947.

20. De Roover, *Medici Bank*, pp. 26-29.

21. Edler, *Glossary*, p. 305.

22. *Ibid.*, p. 355.

23. *Ibid.*, p. 363.

24. *Ibid.*, p. 379.

25. *Loc. cit.*

26. Edler, *Glossary*, p. 385.

27. De Roover, *Speculum*, XVI, 24.

28. *Loc. cit.*

29. Edler, *Glossary*, p. 383.

30. *Loc. cit.*

31. Edler, *Glossary*, p. 376.

32. *Ibid.*, p. 377.
33. De Roover, *Speculum*, XVI, 26.
34. *Ibid.*, p. 33.
35. *Ibid.*, p. 26.
36. *Ibid.*, p. 28.
37. Edward Peragallo, *Origin and Evolution of Double Entry Bookkeeping* (New York: American Institute Publishing Company, 1938), pp. 38-49, has described these records in an excellent fashion. The discussion in this chapter is based upon Peragallo's Chapter IV.
38. *Ibid.*, p. 40.
39. *Ibid.*, pp. 40-42.
40. *Ibid.*, p. 44.
41. *Ibid.*, p. 48.
42. For information about Datini see Robert Brun, "A Fourteenth-Century Merchant of Italy," *Journal of Economic and Business History*, II (1930), 451-466; see also Peragallo, pp. 22-30.
43. Prof. Dr. B. Penndorf, "Die Anfänge der Betriebsbuchhaltung," *Zeitschrift für Handelswissenschaftliche Forschung*, XII (December, 1930), 627-631.
44. *Ibid.*, p. 628.
45. *Ibid.*, p. 630.
46. *Ibid.*, pp. 630-631.
47. Melis, *op. cit.* (above, note 4), pp. 569-574. This is a very complete treatise on the development of accounting in Italy.
48. Translated freely.
49. A number of entries are faded out and indecipherable.
50. Melis, p. 573.
51. Florence Edler, "Cost Accounting in the Sixteenth Century," *The Accounting Review*, XII, 226-237.
52. *Ibid.*, p. 228.
53. *Ibid.*, p. 229.
54. *Ibid.*, pp. 229-230.
55. *Ibid.*, p. 230.
56. *Ibid.*, p. 231.
57. George Hillis Newlove, "Depreciation," *The Journal of Accountancy*, XLIV (December, 1927), 432-437; and Henry Rand Hatfield, "What They Say About Depreciation," *The Accounting Review*, XI (March, 1936), 18-26.
58. Henry Rand Hatfield, *Modern Accounting* (New York and London: D. Appleton and Company, 1909), p. 121.
59. Edler, *Glossary*, p. 234.
60. *Loc. cit.*
61. These accounts have been briefly described by Raymond de Roover in "Aux Origines d'une Technique Intellectual: La Formation et l'Expansion de la Comptabilité à partie double," *Annales d'Histoire économique et sociale*, XLIV-XLV (1937), 172-193, 270-298. See also Prof. Dr. B. Penndorf, *Zeitschrift*, XII, 627.
62. De Roover, *Annales d'Histoire*, XLV, 295.
63. Yamey, pp. 110-113.
64. De Roover, *Speculum*, XVI, 28; see also A. C. Littleton's review of de Roover's "La Formation et l'Expansion de la Comptabilité à partie double," *The Accounting Review*, XII (1937), 440. Yamey, pp. 110-113, presents the same conclusion.
65. Yamey suggests the following objectives (three reference footnotes omitted):
The need to control the movement of merchandise, particularly

where trading transactions seem to have been common, may have given rise to a system of accounts which could serve as a convenient check on merchandise stocks, and provide information about their origin, quantity, location, ownership, etc. The particularized merchandise accounting may have provided the sort of information which perpetual inventory records supply as a supplement to modern systems of accounts. The profit calculations may have been subsidiary products of the system, made necessary as part of the process of balancing. . . . This tentative conclusion is reinforced by the consideration that the type of trading represented in the texts, consisting of a variety of apparently unrelated activities, would have made it difficult if not impossible to base decisions for the future on past results. . . . In short, is it not possible to claim for the system of accounts the advantages claimed today for modern cost accounting systems?

Yamey, pp. 110-113.

66. Yamey states:

This conclusion is not surprising. The majority of merchants were probably so intimately concerned with the details of their own business affairs that they did not need elaborate accounting calculations to inform them of the size of their fortunes or to acquaint them of the results of their enterprise. It is likely, indeed, that the merchant's knowledge of his affairs would have been so sound that he would have been able to detect errors in the calculations of his bookkeeper. It is only when the firm is very large, or where the owner is not actively or continuously in control of his enterprise, that accounting data would be necessary to supply him, however imperfectly and inadequately, with information he would otherwise not possess, and which he would require in the rationalistic pursuit of profits. Accounting techniques, in the period under review, do not seem to have been designed to meet requirements of this order. But at the same time there is little likelihood that this defect had any inhibitory effect on business enterprise and the pursuit of profit.

Yamey, pp. 110-113.

67. Littleton, *The Accounting Review*, XII, 440.

CHAPTER II

1. Cf. A. C. Littleton, *Accounting Evolution to 1900* (New York: American Institute Publishing Company, 1933), *passim*.
2. "Sunk costs" is a term used by Harry Gunnison Brown, *Transportation Rates and Their Regulation* (New York: The Macmillan Company, 1916), pp. 11-12. For a brief but concise explanation of its meaning see John Maurice Clark, *Studies in the Economics of Overhead Costs* (Chicago: The University of Chicago Press, 1923), p. 54.
3. Thomas Southcliffe Ashton, *Iron and Steel in the Industrial Revolution* (Manchester: Manchester University Publications, Economic History Series No. 2, 1924), p. 100.
4. *Ashton*, p. 163.
5. Lyndall Urwick and Edward Franz Leopold Brech, *The Making of Scientific Management* (London: Management Publications Trust, 1945), II, 17-23, draw the same conclusion.

6. Ronald S. Edwards, "Some Notes on the Early Literature and Development of Cost Accounting in Great Britain," *The Accountant,* XCVII (August, 1937), 194.

7. Clark, *op. cit.* (above, note 2), p. 7.

8. Alphonse Perren, "The Development of Cost Accounting in Europe," *N. A. C. A. Bulletin,* XXIV (1944), 1060.

9. Urwick and Brech, II, 17-23.

10. Sir John Mann, "Cost Records or Factory Accounts," *The Encyclopaedia of Accounting,* (London: William Green and Sons, 1903), II, 260-261. Other authorities also commented on this secrecy attitude. See Horace Lucian Arnold, *The Factory Manager and Accountant* (New York: The Engineering Magazine Press, 1903), *passim.* Arnold was an American.

11. Perren, *N.A.C.A. Bulletin,* XXIV, 1061-62, presented in 1944 a somewhat different conclusion:

> In dealing with accounting problems or the accounting profession in Europe, it is necessary to differentiate between the British Isles and the Continent, first, because Britain is the birthplace and the classic land of modern accounting, and secondly, because nowhere else in the world has the accounting profession attained such distinction and recognition. In industrial accounting Britain has, if not led, at least kept step with America. We find indeed, besides pioneer writers on cost accounting, such as Cronhelm in 1818 and Strachan and Whittem Hawkins in our time, many early applications of cost systems. Normal burdens, for instance, were used in England as early as 1886 in the Atlas works of John Brown & Co., Ltd.
>
> As long as industry remained comparatively simple and the management unit small there was not likely to be any demand for costing or cost recording. It was, therefore, only in the latter part of the eighteenth century and on towards the middle of the nineteenth century that the subject of cost accounting was really developed. During these decades the technical developments which were changing the structure of industry were of such character as to make greater capitalisation inevitable. In fact, the whole trend of these early phases of the Industrial Revolution was directed towards the increased application of capital to the processes of manufacturing. Illustrations are readily provided by the major trades of iron making, coal mining, the development of the steam engine, constructional engineering, and the railways. As the size of his technical units increased, and the amount of invested capital grew, the engineer found that costs gradually became more and more important. They provided the basis on which future trade could be conducted, since they became an important constituent of estimating. The need to recover heavy overhead expenses loomed larger as a problem in the control of engineering works.

12. Cited by F. W. H. Saunders (but supplied to him by E. V. Amsdon) in *The Cost Accountant,* XXVI (March-April, 1948), 78. See also an unsigned article called "Costing in the Seventeenth Century," *The Cost Accountant,* XXI (October-November, 1941), 211-212.

13. Urwick and Brech, II, 17.

14. Edwards, *The Accountant,* XCVII, 225-226, has described the contents of this work.

15. See David Murray, *Chapters in the History of Bookkeeping, Accountancy, and Commercial Arithmetic* (Glasgow: Jackson, Wijlie and Company, 1930), p. 262.

16. See Edwards, *The Accountant*, XCVII, 226, for a reproduction of some of the accounts used by North.
17. From Edwards, *loc. cit.*
18. Quoted by Edwards, *loc. cit.*
19. Edwards, *The Accountant*, XCVII, 226-228.
20. *Ibid.*, p. 227.
21. For further examples of the early recognition of depreciation see Littleton, pp. 223-226 (above, note 1).
22. John Mair, *Book-keeping Methodized*, 6th ed. (Edinburgh: 1760), p. 330.
23. *Ibid.*, p. 331.
24. *Loc. cit.*
25. John Mair, *Bookkeeping Modernized* (Edinburgh: Bell and Bradfute and William Creech, 1768).
26. Edwards, *The Accountant*, XCVII, 228.
27. Edwards, p. 229, illustrates the entries.
28. Edwards, p. 253.
29. *Loc. cit.*
30. Hamilton in his early career was a banker. After that he became a Professor of Mathematics at Aberdeen; he was also well known as an economist.
31. Robert Hamilton, *Introduction to Merchandise*, 2nd ed. (Edinburgh: Creech, 1820), p. 486.
32. Summarized in Edwards, *The Accountant*, XCVII, 253.
33. Hamilton, p. 486.
34. Hamilton, p. 491.
35. Edwards, *The Accountant*, XCVII, 253.
36. Littleton, p. 339.
37. *Loc. cit.*
38. Hamilton, pp. v, vii.
39. Edwards, *The Accountant*, XCVII, 254.
40. Littleton, p. 350.
41. Urwick and Brech, II, 35-36.
42. *Ibid.*, pp. 17-23.
43. See *La Grande Encyclopedia*, Vol. 26, s. v. "Anselme Payen." The latter, however, was the son.
44. Littleton, pp. 323-333; R. S. Edwards, *A Survey of the French Contributions to the Study of Cost Accounting During the Nineteenth Century* (London: Gee and Company, 1937), pp. 1-7.
45. Littleton, p. 325.
46. Reproduced by Littleton, p. 324.
47. Reproduced by Littleton, pp. 324-325; Edwards, *Survey*, p. 2.
48. From Littleton, p. 327; Edwards, *Survey*, p. 3.
49. Littleton, p. 327, gives this number as 24; Edwards, *Survey*, p. 3, gives the number as 22. Twenty-four is apparently correct.
50. No indication is given as to how the two barrels of glue were priced.
51. Reproduced in Littleton, pp. 328-329.
52. Reproduced in Littleton, p. 329.
53. Edwards, *Survey*, p. 4.
54. Edwards, *Survey*, p. 5.
55. Littleton, p. 330. The financial or "ledger in money" records have been described on a previous page.
56. *Loc. cit.*
57. Edwards, *Survey*, p. 7.
58. L. F. G. de Cazaux, *De la Comptabilité dans une Enterprise Industrielle et*

spécialement dans une Exploitation Rurale, 1824. Cited by Edwards, *Survey*, pp. 7-10.

59. Translation supplied by Edwards, *Survey*, pp. 8-13.
60. Translation by the author from Edwards, *Survey*, p. 10.
61. Translation supplied by Edwards, *Survey*, p. 12.
62. Mce Jeannin, *Traité de la Comptabilité* (Paris: 1829), cited by Edwards, *Survey*, p. 18.
63. F. N. Simon, *Methode Complête de la tenue des livres* (1832), cited by Edwards, *Survey*, pp. 18-19.
64. Adapted from Edwards, *Survey*, p. 19.
65. Translation by the author from Edwards, *Survey*, p. 14.
66. Louis Meziéres, *Comptabilité Industrielle et Manufacturiere*, 5th ed. (1862), cited by Edwards, *Survey*, pp. 30-32.
67. Edwards, *Survey*, p. 34, states that Guilbault was at one time Chef d' Administration de la Societé Métallurgique de Vierzon and later Chef de Comptabilité, Inspector aux Forges et Chautiers de la Méditerranée. After 25 years of practical experience, he wrote in 1865 a two-volume work called *Traité de Comptabilité et d'Administration industrielles.*
68. M. Dugué, *Traité de Comptabilité et d'Administration à l'usage des Entrepreneurs de Bâtiments et de travant publics* (1872).
69. M. E. Claperon, *Cours de Comptabilité* (1886).
70. H. Lefevre, *La Comptabilité* (1883).
71. Edwards, *Survey*, pp. 35-36.
72. F. W. Cronhelm, *Double Entry by Single* (London: Longmans, Green & Co., 1818), pp. 125-127.
73. This controversy is discussed in Chapter VI.
74. George Jackson, *The Check Journal*, 5th ed. (London: 1836), p. 133. (First edition, 1826; twenty-fifth, 1904.) The 1904 edition also contained a few remarks about manufacturing, and thus will be discussed in a later chapter.
75. Charles Babbage, *The Economy of Machinery and Manufacturers* (London: C. Knight, 1832); as reproduced in Urwick and Brech, I, 25.
76. Charles Babbage, *On the Economy of Machinery and Manufacturers*, 4th ed. (London, 1841), pp. 203-204.
77. Babbage's work foreshadowed a large number of the later, more modern, economists who emphasized the production of consumer goods. He gave stress to the division of labor and the adequate planning of output. For an excellent discussion of this and other relationships of scientific management to economics see E. H. Anderson and Gustav T. Schwenning, *The Science of Production Organization* (New York: John Wiley & Sons, 1938), pp. 40-63.
78. Cf. Earl J. Hamilton, "Profit Inflation and the Industrial Revolution, 1751-1800," *The Quarterly Journal of Economics*, LVI (February, 1942), 267, where he states: "Economic historians agree that a sellers' market prevailed in the second half of the eighteenth century, when real wages were falling steadily—that the great problem was to make goods as fast as they could be sold. There is general recognition that the pressure of demand upon existing modes of production was a major factor in the adoption of the new technique." See also J. C. L. Simonde de Sismondi, *Études sur l'Economie Politique* (Paris, 1837), I, 39.
79. John Fleming, *Bookkeeping by Double Entry* (Pittsburgh: W. S. Haven, 1854), p. 115. Cf. also Littleton, p. 356. Fleming was an American.
80. Cf. Littleton, p. 356.
81. Frederick C. Krepp, *Statistical Bookkeeping* (London: Longman 1858), p.

151. The second edition appeared in 1862, but it was no more complete than the first. Krepp was an Englishman.

82. J. Sawyer, *Bookkeeping for the Tanning Trade*, 2nd ed. (London, 1862). Sawyer was also an Englishman.

83. The term "Dark Age" is used advisedly.

84. Sawyer, quoted in Edwards, *The Accountant*, XCVII, 255.

85. For the sake of completeness, it might be mentioned that in the 1866 edition of *The Science and Practice of Bookkeeping* (Philadelphia: Sower, Barnes and Potts), the author, Lorenzo Fairbanks, expressed the hope that he would be able to publish a separate volume on manufacturing accounting at some later date. So far as can be ascertained, no such work was ever issued. This does indicate, however, that the special needs of industrial firms were recognized. Fairbanks was the president of a business college in Philadelphia.

86. By F. R. Goddard. See "Balance Sheets of Manufacturing Firms," *Proceedings of the Cleveland* (England) *Institution of Engineers*. Referred to in *The Accountant*, XCVII, 284.

87. *Loc. cit.*

88. In the second edition (1874) of a book called *Practical Bookkeeping* (Edinburgh: Simpkin, Marshall, Hamilton, Kent and Company) by F. H. Carter, a Scottish text writer, there was a brief chapter on a costing system for a mine or quarry. The aim of the system was to show the cost of operating the mine on a per level basis. A cost sheet was drawn up, therefore, for each level, and on it were recorded the costs of labor, tools, transportation expenses, and miscellaneous items on a monthly basis. These totals were broken down into per ton figures, both for rough stone and for finished slate. (Carter had in mind a slate quarry.) Another interesting feature of this technique was that overhead costs were collected for each month on a separate sheet, and again divided up on a per ton basis, both for rough stone and slate. These overhead items were then added to the costs incurred on each level (as above) in proportion to the tonnage mined from each. This description, then, foreshadowed the modern "per unit of product" method of allocating overhead. See *The Accountant*, XCVII, 313.

89. Thomas Battersby, *The Perfect Double Entry Bookkeeper and the Perfect Prime Cost and Profit Demonstrator (on the Departmental System) for Iron and Brass Foundries, Machinists, Engineers, Shipbuilders, Manufactures, etc.* (Manchester: 1878).

90. Battersby, p. 33.

91. Battersby, p. 34.

92. *Loc. cit.*

93. *Loc. cit.*

94. *Loc. cit.*

95. Battersby, pp. 34-40.

96. This balance was not called "gross profit" by Battersby; nevertheless, that is what he obviously meant.

97. The work of Garcke and Fells is discussed in later chapters.

98. W. C. Scoville, *Revolution in Glassmaking* (Cambridge: Harvard University Press, 1948), p. 56.

99. J. H. Goodwin, *Goodwin's Improved Bookkeeping*, 4th ed. (Published by the author, 1881). The twenty-sixth edition of 1908 carried exactly the same description. Did Goodwin think no progress in factory accounting had been made in those 27 years? Another example of a sparse treatment of manufacturing accounts is to be found in J. C. Bryant, *Bryant's New Bookkeeping*, 6th ed. (Buffalo: Published by the author, 1880), pp. 161-170.

100. *Ibid.*, p. 15.
101. In a book by D. S. Dow, *Keeping Books* (New York: D. A. Curtis, 1882), p. 80, there is a statement which also indicates the little regard with which American writers treated factory accounting in this period. He stated: "The bookkeeper opens an account which he calls the manufacturing account and treats it exactly as he has the merchandise account . . . that is, he debits it with all it receives and credits it with all it gives." Nothing was said about overhead. Cf., however, Littleton, pp. 356-357, where it is stated: "But the use of an account on the pattern of a merchandise account did not escape criticism. For example, the editors of *The Bookkeeper* (1880) object to the lack of elucidating details and hold that 'systematic accountantship' in a factory calls for . . . 'division of information'."
102. Goodwin, p. 14. He showed only the first two debits and the first credit in his own ledger account; the others were supplied by the present writer, based upon his description.
103. George S. Gibb, *The Whitesmiths of Taunton—A History of Reed and Barton* (Cambridge: Harvard University Press, 1943).
104. *Ibid.*, pp. 267-270.
105. *Ibid.*, pp. 267-270.
106. Thomas R. Navin, *The Whitin Machine Works Since 1831* (Cambridge: Harvard University Press, 1950).
107. *Navin*, p. 27.
108. *Navin*, pp. 149-150.
109. George S. Gibb, *The Saco-Lowell Shops* (Cambridge: Harvard University Press, 1950).
110. *Ibid.*, p. 41.
111. *Ibid.*, p. 42.
112. *Ibid.*, pp. 47, 60-61.
113. *Ibid.*, pp. 50-51.
114. Evelyn H. Knowlton, *Pepperell's Progress* (Cambridge: Harvard University Press, 1948).
115. *Ibid.*, pp. 71-72.
116. *Ibid.*, p. 177.
117. *Loc. cit.*
118. W. W. Cauley, "A Study of the Accounting Records of the Shelby Iron Company," (Unpublished M.B.A. thesis in the University of Alabama Library, 1949).

CHAPTER III

1. See Chapter II, *passim.*
2. Henry Metcalfe, *The Cost of Manufactures* (New York: John Wiley and Sons), first edition. 1885, third edition, 1907. There was almost no change in the two editions.
3. Metcalfe, *passim.*
4. The criticisms can be found in *Transactions American Society of Mechanical Engineers* (1886), *passim.* As a matter of interest, the remarks here of F. W. Taylor were his first published contribution to the literature of management and costing. Later on he became perhaps the most prominent of all the exponents of scientific management. For an excellent, yet brief, discussion

of his contributions, see E. H. Anderson and G. T. Schwenning, *The Science of Production Organization* (New York: John Wiley and Sons, 1938), pp. 226-231. Some authorities regard Taylor's later famous article on "Shop Management" as being one of the early contributions to standard costing. See *Transactions American Society of Mechanical Engineers*, XXIV (1903), 1337-1456.

5. Emile Garcke and J. M. Fells, *Factory Accounts, Their Principles and Practice*, 4th ed. (London: Crosby, Lockwood and Son, 1893), pp. 52-57. (First edition, 1887.) There was substantially no difference between the two editions. See John Whitmore, "Some Cost Accounting Terms," *The Journal of Accountancy*, L, No. 3 (September, 1930), 200. For a brief biographical sketch of Garcke and Fells see David Solomons, *Studies in Costing* (London: Sweet and Maxwell, 1952), p. 35.

6. Garcke and Fells, p. 50.

7. G. P. Norton, *Textile Manufacturers' Bookkeeping*, 4th ed. (London: Simpkin, 1900), pp. 248-262. (First edition, 1889.) The fourth edition was substantially unchanged. Incidentally, Norton's illustrations were dated 1884, and it may be that his manuscript was written several years before it was published in 1889. He was a practicing English Chartered Accountant. He lived from 1858 to 1939.

8. J. Slater Lewis, *Commercial Organisation of Factories*, 3rd ed. (London: E. and F. N. Spon, 1896), p. 376.

9. E. Andrade, "Manufacturing Costs Accounts, Their Use and Treatment," *The Accountant*, Feb. 11, 1899, p. 171.

10. Garcke and Fells, p. 117, had recommended a similar practice.

11. H. Diemer, "The Commercial Organization of the Machine Shop," *The Engineering Magazine*, XIX (1900), 511, 707. Diemer was an American.

12. H. L. C. Hall, *Manufacturing Costs* (Detroit: The Bookkeeper Publishing Company, 1904), pp. 45-50.

13. Henry Spencer, *Commercial Organisation of Engineering Factories* (New York: Spon and Chamberlain, 1907), pp. 40-50.

14. L. W. Hawkins, *Cost Accounts* (London: Gee and Company, 1905), also illustrated a stores ledger similar to that of Spencer—by quantities only. Hawkins did suggest, however, that values could be used as well, if desired.

15. This same technique had been recommended in this country as early as 1905. H. C. M. Vedder, for example, illustrated a "summary sheet of materials consumed" which was designed to permit the posting to the cost ledger once a month, or at some other period. It had columns for date, order number 1, order number 2, order number 3, etc. This sheet would also be used to make the posting to the credit of materials and supplies account, and the debit to the manufacturing account. See "Cost Accounting: an Exposition of its Theories and Principles," *The Accountant*, Nov. 11, 1905, p. 549. Reprinted from the *Business World*.

16. J. L. Nicholson, *Factory Organization and Costs* (New York: Kohl Technical Publishing Company, 1909), p. 274.

17. F. E. Webner, *Factory Costs* (New York: The Ronald Press Company, 1911), p. 92.

18. J. L. Nicholson, *Cost Accounting—Theory and Practice* (New York: The Ronald Press Company, 1913), p. 255. J. B. Green, "The Perpetual Inventory in Practical Stores Operation," *The Engineering Magazine*, XLVIII (1915), 880, illustrated a form similar to Nicholson's except that he added a date column for each section.

19. E. P. Moxey, *Principles of Factory Cost Keeping* (New York: The Ronald Press Company, 1913), pp. 22-39.
20. Moxey, p. 40.
21. J. P. Jordan and G. L. Harris, *Cost Accounting* (New York: The Ronald Press Company, 1920), *passim.*
22. E. T. Elbourne, *Factory Administration and Cost Accounts* (London: Longmans, Green and Company, 1921), pp, 370-398.
23. H. B. Twyford, *Purchasing, Its Economic Aspects and Proper Methods* (New York: D. Van Nostrand Company, 1915); H. H. Farquhar, *Factory Store-Keeping—the Control and Storage of Materials* (New York: McGraw-Hill Book Company, 1922); J. H. Barber, *Economic Control of Inventory* (New York: Codex Book Company, 1925); F. W. Kilduff, *Inventory Practice and Material Control* (New York, McGraw-Hill Book Company, 1925); R. C. Davis, *Purchasing and Storing* (New York: Alexander Hamilton Institute, 1931); and M. Cartmell, *Stores and Materials Control* (New York: The Ronald Press Company, 1922).
24. Metcalfe, p. 171.
25. Metcalfe, p. 176.
26. Garcke and Fells, p. 50.
27. Norton, p. 247. The italics are his.
28. F. G. Burton, *Engineering Estimates and Cost Accounts*, 2nd ed., (Manchester: Technical Publishing Company, 1900), p. 63. (First edition, 1895.)
29. E. Andrade, *The Accountant*, Feb. 11, 1899, p. 171, followed the same practice.
30. Pseudonym of H. L. Arnold, "Cost-keeping Methods in Machine-Shop and Foundry," *The Engineering Magazine*, XIV (1898), 631.
31. W. C. Eddis and W. B. Tindall, *Manufacturers' Accounts* (Toronto: Published by the Authors, 1902), pp. 65, 100.
32. Eddis and Tindall, p. 66.
33. B. C. Bean, *The Cost of Production* (Chicago: A. W. Shaw Company, 1905), p. 35.
34. Joseph MacNaughton, *Factory Bookkeeping for Paper Mills* (London: Wood Pulp, Limited, 1899), p. 12.
35. See S. S. Dawson, "Stock and Cash Accounts of a Flour Miller," *The Accountant*, Apr. 3, 1897, p. 370.
36. H. Stanley Garry, "Factory Costs," *The Accountant*, July 25 and Sept. 12, 1903, p. 956.
37. *Ibid.*, p. 957.
38. Stanley Pedder, "Cost Accounts: Their Advantages and Their Relations to Business Results," *The Accountant*, Apr. 29, 1905, p. 524.
39. John Whitmore, "Factory Accounting As Applied to Machine Shops," *The Journal of Accountancy*, III (1906), 356.
40. W. Strachan, *Cost Accounts* (London: Stevens and Haynes, 1909), p. 19. L. W. Hawkins was not so dogmatic on this point; he gave both viewpoints, and also discussed the pricing at cost and the average cost methods. If the market price were adopted, according to Hawkins, the differences between cost and market would be a profit or loss due to fluctuation. He did not, however, show how such a difference was to be handled on the books. See his *Cost Accounts*, p. 77. Both Hawkins and Strachan were Englishmen.
41. Moxey, p. 28.
42. A. Hamilton Church, *Manufacturing Costs and Accounts* (New York: McGraw-Hill Book Company, 1917), p. 163; and F. H. Baugh, *Cost Accounting* (Baltimore: F. H. Baugh, 1915), p. 64.

43. Cf. C. H. Scovell, *Cost Accounting and Burden Application* (New York: D. Appleton and Company, 1916), p. 28; and Church, 1917, p. 160.
44. Scovell, p. 41.
45. Cf. C. E. Woods, *Unified Accounting Methods for Industrials* (New York: The Ronald Press Company, 1917), p. 78.
46. Jordan and Harris, p. 152.
47. A. C. Ridgway, "Cost Accounts," *The Accountant*, Dec. 6, 1919, p. 488.
48. Hawkins, 1920, p. 76.
49. Elbourne, p. 379.
50. See, e.g., C. O. Wellington, "Actual Costs as Compared with Replacement Costs," *Yearbook National Association of Cost Accountants* (1922), p. 52.
51. See *Proceedings International Congress on Accounting* (1929), *passim*, for a discussion of this method.

CHAPTER IV

1. J. H. Goodwin, *Improved Bookkeeping and Business Manual*, 4th ed. (New York: Published by the author, 1881), pp. 14-15, 32.
2. *Transactions American Society of Mechanical Engineers*, VII (1886), 152-155, 269-272.
3. E. Garcke and J. M. Fells, *Factory Accounts*, 4th ed. (London: Crosby, Lockwood and Son, 1893), pp. 20, 39. (First edition, 1887.)
4. G. P. Norton, *Textile Manufacturers' Bookkeeping*, 4th ed. (London: Simpkin, 1900), pp. 154-155. (First edition, 1889.)
5. The burden cost question will be discussed in Chapter V.
6. *The Acoountant* (1894), p. 633.
7. J. Slater Lewis, *Commercial Organisation of Factories* (London: E. and F. N. Spon, 1896), pp. 298-301.
8. F. G. Burton, *Engineering Estimates and Cost Accounts*, 2d ed. (Manchester: Technical Publishing Company, 1900), p. 64. (First edition, 1895.)
9. H. L. Arnold, *The Complete Cost-Keeper* (New York: The Engineering Magazine Press, 1899), *passim*.
10. H. L. Arnold, *The Factory Manager and Accountant* (New York: The Engineering Magazine Press, 1903), p. 198.
11. W. C. Eddis and W. B. Tindall, *Manufacturers' Accounts* (Toronto: Published by the authors, 1902), pp. 50-53.
12. H. L. C. Hall, *Manufacturing Costs* (Detroit: The Bookkeeper Publishing Company, 1904), p. 113.
13. Henry Spencer, *Commercial Organisation of Engineering Factories* (New York: Spon and Chamberlain, 1907), p. 107.
14. A. G. Nisbet, *Terminal Cost Accounts* (London: Gee and Company, 1906), also gave a description of the nature of, and the advantages of, the premium wage plans. Nisbet, like Spencer, was an English cost authority.
15. G. A. Mitchell, *Single Cost Accounts* (London: Gee and Company, 1907), pp. 82-85.
16. A. Hamilton Church, "Proper Distribution of Establishment Charges," *The Engineering Magazine, XXI* (1901), *passim*. While Church did most of his writing in the United States, he at one time worked for the National Telephone Company in Great Britain. See David Solomon's *Studies in Costing* (London: Sweet and Maxwell, 1952), p. 25.

17. J. Lee Nicholson, *Factory Organization and Costs* (New York: Kohl Technical Publishing Company, 1909), pp. 54-57.
18. J. R. Wildman, *Cost Accounting* (New York: The Accountancy Publishing Company, 1910), p. 42.
19. F. E. Webner, *Factory Costs* (New York: The Ronald Press Company, 1911), pp. 105-139.
20. E. P. Moxey, *Principles of Factory Cost Keeping* (New York: The Ronald Press Company, 1913), p. 61.
21. L. W. Hawkins, *Cost Accounts*, 2nd ed. (London: Gee and Company, 1912), pp. 6-14.
22. S. H. Bunnell, *Cost Keeping for Manufacturing Plants* (New York: D. Appleton and Company, 1911), p. 108.
23. E. T. Elbourne, *Factory Administration and Cost Accounts* (London: Longmans, Green and Company, 1921), p. 735.
24. Cf. F. E. Webner, *Factory Accounting* (Chicago: LaSalle Extension University, 1917), *passim*.
25. Elbourne, pp. 350-355.

CHAPTER V

Part I

1. Because of their importance, interest and rent are considered in the next section of this chapter.
2. J. M. Clark, the well-known American economist, noted in 1923 that "the entire idea of expenses of production is, in a sense, a rather recent one. . . . From the slowness with which economic science has assimilated the facts of overhead expense, one is almost tempted to conclude that its prevalent ideas on expenses of production date back to the domestic system and are not really appropriate to any later stage of industrial development." J. M. Clark, *The Economics of Overhead Costs* (Chicago: The University of Chicago Press, 1923), pp. 1-2.
3. E. P. Moxey, *Principles of Factory Cost Keeping* (New York: The Ronald Press Company, 1913), p. 63.
4. Henry Metcalfe, *The Cost of Manufactures* (New York: John Wiley and Sons, 1885), p. 338.
5. The concept of fixed and variable overhead costs can be traced back at least as far as 1862. In that year Nassau Senior, the noted economist, said that "there are certain expenses upon a mill which go on in the same proportion whether the mill be running short of full time, as, for instance, rent rates and taxes, insurance against fire, wages of several permanent servants, deterioration of machinery, with various other charges upon a manufacturing establishment, the proportion of which to profits increases as the production decreases." *Report of the Inspector of Factories* (Oct. 31, 1862), p. 19. This list of items was also a rather complete summary of the charges to be included in the overhead element of cost. In France, C. A. Guilbault was making, in 1865, a reasonably clear distinction between fixed and variable costs. For references, see Chapter II. David Solomons states that an Irishman named Dionysius Lardner referred to fixed and variable costs as early as 1850. See Solomons, *Studies in Costing* (London: Sweet and Maxwell, 1952), p. 34.

6. Metcalfe, p. 73.

7. E. Garcke and J. M. Fells, *Factory Accounts*, 4th ed. (London: Crosby, Lockwood and Son, 1893). (First edition, 1887.)

8. Garcke and Fells, p. 73.

9. G. L. Fowler in *Transactions American Society of Mechanical Engineers*, IX (1888), 393.

10. G. P. Norton, *Textile Manufacturers' Bookkeeping*, 4th ed. (London: Simpkin, 1900), p. 194. (First edition, 1889.) Norton was an Englishman.

11. F. A. Halsey in *Transactions*, XV (1894), 628.

12. F. G. Burton, *Engineering Estimates and Cost Accounts* (Manchester: Technical Publishing Company, 1895), p. 11. (Second edition, 1900.)

13. J. Slater Lewis, *Commercial Organisation of Factories* (London: E. and F. N. Spon, 1896).

14. Lewis, p. 173.

15. Lewis, p. 179.

16. *Loc. cit.* Italics from the original.

17. H. M. Norris in *Transactions*, XIX (1898), 389.

18. Oberlin Smith in *Transactions*, XIX, 405.

19. Halsey, p. 397.

20. *Loc. cit.*

21. W. S. Rogers in *Transactions*, XIX, 401.

22. Norris, p. 413. Norris reiterated his views in "Simple and Effective System of Shop Cost Keeping," *The Engineering Magazine*, XVI (1898), 394-396.

23. H. M. Lane in *Transactions*, XVIII (1897), 893. Incidentally, this is one of the first references to the use of the term "burden," which later became so popular as descriptive of the miscellaneous expenditures properly included in cost of production.

24. *Loc. cit.*

25. His prior views were discussed *supra*, p. 126.

26. H. L. Arnold, *The Complete Cost-Keeper* (New York: The Engineering Magazine Press, 1899), p. 49.

27. Joseph MacNaughton, *Factory Bookkeeping for Paper Mills* (London: Wood Pulp, Limited, 1899), p. 24.

28. A. G. Charleton, "Principles and Methods of Profitably Working the Mine; Office Organization, Cost-keeping and Records of Work Done," *The Engineering Magazine*, XX (1901), 691.

29. A. Hamilton Church, "Proper Distribution of Establishment Charges," *The Engineering Magazine*, XXI and XXII (1901). This series of articles became famous almost over night.

30. Church, p. 517.

31. Church, p. 374.

32. W. C. Eddis and W. B. Tindall, *Manufacturers' Accounts* (Toronto: Published by the authors, 1902).

33. See their Chapter II.

34. Eddis and Tindall, p. 150.

35. "Oncost" is the English term often used synonymously with "overhead" and "burden." According to *The New Oxford Dictionary* it is a rather old term, having been mentioned in the fifteenth century in the *Aberdeen Register*. As early as 1795, it was in general use in connection with the miscellaneous expenditures of a coal mine. For example, J. F. Erskine stated in that year: "[This] yields but a very small return to the coalmaster on account of the overpowering contingent expenses known in collieries by the name of oncost." *Agriculture Survey Clackmannansh*

(1795), p. 410. Sir John Mann suggests that it may have been derived from the old idea that the manufacturing incidental costs were items to be added "on to cost," taking cost as the total of labor and materials. *The Encyclopaedia of Accounting* (London: William Green and Sons, 1903), s. v., "Oncosts." In this country, a similar viewpoint was expressed by A. Hamilton Church in 1930. See his *Overhead Expense* (New York: Mc-Graw-Hill Book Company, 1930), pp. 3, 4. Cf. also, *The Accountant*, XCVII, 313, 343; and J. U. Nef, *The Rise of the British Coal Industry* (London: George Routledge and Sons, 1932), II, 432. Nef refers to the accounts of the Tulliallan Coal Works (1643-1647) in which the term "oncost" appeared several times.

36. John Urie, "Oncost and Its Apportionment," *The Accountant*, Jan. 11, 1902, p. 51.

37. Urie, p. 52.

38. It should be mentioned, however, that Sir John Mann had written on cost accounts prior to 1903. His pamphlet, *Notes on Cost Records* (which appeared as an article in *The Accountant*, Aug. 29 and Sept. 5, 1891, pp. 619-21, 631-7) was a very important early contribution to the subject. In that work he divided overhead into (1) buying costs, which, he said, varied with the cost of goods bought; (2) selling expenses, which varied with sales; and (3) production expenses.

39. Sir John Mann in *The Encyclopaedia of Accounting*, V, 199.

40. *Loc. cit.*

41. Mann was inconsistent in this respect, however. In one place he stated that indirect expenses were those which could not be applied to a particular contract or department (p. 199). Yet in another place, he stated that one of the reasons for making the distinction was that the allocation of indirect expense was to be handled differently from direct expenses (p. 201). This last statement would imply that both groups were finally to be allocated to product, and it is the opinion of the present writer that that is what he intended should be done.

42. Mann, pp. 201, 202.

43. Reported in *The Accountant*, June 25, 1904, pp. 835-838.

44. J. E. Sterrett in *The Accountant*, June 25, 1904, p. 837.

45. Editorial in *The Accountant* (1904), p. 230.

46. Editorial in *The Accountant* (1905), p. 520, on an essay by Stanley Pedder.

47. *Ibid.*, p. 728.

48. H. Stanley Garry, *Multiple Cost Accounts* (London: Gee and Company, 1906), p. 42.

49. A. G. Nisbet, *Terminal Cost Accounts* (London: Gee and Company, 1906).

50. Nisbet, p. 23.

51. Already discussed, *supra*, p. 129.

52. John Whitmore, "Factory Accounting As Applied to Machine Shops," *The Journal of Accountancy*, III (1907), 21.

53. *Ibid.*, p. 114.

54. John Whitmore, "Shoe Factory Cost Accounts," *The Journal of Accountancy*, VI (1908), 14.

55. Harrington Emerson, "Efficiency As a Basis for Operation and Wages," *The Engineering Magazine*, XXXVI (1908), 173, 336-339. His earlier views are to be found in "Percentage Methods of Determining Production Costs," *The Foundry*, Oct. 1904, pp. 80-81. For a thorough and scholarly treatment of the evolution of standard cost accounting, see Ellis Mast Sowell, *The Evolution of the Theories and Techniques of Standard Costs*, 1944,

an unpublished Ph. D. thesis in the University of Texas Library. See also Solomons, *op. cit.* (above, note 5), pp. 38-50, for an excellent brief summary.

56. Henry Spencer, *Commercial Organisation of Engineering Factories* (New York: Spon and Chamberlain, 1907), p. 152.

57. Spencer, p. 152.

58. G. A. Mitchell, *Single Cost Accounts* (London: Gee and Company, 1907), p. 14.

59. Mitchell, p. 128.

60. Clarence M. Day, *Accounting Practice* (New York: D. Appleton and Company, 1908), p. 114.

61. C. E. Knoeppel, "Cost Reduction Through Cost Comparison," *The Engineering Magazine,* XXXII (1907), 918. Knoeppel was also an American.

62. F. E. Webner, "Obtaining Actual Knowledge of the Cost of Production," *The Engineering Magazine,* XXXV (1908), 255.

63. His more comprehensive views will be described *post,* p. 139.

64. Webner, p. 255.

65. Gershom Smith, "The Distribution of Indirect Costs by the Machine-Hour Method," *The Engineering Magazine,* XXXVII (1909), 384-385.

66. J. Lee Nicholson, *Factory Organization and Costs* (New York: Kohl Technical Publishing Company, 1909), p. 29.

67. Discussed *supra,* p. 132.

68. A. Hamilton Church, *Production Factors in Cost Accounting and Works Management* (New York: The Engineering Magazine Press, 1910), pp. 176-177.

69. See *ibid.,* p. 177.

70. S. H. Bunnell, *Cost-Keeping in Manufacturing Plants* (New York: D. Appleton and Company, 1911), p. 154.

71. Bunnell, pp. 155-158.

72. H. M. Rowe, *Bookkeeping and Accountancy—Cost Accountancy for Manufacturing* (Baltimore: The H. M. Rowe Company, 1910), pp. 204-206.

73. *Supra,* p. 136.

74. F. E. Webner, *Factory Costs* (New York: The Ronald Press Company, 1911), p. 143.

75. *Ibid.,* p. 143.

76. R. R. Keely, "Overhead Expense Distribution with Discussion," *Journal of the American Society of Mechanical Engineers,* June, 1913, p. 983.

77. William Kent in *Journal of the American Society of Mechanical Engineers,* June, 1913, p. 992.

78. L. W. Hawkins, *Cost Accounts,* 2d. ed. (London: Gee and Company, 1912).

79. Hawkins, p. 64.

80. E. P. Moxey, *Principles of Factory Cost Keeping.*

81. F. H. Baugh, *Principles and Practices of Cost Accounting* (Baltimore: F. H. Baugh, 1915), p. 27.

82. But see Baugh, p. 44.

83. It might be mentioned that D. S. Kimball, in *Principles of Industrial Organization* (New York: McGraw-Hill Book Company, 1913), stated that the dividing line between factory and general expenses could not always be sharply drawn, and in cases where the general expenses constituted only a relatively small sum it would not be a large error to include them in the factory expense (p. 116).

84. Nicholas T. Ficker, "Main Divisions of Manufacturing Expense," *The Engineering Magazine,* XLIX (1915), 553.

85. C. H. Scovell, *Cost Accounting and Burden Application* (New York: D.

Appleton and Company, 1916), p. 11. Later on (p. 75) he went on to declare that "it is very important when distributing burden charges that a definite distinction be made between manufacturing and selling expenses. Selling expenses should be kept entirely separate from manufacturing costs . . . "

86. J. P. Jordan and G. L. Harris, *Cost Accounting* (New York: The Ronald Press Company, 1920), p. 22.

87. *Loc. cit.*

88. A. C. Ridgway, "Cost Accounts," address before the Birmingham Chartered Students Society, reported in *The Accountant*, Dec. 6, 1919, p. 485.

89. Ridgway, p. 488.

90. E. T. Elbourne, *Factory Administration and Cost Accounts* (London: Longmans, Green and Company, 1921). This was the most complete treatise on cost accounting published in England in the decade of the 1920's.

91. Discussed *supra*, p. 141.

92. Elbourne, p. 529. Another reason given was that the results of such a practice were misleading in 99 cases out of a hundred.

93. Cf. A. Cathles, "General Principles of Costing," *The Accountant*, Feb. 28, 1920, p. 249. The lecturer here seemed never to have heard of the idea that there was a difference between production costs and commercial expenses. He used the term "costing" in its broad sense as "the designation applied to those methods of accounting by the use of which it is possible to ascertain the actual cost of producing and selling each article . . . " His overhead, therefore, was made up of all the items of expenditure of a firm except material and direct labor, no distinction being made between what were properly production costs and what should be excluded. In addition to this careless bit of thinking, he made no division in his method of allocating the various types of charges—all were to be lumped and added together to get the burden charge (p. 254). The theory displayed in this article became quite rare within a few years. The practice mentioned, however, still recurs. As late as 1933, F. B. Makin was able to state that there were in actual practice "many who fail to distinguish between this type of overhead cost and the productive or general overhead. The tendency has been, and in many cases still remains, for the overhead expenses or constant costs of selling to be included with the administrative cost, and to be considered part of the general overhead cost of production. This practice to the mind of the writer is not correct, for the cost of selling a product does not form any part of the cost of producing that product . . . " *Overhead Costs in Theory and Practice* (London: Gee and Company, 1933), p. 21.

94. Respectively: J. R. Hilgert, *Cost Accounting for Sales* (New York: The Ronald Press Co., 1926); Makin, *op. cit.* (above, note 93); and W. B. Castenholz, *Control of Distribution Costs and Sales* (New York and London: Harper and Brothers, 1930).

Part II

95. Thomas Battersby, *The Perfect Double Entry Bookkeeper* (Manchester: 1878).

96. *The Report of Inspector of Factories*, Oct. 31, 1862, p. 19.

97. Garcke and Fells, *Factory Accounts*.

98. Garcke and Fells, p. 42.

99. Norton, p. 79. Imputed rent also formed an element of cost where the buildings were owned by the firm (p. 213).
100. Cf. Fowler in *Transactions*, IX (1888), 393, who also, in this country, held such a view.
101. For the sake of completeness it is necessary to mention that G. L. Fowler, in 1888, listed interest on borrowed capital as an element of expense which should be included in overhead. He did not elaborate, however, upon this bare statement. *Transactions*, IX, 393.
102. Garcke and Fells, *op. cit.* (above, note 7), p. 74.
103. E. P. Bates in *Transactions*, XV (1894), 626.
104. *Loc. cit.*
105. *The Accountant* (1894), p. 704.
106. Lewis, p. 173, thought this matter so unimportant that he barely mentioned that interest on buildings and machinery formed a part of the legitimate "shop establishment charges," which he said should be spread over jobs turned out. It is evident that he considered interest an element of cost, but that it was not worthy of any emphasis.
107. Oberlin Smith in *Transactions*, XIX (1898), 403.
108. H. M. Norris, "A Simple and Effective System of Shop Cost-Keeping," *The Engineering Magazine*, XVI (1898), 394.
109. Pseudonym of H. L. Arnold, "Cost-Keeping in Machine-Shop and Foundry," *The Engineering Magazine*, XIV (1898), 628.
110. *Ibid.*, p. 628.
111. F. G. Burton, *op. cit.*
112. Burton, p. 12.
113. Burton, p. 80.
114. *Loc. cit.*
115. Burton, p. 81.
116. Burton, p. 82.
117. Church, *The Engineering Magazine*, XXII, 31. Church did most of his writing in this country.
118. Eddis and Tindall, p. 9.
119. H. L. C. Hall, *Manufacturing Costs* (Detroit: The Bookkeeper Publishing Company, 1904), p. 125. Hall was an American.
120. Sir John Mann in *The Encyclopaedia of Accounting*, V, 218. Mann was an English accountant.
121. *Loc. cit.*
122. Garry, *Multiple Cost Accounts*, p. 46.
123. *Ibid.*, p. 47.
124. A. G. Nisbet failed to mention interest as a cost, in spite of the fact that his book was Vol. XLVI of the well-known *Accountants' Library*. Garry's work was Vol. XLII of the same series.
125. Whitmore, "Factory Accounting," *The Journal of Accountancy*, II, 253.
126. Whitmore, III, p. 23. The interest on selling equipment was to be included in distribution expenses.
127. *Loc. cit.* In another issue of the same publication, p. 126, A. A. Murdoch disputed Whitmore's last assertion, and claimed that he had been using exactly the same technique for at least three years.
128. Spencer, p. 150.
129. Mitchell, p. 40.
130. H. Stanley Garry, *Process Cost Accounts* (London: Gee and Company, 1908), p. 52.
131. *Ibid.*, p. 73.

132. Nicholson, p. 33. Nicholson wrote in this country.
133. *Loc. cit.*
134. With two exceptions: Day gave no satisfactory treatment; and Bunnell did not even mention interest.
135. A. Lowes Dickinson, "The Economic Aspects of Cost Accounts," *The Journal of Accountancy*, XI (1911), 335.
136. The material referred to will be treated *post*.
137. Hawkins, p. 113. Hawkins wrote in England.
138. Moxey, p. 73. Moxey was a professor at the University of Pennsylvania.
139. Webner, *Factory Costs*, p. 149. So fas as the present writer can ascertain, Webner was the first to make this point clear.
140. *Ibid.*, pp. 153, 155.
141. *Ibid.*, p. 156.
142. *Ibid.*, p. 157.
143. Church, *Production Factors*, p. 72.
144. Webner, *Factory Costs*, p. 161.
145. Cf., e.g., Clark, who makes the statement that "the discussion of this question is a strange mixture of dogmatic assertion and arguments from expediency, based on assumptions as to how a given policy would work." *Op. cit.* (above, note 2), p. 255. Clark is an American economist.
146. For inclusion: W. M. Cole, A. Hamilton Church, and J. L. Nicholson. For exclusion: W. B. Richards, J. E. Sterrett, J. P. Joplin, H. C. Miller, J. R. Wildman, and H. M. Temple.
147. M. W. Jenkinson in *The Accountant*, Apr. 18, 1914, p. 573.
148. The English term for goodwill and organization expenses is "preliminary expenses."
149. W. H. Hazell, "Printer's Cost Finding System," *The Accountant*, Feb. 28, 1914, p. 314.
150. Nicholas T. Ficker, "Distributing Overhead Expense," *The Engineering Magazine*, L (1915), 259. Ficker was an American.
151. Their views have been discussed *supra*.
152. From what has been stated on the previous pages of this section, there is no doubt that the two groups of persons mentioned had had plenty of thinking done for them, even if, perhaps, they had done little themselves.
153. Scovell, 1916, p. 96.
154. A large number of these are in the appendix to Scovell's volume. The name of the economist was not given.
155. For a clear statement of the viewpoint of an economist, with particular reference to the imputed interest question as it applies to cost accounting, see Clark, *op. cit.* (above, note 2), pp. 255-256. His viewpoint should be quoted here: "Books which do not include interest are primarily adapted to the purposes of financial accounting, and cost accounting, or cost analysis, would in such a case be forced to the keeping of interest in supplementary records. Books which include interest are primarily adapted to the purposes of cost accounting, and the interest must be subtracted in making up the income account. . . . As between charging interest as a cost, and not charging it, the best system is probably the one which best promotes the development of this independent and untrammeled study of costs, and tends most to make accounting outgrow the attitude that cost is one thing for all purposes."
156. Scovell, p. 118. The italics are Scovell's.
157. This included inventories, accounts receivable, and plant and equipment. The interest on accounts receivable, however, was a selling expense.

158. A. Hamilton Church, *Manufacturing Costs and Accounts* (New York: Mc-Graw-Hill Book Company, 1917), p. 394.

159. *Ibid.*, p. 393.

160. *The Accountant* (1918), p. 249.

161. *Ibid.*, p. 322.

162. A. E. Goodwin, "Principles and Practices of Correct Costing," *The Accountant*, March 20, 1920, p. 342.

163. *Supra*, p. 152.

164. Hawkins, p. 113. Hawkins was an Englishman.

165. Hawkins, p. 114.

166. Elbourne, p. 529.

167. Elbourne, p. 575.

168. J. Lee Nicholson and J. D. Rohrbach, *Cost Accounting* (New York: The Ronald Press Company, 1919), p. 139.

169. Jordan and Harris, pp. 428-443.

170. See *Papers and Proceedings of the Third Annual Meeting*, 1918, pp. 12-40.

171. *American Institute of Accountants Yearbook*, 1918, p. 112.

172. *1921 Year Book of the National Association of Cost Accountants*, pp. 45-96.

173. A summary of the results is given in C. H. Scovell, *Interest As A Cost* (New York: The Ronald Press Company, 1924), pp. 122-123.

174. Scovell's views have already been treated *supra*.

175. G. H. Newlove, *Cost Accounting*, second preliminary edition (Washington: The White Press Company, 1928), p. 289. It should be specifically noted, however, that this authority insisted upon the establishment of a valuation reserve (whenever imputed interest was included in the cost of production) in order to avoid an "anticipation of profits due to inflation of the goods in process and finished goods inventories." The valuation reserve (Reserve for Interest on Investment) was to be deducted from the inventories on the balance sheet, and was to be in an amount sufficient to reduce the inventory figures to what they would have been if no imputed interest had been charged. See also his pp. 39-40.

Part III

176. J. H. Goodwin, *Improved Bookkeeping and Business Manual*, 4th ed. (New York: J. H. Goodwin, 1881), Section 90. See also J. C. Bryant, *"Bryant's New Book-keeping*, 6th ed. (Buffalo: Published by the author, 1880), pp. 161-9.

177. Metcalfe, p. 289.

178. Norton, p. 271.

179. See *The Accountant* (1897), p. 604. Broaker was the first Certified Public Accountant in the United States. His certificate was issued by New York State.

180. Lewis, p. 492.

181. Lewis, p. 475.

182. See H. L. Arnold, *The Factory Manager and Accountant* (New York: The Engineering Magazine Press, 1903), *passim*.

183. *The Accountant* (1901), p. 1251. Cowan was an Englishman.

184. Church, *The Engineering Magazine*, XXII, 236. Church did most of his writing in this country. He came to the United States from England about 1900.

185. Eddis and Tindall, p. 33.

186. Eddis and Tindall, p. 25.

187. Glenn H. Frost, "Cost Accounting," *The Business World* (October, 1905). H. C. M. Vedder, "Cost Accounting: An Exposition of Its Theories and Principles," *The Accountant*, Nov. 11, 1905. Vedder was an American professor and accountant.

188. H. Deighton, "Cost System of an Engineering Works," *The Engineering Magazine*, XXIX (1905), 55. Deighton was an American.

189. Knoeppel, *The Engineering Magazine*, XXXII, 920.

190. *Ibid.*, p. 923.

191. John Whitmore, in 1906, referred to an account which he termed "general expense credit." While its use seemed to have had some relation to the present day burden—credit, or burden applied, account, one connot be too sure of such a conclusion in view of his somewhat vague description. The "general expenses" were those charges which were not peculiar to the machinery used in a department of a factory, or which were not peculiar to any special division of the factory. As to the operation of the account, he stated:

> It will be noticed that these debits (departmental general expenses and factory general expenses) to the cost accounts are not posted from a statement previously compiled, but originate in the cost ledgers. It is therefore necessary to create a record of them, and this is done by having an account in the cost ledgers headed general expense credits, and when the debits are made in the cost accounts, corresponding credits are made in this general expense credits account in the cost ledger, and the total of them is thence journalized for the general ledger, as follows:
>
> Manufacturing Account_____xxx
> To General Expense Credit Account_____xxx

So we have a general expense credit account in the general ledger also. *The Journal of Accountancy*, III, 31. Whitmore did not elaborate upon this account, nor did he give any further details as to how it would be handled on either the cost ledger or the general ledger. From the model journal entry given above, however, one would suppose that he had in mind a type of burden applied account.

192. Webner, *The Engineering Magazine*, XXXVI, 79.

193. Webner's later views will be discussed *post*. It will be remembered that Vedder, in 1905, had recommended the use of an account with the same title. Vedder also gave considerable detail as to its use. See *supra*, p. 165.

194. B. A. Franklin, *Cost Reports for Executives* (New York: The Engineering Magazine Press, 1912), p. 111.

195. Although not peculiarly concerned with the topic of burden control accounts, Franklin devoted a paragraph to a topic which is more or less basic to control accounts in general, and thus should be quoted here:

> . . . the best way to build a cost system is from the totals down to the details, and not from the details up to the totals. The former is the logical way for many reasons. It is easier to obtain the totals and to prove them correct, thus obtaining a sure foundation to build on. It is a difficult and discouraging task to gather a great mass of details and prove them with totals, and where this has been undertaken it has usually resulted in the rendering of presumed, but unproven, costs of articles without those values of cost control which are essential to a good system. But if the system starts with the totals of the three general elements—materials, labor, and expense—as proven with the accounting; divides these into sub-totals, and these into still other subdivisions, as circumstances and conditions of organization, of departments and divisions

thereof, and of articles of manufacture demand, then the preceding follows from proof to proof, and from significant total to detailed analysis as is desired.

Franklin, p. 144.

196. H. C. Bentley, *The Science of Accounts* (New York: The Ronald Press Company, 1911), p. 203.

197. L. H. Bosher, "Controlling Accounts in Cost Accounting," *The Journal of Accountancy*, XIII (1912).

198. *Ibid.*, p. 414.

199. J. L. Nicholson, *Cost Accounting—Theory and Practice* (New York: The Ronald Press Company, 1913), p. 197.

200. Scovell, *Cost Accounting*, 1916, p. 194.

201. The substance of the *Bulletin* was given in *The Accountant* (1917), p. 411.

202. C. E. Woods, *Unified Accounting Methods for Industrials* (New York: The Ronald Press Company, 1917), p. 312.

203. F. E. Webner, *Factory Accounting* (Chicago: LaSalle Extension University, 1917), p. 328.

204. Church, *Manufacturing Costs*, p. 310.

205. C. M. Bigelow, "Installing Management Methods in the Woodworking Industry," *Industrial Management*, LVIII (1919), 470.

206. Described by G. L. Harris, *N.A.C.A. Bulletin*, May, 1920, p. 13.

207. D. C. Eggleston, *Cost Accounting* (New York: The Ronald Press Company, 1920), p. 284.

208. Jordan and Harris, p. 247.

209. *Loc. cit.*

210. Jordan and Harris, p. 302.

211. G. H. Newlove, "Manufacturing Accounts," *The Journal of Accountancy*, XXXI (1921), 185.

212. *Ibid.*, p. 186. The same technique was more fully described in his *Cost Accounts*, 3rd ed. (Washington: The White Press Company, 1923), pp. 72-74. This discussion included entries and accounts.

213. Cf. L. W. Hawkins, *Cost Accounts*, 4th ed., 1920.

214. Elbourne, p. 570.

215. Elbourne, pp. 569-570.

216. D. C. Eggleston and F. B. Robinson, *Business Costs* (New York: D. Appleton and Company, 1921), p. 278.

217. Later authorities customarily gave adequate description of both the control accounts for actual burden as well as burden applied accounts. See particularly A. F. Wagner, "Cost Systems and Operating Statistics," *The Journal of Accountancy*, XXXIV (1922), 200; W. B. Castenholz, *Cost Accounting Procedure* (Chicago: LaSalle Extension University, 1922), p. 173; and G. L. Harris, "Calculation, Distribution and Application of Burden," *Management and Administration*, VI (1923), 525. Not all authorities are convinced, however, that the burden applied account should be used,

218. James L. Dohr, *Cost Accounting* (New York: The Ronald Press Company, 1924), p. 102.

219. Dohr, pp. 217-218.

Part IV

220. C. B. Thompson, *How to Find Factory Costs* (Chicago: A. W. Shaw Company, 1916), p. 105.

221. See *The Accountant*, XCVII, 284.

222. *Engineer,* Dec. 23, 1870.   Referred to in *The Accountant,* XCVII, 284.

223. See Chapter II.

224. Battersby wrote in 1878.   See *The Accountant,* XCVII, 286.

225. F. H. Carter, *Practical Bookkeeping,* 2nd ed. (Edinburgh: Simpkin, Marshall, Hamilton, Kent and Company, 1874), *passim.*   Carter was a Scottish Accountant.

226. See Nef, *op. cit.* (above, note 35), *passim.*

227. Metcalfe, p. 73.

228. Metcalfe, p. 329.

229. Metcalfe, p. 338.

230. Metcalfe, p. 352.

231. Garcke and Fells, p. 70.

232. Garcke and Fells, p. 74.

233. G. L. Fowler in *Transactions,* IX (1888), 393.

234. Norton, p. 254.

235. A General Manager, *Engineering Estimates, Costs and Accounts,* 3rd ed. (London: C. Lockwood and Son, 1911), p. 53. (First edition, 1890.)

236. Cf. *The Accountant,* XCVII, 343.   B. C. Bean, *Cost of Production* (Chicago: A. W. Shaw Company, 1905), stated, however that the machine rate plan was the oldest of any burden allocation methods, predating even the direct labor cost basis, and the direct labor time basis.   According to him, the machine hour method originated "before modern methods of accounting and not conforming to them." (p. 63.) Bean did not give the source of his information, and may have been relying upon personal memory of actual conditions.   The present writer, however, disagrees with Bean as to which was first, and prefers the historical development described in this chapter.

237. *The Accountant* (1894), p. 702.   This is an English publication.

258. See Chapter II, *supra.*

239. It may be mentioned that both F. A. Halsey in this country, and F. G. Burton in England, recommended the use of the direct wage cost basis of allocation. For the former see *Transactions American Society of Mechanical Engineers,* XV (1894), 628; for the latter see *Engineering Estimates and Cost Accounts,* 2nd ed. (Manchester: Technical Publishing Company, 1900), p. 11. (First edition, 1895.)

240. Lewis, p. 174.   Lewis was an Englishman.

241. Lewis, p. 185.

242. Lewis, p. 186.

243. Even under his preferred prime cost system Lewis recommended that whenever an addition was made to a factory by the firm's own force of men, a proper proportion of the establishment charges should be taken out of the establishment charges account by means of a credit through the general journal.   The debit, of course, would be to the plant account.   Lewis did not state, however, how to arrive at a "proper proportion." *Ibid.,* p. 383.   Regular factory orders were not to be touched, though, even when they were completed.

244. Lewis, p. 189.

245. Lane in *Transactions,* XVIII (1897), 893.   This was not the first proposal of this sort, however.   As early as 1891 the editor of *Engineering* was advocating a fixed charge per hour for the use of each piece of equipment.   This was to be handled through a "plant charge book." See *Engineering,* (1891), 665.

246. Oberlin Smith, in some comments on Lane's paper, recommended the same technique. *Transactions*, XVIII (1897), 895.
247. The problem of idle time will be considered in a later section.
248. Halsey in *Transactions*, XIX (1898), 398.
249. *Loc. cit.*
250. Norris, *The Engineering Magazine*, XVI, 396.
251. E. Andrade, "Manufacturing Cost Accounts, Their Use and Treatment," *The Accountant*, Feb. 11, 1899, p. 170.
252. G. E. Goode, "Methods of Ascertaining Costs in a Factory," *The Accountant*, June 30, 1900, p. 606.
253. See MacNaughton, pp. 25-26.
254. H. L. Arnold, *The Complete Cost-Keeper*, p. 18.
255. A "Mr. Foote."
256. Arnold, *The Complete Cost-Keeper*, p. 19.
257. *Ibid.*, p. 49.
258. Church, *The Engineering Magazine*, XXI, 911.
259. One English observer has stated: "When I first entered the business [about 1902], this system [Church's] was in its first full flush of enthusiasm. It was developed and refined over the next few years until it became quite unmanageable. "Sir Charles Renold, "Management Accounts," *The Cost Accountant*, XXIX (1950), 113.
260. David Cowan, "Administration of Workshops; With Special References to Oncost," *The Accountant*, Nov. 16, 1901, p. 1249.
261. *Ibid.*, p. 1247.
262. *Ibid.*, p. 1250.
263. Eddis and Tindall, p. 77.
264. Sir John Mann, *Encyclopaedia of Accounting*, V, 207.
265. Hall, pp. 115-117.
266. Hall, p. 126. These will be described in more detail on a later page.
267. J. H. Whitmore, *The Journal of Accountancy*, III, 21-30.
268. C. E. Knoeppel, "Systematic Foundry Operation and Foundry Costing," *The Engineering Magazine*, XXXVI (1908), 215.
269. Gershom Smith, *The Engineering Magazine*, XXXVII, 389-391.
270. Nicholson, *Factory Organization*, p. 55.
271. *Ibid.*, p. 48.
272. A. Hamilton Church, "Organisation by Production Factors," *The Engineering Magazine*, XXXVIII (1909). Reprinted in *Production Factors in Cost Accounting and Works Management*, op. cit. (above, note 68).
273. Church, *Production Factors*, p. 150.
274. Church, p. 153.
275. Webner, *Factory Costs*, p. 245.
276. J. L. Nicholson had called this the "new pay rate" method. See page 193 of this section.
277. Webner, *Factory Costs*, p. 244.
278. F. L. Small, *Accounting Methods* (Boston: L. and S. Printing Company, 1914), p. 131.
279. Garry, *Multiple Cost Accounts*, Chapter VII; Nisbet, Chapter III; Hawkins, Chapter VIII; and Garry, *Process Cost Accounts*, Chapter V.
280. L.R. Dicksee, *Advanced Accounting*, 4th ed. (London: Gee and Company, 1911), p. 242.
281. For instance, George Lisle, *Accounting in Theory and Practice*, revised edition (Edinburgh: William Green and Sons, 1909), p. 261.

282. Taylor's modified plan has been described in several places. See, for example, Keely, *Journal American Society of Mechanical Engineers*, June 1913, p. 986.
283. C. H. Scovell, "Cost Accounting Practice, With Special Reference to Machine Hour Rate," *The Journal of Accountancy*, XVII (1914), 20. Scovell's speech was also printed in the *N. A. C. A. Bulletin*, June 1, 1927.
284. Webner, *Factory Accounting*, p. 212. Webner wrote in this country.
285. William Kent, *Bookkeeping and Cost Accounting for Factories* (New York: John Wiley and Sons, 1918), p. 78. Kent was an American engineer who had previously made some important contributions in his "New Methods of Determining Factory Costs," *Iron Age*, Aug. 24, 1916, Vol. 98, pp. 392-394.
286. D. C. Eggleston, *Problems in Cost Accounting* (New York: D. Appleton and Company, 1918), p. 131.
287. *Ibid.*, p. 232.
288. G. Charter Harrison, "Cost Accounting to Aid Production," *Industrial Management*, LVII (1919), 49. Harrison was born in London, England, but moved to the United States about 1905. He has been a Management Consultant since 1918.
289. G. Charter Harrison, "Bugbear of Burden Distribution; A Plan to Eliminate Its Work and Worry," *Management and Administration*, VI (1923), 49.
290. See also Harrison's *New Wine in Old Bottles* (New York: Privately printed, 1937), *passim*, for another criticism of cost practices.
291. Elbourne, Section VI (F).
292. A comparatively recent monograph by F. B. Makin, *op. cit.* (above, note 93), should not be overlooked. It represents the more modern English viewpoint on the overhead problem. It deals to some extent, also, with differential costs, fixed and varying costs, and the question of idle capacity.
293. Church, *Overhead Expense;* and Clark, *The Economics of Overhead Costs.* Cf., also, F. E. Webner, *Factory Overhead* (Washington: The White Press Company, 1924).

Part V

294. Certain English economists, however, had noted that there was a perplexing problem involved in connection with idle time. Robert Torrens, for instance as early as 1834, stated: "It is self-evident that, amid the ebbings and flowings of the markets and the alternate expansions and contractions of demand occasions will constantly recur in which the manufacturer may employ additional floating capital without employing additional fixed capital . . . if additional quantities of raw material can be worked up without incurring an additional expense for buildings and machinery." *On Wages and Combinations* (London: 1834), p. 63. And Nassau Senior noted that "there are certain expenses upon a mill which go on in the same proportion whether the mill be running short or full time." *Report of the Inspectors of Factories*, Oct. 31, 1862, p. 19.
295. Battersby, p. 34. Referred to in *The Accountant*, XCVII, 284.
296. Garcke and Fells, *Factory Accounts, passim*.
297. Norton, p. 258.
298. Alphonse Perrin, "'The Development of Cost Accounting in Europe," *N.A. C.A. Bulletin*, XXIV (1944), 1062.
299. Metcalfe, p. 166.
300. Fowler, *Transactions*, IX, 393. Fowler was an American.
301. *Ibid.*, p. 393.
302. *The Accountant* (1894), p. 702.
303. Burton, p. 49.

304. "A General Manager" had made the same observation in 1890: "A remark that applies . . . and that is sufficiently obvious, is that these percentages will be higher when there is little doing than when business is good." *Engineering Estimates, Costs, and Accounts* (1890), p. 53. This work is not at hand. The quotation is given in *The Accountant*, XCVII, 343. The "percentages" referred to were direct wage percentages.
305. Burton, p. 49.
306. F. G. Burton, *Engineers' and Shipbuilders' Accounts*, 2nd. ed. (London: Gee and Company, 1911), p. 92. (First edition, 1902.) Kent, *Bookkeeping and Cost Accounting for Factories*, p. 80, accused Burton of entirely ignoring idle time, but, of course, that criticism was not altogether valid.
307. Oberlin Smith in *Transactions*, XVIII (1897), 893. Smith was an American engineer.
308. *Ibid.*, pp. 839, 387.
309. *Ibid.*, p. 897.
310. *Ibid.*, p. 897. This quotation is illustrative of the cost thinking of the period.
311. *Ibid.*, p. 400.
312. See A. C. Littleton, *Accounting Evolution to 1900* (New York: American Institute Publishing Company, 1933), p. 351; and DR Scott, *The Cultural Significance of Accounts* (New York: Henry Holt and Company, 1916), pp. 140-150.
313. It is an interesting commentary that Arnold's *The Complete Cost-Keeper* and *The Factory Manager and Accountant,* although being concerned with the cost accounting actually used by some fifteen American manufacturing firms of the day, mentioned only once the method by which one of the firms handled the problem of idle time. The technique mentioned, moreover, was rather superficial.
314. G. S. Gibb, *The Saco-Lowell Shops* (Cambridge: Harvard University Press, 1950), pp. 130, 429.
315. Alfred P. Sloan, Jr., *Adventures of a White-Collar Man,* (New York: Doubleday, Doran and Company, 1941), pp. 73-76.
316. Church, *The Engineering Magazine*, XXI, 908.
317. *Loc. cit.*
318. *Loc. cit.*
319. *Ibid.*, p. 911.
320. Church, *The Engineering Magazine*, XXII, 39. For a convincing criticism of Church's system see Sir Charles Renold, *op. cit.* (note 259, above), pp. 113-116.
321. In addition to the English authorities discussed above, it should be noted that MacNaughton mentioned that idle time was an important aspect of costing paper in a paper mill. He was more concerned, however, with the lost time caused by washing the machines or passing from one make to another. See MacNaughton, p. 26.
322. Cowan, *The Accountant*, Nov. 16, 1901, p. 1252.
323. *Loc. cit.*
324. *Loc. cit.*
325. H. S. Garry, "Factory Costs," *The Accountant*, July 25, 1903, p. 957.
326. *Ibid.*, p. 959.
327. Sir John Mann in *The Encyclopaedia of Accounting*, V, 210.
328. *Ibid.*, p. 212.
329. *Ibid.*, p. 212.
330. *Ibid.*, p. 202.
331. Stanley Pedder, "Cost Accounts; Their Advantages and Their Relations to

Business Results," *The Accountant,* Apr. 29, 1905, p. 526. A. G. Nisbet, p. 22, made the same distinction.

332. *The Accountant* (1905), p. 729.

333. *Loc. cit.*

334. Garry, *Multiple Cost Accounts,* p. 43; Nisbet, p. 22; Spencer, p. 150; Mitchell, p. 74; and Garry, *Process Cost Accounts,* p. 88. Nisbet was particularly emphatic in stating that the burden rate should be determined in advance of the end of a fiscal period, based upon past experiences, rather than estimated future conditions. He thought the former to be a more accurate procedure in that the firm would not have to predict what it would incur the coming year. Also, Nisbet could see only confusion resulting from preparing each month, or even more often, the shop expense account, as the editor of *The Accountant* had suggested. In summary, "the past year's figures are taken as a basis for tendering and as a basis for costing during the year, on the assumption that it is more correct to work on actual figures of a previous year than estimated figures for the current." Nisbet, p. 23. This last statement is in direct contradiction to the editor's views.

335. O. N. Manners in *System,* (1904), p. 238.

336. Whitmore, *The Journal of Accountancy,* II, 255.

337. *Ibid.,* p. 255.

338. *Ibid.,* p. 257.

339. *Ibid.,* p. 438.

340. *Ibid.,* p. 21.

341. A. A. Murdoch, "Proper Treatment of Machine Costs: A Criticism and a Theory," *The Journal of Accountancy,* III (1906), 127.

342. Whitmore gave his rebuttal in a later issue of *The Journal of Accountancy* in "Some Details of Machine Shop Cost," III (1907), 294, insisting that his technique was entirely practicable.

343. D. C. Eggleston, "System of Factory Cost Accounting," *The Journal of Accountancy,* III (1906), 121.

344. P. J. Darlington, "Developing New Products and Determining Shop Cost," *The Engineering Magazine,* XXXV (1908), 65.

345. *Supra,* p. 216.

346. See C. E. Knoeppel, "Graphic Production Control," *Industrial Management,* LVII (1919), 57. J. P. Jordan and W. J. Gunnell had also considered the under or over absorbed burden to be a profit and loss item as early as 1906. See Jordan and Harris, p. 398.

347. Gershom Smith, *The Engineering Magazine,* XXXVII, 389.

348. But if Smith had used exactly the same practice in 1902 in The Pennsylvania Steel Company (the company for which he worked), and he indicated that he had, he was probably one of the first to adopt the principle that idle time was a loss instead of a cost. Kent, *Bookkeeping,* p. 80, stated that Smith was the first to use the theory mentioned. A sharp controversy arose a few years later as to just who was the first; this controversy is examined later in this section.

349. Nicholson, *Factory Organization and Costs,* p. 55.

350. *Cyclopedia of Accounting* (Chicago: American Technical Society, 1909), p. 186.

351. Henry R. Hatfield, *Modern Accounting* (New York: D. Appleton and Company, 1909), p. 304.

352. *Loc. cit.*

353. William Kent in *Iron Trade Review,* Feb. 4, 1909. Kent was a consulting engineer (American).

354. Kent, *Bookkeeping*, p. 243.

355. Church, *Production Factors*, p. 121. The substance of this book had been presented, however, in the latter part of 1909, in *The Engineering Magazine*.

356. *Loc. cit.*

357. Church, p. 153.

358. *Loc. cit.*

359. *Loc. cit.*

360. In order to show the inconclusive character of his 1910 views, however, and to illustrate that he was not in sympathy with most of his critics, the following might be quoted: "It must never be forgotten that the supplementary rate, the moment it rises above the normal, represents shop inefficiency. It represents *that portion of the cost of the job* which is due to abnormal conditions. Church, p. 184. (Italics supplied.)

361. Rowe, p. 229. Rowe was an American.

362. J. R. Wildman, *Cost Accounting Problems* (New York: The Accountancy Publishing Company, 1910), p. 62.

363. Wildman, p. 88.

364. Bentley, p. 231.

365. C. H. Scovell in *1913 Annual Report of the National Association of Machine Tool Builders*, and in *The Iron Age*, Oct. 30, 1913. Scovell's speech can also be found in *N.A.C.A. Bulletin*, June 1, 1927, pp.889-893; and in *The Journal of Accountancy*, XVII (1914), 21.

366. See particularly Scovell, *Cost Accounting and Burden Application, passim.*

367. Webner, *Factory Costs*, p. 242.

368. H. A. Evans, *Cost-Keeping and Scientific Management* (New York: Mc-Graw-Hill Book Company, 1911), p. 48. Obviously, he meant some kind of a reserve account or an under or over applied burden account. Evans was an American.

369. Hawkins, p. 26. The 1912 edition contained practically the same description as the first edition, 1905.

370. Dicksee, p. 342.

371. S. H. Bunnell in the *Journal American Society of Mechanical Engineers* (1912), p. 544.

372. S. H. Bunnell, *Cost-Keeping in Manufacturing Plants* (New York: D. Appleton and Company, 1911), p. 161. Bunnell's early views are also to be found in "Standardizing Factory Expense and Cost," *Iron Age*, Nov. 16, 1911.

373. Nicholson, *Cost Accounting*, p. 67.

374. Moxey, p. 86.

375. See *supra*, p. 218.

376. *The Accountant* (1913), pp. 392, 469.

377. Jenkinson did say, however, that it should be based on the amount of work which should be done during the year as indicated by previous records.

378. Jenkinson in *The Accountant*, Apr. 18, 1914, p. 569.

379. H. L. Gantt in *Transactions*, XXXVII (1915), 115-20.

380. *Loc. cit.*

381. Ficker, *The Engineering Magazine*, L, 390.

382. *Ibid.*, p. 390.

383. *Ibid.*, 1916, p. 538.

384. F. C. Belser was not so indefinite. He recommended that no unabsorbed burden be carried forward from one year to another. It should be carried forward, however, from one month to another. "Cost Accounting for Fertilizer Manufacturers," *The Journal of Accountancy*, XIX (1915), 172.

385. H. L. Gantt, "Production and Sales," *The Engineering Magazine*, L (1916) 599.
386. Gantt wrote as though practically nothing had been said on the subject in previous years; he seemed unfamiliar especially with the work of C. H. Scovell and William Kent. In fact, Scovell took care in a footnote to his *Cost Accounting and Burden Application*, to state that "in view of certain articles, put forth in the fall of 1915, by a well-known engineer [evidentally Scovell meant Gantt], apparently taking credit for the discovery or first statement of this principle [that is, that idle time was a loss and not a cost], the author [Scovell] wishes to state that he made practical and effective applications of the idea in the spring of 1911, and gave it wide publicity in an address before the National Association of Machine Tool Builders on October 13, 1913." (p. 71.) But Scovell had been anticipated by several years by a half dozen authorities. See, for example, Gershom Smith, *supra*, p. 222. Also, according to the editor of *The Engineering Magazine*, Gantt and Ficker did not know of each other's work; yet each pointed out the same fundamental defect in most of the then existing cost systems, and in the same issue of the same publication—a rather remarkable coincidence. See the Introduction to N. T. Ficker's *Shop Expense Analysis* (New York: The Engineering Magazine Press, 1917), for the editor's statement.
387. R. E. Flanders in *Transactions*, XXXVII (1915), 122.
388. *Loc. cit.*
389. W. E. McHenry, "Is Your Cost System Scientific?" *The Engineering Magazine*, LI (1916), 686. McHenry was an American.
390. See particularly Emerson, *The Engineering Magazine*, XXXVI, 173; and Garry, *The Accountant*, July 25, 1903, p. 956.
391. The pamphlet said "trading account." This bulletin is not at hand; the substance of it was reprinted in *The Accountant* (1917), p. 411.
392. D. S. Kimball, *Cost Finding* (New York: Alexander Hamilton Institute, 1918), p. 244.
393. Kimball, p. 247.
394. Kimball, p. 248.
395. Church, *Manufacturing Costs*, pp. 348-54.
396. Kent, *Bookkeeping and Cost Accounting*, p. 81.
397. Cathles, *The Accountant*, Feb. 28, 1920, p. 255.
398. C. S. Hattersley, "Costing," *The Accountant*, May 28, 1921, p. 685.
399. Elbourne, p. 551.
400. *Loc. cit.*
401. By 1920, L. W. Hawkins, another English cost authority, was also recommending standard overhead rates. These were to be based on "normal trade conditions." Hawkins, however, was not so explicit as to details as Elbourne. See his *Cost Accounts*, p. 82.
402. Cf. (Author not given) *International Accountants Society Textbook*, pp. 12 (58); 13 (58); Jordan and Harris, p. 219; Nicholson and Rohrbach, p. 182; Eggleston and Robinson, p. 282; Dohr, pp. 396-413.
403. Cf. G. W. Greenwood, "On What Should Selling Prices Be Based?" *Administration*, III (1922), 508; and C. B. Williams, "Treatment of Overhead When Production is Below Normal," *The Journal of Accountancy*, XXXI (1921), 339.
404. See, e. g., A. F. Stock and J. M. Goffey in *N.A.C.A. Bulletin*, Feb. 16, 1925.
405. Church, *Overhead Expense*, p. 383.

Part VI

406. It is not clear just what is meant by that statement. See *The Engineer*, XXX (Dec. 23, 1870), p. 428 or *The Accountant*, XCVII, 284.
407. Battersby, pp. 34-43. See also *The Accountant*, XCVII, 285.
408. Battersby's views are discussed more at length in Chapter II.
409. Metcalfe, p. 330; or *Transactions*, VII (1886), *passim*.
410. See Part IV, this Chapter.
411. Norton, p. 222.
412. Norton, p. 223.
413. Norton, p. 226.
414. Incidentally it may be noted that Norton's illustrations were all dated 1884, some five years before the first edition of his work was published. It may be that this book thus represents the techniques used in that earlier period, although Norton did not mention the reason for the predating of the entries and statements.
415. Burton, *Engineering Estimates*, p. 74.
416. F. G. Burton, *Engineers' and Shipbuilders' Accounts.*
417. Lewis, p. 178.
418. Arnold, *The Complete Cost-Keeper*, p. 188.
419. Church, *The Engineering Magazine*, XXI and XXII, *passim*.
420. See Spencer, p. 151; Garry, *Multiple Cost Accounts*, and *Process Cost Accounts, passim*.
421. Whitmore, *The Journal of Accountancy*, II and III, *passim*. See also H. Deighton, *The Engineering Magazine*, XXIX, 55.
422. Day, p. 140.
423. Nicholson, *Factory Organization*, p. 31.
424. Webner, *Factory Costs*, p. 213.
425. Nicholson, *Cost Accounting*, p. 48.
426. F. J. Knoeppel, "Industrial Accounting," *The Journal of Accountancy*, LII (1916), 94.
427. Webner, *Factory Accounting*, p. 340.
428. *Internationl Accountants Society Textbook*, p. 13 (53).
429. Elbourne, pp. 540-60.
430. Cf. L. W. Hawkins, *Cost Accounts*, 4th ed., 1920.
431. G. Charter Harrison, "Bugbear of Burden Distribution," *Magazine of Management and Administration*, VI (1923), p. 50. This was not the first criticism of this type. As early as 1910 an English accountant, W. R. Hamilton stated that it was easy to carry the distribution too far. See his "Some Economic Considerations Bearing on Costing," *The Accountant*, Feb. 5, 1910, pp. 200-206.
432. See particularly, E. A. Camman, *Basic Standard Costs* (New York: American Institute Publishing Company, 1932); and G. Charter Harrison, *Standard Costs* (New York: The Ronald Press Company, 1930).

CHAPTER VI

1. Henry Metcalfe, *The Cost of Manufactures* (New York: John Wiley and Son, 1885), p. 290.

2. Metcalfe, p. 289.
3. *Loc. cit.*
4. Emile Garcke and J. M. Fells, *Factory Accounts*, 4th ed. (London: Crosby, Lockwood and Son, 1893), p. 7. (First edition, 1887.)
5. Cf. A. C. Littleton, *Accounting Evolution to 1900* (New York: American Institute Publishing Company, 1933); p. 350.
6. F. R. Goddard, "Defalcations and How to Prevent Them," *The Accountants' Journal*, March 1, 1887.
7. G. P. Norton, *Textile Manufacturers' Bookkeeping*, 4th ed. (London: Simpkin, 1900), p. 219. (First edition, 1889.)
8. *Loc. cit.*
9. *The Accountant* (1894), p. 655.
10. *Loc. cit.* This statement reminds one of the intense controversy which has prevailed for the past decade or so in regard to the responsibility of accountants for inventory quantities and valuation. Valuation involves a still greater intimacy and familiarity with a company's products and records.
11. *The Accountant* (1894), p. 656.
12. He stated: "Costs should never be permitted to usurp the place of perfect double-entry financial records." F. G. Burton, *Engineering Estimates and Cost Accounts*, 2nd ed. (Manchester: Technical Publishing Company, 1900), p. 102. (First edition, 1895.)
13. Burton, p. 105.
14. Burton, p. 106.
15. J. Slater Lewis, *The Commercial Organisation of Factories* (London: E. and F. N. Spon, 1896), *passim*.
16. At the old Hotel Waldorf. The address was reported in *The Accountant*, 1897, p. 605. Broaker was the first Certified Public Accountant in the United States.
17. *Loc. cit.*
18. "The design and application of the consumption journal afford a magnificent field for the exercise of study and ingenuity, its form varying for every class of business. . . . The application of the consumption journal, the costing records, and double-entry control of the manufacturing records, involve no new mathematical problems . . . but bring into exercise those faculties which are most enjoyable for an accountant to employ and give additional emphasis to the words of John Locke, who said: 'The skill of keeping accounts is a business of reason more than arithmetic.' " *Loc. cit.*
19. The DeLaval Cream Separator Company.
20. E. Andrade, "Manufacturing Cost Accounts, Their Use and Treatment," *The Accountant*, Feb. 11, 1899, p. 171. Andrade was an English Chartered Accountant.
21. *The Acountant* (1900), p. 730.
22. G. Lisle, ed., *Encyclopaedia of Accounting* (London: William Green and Sons, 1903), II, 265.
23. L. W. Hawkins, *Cost Accounts* (London: Gee and Company, 1905); G. A. Mitchell, *Single Cost Accounts* (London: Gee and Company, 1907); H. S. Garry, *Multiple Cost Accounts* (London: Gee and Company, 1906), and *Process Cost Accounts* (London: Gee and Company, 1908); and W. Strachan, *Cost Accounts* (London: Stevens and Haynes, 1909).
24. Stanley Pedder, "Cost Accounts; Their Advantages and Their Relations to Business Results," *The Accountant*, Apr. 29, 1905, p. 519. The italics are supplied.
25. See, e.g., Garry, *Multiple Cost Accounts*, p. 10.

26. W. C. Eddis and W. B. Tindall, *Manufacturers' Accounts* (Toronto: Published by the authors, 1902), pp. 35-48.

27. The textual exposition stated that the trading account was debited (for the underapplied burden), but the illustration on pp. 104-5 indicated that the "manufactured stock" account was to be debited. It is the present writer's opinion that the illustration was in error, and that Eddis and Tindall preferred the treatment as given in the text.

28. J. E. Sterritt, "Cost Accounts," *The Accountant*, June 25, 1904, p. 836.

29. *Loc. cit.*

30. *Loc. cit.*

31. H. L. C. Hall, *Manufacturing Costs* (Detroit: The Bookkeeper Publishing Company, 1904), p. 79.

32. Glenn H. Frost, "Cost Accounting," *The Business World*, October, 1905, *passim*. H. C. M. Vedder, "Cost Accounting: An Exposition of Its Theories and Principles," *The Accountant*, Nov. 11, 1905, p. 545. A criticism of the article, on account of its generalities, can be found in *The Accountant*, 1905, p. 568.

33. John Whitmore, "Factory Accounting As Applied to Machine Shops," *The Journal of Accountancy*, II (1906), 345.

34. A. Hamilton Church, "Proper Distribution of Establishment Charges," *The Engineering Magazine*, XXI and XXII (1901), *passim*.

35. C. M. Day, *Accounting Practice* (New York: D. Appleton and Company, 1908), p. 101.

36. H. M. Rowe, however, was one who still insisted that the cost books and records should be maintained separate and distinct from the commercial or financial ledgers, even though they might be interwoven along certain nondescribed lines. See his *Bookkeeping and Accountancy* (Baltimore: The H. M. Rowe Company, 1910), p. 202. In addition, A. Hamilton Church, in spite of his pronouncement that the financial accounts were the control accounts while the cost accounts were the detailed accounts, proceeded to show a trading account in which the sales and costs were entered; that is, he did not even use a work in process account. In general, Church, even though he had a whole chapter of his *Production Factors* devoted to "Costs and the Financial Books," treated the present topic with much less originality and care than his contemporaries. See his *Production Factors* (New York: The Engineering Magazine Company, 1910), pp. 163-180.

37. F. S. Small, *Accounting Methods* (Boston: L. and S. Printing Company, 1914), p. 15.

38. Strachan, *op. cit.* (above, note 23), p. 41.

39. Hawkins, *Cost Accounts*, *passim*.

40. See especially the fourth edition of L. W. Hawkins, *Cost Accounts*, *passim*.

41. L. R. Dicksee, *Advanced Accounting*, 4th ed. (London: Gee and Company, 1911), p. 249.

42. M. W. Jenkinson, "Some Principles of Accounting Affecting Cost Accounts," *The Accountant*, 1914, p. 576.

43. In addition to those already mentioned, the work of F. E. Webner should be noted. His system contemplated the full integration of the cost and financial records and ledgers. See his *Factory Costs* (New York: The Ronald Press Company, 1911), *passim*.

44. E. P. Moxey, *Factory Cost Keeping* (New York: The Ronald Press Company, 1913), p. 17.

45. J. Lee Nicholson, *Cost Accounting* (New York: The Ronald Press Company, 1913), pp. 120-128.

46. Stephen Gilman, "What the Executive Should Know About Costs." *Industrial Management*, LIII (1917), 669. Gilman is an American.

47. Strangely enough, very few references were made to Nicholson's reciprocal account arrangement until well up into the 1920's; for some reason it was almost entirely ignored, or dismissed as being too complicated, until around 1925. One exception, however, was G. H. Newlove, who gave model journal entries for both the general ledger and the factory ledger in his *Cost Accounts* (Washington: The White Press Company, 1921), *passim*. See also D. C. Eggleston and F. B. Robinson, *Business Costs* (New York: D. Appleton and Company, 1921), pp. 390-4.

48. Nicholson, it will be remembered, suggested only the "cost" technique.

49. The cost-of-sales term was more inclusive than the first.

50. William Kent, *Bookkeeping and Cost Accounting for Factories* (New York: John Wiley and Sons, 1918), p. 35. Kent did not mention what type of inventory he had in mind.

51. E. T. Elbourne, *Factory Administration and Cost Accounts* (London: Longmans, Green and Company, 1921), p. 570.

52. Elbourne, p. 19.

53. James L. Dohr, *Cost Accounting* (New York: The Ronald Press Company, 1924), p. 140.

54. Cf., e.g., Newlove, *op. cit.* (above, note 47), p. 107.

55. As a matter of interest, the opinion of an economist in regard to the coördination of the cost and the financial records may be cited here as illustrative of a different point of view from that taken by most cost accountants. J. M. Clark states, for example, that the

> . . . Costs as reported in the cost accounts shall agree with the costs as set down in the general books from which the income account and the balance sheet are made up. This is not absolutely necessary, but is extremely convenient, and furnishes a valuable check. And yet, as we have already seen, if cost accounting includes interest it must be excluded again before making up the income account. So far as operating expenses go, the cost accounts can be made to check with the general books, but they need to be free on particular occasions and for particular purposes to do something more than this. Wherever the cost accountant uses a standard or normal burden rate instead of the actual burden, this agreement between cost accounts and financial accounts becomes rather nominal. The sum of the actual financial costs of the business is one thing, the sum of the cost-accounting "costs" of the different products (including the "normal" burden, not the actual) is a different thing, and the books are balanced by setting down the discrepancy as a discrepancy, calling it "unabsorbed burden" or "over-absorbed burden" as the case may be. The wide differences of opinion as to how this discrepancy should be treated are evidence that the tying together of these two kinds of costs is a union of two essentially different things.

J. M. Clark, *The Economics of Overhead Costs* (Chicago: The University of Chicago Press, 1923), p. 243. It should be noted that Clark used the term "cost accounts."

56. Katsuji Yamashita, "Evolution of the Third Form of the Profit and Loss Accounting System." *Kokumin-Keizai Zasshi*, LXXXIII, No. 4 (April, 1951), 15.

CHAPTER VII

1. G. P. Norton, *Textile Manufacturers' Bookkeeping,* 4th ed. (London: Simp-kin, 1900), pp. 219-20. (First edition, 1889.)
2. Norton referred to the trade price as a "standard price," but of course he did not have in mind the modern connotation of "standard." *Ibid.,* p. 222.
3. *The Encyclopaedia of Accounting* (London: William Green and Sons, 1903), V, 2, 1. The article was unsigned, but the editor, George Lisle, advocated the same technique in his *Accounting in Theory and Practice,* rev. ed. (Edin-burgh: William Green and Sons, 1909), p. 255. (First edition, 1899.) It is thus very probable that he was the author of the section in *The Encyclo-paedia of Accounting.*
4. *Ibid.,* pp. 1 ,2.
5. *Ibid.,* p. 3.
6. This whole concept has had an interesting history. The final outcome, of course, was the gradual introduction of standard costing arrangements. For the British viewpoint at a later date, see several editorials in *The Accountant* (1912), *passim.*
7. H. Stanley Garry, *Process Cost Accounts* (London: Gee and Company, 1908), *passim.* Garry was an Englishman.
8. For the sake of completeness it might be noted here that C. E. Knoeppel, in 1908, had adopted the theory or idea that in a machine shop, which also included a foundry, the foundry should be considered independent of the machine shop, and should "sell" its castings to the shop at "market rates" (his terms). He did not mention, however, what should be done with any of the interdepartmental profits which might be involved. See his "Graphic Production Control," *Industrial Management,* LVII (1919), 56.
9. L. R. Dicksee, *Advanced Accounting,* 4th ed. (London: Gee and Company, 1911), p. 236.
10. *Loc. cit.* Italics supplied.
11. F. E. Webner, *Factory Costs* (New York: The Ronald Press Company, 1911), p. 280.
12. Webner, p. 279.
13. J. Lee Nicholson, *International Text* (New York: International Textbook Company, 1913), Section 20, p. 46.
14. F. S. Small, *Accounting Methods* (Boston: L. and S. Printing Company, 1914), p. 18.
15. See, e. g., the opinions given in *The Accountant* (1915), p. 186.
16. M. W. Jenkinson, "Some Principles of Accounting Affecting Cost Accounts," *The Accountant* (1914), pp. 573-577.
17. See, e. g., E. W. Newman, "Functions of Costing," *The Accountant,* Mar. 19, 1921, p. 335.
18. This was essentially the proposition which M. W. Jenkinson had in mind. Jenkinson's technique has already been discussed.
19. *N.A.C.A. Bulletin,* Apr. 15, 1922. F. E. Webner had also mentioned the doctrine in 1917, but had refused to give it his recommendation. Webner did mention, however, that the meat packing industry was then using it. He referred to it as the "utilitarian cost" transfer technique. See his *Factory Accounting* (Chicago: La Salle Extension University, 1917), p. 186.
20. James H. Bliss, *N.A.C.A. Bulletin,* Apr. 15, 1922, *passim.*
21. James L. Dohr, *Cost Accounting* (New York: The Ronald Press Company, 1924), p. 118.

CHAPTER VIII

1. This term is fairly old. In addition to the references cited in this chapter, see E. Acton, *English Breadbaking*, II (1857), 95, where it was stated: "German yeast . . . in many distilleries forms an important by-product." Cf., also, *The Standard*, for Aug. 24, 1882, where a reference was made to the "by-products of gas manufacture."

2. As a matter of interest, John Arch White, in his *Accounting for By-Products* (an unpublished master's thesis presented to the University of Texas, 1930), made a distinction between what he called "by-products" and "co-products," which, although it has considerable merit along terminological lines, is hardly of importance in the present discussion. The dichotomy, therefore, will not be strictly observed here.

3. M. E. Claperon, *Cours de Comptabilité* (1886), pp. 105-110.

4. S. S. Dawson, "Stock and Cost Accounts of a Flour Miller," *The Accountant*, Apr. 3, 1897, p. 369. His illustrations are dated 1896, however.

5. *Ibid.*, p. 369.

6. He did say, however, that the pricing required considerable care in case a different price were paid for the same grade of wheat. Witness his handling of the California and River Plate types in the illustration in the text.

7. *Ibid.*, p. 369.

8. *Ibid.*, p. 370.

9. As was described in Chapter V, this was a common practice in the nineteenth century.

10. J. Slater Lewis, *Commercial Organisation of Factories* (London: E. and F. N. Spon, 1896), p. 269. Lewis was an English accountant and factory manager.

11. *Loc. cit.*

12. Joseph MacNaughton, *Factory Bookkeeping for Paper Mills* (London: Wood Pulp, Limited, 1899), p. 18. MacNaughton did not use the term "by-products."

13. *Loc. cit.*

14. H. Stanley Garry, "Factory Costs," *The Accountant*, July 25, 1903, pp. 955-7. Garry was an English accountant.

15. He used this term.

16. Free from admixture or adulteration.

17. This is discussed at length in Chapter V, *supra*.

18. G. A. Mitchell, *Single Cost Accounts* (London: Gee and Company, 1907), p. 32. The screenings, or small barley, were handled similarly.

19. Cf. H. L. C. Hall, *Manufacturing Costs* (Detroit: The Bookkeeper Publishing Company, 1904), p. 129, where he stated that it was the custom to consider revenue arising from the sale of "by-products" (his term) as "found money."

20. *Loc. cit.* Care had to be taken, however, to credit the proper department which used the raw material in the first instance.

21. J. B. Griffith, *Cyclopedia of Commerce, Accountancy, and Business Administration* (Chicago: American Technical Society, 1909), II, 183.

22. He did not state what this included.

23. *Loc. cit.*

24. He did not use this term.

25. F. E. Webner, *Factory Costs* (New York: The Ronald Press Company, 1911), pp. 102-4.

26. He meant the Reserve for Variations in Weights and Measures and the Reserve for Over, Short, and Damage.

27. Or over, short, and damage account.

28. H. C. Bentley, *The Science of Accounts* (New York: The Ronald Press Company, 1911), pp. 216-17; 240-41.

29. *Ibid.*, p. 216.

30. *Ibid.*, p. 216.

31. *Ibid.*, p. 240.

32. *Ibid.*, p. 240.

33. *Ibid.*, p. 240.

34. *Ibid.*, p. 217.

35. J. Lee Nicholson, *Cost Accounting* (New York: The Ronald Press Company, 1913), p. 50.

36. A. Hamilton Church, *Manufacturing Costs and Accounts* (New York: Mc-Graw-Hill Book Company, 1917), pp. 94-95.

37. Reported in "Costings," *The Accountant,* Jan. 18, 1919, p. 44. Jenkinson was a Chartered Accountant, and, during the First World War, Controller of Factory Audits and Costs in the Ministry of Munitions.

38. E. T. Elbourne, *Factory Administration and Cost Accounts* (London: Longmans, Green and Company, 1921), p. 454.

39. Cf. both Jenkinson, *op. cit.* (above, note 37), p. 45; and Elbourne, p. 454.

40. *N.A.C.A. Bulletin,* Aug. 16, 1920.

41. J. P. Jordan and G. L. Harris, *Cost Accounting* (New York: The Ronald Press Company, 1920), pp. 244-50.

42. W. B. Castenholz also gave an unusually thorough treatment of the topic under review. It was not, however, so comprehensive as that of Jordan and Harris. See W. B. Castenholz, *Cost Acoounting Procedure* (Chicago: La-Salle Extension University, 1922), pp. 314-316; and James L. Dohr, *Cost Accounting* (New York: The Ronald Press Company, 1924), p. 416.

43. *N.A.C.A. Bulletin,* Dec. 1, 1922.

44. The weight basis had been hinted at by other authorities. Cf. W. B. Castenholz, p. 315.

45. Cf. White, *op. cit.* (above, note 2). See also his article in *The Journal of Accountancy,* LI (February, 1931).

CHAPTER IX

1. Emile Garcke and J. M. Fells, *Factory Acoounts,* 4th ed. (London: Crosby, Lockwood and Son, 1893), p. 50. (First edition, 1887.) On another page they implied that the prime cost ledger would be credited on account of the scrap, but again no details were given. See their p. 68.

2. G. P. Norton, *Textile Manufacturers' Bookkeeping,* 4th ed. (London: Simpkin, 1900), p. 96. (First edition, 1889.) Norton was a practicing English accountant.

3. Another Englishman, F. G. Burton, recommended a similar plan in 1895. See his *Engineering Estimates and Cost Accounts,* 2nd ed. (Manchester: Technical Publishing Company, 1900), p. 100. (First edition, 1895.)

4. J. Slater Lewis, *Commercial Organisation of Factories* (London: E. and F. N. Spon, 1896), p. 268. Lewis was an English factory manager and accountant.

5. Later Sir John Mann. See *The Encyclopaedia of Accounting* (London: William Green and Sons, 1903), V, *passim*.

6. H. L. C. Hall, *Manufacturing Costs* (Detroit: The Bookkeeper Publishing Company, 1904), p. 108.

7. Hall, p. 122.

8. B. C. Bean, *The Cost of Production* (Chicago: A. W. Shaw Company, 1905), p. 39.

9. *Loc. cit.*

10. C. M. Day, *Accounting Practice* (New York: D. Appleton and Company, 1908), p. 111.

11. F. E. Webner, *Factory Costs* (New York: The Ronald Press Company, 1911), p. 95, emphasized particularly the importance of this factor.

12. J. Lee Nicholson, *Factory Organization and Costs* (New York: Kohl Publishing Company, 1909), p. 166.

13. J. R. Wildman, *Cost Accounting* (New York: The Accountancy Publishing Company, 1911), p. 58.

14. S. H. Bunnell, *Cost-Keeping for Manufacturing Plants* (New York: D. Appleton and Company, 1911), p. 154.

15. Webner, *Factory Costs, passim*.

16. L. W. Hawkins, *Cost Accounts* (London: Gee and Company, 1912), pp. 89, 105, 113.

17. J. Lee Nicholson, in this country, advocated at about the same time a similar procedure, but insisted that the total factory cost should be taken into account, instead of merely the prime cost. See his *Cost Accounting* (New York: The Ronald Press Company, 1913), p. 113.

18. E. T. Elbourne, "Approximation in Factory Accounting," *The Accountant,* Mar. 20, 1915, p. 391.

19. A. Hamilton Church, *Manufacturing Costs and Accounts* (New York: McGraw-Hill Book Company, 1917), pp. 86-93.

20. Nicholas T. Ficker, *Shop Expense Analysis and Control* (New York: The Engineering Magazine Company, 1917), p. 33.

21. F. W. Kilduff, "Spoilage, the Fourth Factor of Cost," *The Journal of Accountancy,* XXV (1918), 192.

22. A. Hamilton Church had not altogether followed this principle. Cf. Church, p. 86.

23. F. W. Kilduff, *Inventory Practice and Material Control* (New York: McGraw-Hill Book Company, 1925), p. 195.

24. *Ibid.*, p. 194.

25. J. P. Jordan and G. L. Harris, *Cost Accounting* (New York: The Ronald Press Company, 1920), p. 358, followed Kilduff's procedure as to the handling of normal and abnormal spoilage; that is, the normal spoilage was an overhead item, while the unusual spoilage was a charge against the job causing it.

26. Cf. G. H. Newlove, *Cost Accounts*, 3rd ed. (Washington: The White Press Company, 1923), p. 95; and D. C. Eggleston and F. B. Robinson, *Business Costs* (New York: D. Appleton and Company, 1921), p. 182.

27. Cf. D. S. Kimball, *Cost Finding* (New York: Alexander Hamilton Institute, 1919), p. 76; Jordan and Harris, p. 280; W. B. Castenholz, *Cost Accounting Procedure* (Chicago: LaSalle Extension University, 1922), p. 318; Eggleston and Robinson, p. 182; C. B. Williams, *N.A.C.A. Bulletin,* May, 1921, p. 5; and James L. Dohr, *Cost Accounting* (New York: The Ronald Press Company, 1924), p. 417.

28. J. Lee Nicholson and J. F. D. Rohrbach, *Cost Accounting* (New York: The Ronald Press Company, 1919), p. 128.
29. Nicholson and Rohrbach did state, however, that if the scrap were used in a by-product, its value was to be credited to the original job or process. See their pp. 92, 128.
30. Cf. Newlove, p. 92; Jordan and Harris, p. 358; Castenholz, *op. cit.* (above, note 27), p. 306; and Kimball, p. 111.
31. Newlove, p. 92. Cf., also Jordan and Harris, p. 359, for a similar distinction.
32. *N.A.C.A. Bulletin*, May, 1921, p. 3.
33. *Ibid.*, p. 4.

CHAPTER X

1. One reason for the lack of interest in the matter of inventory pricing is that so-called venture accounting dominated accounting procedure for such a long period of time. For example, De Roover states:

> It was the custom of Medieval merchants, including the Medici, to open a separate account for each venture. Such accounts were charged with all outlays, costs, and expenses, and credited with the proceeds from sales. The difference that remained after conclusion of the venture represented either a profit or a loss and was transferred to an account "Profit and Loss on Merchandise." Thus profits from trade and from exchange were kept separate. This system of opening a separate account to each venture has been called "venture accounting" by accountants and students of the history of accounting. Venture accounting eliminates the necessity of inventory valuation. Since records were generally kept according to this system, it is not surprising that Paciolo and other early authors on bookkeeping are silent on the subject of inventory valuation. Neither is it surprising that there are no examples of it in the Medici records.

Raymond de Roover, *The Medici Bank* (New York: New York University Press, 1948), p. 44. Cf. Frederic C. Lane, "Venture Accounting in Medieval Business Management," *Bulletin of the Business Historical Society*, XIX (1945), 164-73. For a description of the Medici industrial records, see Chapter I of this volume.

2. Cf., however, J. L. Weiner, "Balance-sheet Valuation in German Law," *The Journal of Accountancy*, XLVIII (1929), 195, where he states that "in 1857, prior to the unification of Germany, a conference was called to draft a uniform commercial code for the then independent German states. The basis of the conference discussions was a draft prepared by the Prussian representatives. This draft contained only a few valuation rules, to wit, goods and materials were to be carried at the lower of cost or market . . . " This recommendation was not, however, adopted at the time. Obviously, also, it might have applied only to mercantile or trading concerns. Weiner did not make the point clear, and no further evidence is available. The 1857 draft of the code is significant, however, in that it is one of the early references to the "cost or market, whichever is lower" rule. For further details on cost or market, whichever is lower, see A. C. Littleton, "A Genealogy for Cost or Market," *The Accounting Review*, XVI, No.

2 (June, 1941), 161-67; and L. L. Vance, "The Authority of History in Inventory Valuation," *The Accounting Review,* XVIII, No. 3 (July, 1943), 219-228.

3. J. Sawyer, *Bookkeeping for the Tanning Trade,* 2nd ed. (London: 1862), *passim.* Sawyer was an Englishman.

4. Sawyer, *ibid.*

5. Evelyn H. Knowlton, *Pepperell's Progress* (Cambridge: Harvard University Press, 1948), p. 114. In later years this firm adopted a rather unusual inventory "reserve" technique involving the write-down of the inventory when profits were good, and the reversal of this reserve when profits were at a low ebb. See her p. 177.

6. Cf. George Lisle, *Accounting in Theory and Practice* (Edinburgh: William Green and Sons, 1899), p. 53.

7. In 1886, however, J. W. Best made the statement that the cost price should be adopted for valuing factory inventories if the market price was higher; but, on the other hand, the market price should be used in the event the cost price exceeded the market. *The Accountants' Journal,* Jan. 1, 1886.

8. In modern terminology, "taking inventory." Emile Garcke and J. M. Fells, *Factory Accounts,* 4th ed. (London: Crosby, Lockwood and Son, 1893), pp. 115-25. (First edition, 1887.)

9. Garcke and Fells, p. 124.

10. Garcke and Fells, p. 122.

11. G. P. Norton, *Textile Manufacturers' Bookkeeping,* 4th ed. (London: Simpkin, 1900), *passim.* (First edition, 1889.)

12. Norton did not state whether he referred to cash or trade discounts or both. See his p. 259.

13. *Loc. cit.* The italics are Norton's.

14. This was discussed *in extenso* in Chapter VI.

15. These had been hinted at by Garcke and Fells.

16. Norton, p. 259.

17. It should be noted, however, that Norton's many illustrations were all dated 1884, some five years before the first edition of his work was published, and three years before Garcke and Fells. It may be that his plan was the practice some years before 1889. He suggested no reason for pre-dating his entries and forms, and did not refer to Garcke and Fells' work.

18. Norton, p. 260.

19. J. Slater Lewis, *The Commercial Organisation of Factories* (London: E. and F. N. Spon, 1896). Lewis was an English factory manager and accountant.

20. Lewis, p. 180.

21. Lewis did state, however, that a percentage-on-labor method would probably be adopted. See his p. 181.

22. Lewis, p. 180.

23. Cf. H. L. Arnold, *The Complete Cost-Keeper* (New York: The Engineering Magazine Press, 1899), *passim;* and H. L. Arnold, *The Factory Manager and Acountant* (New York: The Engineering Magazine Press, 1903), *passim.*

24. T. R. Navin, *The Whitin Machine Works Since 1831* (Cambridge: Harvard University Press, 1950), p. 153.

25. H. M. Norris in *Transactions American Society of Mechanical Engineers,* XIX (1898), 391.

26. F. A. Halsey, *Transactions,* XIX, 397.

27. Norris, *Transactions,* XIX, 413. (Italics supplied.)

28. A. Hamilton Church, "The Proper Distribution of Establishment Charges," *The Engineering Magazine,* XXI (1901), 515.

29. John Whitmore, "Factory Accounting As Applied to Machine Shops," *The Journal of Accountancy*, II (1906), 355.

30. For a discussion of the influence of these factors see A. C. Littleton, *Accounting Evolution to 1900* (New York: American Institute Publishing Company, 1933), pp. 288-315.

31. John A. Walbank, "Stock and Stocktaking," in *The Encyclopaedia of Accounting* (London: William Green and Sons, 1903), VI, 175.

32. As noted *supra*, J. L. Weiner states that this term was used in Germany as early as 1857. See Weiner, *The Journal of Accountancy*, XLVIII, 195.

33. Walbank, *op. cit.* (above, note 31), p. 168.

34. Lisle, p. 53.

35. G. A. Mitchell, *Single Cost Accounts* (London: Gee and Company, 1907), pp. 127-31.

36. Mitchell followed Norton (1889) in regard to a number of his proposals.

37. Mitchell, p. 131. In addition to Mitchell's chapter on this topic, H. Stanley Garry also devoted several pages at about the same time to the valuation problem in a continuous process industry. See his *Process Cost Accounts* (London: Gee and Company, 1908), pp. 99ff.

38. L. W. Hawkins, *Cost Accounts*, 2nd ed. (London: Gee and Company, 1912), pp. 77. (First edition, 1905.)

39. S. H. Bunnell, *Cost Keeping for Manufacturing Plants* (New York: D. Appleton and Company, 1911), pp. 155, 169.

40. Cf. Bunnell, pp. 164-172.

41. S. H. Bunnell, "Expense Burden: Its Incidence and Distribution," *Journal American Society of Mechanical Engineers* (1912), p. 558.

42. Respectively, F. E. Webner, *Factory Costs* (New York: The Ronald Press Company, 1911); and J. Lee Nicholson, *Cost Accounting* (New York: The Ronald Press Company, 1913).

43. Cf. F. H. Baugh, *Principles and Practices of Cost Accounting* (Baltimore: F. H. Baugh, 1915), pp. 6-7, for a similar viewpoint.

44. In addition to the British experts cited previously, see M. W. Jenkinson in *The Accountant* (1914), p. 568 for an opinion similar to that of Hawkins, that is, that the lower of average cost or market should be adopted. Jenkinson's average cost, however, was the average price paid for the articles (material) purchased during the last month of the fiscal period. This last was a rather novel method which never attained much standing.

45. E. P. Moxey, *Principles of Factory Cost Keeping* (New York: The Ronald Press Company, 1913), p. 40.

46. Moxey, p. 43.

47. William Kent, *Bookkeeping and Cost Accounting for Factories* (New York: John Wiley and Sons, 1918), p. 53.

48. For a further discussion of this method see *N.A.C.A. Yearbook*, 1922, pp. 66-70; and *Proceedings International Congress on Accounting*, 1929, *passim*.

49. S. G. H. Fitch, "Present-day Problems in Industrial Accounting," *The Journal of Accountancy*, XXXIV (1922), 6.

50. Cf. in England, E. T. Elbourne, *Factory Administration and Cost Accounts* (London: Longmans, Green and Company, 1921), pp. 371-398; and in this country, J. P. Jordan and G. L. Harris, *Cost Accounting* (New York: The Ronald Press Company, 1920), pp. 158-78; James L. Dohr, *Cost Accounting* (New York: The Ronald Press Company, 1924), pp. 196-197.

CHAPTER XI

1. Henry Metcalfe, *The Cost of Manufactures* (New York: John Wiley and Sons, 1885), pp. 142-143.
2. Metcalfe, p. 306.
3. S. A. Hand in *Transactions American Society Mechanical Engineers*, VII (1885), 483.
4. Emile Garcke and J. M. Fells, *Factory Accounts*, 4th ed. (London: Crosby, Lockwood and Son, 1893), p. 65. (First edition, 1887.)
5. G. P. Norton, *Textile Manufacturers' Bookkeeping*, 4th ed. (London: Simpkin, 1900), p. 267. (First edition, 1889.)
6. Norton, p. 254.
7. Unsigned article in *The Accountant* (1894), p. 689.
8. *Ibid.*, p. 704.
9. J. S. Lewis, *The Commercial Organisation of Factories* (London: E. and F. N. Spon, 1896), p. 289.
10. H. M. Norris, "A Simple and Effective System of Shop Cost Keeping," *The Engineering Magazine*, XVI (1898), 392.
11. *Ibid.*, p. 393.
12. H. L. Arnold, *The Complete Cost-Keeper* (New York: The Engineering Magazine Press, 1899), *passim*.
13. Arnold, p. 218.
14. Arnold, p. 337.
15. Arnold, p. 304.
16. Arnold, p. 47.
17. Arnold, p. 306.
18. Joseph MacNaughton, *Factory Bookkeeping for Paper Mills* (London: Wood Pulp, Limited, 1899), *passim*.
19. MacNaughton, p. 27.
20. H. Diemer, "Commercial Organization of the Machine Shop," *The Engineering Magazine*, XIX (1900), 344-346.
21. *Ibid.*, pp. 344-346.
22. *Ibid.*, pp. 344-346.
23. *Ibid.*, p. 895.
24. H. L. C. Hall, *Manufacturing Costs* (Detroit: The Bookkeeper Publishing Company, 1904), pp. 74-85.
25. H. Deighton, "Cost System of an Engineering Works," *The Engineering Magazine*, XXIX (1905), 50-52. Deighton was an American engineer.
26. Stanley Pedder, "Cost Accounts; Their Advantages and Their Relation to Business Results," *The Accountant*, Apr. 29, 1905, p. 529.
27. Clarence Day, *Accounting Practice* (New York: D. Appleton and Company, 1908), p. 92.
28. Day, p. 161.
29. J. Lee Nicholson, *Factory Organization and Costs* (New York: Kohl Technical Publishing Company, 1909), pp. 102-315.
30. Nicholson, p. 102.
31. Nicholson, p. 307.
32. Nicholson, p. 315.
33. Nicholson, p. 341.
34. W. Strachan, *Cost Accounts* (London: Stevens and Haynes, 1909), *passim*.
35. Strachan, p. 48.
36. Strachan, p. 60.

37. F. E. Webner, *Factory Costs* (New York: The Ronald Press Company, 1911), pp. 251-300.
38. H. C. Bentley, *The Science of Accounts* (New York: The Ronald Press Company, 1911), pp. 246-247.

CHAPTER XII

1. Cf. *supra*, p. x (Preface).
2. As a matter of fact, several authorities, as late as 1900, noted the attitude of secrecy which seemed to surround the subject of costing in the years prior to the turn of the century. See Chapter II.
3. These and others are detailed in previous chapters.
4. The contents of these three works are described at length in Chapters III through XI. Cf., also, S. Paul Garner, "Has Cost Accounting Come of Age?" *N.A.C.A. Bulletin*, XXXIII (1951), pp. 287-292.
5. Emile Garcke and J. M. Fells, *Factory Accounts*, 4th ed. (London: Crosby, Lockwood and Son, 1893). (First edition, 1887).
6. A. Hamilton Church, "The Proper Distribution of Establishment Charges," *The Engineering Magazine*, XXI and XXII (1901), *passim*.
7. John Whitmore, "Factory Accounting As Applied to Machine Shops," *The Journal of Accountancy*, II and III (1906), *passim*.
8. The system advocated by J. S. Lewis, *The Commercial Organisation of Factories* (London: E. and F. N. Spon, 1896), is an illustration in point. Lewis was an English factory manager and accountant.
9. Some of the reasons for this lack of interest are discussed in Chapter V.
10. In this connection, A. C. Littleton notes that "methods of allocating cost units to product units were devised with such skill that cost accounting has become a veritable symphony of analysis and synthesis." *Accounting Evolution to 1900* (New York: American Institute Publishing Company, 1933), p. 368.
11. "The Commercial Aspects of an Engineer's Training," *Engineering*, LV (Feburary, 1893). For a more detailed treatment of this matter see Richard E. Gaylord, *Historical Development of Cost Accounting with Particular Reference to Its Relations to Industrial Engineering* (New York: An unpublished manuscript of 34 pages, January, 1952).
12. Cf. Emile Garcke and J. M. Fells, *passim*.
13. Littleton, p. 359.
14. Littleton, p. 368.

SELECTED
BIBLIOGRAPHY

No author given, "Costing in the Seventeenth Century," *The Cost Accountant,* XXI (October-November, 1941)

No author given, *Factory Cost Accounting* (Detroit: Bookkeeper Publishing Company, 1900)

No author given, *International Acoountants Society Textbook* (New York: International Textbook Co., 1920)

Acton, E., *English Breadbaking,* II (1857)

American Institute of Accountants, *Yearbook* (1918)

American School of Correspondence, *Cyclopedia of Practical Accounting* (Chicago: American Technical Society, 1912)

Amsdon, Edward, *Amsdon's Guide to Brewers' Book-keeping* (London: 1881)

Anderson, E. H. and Schwenning, Gustav, *The Science of Production Organization* (New York: John Wiley & Sons, 1938)

Andrade, E., "Manufacturing Cost Accounts, Their Use and Treatment," *The Accountant* (February 11, 1899)

Armstrong, George Simpson, *Essentials of Industrial Costing* (New York: Appleton, 1921)

Arnold, H. L., "Cost-Keeping in Machine-Shop and Foundry," *The Engineering Magazine,* XIV (1898)

    The complete Cost-Keeper (New York: The Engineering Magazine Press, 1899)

    The Factory Manager and Accountant (New York: The Engineering Magazine Press, 1903)

Ashton, Thomas Southcliffe, *Iron and Steel in the Industrial Revolution* (Manchester: Manchester University Publications, Economic History Series No. 2, 1924)

Atkins, Paul Moody, *Industrial Cost Accounting for Executives* (New York: McGraw-Hill Book Company, 1923)

    Textbook of Industrial Cost Accounting (New York: McGraw-Hill Book Company, 1924)

Babbage, Charles, *On the Economy of Machinery and Manufactures,* 4th ed. (London, 1841)

Baillet, Henry F., *Overhead Expense and Percentage Methods: A Lecture on the Cost of Doing Business* (New York: D. Williams, 1915)

Baltes, F. W., *The Cost of Printing* (Portland: Baltes, 1894)

Baruch, Alfred, *Standard Costs for Sheet Metal Workers* (New York: U. P. C. Book Company, 1923)

Basset, W. R., *Accounting as an Aid to Business Profits* (Chicago: A. W. Shaw Company, 1918)

Bates, E. P., "Discussion on Cost of Manufacture," *Transactions American Society of Mechanical Engineers*, XV (1894)

Battersby, Thomas, *The Perfect Double Entry Bookkeeper* (Manchester: 1878)

Baugh, F. H., *Principles and Practices of Cost Accounting* (Baltimore: F. H. Baugh, 1915)

Bean, B. C., *The Cost of Production* (Chicago: A. W. Shaw Company, 1905)

Belser, F. C., "Cost Accounting for Fertilizer Manufacturers," *The Journal of Accountancy*, XIX (1915)

Belt, Robert E., *Foundry Cost Accounting Practice and Procedure* (Cleveland: Penton Press, 1919)

Bentley, H. C., *Basic Cost Accounting*, 3rd ed. (Chicago: International Accountants Society, 1920)

The Science of Accounts (New York: The Ronald Press Company, 1911)

Berndt, Irving A., *Costs: Their Compilation and Use in Management* (Chicago: H. P. Gould, 1920)

Best, J. W., *The Accountants' Journal* (January 1, 1886)

Cost Accounts, 2nd ed. (London: Gee and Company, 1911)

Bigelow, C. M., "Installing Management Methods in the Woodworking Industry," *Industrial Management*, LVIII (1919)

Blanchard, Isaac H., *Actual Costs in Printing and How to Discover and Reckon Them* (New York: Blanchard, 1901)

Bliss, James H., "Cost Methods in the Packing Industry," *N.A.C.A. Bulletin* (April 15, 1922)

Book-keeper Publishing Company, Ltd., *Improved Balance System of Cost Accounting* (Detroit: Book-keeper Publishing Company, 1905)

Borton, E. J., *Cost Accounting Principles and Methods* (Chicago: Lyons & Carnahan, 1923)

Bosher, L. H., "Controlling Accounts in Cost Accounting," *The Journal of Accountancy*, XIII (1912)

Brierley, John Thomas, *Manufacturing Cost Accounts* (Brooklyn: Published by the author, 1913)

Broaker, Frank, "Cost and Factory Accounts," *The Accountant* (June, 1897)

Brown, Harry Gunnison, *Transportation Rates and Their Regulation* (New York: The Macmillan Company, 1916)

Brown, Richard, *A History of Accounting and Accountants* (Edinburgh: T. C. & E. C. Jack, 1905)

Brun, Robert, "A Fourteenth-Century Merchant of Italy," *Journal of Economic and Business History*, II (1930)

Bryant, J. C., *Bryant's New Bookkeeping*, 6th ed. (Buffalo: Published by the author, 1880)

Bunnell, S. H., *Cost Keeping for Manufacturing Plants* (New York: D. Appleton and Company, 1911)

"Expense Burden: Its Incidence and Distribution," *Journal American Society of Mechanical Engineers* (1912)

"Standardizing Factory Expense and Cost," *Iron Age* (November 16, 1911)

Burton, F. G., *Engineering Estimates and Cost Accounts* (Manchester: Technical Publishing Company, 1895) (2nd ed. 1900)

Engineers' and Shipbuilders' Accounts, 1st ed., 1902, 2nd ed. (London: Gee and Company, 1911)

The Commercial Management of Engineering Works, 2nd ed. (Manchester: The Scientific Publishing Company, 1905)

Byrne, E. H., *Genoese Shipping in the Twelfth and Thirteenth Centuries*, Publication No. 5, Monograph No. 1 (Cambridge, Massachusetts: Mediaeval Academy, 1930)

Camman, E. A., *Basic Standard Costs* (New York: American Institute Publishing Company, 1932)

Carpenter, C. U., *Increasing Production Decreasing Costs* (New York: The Engineering Magazine Company, 1920)

Carter, F. H., *Practical Bookkeeping*, 2nd ed. (Edinburgh: Simpkin, Marshall, Hamilton, Kent and Company, 1874)

Cartmell, M., *Stores and Materials Control* (New York: The Ronald Press Company, 1922)

Castenholz, W. B., *Control of Distribution Costs and Sales* (New York and London: Harper and Brothers, 1930)

Cost Accounting Procedure (Chicago: LaSalle Extension University, 1922)

Cathles, A., "General Principles of Costing," *The Accountant* (February 28, 1920)

Cauley, W. W., *A Study of the Accounting Records of the Shelby Iron Company*, (Unpublished M.B.A. thesis in the University of Alabama Library, 1949)

Chamber of Commerce of the United States, Department of Manufacture, *Cost Accounting Through the Use of Standards* (Washington: Chamber of Commerce, 1925)

Chamber of Commerce of the United States, *The Evolution of Overhead Accounting* (Washington: Chamber of Commerce, 1927)

Charleton, A. G., "Principles and Methods of Profitably Working the Mine; Office Organization, Cost-keeping and Records of Work Done," *The Engineering Magazine*, XX (1901)

Chase, W. A., *Auditing and Cost Accounting* (Chicago: LaSalle Extension University, 1922)

Child, F. W., *Elements of Cost* (New York: Office Co., 1887)

Church, A. Hamilton, *Manufacturing Costs and Accounts* (New York: McGraw-Hill Book Company, 1917)

"Organisation by Production Factors," *The Engineering Magazine*, XXXVIII (1909); Reprinted in *Production Factors in Cost Accounting and Works Management* (New York: The Engineering Magazine Press, 1910)

Overhead Expenses (New York: McGraw-Hill Book Company, 1930)

Production Factors in Cost Accounting and Works Management (New York: The Engineering Magazine Press, 1910) (Works Management Library)

"The Meaning of Commercial Organization," *The Engineering Magazine*, XX, December, 1900)

"The Proper Distribution of Establishment Charges," *The Engineering Magazine*, XXI and XXII (1901)

Claperon, M. E., *Cours de Comptabilité* (1886)

Clark, J. M., *The Economics of Overhead Costs* (Chicago: University of Chicago Press, 1923)

Cleary, P. Roger, *How To Figure Profit: A Comprehensive Reference Book for Business Men, Teachers and Students* (Ypsilanti, Michigan: Cleary, 1918)

Cole, William Morse, *Cost Accounting for Institutions* (New York: The Ronald Press Company, 1913)

Cook, Charles Bannister, *Factory Management* (Detroit: Bookkeeper Publishing Company, 1906)

Corsani, Gaetano, *I fondaci e i banchi di un mercante pretese del Trecento* (Prato: Archivio Storico Pratese, Supplement II, 1922)

Cowan, David, "Administration of Workshops; With Special References to Oncost," *The Accountant* (November 16, 1901)

Cronhelm, F. W., *Double Entry by Single* (London: Longmans, Green and Company, 1818)

Cyclopedia of Commerce, Accountancy, Business Administration (Chicago: American Technical Society, 1909)

Dale, Samuel Sherman, *Cost Finding for Textile Mills* (Boston: Textiles, 1916)
Cost Finding in Woolen and Worsted Mills (Boston: Textiles, 1918)

Dana, R. T. and Gillette, H. P., *Cost Analysis Engineering* (Chicago: American Technical Society, 1918)

Dando, J. Clifford, *Fundamental Principles of Ascertaining Cost of Manufacturing* (Philadelphia: Dando Printing and Publishing Company, 1901)

Darlington, P. J., "Developing New Products and Determining Shop Cost," *The Engineering Magazine*, XXXV (1908)

Davis, Albert Eugene, *How To Find Cost in Printing* (New York: Oswald Publishing Company, 1914)

Davis, R. C., *Purchasing and Storing* (New York: Alexander Hamilton Institute 1931)

Dawson, S. S., "Stock and Cash Accounts of a Flour Miller," *The Accountant* (April 3, 1897)

Day, C. M., *Accounting Practice* (New York: D. Appleton and Company, 1908)
Silk Mill Costs (New York: Day, 1912)

De Cazaux, L. F. G., *De la Comptabilité dans une Enterprise Industrielle et specialement dans une Exploitation Rurale* (Toulouse: 1824)

De Roover, Raymond, "A Florentine Firm of Cloth Manufactures," *Speculum*, XVI (January, 1941)
"Aux Origines d'une Technique Intellectual: La Formation et l'Expansion de la Comptabilité à partie double" *Annales d'Histoire économique et sociale*, XLIV-XLV (1937)
The Medici Bank (New York: New York University Press, 1948)

Deighton, H., "Cost System of an Engineering Works," *The Engineering Magazine*, XXIX (1905)

Denham, Robert Scudder, *Fundamentals of Cost and Profit Calculations* (Cleveland: Cost Engineer Publishing Company, 1918)
The A-B-C of Cost Engineering (Cleveland: Denham Cost-Finding Company, 1919)
The Science of Cost-finding Applied to Factories Making Products to Special or Shop Orders (Cleveland: Denham Costfinding Company, 1911)

Dickinson, A. Lowes, "The Economic Aspects of Cost Accounts," *The Journal of Accountancy*, XI (1911)

Dicksee, L. R., *Advanced Accounting*, 4th ed. (London: Gee and Company, 1911)

Diemer, H., *Factory Organization and Administration*, 3rd ed., (New York: McGraw-Hill Book Company, 1920)
"The Commercial Organization of the Machine Shop," *The Engineering Magazine*, XIX (1900)

Dodson, James, *The Accountant, or the Method of Book-keeping* (London: 1750)

Dohr, James L., *Cost Accounting* (New York: The Ronald Press Company, 1924)

Dow, D. S., *Keeping Books* (New York: D. A. Curtis, 1882)

Dugué, M., *Traité de Comptabilité et d'Administration à l'usage des Entrepreneurs de Bâtiments et de Travant publics* (1872)

Duncan, J. C., *The Principles of Industrial Management* (New York: D. Appleton and Company, 1911)

Eddis, W. C. and Tindall, W. B., *Manufacturers' Accounts* (Toronto: Published by the authors, 1902)

Editorial, *The Accountant* (1904)

Editorial, *The Accountant* (1905)

Editorial, "The Commercial Aspects of an Engineer's Training," *Engineering*, LV (February, 1893)

Editorial, "Practical Prime Costs," *Engineering* (December 4, 1891)

Editorials, *The Accountant* (1912)

Editors, *The Bookkeeper* (1880)

Edler, Florence, "Cost Accounting in the Sixteenth Century," *The Accounting Review*, XII (September, 1937)

   Glossary of Mediaeval Terms in Business, Italian Series, 1200-1600 (Cambridge: The Mediaeval Academy of America, 1934)

Edwards, Ronald S., *A Survey of the French Contributions to the Study of Cost Accounting During the Nineteenth Century* (London: Gee and Company, 1937)

   "Some Notes on the Early Literature and Development of Cost Accounting in Great Britain," *The Accountant*, XCVII (July-December, 1937)

Eggleston, D. C. and Robinson, F. B., *Business Costs* (New York: D. Appleton and Company, 1921)

Eggleston, D. C., *Cost Accounting* (New York: The Ronald Press Company, 1920)

   "Motor Manufacturing Costs," *Business Man's Magazine* (October, 1907)

   Problems in Cost Accounting (New York: D. Appleton and Company, 1918)

   "System of Factory Cost Accounting," *The Journal of Accountancy*, III (1906)

Ehrenberg, Richard, *Das Zeitalter der Fugger*, 2 vols. (Jena: 1896)

Elbourne, E. T., "Approximation in Factory Accounting," *The Accountant* (March 20, 1915)

   Factory Administration and Cost Accounts, new ed. (London: Longmans, Green and Company, 1921)

Eldridge, H. J., *The Evolution of the Science of Bookkeeping* (London: Institute of Bookkeepers, Ltd., 1931)

Emerson, Harrington, "Efficiency as a Basis for Operation and Wages," *The Engineering Magazine* (July, 1908-March, 1909)

   "Percentage Method of Determining Production Costs," *The Foundry* (October, 1904)

Evans, H. A., *Cost-Keeping and Scientific Management* (New York: McGraw-Hill Book Company, 1911)

Everitt, Frank and Heywood, Johnson, *Cost Control for Foundries* (New York: McGraw-Hill Book Company, 1923)

Fairbanks, Lorenzo, *The Science and Practice of Bookkeeping* (Philadelphia: Sower, Barnes and Potts, 1866)

Farquhar, H. H., *Factory Storekeeping—the Control and Storage of Materials* (New York: McGraw-Hill Book Company, 1922)

Fells, John Manger, "Cost Accounting: Its Evolution and Its Trend," *The Accountant*, LX (1919)

Ferguson, W. B., *The Art of Estimating* (New York: McGraw-Hill Book Company, 1915)

Ficker, Nicholas T., "Distributing Overhead Expense," *The Engineering Magazine*, L (1915)

   Industrial Cost-Finding (New York: Industrial Extension Institute, 1917)

   "Main Divisions of Manufacturing Expense," *The Engineering Magazine*, XLIX (1915)

   Shop Expense Analysis and Control (New York: The Engineering Magazine Press, 1917)

Fink, Albert, *Cost of Railroad Transportation* (Louisville: J. P. Morton & Co., 1875)

Fitch, S. G. H., "Present-day Problems in Industrial Accounting," *The Journal of Accountancy*, XXXIV (1922)

Flanders, R. E., "Discussion on Production and Costs," *Transactions American Society of Mechanical Engineers*, XXXVII (1915)

Fleming, John, *Bookkeeping by Double Entry* (Pittsburgh: W. S. Haven, 1854)

Fowler, G. L., "Estimating the Cost of Foundry Work," *Transactions American Society of Mechanical Engineers*, IX, (1888)

Franklin, Benjamin Alvey, *Cost Reports for Executives As a Means of Plant Control* (New York: The Engineering Magazine Press, 1913)

   Cost Reports for Executives (New York: The Engineering Magazine Press, 1912)

Frost, Glenn H., "Cost Accounting," *The Business World* (October, 1905)

Gantt, H. L., "Production and Sales," *The Engineering Magazine*, L (1916)

   "The Relation Between Production and Costs," *Transactions American Society of Mechanical Engineers*, XXXVII (1915)

Garcke, Emile and Fells, J. M., *Factory Accounts, Their Principles and Practice*, 1st ed., 1887; 4th ed. (London: Crosby, Lockwood and Son, 1893)

Garner, S. Paul, "Has Cost Accounting Come of Age?", *N.A.C.A. Bulletin*, XXXIII (1951)

   "Historical Development of Cost Accounting," *The Accounting Review*, XXII (1947)

Garry, H. Stanley, "Factory Costs," *The Accountant* (July 25 and September 12, 1903)

   Multiple Cost Accounts (London: Gee and Company, 1906)

   Process Cost Acoounts (London: Gee and Company, 1908)

Gaylord, R. E., *Historical Development of Cost Accounting with Particular Reference to its Relation to Industrial Engineering* (New York: An unpublished manuscript of 34 pages, January, 1952)

General Manager, *Engineering Estimates, Cost and Accounts*, 1st ed., 1890; 3rd ed. (London: C. Lockwood and Son, 1911)

Gibb, George S., *The Saco-Lowell Shops* (Cambridge: Harvard University Press, 1950)

   The Whitesmiths of Taunton—A History of Reed and Barton (Cambridge: Harvard University Press, 1943)

Gillette, Halbert Powers and Dana, Richard Turner, *Cost Keeping and Management Engineering* (New York: M. C. Clark, 1909)

Gilman, Stephen, "What the Executive Should Know About Costs," *Industrial Management*, LIII (1917)

Godard, M., *Traité Général et Sommaire de la Comptabilité Commerciale* (Paris: 1827)

Goddard, F. R., "Balance Sheets of Manufacturing Firms," *Proceedings of the Cleveland (England) Institution of Engineers* (Middlesbrough: 1872-1873)

   "Defalcations and How to Prevent Them," *The Accountants' Journal* (March 1, 1887)

Goggin, Walter John, *Cost Accounting* (New York: La Fayette Institute, 1921)

Going, C. B., *Principles of Industrial Engineering* (New York: McGraw-Hill Book Company, 1911)

Goode, G. E., "Methods of Ascertaining Costs in a Factory," *The Accountant* (June 30, 1900)

Goodwin, A. E., "Principles and Practice of Correct Costing," *The Accountant* (March 20, 1920)

Goodwin, Frank Elbert, *Cost Accounting Pathfinder* (St. Louis: Midland Publishing Company, 1910)

Goodwin, J. H., *Improved Bookkeeping and Business Manual*, 4th ed. (New York: Published by the author, 1881)

Green, J. B., "The Perpetual Inventory in Practical Stores Operation," *The Engineering Magazine*, XLVIII (1915)

Greenwood, G. W., "On What Should Selling Prices Be Based?" *Administration*, III (1922)

Griffith, J. B., *Cyclopedia of Commerce, Accountancy, and Business Administration*, Vol. II (Chicago: American Technical Society, 1909)

Grover, P. H., *Corporation Bookkeeping in a Nutshell; With an Appendix on Manufacturing Accounts* (Detroit: Bookkeeper Co., 1897)

Guilbault, *Traité d'Comptabilité d'Administration Industrielles* (Paris: 1865)

Hall, H. L. C., *Manufacturing Costs* (Detroit: The Bookkeeper Publishing Company, 1904)

Halsey, F. A., "Discussion on Cost of Manufacture," *Transactions American Society of Mechanical Engineers*, XV (1894)

"Principles of Cost Accounting," *American Machinist* (June 20, 27, 1901)

Hamilton, Earl J., "Profit Inflation and the Industrial Revolution, 1751-1800," *The Quarterly Journal of Economics*, LVI (February, 1942)

Hamilton, Robert, *Introduction to Merchandise* (Edinburgh: 1788)

Hamilton, W. R., "Some Economic Considerations Bearing on Costing," *The Accountant* (February 5, 1910)

Hand, S. A., "Discussion on the Shop-Order System of Accounts," *Transactions American Society Mechanical Engineers*, VII (1885)

Harris, G. L., "Calculation, Distribution and Application of Burden," *Magazine of Management and Administration*, VI (1923)

Harrison, G. Charter, "Bugbear of Burden Distribution," *Magazine of Management and Administration*, VI (1923)

"Cost Accounting to Aid Production," *Industrial Management* (October, 1918-June, 1919)

New Wine in Old Bottles (New York: Privately printed, 1937)

"Scientific Basis for Cost Accounting," *Industrial Management* (December, 1918)

Standard Costs (New York: The Ronald Press Company, 1930)

Hatfield, Henry Rand, *Accounting* (New York: D. Appleton and Company, 1927)

Modern Accounting (New York: D. Appleton and Company, 1909)

"What They Say About Depreciation," *The Accounting Review*, XI (March, 1936)

Hathaway, Charles E. and Griffith, James Bray, *Factory Accounts: A Working Handbook of Departmental Organization and Methods as Applied to Factories* (Chicago: American School of Correspondence, 1910)

Hattersley, C. S., "Costing," *The Accountant* (May 28, 1921)

Hawkins, L. W., *Cost Accounts*, 2nd ed. (London: Gee and Company, 1912)

Hazell, W. H., *Costing for Manufacturers* (London: Nisbet and Co., Ltd., 1921)

"Printer's Cost Finding System," *The Accountant* (February 28, 1914)

Hess, Henry, "Manufacturing: Capital, Costs, Profits and Dividends," *The Engineering Magazine* (December, 1903)

Hilgert, J. R., *Cost Accounting for Sales* (New York: The Ronald Press Co., 1926)

International Library of Technology, *Cost Accounting* (New York: International Textbook Company, 1904)

Jackson, G., *A Practical System of Bookkeeping*, 24th ed. (London: Effingham Wilson, 1906)

Jackson, George, *The Check Journal*, 5th ed. (London: 1836)

Jackson, J. Hugh, "A Quarter-Century of Cost-Accounting Progress," *N.A.C.A. Bulletin*, XXVIII (June 1, 1947)

Jeannin, Mce, *Traité de la Comptabilité* (Paris: 1829)

Jenkinson, M. W., "Costing," *The Accountant* (January, 1919)

"Some Principles of Accounting Affecting Cost Accounts," *The Accountant* (April 18, 1914)

Jones, Arthur Francis, *Lumber Manufacturing Accounts* (New York: The Ronald Press Company, 1914)

Jordan, J. P. and Harris, G. L., *Cost Accounting* (New York: The Ronald Press Company, 1920)

Kelly, R. R., "Overhead Expense Distribution," *Journal American Society of Mechanical Engineers* (June, 1913)

Kemp, William S., *Departmental and Standard Costs* (New York: National Association of Cost Accountants, 1923)

Kent, William, *Bookkeeping and Cost Accounting for Factories* (New York: John Wiley and Sons, 1918)

Iron Trade Review (February 4, 1909)

"Discussion on Overhead Expense Distribution," *Journal of the American Society of Mechanical Engineers* (June, 1913)

"New Methods of Determining Factory Costs," *Iron Age*, Vol. 98 (August 24, 1916)

Kilduff, F. W., *Inventory Practice and Material Control* (New York: McGraw-Hill Book Company, 1925)

"Spoilage, the Fourth Factor of Cost," *The Journal of Accountancy*, XXV (1918)

Kimball, D. S., *Cost Finding* (New York: Alexander Hamilton Institute, 1918)

Principles of Industrial Organization (New York: McGraw-Hill Book Company, 1913)

Knoeppel, C. E., "Cost Reduction Through Cost Comparison," *The Engineering Magazine*, XXXII (1907)

"Graphic Production Control," *Industrial Management*, LVII (1919)

Maximum Production in Machine Shop and Foundry (New York: The Engineering Magazine Press, 1911)

"Systematic Foundry Operation and Foundry Costing," *The Engineering Magazine*, XXXVI (1908)

Knoeppel, F. J., "Industrial Accounting," *The Journal of Accountancy*, LII (1916)

Knowlton, Evelyn H., *Pepperell's Progress* (Cambridge: Harvard University Press, 1948)

Konopak, Lother Theodore, *Cost Accounting Fundamentals from the Standpoint of Management* (New York: The Ronald Press Company, 1924)

Krepp, Frederick C., *Statistical Bookkeeping* (London: Longman, 1858)

Lane, Frederic C., "Venture Accounting in Medieval Business Management," *Bulletin of the Business Historical Society*, XIX (1945)

Lane, H. M., "A Method of Shop Accounting to Determine Shop Cost," *Transactions American Society of Mechanical Engineers*, XVIII (1897)

Lardner, Dionysius, *Railway Economy* (New York and London: 1850)

Larson, Carl William, *Milk Production Cost Accounts* (New York: Columbia University Press, 1916)

Lawrence, William Beaty, *Cost Accounting* (New York: Prentice-Hall, 1925)

Lefevre, H., *La Comptabilité* (1883)

Lewis, E. S. E., *Efficient Cost Keeping*, 3rd ed. (New York: Burroughs Adding Machine Company, 1914)

Lewis, J. Slater, *Commercial Organisation of Factories* (London: E. and F. N. Spon, 1896)

Lisle, George, *Accounting in Theory and Practice,* 1st ed. 1899; rev. ed. (Edinburgh: William Green and Sons, 1909)

Editor, *Encyclopaedia of Accounting,* Vol. II (London: William Green and Sons, 1903)

Littleton, A. C., "A Genealogy for Cost or Market," *The Accounting Review,* XVI (June, 1941)

Accounting Evolution to 1900 (New York: American Institute Publishing Company, 1933)

Review of de Roover's "La Formation et l'Expansion de la Comptabilité à partie double," *The Accounting Review,* XII (1937)

Longmuir, Percy, "Recording and Interpreting Foundry Costs," *The Engineering Magazine* (September, 1902)

Loughry, James Cooper, *How To Install a Foundry Cost System* (New York: W. W. White Manufacturing Company, 1910)

Low, Edward, *Theorie des Rechnungswesens* (1860)

MacNaughton, Joseph, *Factory Bookkeeping for Paper Mills* (London: Wood Pulp, Limited, 1899)

Mair, John, *Bookkeeping Methodized,* 6th ed. (Edinburgh: 1760)

Makin, F. B., *Overhead Costs in Theory and Practice* (London: Gee and Company, 1933)

Mann, Sir John, "Cost Records or Factory Accounts," *The Encyclopaedia of Accounting,* II (London: William Green and Sons, 1903)

"Notes on Cost Records," *The Accountant* (August 29 and September 5, 1891)

"Oncosts," *The Encyclopaedia of Accounting* (London: William Green and Sons, 1903)

Manners, O. N., *System* (1904)

Manning, Anthony B., *Elements of Cost Accounting* (New York: McGraw-Hill Book Company, 1924)

McGrath, Thomas Orrin, *Mine Accounting and Cost Principles* (New York: McGraw-Hill Book Company, 1921)

McHenry, W. E., "Cost per Ton," *The Engineering Magazine* (August, 1914)

"Is Your Cost System Scientific?" *The Engineering Magazine* (August, 1916)

McIntosh, R. J., *Reference Book of Accounts for Manufacturing and Mercantile Companies* (Toledo: Robert McIntosh and Company, 1914)

Metcalfe, Henry, *The Cost of Manufactures,* 1st ed. 1885; 3rd ed. (New York: John Wiley and Sons, 1907)

"The Shop-Order System of Accounts," *Transactions American Society of Mechanical Engineers,* VII (1886)

Melis, Federigo, *Storia della Ragioneria* (Bologna: Dott, Cesare Zuffi, 1950)

Mezieres, Louis, *Comptabilité Industrielle et Manufacturiere,* 5th ed. (Paris: 1862)

Millener, C. A., "Evolution of Cost Accounts," *Business* (July-November, 1895)

Mitchell, G. A., *Single Cost Accounts* (London: Gee and Company, 1907)

Moxey, E. P., *Principles of Factory Cost Keeping* (New York: The Ronald Press Company, 1913)

Murdoch, A. A., "Proper Treatment of Machine Costs: A Criticism and a Theory," *The Journal of Accountancy,* III (1906)

Murray, David, *Chapters in the History of Bookkeeping, Accountancy, and Commercial Arithmetic* (Glasgow: Jackson, Wijlie and Company, 1930)

National Association of Cost Accountants, *Yearbook* (New York: 1921)

Navin, T. R., *The Whitin Machine Works Since 1831* (Cambridge: Harvard University Press, 1950)

Nef, J. U., *The Rise of the British Coal Industry*, Vol. II (London: George Routledge and Sons, 1932)

Newlove, G. H., and Pratt, Lester Amos, *Industrial Accounting* (New York: D. Appleton, 1921)

Newlove, G. H., *Cost Accounting*, preliminary ed. (Baltimore: The Author, 1927)
Cost Accounting, second preliminary ed. (Washington: The White Press Company, 1928)
Cost Accounts (Washington: The White Press Company, 1921)
Cost Accounts, 2nd ed. (Washington: The White Press Company, 1922)
Cost Accounts, 3rd ed. (Washington: The White Press Company, 1923)
"Depreciation," *The Journal of Accountancy*, XLIV (December, 1927)
"Manufacturing Accounts," *The Journal of Accountancy*, XXXI (1921)

Newman, E. W., "Functions of Costing," *The Accountant* (March 19, 1921)

Nichols, Henry Wyman, *A Method of Determining Costs in a Cotton Mill* (New Bedford, Massachusetts: E. Anthony & Sons, 1915)

Nichols, W. G., *Methods of Cost Finding in Cotton Mills* (Waltham: E. L. Barry, 1900)

Nicholson, J. Lee and Rohrbach, J. D., *Cost Accounting* (New York: The Ronald Press Company, 1919)

Nicholson, J. Lee, *Cost Accounting—Theory and Practices* (New York: The Ronald Press Company, 1913)
Factory Organization and Costs (New York: Kohl Technical Publishing Company, 1909)
International Text (New York: International Textbook Company, 1913)

Nisbet, A. G., *Terminal Cost Accounts* (London: Gee and Company, 1906)

Norris, H. M., "A Simple and Effective System of Shop Cost-Keeping," *The Engineering Magazine*, XVI (1898)
"Discussion on an Accurate Cost-Keeping System," *Transactions American Society of Mechanical Engineers*, XIX (1898)

Norton, G. P., *Textile Manufacturers' Bookkeeping*, 1st. ed., 1889; 4th ed. (London: Simpkin, 1900)

Payen, Anselme, *Essai sur la Tenue des Livres d'un Manufacturer* (Paris: 1817)

Pedder, Stanley, "Cost Accounts: Their Advantages and Their Relations to Business Results," *The Accountant* (April 29, 1905)

Penndorf, Baldwin, *Geschichte der Buchhaltung in Deutschland* (Leipzig: 1913)
"Die Anfange der Betriebsbuchhaltung," *Zeitschrift fur Handelswissenschaftliche Forschung*, XII (December, 1930)

Peragallo, Edward, *Origin and Evolution of Double Entry Bookkeeping* (New York: American Institute Publishing Company, 1938)

Perren, Alphonse, "The Development of Cost Accounting in Europe," *N.A.C.A. Bulletin*, XXIV (1944)

Pirenne, H., "L'Instruction des Merchands au Moyen Age," *Annales d'Histoire économique et sociale* (1929)

Racine, Samuel Frederick, *Cost Accounts* (Seattle: Western Institute of Accountancy, Commerce and Finance, 1921)

Renold, Sir Charles, "Management Accounts," *The Cost Accountant*, XXIX (1950)

Ridgway, A. C., "Cost Accounts," *The Accountant* (December 6, 1919)

Rogers, W. S., "Discussion on an Accurate Cost-Keeping System," *Transactions American Society of Mechanical Engineers*, XIX (1898)

Roland, Henry, "An Effective System of Finding and Keeping Shop Costs," *The Engineering Magazine*, XV (May, 1898)
"Cost Keeping Methods in Machine-shop and Foundry," *The Engineering Magazine*, XIV (May, 1898)

Ross, George Edward, *Cost Keeping and Construction Accounting* (Salem, Oregon: 1917)

Rowe, H. M., *Bookkeeping and Accountancy—Cost Accountancy for Manufacturing* (Baltimore: The H. M. Rowe Company, 1910)

Commercial and Industrial Bookkeeping (Baltimore: Sadler-Rowe Company, 1899)

Sanders, T. H., *Industrial Accounting* (New York: McGraw-Hill Book Company, 1929)

Problems in Industrial Accounting (Chicago: A. W. Shaw Company, 1923)

Sapori, Armando, *Una Compagnia di Calimala ai primi del Trecento* (Florence: Olschki, 1932)

Saunders, F. W. H. (but supplied to him by E. V. Amsdon) in *The Cost Accountant*, XXVI (March-April, 1948)

Sawyer, J., *Bookkeeping for the Tanning Trade*, 1st ed. (London, 1851); 2nd ed. (London, 1862)

Scheuermann, Ludwig, *Die Fugger als Montanindustrielle in Tirol und Karnten* (Munich: Duncker and Humbolt, 1929)

Schlatter, C. F., *Elementary Cost Accounting* (New York: John Wiley and Sons, 1927)

Schmalenbach, Eugen, "Buchfuhrung und Kalkulation im Fabrikgeschäft," *Deutsche Metallindustriezeitung* (1899)

Scott, DR, *The Cultural Significance of Accounts* (New York: Henry Holt and Company, 1916)

Scott, Walter, *The Principles and Practice of Cost Accounting* (Sydney, Australia: Law Book Company of Australasia Pty., Ltd., 1947)

Scovell, C. H., *Cost Accounting and Burden Application* (New York: D. Appleton and Company, 1916)

"Cost Accounting Practice, With Special Reference to Machine Hour Rate," *The Journal of Accountancy*, XVII (1914); also printed in *N.A.C.A. Bulletin* (June 1, 1927); also printed in *1913 Annual Report of the National Association of Machine Tool Builders;* also printed in *The Iron Age* (October 30, 1913)

Interest As A Cost (New York: The Ronald Press Company, 1924)

Scoville, W. C., *Revolution in Glassmaking* (Cambridge: Harvard University Press, 1948)

Senior, Nassau, *Report of the Inspector of Factories* (October 31, 1862)

Shaw, A. W. Company, *Operation and Costs* (Chicago: A. W. Shaw Company, 1915)

Simon, F. N., *Methode Complète de la tenue des livres* (1832)

Simonde de Sismondi, J. C. L., *Études sur l'Economie Politique,* Vol. I (Paris: 1837)

Sloan, Alfred P., Jr., *Adventures of a White-Collar Man* (New York: Doubleday, Doran and Company, 1941)

Small, F. S., *Accounting Methods* (Boston: L. and S. Printing Company, 1914)

Smallpiece, Basil, "The Evolution of Industrial Accounting," *The Accountant* (October, 1949)

Smith, Gershom, "The Distribution of Indirect Costs by the Machine-Hour Method," *The Engineering Magazine*, XXXVII (1909)

Smith, Oberlin, "Discussion on an Accurate Cost-Keeping System," *Transactions American Society of Mechanical Engineers*, XIX (1898)

Solomons, David, *Studies in Costing* (London: Sweet and Maxwell, 1952)

"Uniform Cost Accounting—A Survey," *Economica* (August and November, 1950)

Sowell, Ellis Mast, *The Evolution of the Theories and Techniques of Standard Costs* (Unpublished Ph.D. thesis in the University of Texas Library, 1944)

Spencer, Henry, *Commercial Organisation of Engineering Factories* (New York: Spon and Chamberlain, 1907)

Sterritt, J. E., "Cost Accounts," *The Accountant* (June 25, 1904)

Stewart, Ethelbert, *Tannery Production Costs and Methods of Accounting* (Boston: Rogers and Atwood, 1913)

Stock, A. F. and Goffey, J. M., "Overhead During Low Volume Production," *N.A.C.A. Bulletin* (February 16, 1925)

Strachan, W., *Cost Accounts* (London: Stevens and Haynes, 1909)

Taylor, F. W., "Shop Management," *Transactions American Society of Mechanical Engineers*, XXIV (1903)

"Comments," *Transactions American Society of Mechanical Engineers*, VII 1886)

Theiss, Edwin Leodgar, *Elements of Accounting Practice*, Pamphlets 23 and 24 (Chicago: LaSalle Extension University, 1922)

Thompson, C. B., *How to Find Factory Costs* (Chicago: A. W. Shaw Company, 1916))

Thompson, Wardhaugh, *The Accountant's Oracle: Or Key to Science* (York, England: 1777)

Thornton, Frank Weldon, *Brewery Accounts* (New York: The Ronald Press Company, 1913)

Timken, Frank Herrmann, *General Factory Accounting* (Chicago: Trade Periodical Company, 1914)

Torrens, Robert, *On Wages and Combinations* (London: 1834)

Twyford, H. B., *Purchasing, Its Economic Aspects and Proper Methods* (New York: D. Van Nostrand Company, 1915)

Unckless, Leslie, *How to Find Manufacturing Costs and Selling Costs* (Detroit: Modern Methods Publishing Company, 1909)

U. S. Federal Trade Commission, *Fundamentals of a Cost System for Manufacturers* (Washington: Government Printing Office, 1916)

Urie, John, "Oncost and Its Apportionment," *The Accountant* (January 11, 1902)

Urwick, Lyndall and Brech, Edward Franz, *The Making of Scientific Management*, Vol. II (London: Management Publications Trust, 1945)

Usher, Abbott Payson, *Industrial History of England* (Boston: Houghton Mifflin Company, 1920)

Vedder, H. C. M., "Cost Accounting: An Exposition of its Theories and Principles," *The Accountant* (November 11, 1905)

Vincent, John P., *Cost Accountancy and Profit Figuring* (Cincinnati: Campbell Commercial School, 1919)

Wagner, A. F., "Cost Systems and Operating Statistics," *The Journal of Accountancy*, XXXIV (1922)

Walbank, John A., "Stock and Stocktaking," *The Encyclopaedia of Accounting*, Vol. VI (London: William Green and Sons, 1903)

Waldron, Frederick A., *Simplified Factory Accounting and Routing* (New York: The Ronald Press Company, 1925)

Watts, Charles J., *The Cost of Production* (Muskegon, Michigan: Shaw-Walker, 1902)

Webner, F. E., *Factory Accounting* (Chicago: LaSalle Extension University, 1917)

Factory Costs (New York: The Ronald Press Company, 1911)

Factory Overhead (Washington: The White Press Company, 1924)

"Obtaining Actual Knowledge of the Cost of Production," *The Engineering Magazine* XXXV (1908)

Weiner, J. L., "Balance-sheet Valuation in German Law," *The Journal of Accountancy*, XLVIII (1929)

Wellington, C. O., "Actual Costs as Compared with Replacement Costs," *Yearbook National Association of Cost Accountants* (1922)

White, John Arch, *Accounting for By-Products* (Unpublished master's thesis presented to the University of Texas, 1930)

"Accounting for By-Products," *The Journal of Accountancy*, LI (February, 1931)

Whitmore, John, "Factory Accounting As Applied to Machine Shops," *The Journal of Accountancy*, III (1907)

"Shoe Factory Cost Accounts," *The Journal of Accountancy*, VI (1908)

"Some Cost Accounting Terms," *The Journal of Accountancy* (September, 1930)

"Some Details of Machine Shop Cost," *The Journal of Accountancy*, III (1907)

Wildman, John Raymond, *Cost Accounting* (New York: The Accountancy Publishing Company, 1910)

Principles of Cost Accounting (New York: New York University Press, 1914)

Williams, C. B., "Method of Accounting for Scrap," *N.A.C.A. Bulletin* (May, 1921)

"Treatment of Overhead When Production is Below Normal," *The Journal of Accountancy*, XXXI (1921)

Winchell, Samuel Dixon, *The Model System of Bookkeeping and Cost Finding* (Philadelphia: T. A. Winchell, 1913)

Woods, Clinton Edgar, *Practical Cost Accounting for Accountant Students* (New York: Universal Business Institute, 1908)

Unified Accounting Method for Industrials (New York: The Ronald Press Company, 1917)

Manufacturing Cost (Detroit: The Business Man's Publishing Company, 1904)

Woolf, A. H., *A Short History of Accountants and Accountancy* (London: Gee and Company, 1912)

Wright, H. Winfield, *Cost Accounting Theory and Practice* (Philadelphia: Bennett Accountancy Institute, 1924)

Yamashita, Katsuji, "Evolution of the Third Form of the Profit and Loss Accounting System," *Kokumin-Keizai Zasshi*, LXXXII, No. 4 (April, 1951)

Yamey, Basil S., "Scientific Bookkeeping and the Rise of Capitalism," *Economic History Review*, Second Series, I (1949)

INDEX